THE
HUMAN
EDGE

THE HUMAN EDGE

Information Technology and Helping People

Edited by
Gunther R. Geiss
Narayan Viswanathan
School of Social Work
Adelphi University

The Haworth Press, Inc.
New York   1986

HV
29.2
.H86
1986

Permission to use excerpts from the following works is gratefully acknowledged:

The Ascent of Man, by J. Bronowski. Copyright © 1973 by J. Bronowski. Reprinted by permission of Little, Brown and Co.

Case Studies in Medical Ethics, by R. Veatch. Cambridge, MA: Harvard University Press, 1977. Reprinted by permission of publisher.

"Choruses from 'The Rock,'" in *Collected Poems* 1909-1962, by T. S. Eliot, page 163. Copyright © 1936 by Harcourt Brace Jovanovich, Inc.; copyright © 1963, 1964 by T. S. Eliot. Reprinted by permission of publisher.

"Computer Software," by A. Kay. In *Scientific American, 251* (3), W. H. Freeman and Co., 1984. Reprinted by permission of publisher.

"A Computerized Tracking System for Deinstitutionalized Clients," by NASW. In *Practice Digest, 6*(3), 1983. Reprinted by permission of the publisher.

"Computers and Social Options," by H. Sackman. In E. Mumford and H. Sackman (Eds.), *Human Choice and Computers*, 1975. Amsterdam: North Holland; New York: Elsevier Science Publishing Co., Inc.

"Current and Future Trends in Clinical Social Work" by S. Briar (Ed.). In A. Rosenblatt & D. Waldfogel (Eds.), *Handbook of Clinical Social Work*, 1983. San Francisco: Jossey Bass. Reprinted by permission of publisher.

"The Issues We Avoid," by D. Christiansen. In *IEEE Spectrum, 21*(6), June 1984. Copyright © 1984 by IEEE. Reprinted by permission of publisher.

"Living with the Computer," by P. Morrisroe. In *New York*, Jan. 9, 1984. Copyright © 1985 by News Group Publications, Inc. Reprinted with permission of *New York* magazine.

Making the Future Work: Unleashing Our Powers of Innovation for the Decade Ahead, by John Diebold. New York: Simon and Schuster, 1984. Reprinted by permission of publisher.

The Micro Millennium, by Christopher Evans. Copyright © 1979 by Christopher Evans. Reprinted by permission of Viking Penguin, Inc.

"New Views, Computers and New Media," by Kerstin Anér. In a Report by the Commission on New Information Technology, Sweden, 1979. Liber Förlag Stockholm. Reprinted by permission of the author.

"Next-Generation Impacts," by F. Guterl. In *IEEE Spectrum, 20*(11), Nov. 1983. Copyright © IEEE, 1983.

"Perspective on Business Computing," by G. A. Champine. In *Computer 13*(11), November 1980. Copyright © 1980 by IEEE. Reprinted by permission of publisher.

The Professions, by A. M. Carr-Saunders & P. A. Wilson. Oxford University Press, 1933. Used by permission of publisher.

"A Program for Research on Management Information Systems," by R. O. Mason and I. F. Mitroff. In *Management Science*, 19, 1973. Copyright © 1973 by The Institute of Management Sciences. Reprinted by permissions of authors and publishers.

"Technological Advances in I & R: An American Report," by W. Garrett. In R. Levinson and K. S. Haynes (Eds.), *Accessing Human Services: International Perspectives*, 1984. Beverly Hills: Sage. Copyright © 1984 by Sage Publications. Reprinted by permission of Sage Publications, Inc.

The Widening Gap: Development in the 1970's, B. Ward, J. D. Runnullo, L. D'Anjou (Eds.). Copyright © 1971, Columbia University Press. Reprinted by permission of publisher.

Library of Congress Cataloging-in-Publication Data

The Human edge.

Papers from the Information Technology and Social Work Practice Conference, held in Queenstown, MD, June 9–12, 1984, which was sponsored by the Lois and Samuel Silberman Fund.

Bibliography: p.
Includes index.

1. Social service — Data processing — Congresses.
I. Geiss, Gunther. II. Viswanathan, Narayan.
III. Information Technology and Social Work Practice Conference (1984 : Queenstown, Md.) IV. Lois and Samuel Silberman Fund.

HV29.2.H86 1986   361'.0028'.5   86-9905
ISBN 0-86656-404-7
ISBN 0-86656-407-1 (pbk.)

The Haworth Press, Inc.   EUROSPAN/Haworth
28 East 22 Street   3 Henrietta Street
New York, New York 10010   London WC2E 8LU England

Technical editing by Carole A. Geiss
Designed, composed, and produced by The Bookmakers, Incorporated, Wilkes-Barre, Pa.
Manufactured in the United States of America

This volume is dedicated to two groups of special people

**Those who have the strength to cope and endure,
while others think, study, and try**

and

**Those whose unseen support in thought, word, and deed
make it possible for others to do their very visible best**

They know who they are,
and we thank them for making this possible.

CONTENTS

APPENDIXES, REFERENCES, BIBLIOGRAPHY, INDEX

LIST OF FIGURES

LIST OF TABLES

FOREWORD

Information technology, spearheaded by computers, is a subject that fascinates almost everybody. Rarely has science traveled so quickly from laboratory research to broad applications that affect almost every aspect of our daily lives. The effect on our society has already been profound, although it is only beginning to be felt. Without question, it will intensify and become even more pervasive. Experimentation has occurred at all levels, from the most sophisticated high-tech university and corporate research centers to the individual software programmers serving the personal-computer market. In this context, the Grant Committee of The Lois and Samuel Silberman Fund was flooded with an incredible number of diverse requests, all of them computer-related. The only feature they had in common was an almost compulsive desire either to spread this technology to new applications or to increase the abilities of more people to use what is already known.

The Grant Committee, a group of distinguished persons of diverse expertise, felt that even a small foundation such as ours has a role to play in addressing the future of so awesome a development, particularly since The Fund has focused its interest on social services and the development of personnel for the field. In our Committee discussions, the questions raised were quite different from the questions which the grant requests sought to answer. Our questions for the most part looked broadly at the impact—or potential impact—of information technology on social services. Could future computer use in social services benefit the client, or would it be limited to administrative accountability and control? What problems are inherent in transferring to human applications the tools and methods developed for impersonal uses? Would differences in the cultures and value systems of institutions make such a transfer impossible? What are the ethical issues? Who should have access to information? What are the client's rights? Who controls the design of a system, and should that design be conceived as top-down or bottom-up?

Obviously, it was far easier to raise questions such as these than to answer them. The Committee was nevertheless convinced that these were the types of questions that needed to be addressed. We decided to initiate a dialog with those individuals who were concerning themselves with these issues in an effort to determine what, if anything, The Fund might do to deploy its resources in a helpful and constructive way. It was clear that we needed a consultant who could educate us further about what was happening in the field and help us decide what action might be appropriate.

A member of the Committee, Dr. Thomas Horton, formerly Vice-President of IBM and currently President of the American Management Association, joined me in meeting with Dr. Gunther Geiss. It became clear almost immediately that we had found fertile ground. According to Dr. Geiss, a number of individuals had considered various aspects of our questions, but their exchange of ideas had been limited. Nothing of a comprehensive nature had been done. Starting with that meeting, a process was designed and implemented that has ultimately resulted in this book. To insure that he was current, Dr. Geiss spent more than six months attending every important computer conference concerning social services, going both to learn and to contribute. The Planning Committee he formed for the project then identified the most knowledgeable people in the subject-matter areas and invited them to the Wye Plantation of the Aspen Institute where they would discuss the invited papers, which they read prior to the Conference, and the keynote presentations, which were given at the Conference. Others prepared hypothetical cases based on actual experiences to provide a test for whatever theories or applications might evolve. Then came the long digestive process, and the ultimate writing. It should be emphasized that preparation of this text for publication was the original objective of the project. An outline of the scope of this volume was prepared and agreed upon long before there was any commitment about its exact contents. All those involved were aware of this. On behalf of The Fund, I express deep appreciation to all the participants, not only for their considerable contributions but also for their willingness to submit themselves to the discipline necessary to produce this outcome in less than two years from the time of the Conference to this printed volume.

It is our collective hope that *The Human Edge: Information Technology and Helping People* will serve as a basis for establishing some new directions in social work education and practice and for opening the discussion of critical issues in the classroom, in the practice professions, in the institutions (at both their executive and their administrative levels), and among those actually involved in designing information systems. It is our goal that the ideas contained in this volume reach all persons concerned with and committed to the future of human services. Only if we as a society are willing to consider the serious questions and issues involved in bringing information technology to human-service applications can we dare hope for its optimum contribution to improving the human condition. Perhaps this document will serve as a catalyst in shaping the way we think about human services in the future.

Samuel J. Silberman, President
The Lois and Samuel Silberman Fund

PREFACE

The Human Edge: Information Technology and Helping People is the title that we have bestowed on this book to reflect its content, our vision of opportunity, and our sustained efforts over a decade to come to terms with innovations in information technology and their relevance and utility for the helping professions. The intellectual origins of this effort extend back to the year 1975, when we, an electrical engineer and a social worker, began to design and teach a seminar course on technological aspects of management in the doctoral program of the Adelphi University School of Social Work. The experience of jointly teaching this course for the last 10 years led us to recognize that most of the literature on the subject reflected the dominance of a rationalist perspective. Major contributors to the literature saw information technology largely as an apolitical technology for improving the rationality of decision-making and the efficiency of operations in organizations. It was unclear how useful or relevant this literature was to social work students because it was markedly apolitical, and because it also tended to reflect only the experiences of organizations largely outside the sphere of human-service organizations. A recurring contention in the class was that the political and value considerations that govern human-service organizations are distinctly different from those that govern organizations with other missions. An additional contention was that the primary mission of professional workers in human-service organizations was effective or improved practice — helping the clients — and hence that the concerns for organizational rationality and efficiency were subservient to the more fundamental concern for professional practice.

Efforts were initiated to address these concerns through field studies and case studies of specific attempts that were being made by human-service organizations to experiment with the transfer of technological innovations into their organizational environments. While this shift in focus yielded some useful results, we also discovered that the preoccupation with field studies and case studies did not permit the movement toward a more fundamental conceptual understanding of the processes of technology innovation and transfer. We felt that it would be useful to begin to address this task with the goals of advancing the knowledge base of the profession and, at the same time, contributing to the developing knowledge bases in related fields of service delivery.

The Lois and Samuel Silberman Fund gave the much needed stimulus and resources to extend this effort beyond the classroom by suggesting that a book on computers in social work be written, and that a national conference on the subject be organized to support that effort. A conference planning committee was formed to design such a conference, and it decided that information technology and social work practice ought to be the focus. We will say more on this later. What is important now is to provide some amplification of the directions of our search.

Technological genius is one of the glories of mankind. It has reduced the separations that are due to distance by means of flight and telecommunications, expanded the range of human capacities with the computer and its software, opened up new biological frontiers with DNA recombinant technology, and made it possible, via the green revolution, to produce sufficient food to prevent famine and starvation. The dramatic advances in computers and biotechnology of recent years have been the center of much media as well as professional attention, hence overshadowing equally dramatic though much less publicized advances in cutting-edge technologies in other fields. Rapid change is occurring in many scientific, engineering, and technological fields. The paces of scientific discovery and technological development and application have accelerated beyond any historic precedent. As the rate of change accelerates, specialists in particular fields find it more difficult to keep abreast of the increases in knowledge and technique. It is even more difficult for professional practitioners to understand how developments outside their fields of specialty are likely to affect what they do and how they do it. Nevertheless, it is vitally important that our professional and technical personnel remain on the cutting edge of scientific and technical progress and, in fact, that all citizens have the scientific and technical understanding necessary to participate in our increasingly complex technological society.

Virtually everyone everywhere has been drawn into the orbit of modern science and technology. Technological development is faster than ever, and we are confronted with its impact every day. The effects of innovations upon both the natural and social environments are now far more massive and immediate than ever before in the history of mankind. It is then essential that we investigate how technological developments can be used to directly benefit people, especially those who need help. We are morally and professionally bound to ask how technology can be utilized to help — to help those in need, to help those who will help themselves, to help those who help others, and to help those who provide professional help. The human ability to create and utilize tools to human advantage makes the human unique, it is *the human edge*.

Information technology, a double-edged innovation combining computers and information systems with telecommunications, has become a fact of everyday life. It has also become a kind of staple in the American home. Most importantly, the technology affects virtually every industry and service in the economy. One would be hard pressed to name an enterprise today that does not depend on the effective use and communication of information: to design products and services, to track and respond to market demands, or to make well-informed decisions. Computers and communications constitute tools for manipulating and transmitting that information. What's more, the combination of computers and communications (compunication is a new hybrid term; the French introduced *telematique,* or *telematics*) is creating wholly new industries — for example, computer-based literature retrieval, catalogue shopping, electronic mail and conferencing, and so forth. As new industries based on information technology are formed, their technological advances are incorporated into or transferred to existing industries. The resulting diffusion of technology in the wider culture from industry to industry is shaping the evolution of our economy as well as our social and cultural landscapes.

Information technology is one of the most important scientific determinants of social change in our times. Although the roots of research in this field have had a long history, it is only in recent years that the real explosions have started, ushering in a period of significant social change. Illustrative is the development of more effective research methodologies and tools for the study of human learning, as well as recent advances in hardware capabilities, which are opening up the possibility of using new information technologies to help solve pervasive educational problems. Parallel work in artificial intelligence and the cognitive sciences has set the stage for qualitatively new applications of technology to education and human change, in general. While success in this arena will probably not solve all educational or human-change problems, it will provide a new scientific basis for instructional systems design, teacher training, curricular restructuring, and other human-change processes.

When change becomes extensive and pervasive, it must obviously influence and even alter the ways in which we understand, organize, and evaluate the world around us. It will have an impact on our sensibilities and ideas, our institutions and practices, and our politics and values. It is small wonder, indeed, that many of us feel the need to look ahead. With the existing rapid pace of technological change, we are more convinced than ever that we may be taken by surprise and experience future culture shock as a consequence of the changes.

There is little doubt that information technology, like other, similar science-based technologies before and concurrent with it, has opened new windows of opportunity. Advanced systems combining symbolic computational capabilities, artificial intelligence, and cognitive theory have begun to be developed in a few well-equipped laboratories. Methods for constructing expert systems have developed particularly rapidly. The construction of an expert system requires an explicit representation of the knowledge that constitutes expertise. This work, along with empirical studies of human expert performance, has been a means of gaining crucial insights into skilled diagnoses and problem-solving, reasoning, and the nature of human knowledge. The cumulative result of these and other convergent efforts could bring about major advances in our ability to use information technology in professional education and practice, that is, for helping people, in helping people, and with helping people.

Yet, even as the technology advances, there are new doubts and uncertainties about the extent to which society must embrace it. Even at this early stage, the use of information technology has stirred some important debates. Will increasingly sophisticated communications, surveillance, and information technology turn governments into all-powerful watchdogs? Will the rise of new high-tech industries and service-related sectors increase existing uneven distribution of income and political power? Or will computers and information technology end up serving as adaptable and useful tools—vastly improving our professional, community, and personal lives, making work more flexible and less arduous, and decentralizing power by allowing individuals access to greater information? Is information technology delivering—or can it deliver—its promised benefits? Does the technology favor or foster service-delivery systems that lead to dehumanization and dependence

of the clients under their jurisdiction? To whom do we assign ownership of information, and how can ownership be exercised in a world of
computer networks? How do we measure the value of such a unique
commodity as information? Does information foster or favor systems
that help serve people, or does it merely create new forms of professional control or coalescence of elite groups? How do we ensure that information does not get into the wrong hands—or, perhaps, into the
wrong computer? How sure can we be that the client's right to privacy
and confidentiality will be protected? Is the technology outpacing or
outrunning our ability to manage it for the betterment of the human
condition? As information and related technologies have become more
sophisticated and widely available, and as they bring about far-reaching
changes in the world economy, these questions become all the more
urgent.

Information technology is making inroads into what some consider
the last professional bastion of human values and human concern,
social work practice. What is or should be the response of social work to
this uninvited guest? Should social work treat this uninvited guest as an
unwelcome intruder or as a welcome new face? Quite obviously, opinions
on the questions are divided and varied. There are those who would like
to obstruct the intrusion of this technology. Are those who valiantly defend us against what they perceive to be the onslaught of mechanistic
thinking, automation, and dehumanization the Luddites of today, or are
they the visionaries who may protect us against an undesirable future?
On the other side, there are some who propose creative new applications
of technology to better fulfill the mission of practice. If we accept their
proposals, how shall we proceed with the construction of a new scheme
of practice suited to the needs and resources of a new era? The opportunities offered to us by information technology are quite attractive; yet
we know that there are substantial and, often, hidden costs attached.
Must we, therefore, concern ourselves with defining the appropriate applications of information technology to helping people, especially in
social work?

These are only a few of the questions raised by information
technology—questions often so novel, complex, and interrelated that
no ready answers are yet apparent. To explore these and other questions, we outlined the proposed book, and organized the Information
Technology and Social Work Practice Conference to invite some fresh
thinking, and to disseminate the results of that effort to the professional
community. The Lois and Samuel Silberman Fund gave us the encouragement and support to bring together a group of educators and
practitioners concerned with the helping professions to examine the

issues. Humanistic and radical feelings prompted us to be expectant and hopeful, but our knowledge that the field had not developed in directions where technology could be readily adapted gave us some initial trepidations and doubts about the wisdom of such a course of action. In retrospect, we cannot help feeling that our rashness in initiating this search for a new paradigm of helping in the Information Age was far less extreme than we had initially imagined or anticipated.

From the conference itself, we have recollections of stimulating comments, critiques, and suggestions floating across and around the circular table located in a lovely setting on the Maryland shore. All of these elements clarified our thoughts and jolted our analysis into better focus.

It soon became obvious that the prepared conference papers represented the kernel of a volume with a much wider potential audience. However, we needed to invite contributions on several themes that had emerged during the discussions; we needed, also, additional writings to provide a more integrated view of the subject matter.

The response to our resulting invitations was to prove overwhelming. Each of the authors revised or reworked his or her paper to reflect more fully the concerns and issues that were expressed at the conference. A few postconference reflections were also submitted, reviewed, and included. It was our responsibility, of course, as the editors, to pull these diverse efforts and contributions together into a volume that has a unity and coherence much beyond that of a conference report or proceedings. We have endeavored to produce a text that fulfills the dual purposes of stimulating discussions and action in the helping professions and providing a classroom text to stimulate teaching and learning of new ideas.

We have organized the materials into three major parts:

> I. Foundations
> II. Views of Present and Future
> III. Issues and Options

These parts meet the varied interests of readers. Part I, "Foundations," presents the context and premises of what follows. It introduces the fundamental ideas and definitions that support our explorations, and it provides introduction to the subject areas for those with no prior background in either helping people or in information technology.

Part II, "Views of Present and Future," provides the substance from which discussions began at the Information Technology and Social Work Practice Conference. The keynotes provide challenges from experts, in philosophy (especially ethics) and information technology (particularly networking and decision support), that bring our knowledge up to date and unsettle our complacency about that knowledge. The scenarios that follow further challenge and disturb our thinking as they display problems, possibilities, opportunities, barriers, and threats drawn from the practice experiences of conference participants. Part II closes with descriptions, in detail, of innovations in social work practice that are based upon utilizing information technology. Each of the first four papers is a unique and carefully chosen representative of a major category of practice innovation: facilitation of professional work; preparation for service delivery; support of service decision-making; and direct delivery of services. The fifth presents an example of a major innovation that is in the public domain (VA Hospital Computer System) and ready for transfer to other settings. Thus Part II brings us from varied views of what may be to what is, and what is ready for transfer.

Part III, "Issues and Options," presents the distillation of our explorations, at the conference and, thereafter, in the form of an "Encyclopedia of Ignorance." We identify issues, raise questions, and also consider options in the context of a model derived from a synoptic overview of our discussions. There are five components of this model:

Information Technology/Social Work Practice/Social Work Education
Value/Ethics
Science/Knowledge
Management/Resource Development
Actions/Applications

These components are the bases for the ensuing chapters which elaborate the issues in, and our ignorance of, each component. The first of these, Chapter 7, also includes contributions regarding social work education that were written by two educators and a practitioner. Chapter 8 includes a contribution regarding information technology and human values; it was written by a practitioner, and it proposes a position statement for discussion and action by practicing professionals. The final chapter presents agreements reached at the conference that provide clarification of purpose, a design philosophy, and actions suggested or next steps.

Given this content and organization, our volume may be used in a variety of ways. For example, an introductory course in information technology and professional practice might make use of portions of Chapter 1, Chapters 2, 3, and 5, selected scenarios from Chapter 4, and Chapter 8. An advanced or subsequent course might focus on Chapters 1, 3, and 5, and then use Chapter 4 as case studies for discussion and brainstorming. A doctoral research seminar might use Chapters 1 through 5 as background for detailed discussions of the issues and options in Chapters 6 through 11. We hope that at least some of these issues will become the subjects of doctoral research.

The use of this volume in practice settings, that is, agency board meetings, executive planning and policy implementation, professional supervision, and so forth, is perhaps less obvious. Certainly Chapters 1, 2, and 3 provide a foundation for considerations of technology utilization at all agency levels. Chapter 4 provides stimuli for needs assessments and broadening the currently held views of opportunities, threats, and barriers. Those ready to engage in practice applications of technology will concern themselves with Chapters 5, 6, 8, 10, 11, and the practice portion of Chapter 7. Board members and executives concerned with planning and policymaking will be concerned with Chapters 3, 4, 5, 6, 7, 8, and 10. Chapters 4, 5, and 8 will be valuable stimuli for supervisory sessions devoted to engaging professional staff in the design process.

Technologists interested in developing applications for helping people may use Chapter 4 to gain knowledge of the breadth of problems faced. Chapter 5 describes the current state of the art, while Chapters 1, 3 (especially the Christensen paper), and 6 through 11 yield insights regarding the intercultural technology-transfer problems and the centrality of value issues.

The breadth and variety of the content provides material and cases for a variety of interests, from clinical or micro practice through community organizing or macro practice; from therapeutic problem-solving and counseling through preventive services; from advocacy through policy-making and planning; from concrete services through value analysis, moral thinking, and ethical behavior; and, finally, from specific applications through intercultural technology transfer.

We hope that the papers and the editors' reflections contained in this volume can place in perspective the present state of development of information technology and its relationship with helping people and how that is likely to evolve over the next several decades. If the individual and collective effects of the papers also communicate the vitality of the multiple streams of technological development taking place, then a major goal of the conference will have been achieved. Just as importantly, however, the collection of papers in this volume foreshadows the changing technological environment that will enhance our society in the years ahead.

We are painfully aware that we have raised many more questions regarding information technology than we have answered. However, we have provided some suggestions, albeit tentative ones, to a vast range of issues related to the question of proper interfaces between information technology and social work practice; and we have approached these issues from a number of perspectives and thematic standpoints. If in so doing we move more individuals into serious examination of these critical issues, and if we raise the level of debate in the professions and the community at large regarding the uses or abuses of this technology, then this book will serve its intended purpose.

Gunther R. Geiss
Narayan Viswanathan

ACKNOWLEDGMENTS

Whenever adventurers undertake a journey on the high seas of life to reach a new land, there are many to whom they owe so much — the many who in a variety of ways make the journey possible, whether they be upon the decks, below the decks, on the dock, or "tending the fires" at home. Because it is so difficult to value them in any orderly way, it is difficult to thank each appropriately, or even proportionately, for his or her contributions. Therefore, we can only thank each, and hope that readers will not infer an ordering when none is intended. Each journey begins with just one step, but which is the first? Each journey is the product of facilitative and supportive acts, but which is the key act?

We begin by recognizing Dean Joseph L. Vigilante, whose strong orientation toward risk and opportunity permitted him to make a place for an engineer in a school of social work. He is the kind of person who is always willing to shake the "tree of life" very vigorously to discover its fruits. He has taught us much.

Dr. Beulah Rothman undertook the special job of "socializing" that engineer to the social work profession and thereby taught the value and skills of group work by demonstration and with art. She also created and nurtured the doctoral program that stimulated and accommodated our innovative joint teaching effort.

The Lois and Samuel Silberman Fund has not only financed the journey but also through three members of its Grant Committee provided support and guidance. Mr. Samuel J. (Buddy) Silberman has by word, deed, and style illuminated the highest meaning of working partner and of mentor. Dr. Thomas Horton provided invaluable insights into the conferencing process, which led to a unique conference design and ultimately to this text. Each journey requires, at least on occasion, a navigator with exceptional knowledge of the stars, shoals, and reefs. Dean Harold Lewis has served us well in this capacity by keeping us on course throughout the process of conference design, execution, and documentation. In fact, he had much to do with the initiation of the journey as well.

The members of the Planning Committee, Mr. Richard H. Calica, Ms. Connie Cobb, Drs. Walter LaMendola, Charles O'Reilly, Dick Schoech, and Lynn Harold Vogel have contributed greatly through their creativity, their endurance during marathon teleconferences, their knowledge of the field, their patience in learning to conference via computer, and their support during the entire process. They are the crew leaders whose skill, knowledge, and loyalty to purpose have made this a complete and successful journey.

The motivation to undertake a major new journey usually comes from thoughts of visionaries and tales from the explorers—those who dare to go first in concept or deed. Ours is no exception, as we are deeply indebted to Drs. Kathleen Christensen, John C. Henderson, and Jacques Vallee for sharing their visions with us, and to William J. Garrett, Dr. Kenric Hammond, Patricia Lynett, Jim Newkham, and Dr. Robert Pruger for sharing paths and experiences. Each told us of a new and exciting land.

Each conference participant contributed significantly via scenario, discussion, and process insights. Some members of this crew—Dr. Joan DiLeonardi, Dr. Marilyn Flynn, Dean Joseph Palombo, and Dean Charles O'Reilly—contributed additional papers to this volume.

Major structural elements for our vessel were provided by the staff of the Electronic Information Exchange System (EIES) at New Jersey Institute of Technology. Dr. Bill Savin of the Physics Department introduced us to EIES. Dr. Murray Turoff provided a generous start to our experiments and created the medium we used to accomplish them. Anita Graziano and the collective support, named HELP, answered many questions for us, the novice sailors. The amenities and services of the Aspen Institute for Humanistic Studies' Wye Plantation contributed significantly to the success of the conference.

This document owes much to colleagues and students who provided critical comments and suggestions, especially Drs. Harold Lewis, Bert Kaplan, and Walter LaMendola who read an early draft. In addition to his careful review of our manuscript, we are particularly indebted to Dr. LaMendola for his early explorations and commitment to its use in teaching. We also must recognize the many students who, over the last ten years, shared enthusiasm and ideas while participating in our various experiments in teaching this content, and the graduate assistants who gave diligence, care, and a mighty effort to the timely preparation of the index via dBASE II.

The Bookmakers, Incorporated, particularly John Beck and Richard Johnson, provided varied services in preparation of this volume — from transcribing tapes, through typesetting, to creating the graphic design and cover art. They traveled the bumpy road of "electronic publication" with us in good cheer and with informed judgment and creativity.

Finally, thanks to those who helped by simply "being there," or pitching in when it was time to "bail" — the crew at home: Gertrude ("Grandma"), Carole, Chris, and Karin Geiss; and Nalini, Bhamati, and Aditi Viswanathan — especially Carole, who shared the beauty of morning sunrise and evening sunset on deck, and, more importantly, our "mal de mer" from heavy seas as wife, friend, partner, and technical editor.

Thank you all.

Gunther R. Geiss
Narayan Viswanathan

PART ONE

THE FOUNDATIONS

by
Gunther R. Geiss
and
Narayan Viswanathan

CHAPTER 1

INTERCULTURAL TECHNOLOGY TRANSFER

> Technological innovations have often led to changes in society. Seldom, however, have so many fundamental social issues been posed so rapidly as has been the case in the veritable explosion of information technology—computers and communications. The technology is changing far more rapidly than the rules that are supposed to contain it, often leaping over national as well as regulatory boundaries. Dealing as they do with the principal determinant of human organization— information and its communication—this technology promises to change the very fabric of society, and in the process a wide range of the most basic ethical, legal, and moral questions must be faced if we are to make our future work.
> —John Diebold (1984, p. 308.)

The subject of this chapter—the transfer of technology from the scientific to the professional culture—has received increasing attention in recent years. Louise Russell (1979), for example, provides an examination of how new techniques and technologies have wrought changes in hospital practices in the last several decades. The rapid diffusion of intensive-care units, renal dialysis, open-heart surgery, and many other innovations have been part of the revolution in what hospitals can provide and what the public expects.

As the helping professions have become more widely dispersed around the world, and as the technological capacity of the helping professions has come to be seen as one key to their overall development, educators and practitioners alike have begun to ask questions about the technology-transfer process and its consequences. In particular, interest has focused on the extent to which transfer mechanisms affect the ability of helping professions to acquire technology and to use it effectively toward the fulfillment of their human-service mission.

This chapter contributes directly to the debate about the consequences of technology transfer — a debate that has sometimes generated more heat than light. Our aim is to illuminate the complexity of the mechanisms and motivations involved in the transfer process, a topic on which relatively little hard information is available.

The Conceptual Framework

Cortes and Bocock (1984) rightly caution us that one of the problems of discussing technology transfer is that the terms used in the discussion are not easily defined and are frequently used differently by different participants in the discussion. Technology may be defined very broadly as "knowledge of how to do all those things associated with economic activity" (Stewart, 1979, p. i); or, it may be defined much more specifically as "a collection of physical processes which transforms inputs into outputs, together with the social arrangements — that is, organizational modes and procedural methods — which structure the activities involved in carrying out these transformations" (Dahlman and Westphal, 1981, p. 13). What these and other similar definitions have in common, however, is the idea that technology is much more than a collection of blueprints, machinery, and equipment. It is, in fact, organized and replicable knowledge. It also has a transmittable quality. That is, technology can be transferred. The transfer or movement of technology occurs both horizontally and vertically within organizations and, at a more complex level, technology transfer may be transnational (international), that is, taking place between countries, as well as intranational (domestic), that is, occurring within a country. Mogavero and Shane (1982) provide several models of the technology-transfer process. The important element in the technology-transfer process is not simply the transfer of the technology but also the transfer of the knowledge that will enable the recipient to use those physical objects, processes, and techniques effectively.

Moreover, what is transferred and the way in which it is transferred may be very different in the case of transfers between one culture and another. We use the term *intercultural technology transfers* advisedly to designate the transfer of knowledge and know-how from the scientific to the professional culture. The process extends from the invention of new knowledge in the sciences to the transfer of that knowledge to the applied sciences, and the movement of that knowledge from the laboratory to the outside world in the form of technological innovation, and the utilization and application of such innovations in professional education and practice.

It is also our premise that intercultural technology transfer also transmits knowledge and know-how from the professional to the scientific culture. Last but not the least in importance, the use of the term *culture* is a reminder to the participants in the technology-transfer process of the importance of values in the assimilation, integration, and utilization of scientific knowledge and technological know-how. A technology-transfer process that is devoid of or misinformed about the relevant values of both the recipient and the transmitting cultures is sterile.

The conceptual model, as envisioned above, is displayed in Figure 1.

The Scientific Culture

What defines the twentieth century uniquely is science. As Horace Judson (1984) suggests, the rise of science may be the true hallmark of our times, the most potent force at work in the world today. Or, rather, the sciences, for they are many and varied. They have become a critical social force because they fundamentally transform the way we perceive the world, the nature of the questions we ask, and even the expectations we hold. In a tribute to our century, the fifth anniversary issue (November) of *Science '84* is devoted to significant discoveries in the "Century of the Sciences."

The exponential growth of the enterprise of science marks the modern era. In the decades since World War II, the enterprise has increased greatly in size, complexity, and diversity. Changes in the workings of the enterprise are evidenced in areas as varied as the financing of science, science policy, scientific instrumentation, the links of science and technology, the education of scientists, and the public understanding and following of science. As the pace and impact of scientific and technological changes quicken, it becomes harder than ever before to grasp their real meanings and significances. That pace underlines the need for a fuller and richer historical perspective from which to see the steady scientific process as a whole.

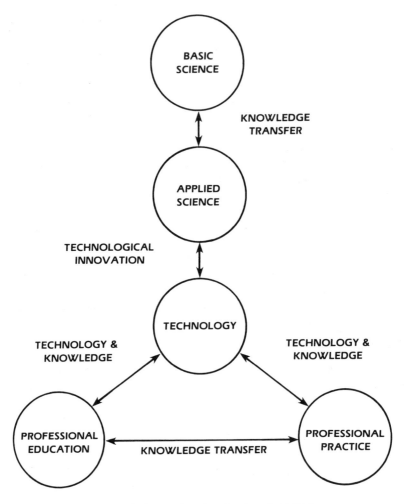

Figure 1. **Intercultural technology transfers**

More than a decade ago, I. I. Rabi (1970) claimed—and many individuals have agreed with him—that "science is the center of culture." Not everyone sees science as the center of culture, however, for many assert that science per se—the exciting and personal search for knowledge—is not the center of our culture so much as technology—the useful fruits of that search. Still another opinion asserts that science and technology are not at the center of the wider culture but rather that the wider culture is at the center of science and technology. Since the work of Thomas Kuhn (1970) on the Copernican revolution, historians of science have been acutely aware that science and technology are the creatures of the cultures in which they developed. Some critics also maintain that science and technology are threats to our culture, even plagues on our culture. Opinions about the subject of the benefits and harmful effects of scientific and technological progress range, however, from a Hobbesian insistence that they are "nasty, brutish, and short" to Bronowski's (1973) vision of them as creative and liberating. No matter which view or perspective one adopts, both the nourishing fruits and the toxic fruits of scientific and technological advances increasingly affect all the other elements of culture.

Images of Yesterday's Future

Visitors to Paris in 1984 were treated to a series of special events and exhibitions chronicling the modern contributions of France's scientific community to science and technology. Each of these separate events, along with others throughout the country, was part of a government-inspired campaign in France to stimulate *la culture scientifique et technique*, a phrase that translates as "scientific and technical culture." As explained in *Science*: "At the center of many of these efforts currently stands the figure of the eighteenth-century polymath and philosopher Denis Diderot, the bicentenary of whose death in 1784 is being used as a vehicle for conveying the message that technological change is an essential part of human culture and social evolution, and should not be seen as a threat to either" ("France puts Diderot," 1984, p. 1132).

1984 is also the title of George Orwell's literary masterpiece. Written in 1948, the novel is a nightmare vision of the future. Extrapolating from his experiences in Spain and from what he had learned in England of Soviet behavior, Orwell felt that a communist system that attained world dominion and went to its logical limits might seek to destroy memory, the meaning of language, independent thought, individuality—everything unique to human beings. The novel's most celebrated lines are INGSOC's (English Socialism) ominous maxim: "Who controls the past, . . . controls the future: who controls the present controls the past" (p. 35). The Orwellian image of the future is a frightening satire of the naive idea that equated social progress with a maximalist state and its attendant depersonalized or faceless bureaucracy. Orwell's vision provided an intellectual challenge that we had to confront for more than three decades. Since we have passed the year of his futurist scenario, we hope that his grim predictions will never be borne out.

Today's Future: The Information Revolution and High Technology

As we approach the end of the twentieth century and the dawn of the twenty-first, we witness the beginning of another new and challenging era in world history. The trigger for this era is the information revolution, which encompasses a group of revolutions, variously called the electronic and microelectronic revolution, the telecommunications revolution, and the computer revolution. There is growing agreement in the scientific community that the dawn of the new era is marked by the development of new technologies in electronics, biology, and materials. A symposium on Cutting Edge Technologies, convened in 1983 by the National Academy of Engineering, foreshadowed the changing technological environment in which scientists, engineers, and professional practitioners will be working in the years ahead. The published report of the National Academy of Engineering (1984) provides an overview of general trends, and it also provides a detailed look at current technologies and how they are likely to evolve.

One strong point in Karl Marx's social philosophy has been his view that technological development is a powerful driving force in social development. Such development tends to act explosively in social institutions, which are no longer the best frame for the new production processes. Other sociologists since Marx have utilized the "cultural lag" hypothesis in their discussions of the impact of technology on culture. The pervasive influence of the scientific and technical culture upon the broader culture shows no signs of abating. Whether in terms of its impact on the natural environment, its contribution to the transformation of social and political relations, or its effects on patterns of work, leisure, and emerging lifestyles, the cultural impact of science and technology has been profound and promises to be of even greater import in the future. The pace of technological advancement has been bewilderingly rapid during the past 30 years and still appears to be accelerating. The vision that Joseph Schumpeter (1935, pp. 2–10; Clemence, 1951, pp. 125–133) had of major innovations—steam power in the nineteenth century, or electricity in this century—followed by a wave of applications of new products, new processes, and new vertical linkages between providers of economic inputs and outputs, fits the world of integrated circuits and digital and information technologies. The times between major events have shrunk, however, along with the sizes of the new devices.

The upsurge of new scientific and technological thresholds has opened up the new frontiers of a high-tech society. *High tech* is a term that connotes the technology considered to be nearer to the leading edge of

Table 1 **Societal Shifts Now in Progress**

Industrial Society	Information Society
Forced Technology	High-Tech/High-Touch
National Economy	World Economy
Short-Term	Long-Term
Centralization	Decentralization
Institutional Help	Self-Help
Representative Democracy	Participatory Democracy
Hierarchies	Networking
North	South
Either/Or	Multiple Options

science; it is the technology emerging from the laboratory into practical application. Fiber optics, gene-splicing, artificial intelligence, lasers, robotics, satellites, space vehicles, and weapons systems are manifestations of the high-tech society. The United States, which is a prototype of this new kind of social order, is a prime instigator of the changes that are reshaping society and culture. The United States is once again a frontier society. In this postmodern era, information and ideas replace physical resources as the new frontier. What we need now, therefore, is a new understanding of the structural features of our society that will influence the future development of science and technology.

John Naisbitt (1984) provides one view of our future culled from what he sees as the indicators of long-term durable changes—the local newspapers—and not from the outputs of Washington, D.C., and New York City, which he claims only generate short-lived fads. Table 1 shows major social changes now in progress.

These are major social changes that affect our professional and personal lives. Of most concern to the helping professions are the shift from an imposed technology to technology introduced along with countervailing human aspects (touch), the shift from institutional forms of help to self-help, the shift to more participation in decision-making, and the movement from institutionalized hierarchies to more flexible network forms of organization. Each of these shifts is enabled, supported, or facilitated by information technology.

Impact on Professions

Information and communications technologies are already changing society in important ways. Regardless of what one chooses to call the product of this transformation (the new information society, high-tech society, postindustrial period, postmodern era), far-reaching impacts on economic, political, and social institutions, as well as individuals, are inevitable. As the new information society generates new demands and expectations, various professions—medicine, law, engineering, business, to cite only a few—are experiencing destabilization. Recent advances in science and technology have exposed new ignorance and uncertainties, new opportunities, new risks, and new value dilemmas. Traditional assumptions about the proper mission and function of a profession have to be reexamined with both traditional and novel methods. These introspections are already underway in various spheres of professional education and practice. (See, for example, LaMendola [1985] and Geiss [in press].)

The health of science and technology and the health of the professions are closely linked: progress in the former generates growth in the latter, which in turn provides further resources for research and development. Scientific research, technological innovation, and their utilization and application in professional practice have been responsible for improvements in our standard of living. People in the industrial world are fed better, they are healthier, and they live longer than human beings have at any other time. Our ability to solve many of our national problems—energy availability, environmental pollution, agricultural pest control—also depends on our continuing support for scientific research and technological development. Numerous areas of public and private life—income security, employment, health, standard of living, education, and social welfare—would suffer from the absence or diminution of scientific research and technological development. Science and technology are of vital importance to almost every profession. The professions must therefore have scientific and technical capabilities as well as the operational capabilities needed to accomplish their missions.

C. P. Snow (1959, 1963), a sharp observer of society as well as of science, coined the expression "The Two Cultures" to suggest an intellectual segregation of the two moieties of the intellectual enterprise, the humanistic and the scientific. Science, he observed, may be at the center stage of modern culture but, paradoxically, it stands aloof. The result is what he called the two-culture problem, and he challenged the world community to work toward a unification of the two cultures. Efforts to resolve the discord between the scientist and the humanist still persist. With too few exceptions, C. P. Snow's two cultures are still far apart. But what about science and other areas of human endeavor? Is there perhaps a similar bipolarity between the scientific culture and the culture of the helping professions? At yet another level, we have the culture of administration and the culture of helping, and the question may be asked again. If we answer "yes" to any or all of these, then what is the magnitude of this two-culture problem? And, what are the prospects for bridging these cultures?

Bridging Cultures

An underlying premise of the authors of this volume—and of The Lois and Samuel Silberman Fund, which sponsored the Information Technology and Social Work Practice Conference and provided the impetus and resources to produce this volume—is that the two cultures do exist and are in fact separate, although they are not mutually exclusive or incomprehensible. Integral to this premise is also the belief that a clear definition of the content and methodology of each of the two cultures can make them mutually supportive and enhance our understanding of both. In focusing our attention upon the helping process as a unifying theme of the two cultures, we begin to see the human aspect of science and technology—its human interface—not the cutting edge or leading edge but rather the human edge.

Several years ago, James Shannon (1973), of Rockefeller University, echoed the prevailing view that "the science enterprises of the nation are vigorous, diversified, and generally characterized by excellence" (p. vii). Scientific and technological advances have moved forward on several frontiers encompassing research, development, and associated educational enterprises. The profound influences of science and its derived technologies are obvious, but the reverse, the pervasive influences of human need and human attitude on science and technology, less evident. The changing context of science and technology has been accompanied by a steady transfer of scientific knowledge and technical know-how to the helping professions. Advances in professional practice also have contributed to a reverse flow of knowledge from professional disciplines to the sciences. This leads us to the statement of our next premise: knowledge transfer is a combination of knowledge processes, technological processes, and helping processes that allows for a reciprocal flow of influences.

While we affirm our belief in the value of blending scientific and professional cultures, we shall also introduce the proposition that the two cultures can (and even should) maintain their distinctive cultural identities and social commitments. At the same time they can cooperate in their respective cultural spheres and practice domains to permit mutual learning, innovation, adaptation, and growth. *Technology transfer*, as envisioned by the authors of this volume, is a mediating mechanism for a synergistic unification of the two cultures. The authors believe that the goal of bridging cultures is best achieved through cultural pluralism rather than the hegemony of one culture over another.

In advancing the theme of unification of cultures, the authors do not set aside the moral, ethical, or human concerns that are of paramount importance to the helping professions; instead, they are identified and addressed. We attempt to incorporate what social philosophers have called "first principles" into our thinking and analysis. The classical first principles of truth, beauty, and justice take a different form in the helping professions, for example, privacy, dignity, respect, equity, self-determination, freedom, and confidentiality. There is explicit recognition throughout this volume that the transference of technology to serve people must take into consideration value judgments, value systems, and social processes. Any attempt to bridge cultures is at peril unless there is due regard and consideration of the values underpinning professional practice.

Another important concept in technology transfer is *technological innovation*, a term that describes the activities that bring a new element of technology from conceptualization into actual use. Research and development (R&D) is a useful term for describing the earlier state of this process, but successful innovation requires additional steps that are usually labeled commercialization or utilization and which include process design and development, program development, and market development. We will restrict the definition of technological innovation to "technology new to a given organization" (NSF, 1983, p. 2). The technology may not be new to the culture that developed it. It is noteworthy, however, if the technology is new to the recipient culture, which may use the technology in ways that were not intended or anticipated by its inventors.

The objectives in adopting technological innovations are to safeguard and improve the activities of an enterprise within its overall mission. From a broader societal viewpoint, technological innovation is increasingly seen as a major contributor to economic growth and as an element in international competition and international prestige (Long, 1978, pp. 106–142). The activities leading to innovation usually involve a long-term process incorporating the various stages of research, development, capital investment, education, and utilization. The successful adoption and diffusion of innovations require adaptation to external constraints, linkage with broader development efforts, initiative and partnership, and sustained effort over a period of decades (Office of Technology Assessment, 1984). The authors' intent in this volume is to explore this new frontier of technological innovation in the helping professions, and to illuminate critical factors that contribute to or inhibit the innovation process.

The essential thrust of the present volume is to examine the interplay between a single technology—information technology—at the leading edge of science, and a single helping profession—social work. However, many of the observations and discussions here may be generalized to other technologies and allied service enterprises. The significance of our inquiry must be understood in the context of the rapid emergence of new technologies and the changing cultural landscape of society.

The Social Work Profession

The social work profession, too, faces many fast-paced social changes that beset a society undergoing transition or, as some might say, transformation. The phenomenon of social change is neither new nor uniquely a concern of the social work profession, but throughout its history social work has had much turbulence about its mission, function, and place in society within its own ranks. These internal struggles have led to useful debates and new initiatives that have moved the profession into new periods of change and growth. When suggested changes were slow in coming, some in the social work community criticized the conservative ideology that militated against the adoption of new practices. Thus, the strengths and weaknesses of social work have been attributed to the profession's ability, or inability, to adapt to new aspects of society that affect its organizational and social milieu.

The 25-year period from 1957 to 1982 was a time of unparalleled growth and development in the social work profession. During this period, significant strides were made to develop a knowledge base, gain social legitimacy and respect, expand the arenas of practice, and refine and strengthen the education of social workers for practice. While this process of consolidation and steady growth must continue, the decade of the 1980's could see a vast social transformation triggered by advances in science and technology. It is important for social work practitioners and educators to come to terms with the magnitude and reality of the changes that are being wrought in the social order as a result of the emergence of the postmodern era. These changes are not transitory; they are deep-seated and far-reaching, anchored in fundamental advances in scientific knowledge. Recent developments in computers, information systems, expert systems, artificial intelligence, image processing, and the like, presage the possibility of newer scientific discoveries and inventions. Their rapid diffusion to numerous areas has already become commonplace. The profession must meet its responsibility to develop a well-considered plan to incorporate appropriate technologies.

An Agenda for Change

The immediate agenda of social work should be to align the functions, tasks, and missions of social work education and practice with the problems, needs, and opportunities of a high-tech society. Unprecedented demands for talent, resourcefulness, and innovation press upon us to play our part in the scientific and technological revolutions, even as we reflect about their implications; to seek solutions to the most complex problems that the profession confronts; and to prepare the next generation for the rapid changes engulfing us. Our response will determine the future shape and strength of social work.

An agenda for change in social work must first meet the challenge of the production of new knowledge relevant to the postmodern era. A related task is the distribution of that knowledge to all present and future members of the profession, as well as the creation of proper rewards and incentives for the effective utilization of that knowledge in a variety of practice situations and settings. An added impetus to creating such an agenda is its potential for disseminating that knowledge to social work practitioners and educators in other parts of the world. Science, technology, and professional education are important factors in shaping relations among nations. American models of social work education and practice have long exerted profound influences on social work abroad. As other countries experience the push and pull of the postmodern era and gain access to the new information and communications technologies, they too will have to resolve hitherto unanticipated issues and concerns. Therefore, the consideration of changes in the United States will probably catalyze changes in other parts of the world. The United States once again has the opportunity to be the leader and steward of the social work profession, and thereby lead in the development and maintenance of the human edge.

Social work in the American tradition has usually entailed a struggle to maintain a reasonable balance between the needs of the society at large and the internal needs of the professional community. A profession turned inward has trouble relating to broader social changes. A new dynamic equilibrium can and must be established in social work education and practice through an orderly examination of relevant scientific and technological advances that are occurring in today's new information society.

Intercultural Technology Transfers

As the world moves into a postindustrial age that relies more and more on information gathering, analysis, and transmission, social institutions must prepare themselves to share in the powerful new technology involving computers, telecommunications, semiconductors, solar cells, fiber optics, and so forth. The importance of these applications is already evidenced in their use in trade, banking and finance, manufacturing, and university and civil-service functions.

Social-service organizations and agencies, both public and private, have also begun to utilize these technologies (LaMendola, 1979), albeit very slowly. These changes in the modes of delivering services will both benefit consumers and create problems for them. New delivery systems are designed to be more convenient, but consumers will have to be better informed to understand them and to choose among them. Also, public-policy issues stemming from changes in social services involve new questions about access to services, system security, privacy and confidentiality, and the effects of fundamental changes in information-processing and telecommunications technologies.

The effects of information technology on social services need to be understood. Social work educators and practitioners must turn their attentions to the processes that foster or inhibit the transfer of technology, to analyses of the resources that are necessary to produce orderly transfers, to the knowledge and skills that managers and practitioners need to effectively use the technology, and to assessment of the impact the technology has on administrative and clinical practice.

The Expanding Horizon for Social Work Education and Practice

The subject of knowledge and technology transfer is an underexplored domain in social work education and practice. The demanding questions and the elements of crisis that challenge us today in creating an educational policy for the profession are the most extensive, and quite possibly the most difficult, that we have experienced. It is worth recalling, in this context, Whitehead's (1929) prophetic view that "In the conditions of modern life the rule is absolute; the race which does not value trained intelligence is doomed.... Today we maintain ourselves. Tomorrow science will have moved forward yet one more step, and there will be no appeal from the judgment which will then be pronounced ... on the uneducated" (pp. 22–23).

A new phase is imminent for social work education and practice, a phase in which technological innovations of an unprecedented nature open up new frontiers of application. It is probable that the professional culture will be deeply affected by the products of electronics and information technology. In this respect, the integration of technology and the professional culture raises some problems. These problems would not necessarily lead to disharmony, although they might result in some destabilization. Adaptation and selective emphasis of the harmonious aspects may permit a blending of the professional culture and the technology, with benefits for the profession and society as a whole. Among professions, social work has demonstrated its ability to accommodate greater diversity within a commitment to human values and common principles. In the decades ahead, no goal will be more important to social work than its ability to respond creatively to the needs, characteristics, and expectations of the new information society.

The exploration and elaboration of the foregoing themes set the context for the identification, in subsequent chapters, of issues, opportunities, constraints, implications, and future challenges and options. An array of issues has been distilled from the keynote papers, the background papers, the scenarios, and the conference-participant discussions included in this book. Each issue warrants continued study and development. No grand conclusion or resolution of issues can be arrived at in a ground-breaking volume of this kind, but we anticipate that the reader will appreciate a revealing juxtaposition of assumptions, challenges, and viewpoints.

Finally, we return to the overarching theme that initiated this effort — bridging the cultures of technology and the helping professions. How is this objective to be realized? While there is no finality to the answers that are provided in this volume, many suggestions are made for reform and new initiatives in the helping professions. Whether such reform or initiative in professional education and practice follows the outlines presented here or takes some other form should not obscure the fact that the two-culture problem is one of escalating importance; the problem will not be resolved until greater attention is paid to learning from those individuals who are attempting to bridge cultures and to the processes by which they do so.

Needed: A Guidance Mechanism for Change

We have few enough replies for all the questions that impose themselves as we begin to explore new directions and frontiers in social work education and practice. Almost the only specific guides that we can muster, in the new world that we enter, are some striking bits of historical evidence. But perhaps it is proper to suspect that even in a universe that appears to change so rapidly there are relatively durable and invariant elements, and these may be the very elements of deepest import for us. The social work profession still embodies the old spirit of humane service that illuminated the arts of healing and caring. Perhaps newer advances in science and technology may be harnessed to this spirit to develop and maintain the human edge.

It is hoped that this publication achieves our objective to open this domain for future investigation. The responsibility for mapping this domain falls squarely on the shoulders of each of us who identifies with the social work profession, as educators and practitioners. For the architects of the future of social work, the message is that *the future is now.*

CHAPTER 2

INFORMATION TECHNOLOGY AND HELPING PEOPLE

> After all, this is a world run by specialists: is that
> not what we mean by a scientific society? No, it is
> not. A scientific society is one in which specialists
> can indeed do the things like making the electric
> light work. But it is you, it is I, who have to know
> how **nature** works, and how (for example)
> electricity is one of her expressions in the light
> **and** in my brain.
> —J. Bronowski (1973, pp. 435–436)

Helping people may signify the group that provides assistance to others, or it may mean the act of doing so; we use both of these definitions. *Helpers* have a variety of relationships to those they help — for example, strangers, acquaintances, relatives, selves, volunteers, or professionals — and they may act from motivations such as altruism, empathy, exercise of training and skills, charity, or self-interest. What they share as a group, at least in part, is the goal of improving the lot of self, another, or group of others by relieving wants, providing comfort, and facilitating the achievement of desired ends for those they seek to help.

Another common bond is the need for information — information about needs, strategies for helping, methods of helping, available resources, and so on. In this regard information technology becomes a medium for helping that should be readily available to helping people.

The Helping Professions

Lynn (1965) introduced his study of the professions with the observation that "Everywhere in American life, the professions are triumphant" (p. ix). Professions are as characteristic of the modern world as the crafts were of the ancient. Alfred North Whitehead (1948), in developing the distinction between the two, suggested the importance of the social transformation from crafts to professions. A craft, he explained, was "an avocation based upon customary activities and modified by the trial and error of individual practice"; a profession, in contrast, was "an avocation [EDITORS' NOTE: archaic for profession] whose activities are subject to theoretical analysis, and are modified by theoretical conclusions derived from that analysis" (pp. 73–76). If this is so, one can ask the question, "Is the vocation of helping people a craft or a profession?" Sociologists have developed indicators of professionalization and professionalism; measured against these indices, social work and other kindred helping professions closely approximate full-fledged professional status.

One of the factors that promotes professionalization in modern society is technological change, especially the rapid and advanced technological changes that have occurred in the second half of the twentieth century. In a pioneering study of professionalism from a historical perspective, Carr-Saunders and Wilson (1933) noted the importance of technology for professionalization:

> In the long run technical advance implies an increase in the number of those doing more or less specialized intellectual work relative to the number of those who are engaged in manual labor or in unspecialized intellectual routine. It may be that, while the extension of professionalism upwards and outwards will be fairly rapid, its extension downwards, though gradual and almost imperceptible, will be continuous. Thus, taking the long vision, the extension of professionalism over the whole field seems in the end not impossible. (pp. 493–494)

Blumer (1966) makes a similar connection between social change and professionalization from a slightly different historical perspective: "Professionalization represents an indigenous effort to introduce order into areas of vocational life which are prey to the free-playing and disorganizing tendencies of a vast, mobile, and differentiated society undergoing continuous change" (p. xi).

Helping people depends, at least in part, on information. Helpers certainly require information on needs, methods, and effects. Information may be drawn from observations, statements of individuals, empirical measurements, data analysis, practice wisdom, intuitions, feelings, theories, conceptualizations, literature, and religious and humanitarian values. The codification of that information into a body of systematic theory to be communicated, transferred, applied, tested, verified, grounded, and further developed is used by Ernest Greenwood (1957) as one of five characteristics that distinguish the professions.

Technological Innovation

Much of the work involving computer technology and mental-health applications is documented in Sidowski, Johnson, and Williams (1980). In that volume Sines (1980, pp. 3–4) identifies, from three key studies, the background conditions requisite for innovation. One study identifies the key factors as available knowledge, public need and recognition, and economic influences. Another study identifies scientific advancement as dependent upon tools, both conceptual and physical, and systems of classification. The third examines uncertainties— technical feasibility, monetary cost, benefits to accrue, impacts on organizations, and external effects not included in pricing—that may impede adoption of technological innovations. Sines points to technical feasibility and the external effects as the key uncertainties in applying computers in mental-health settings.

Sines concludes that three factors, in addition to the availability of computers, are necessary to the application of technology to the delivery of mental-health services: "(1) the perceived need for mental health services, (2) the availability of adequate funds . . . , (3) the availability of a particular set of conceptual tools" (p. 3). The conceptual tools, Sines points out, are those that permit investigators and practitioners to think of mental-health activities in terms of specifiable discrete steps that can be reduced to sets of rule-determined responses at each of the many specifiable decision points (Sines, 1980, p. 15). Stein and Rzepnicki (1983) provide a statement of such steps and decision points for child-welfare intake, and other descriptions of human-service activities will follow. In this volume, Pruger describes a method of developing such understanding with regard to service awards.

In introducing the section, "Current and Future Trends in Clinical Social Work," in the *Handbook of Clinical Social Work*, Scott Briar (1983) identifies a trend toward empirically based practice models in clinical social work as well and notes:

> It seems clear that implementation of data-based practice models will bring many changes in clinical practice, and it seems almost as clear that

these changes are likely to bring about a pattern of practice that is more accountable and probably more effective. What is different now compared to a decade ago is that new data-based approaches to clinical practice are feasible and not merely hypothetical. (p. 1058)

Helping depends on more than caring. It must be informed to be effective, and the more complex the society the more dependent helping becomes upon information and the technology that provides ready access to that information. We are now at the confluence of technological capability and the realization of the need for information for helping people. The conditions for innovation in social work and the other human services, especially with regard to use of information technology, can now be satisfied. We must now turn to establishing the knowledge base for the discussions of information-technology utilization in helping people, particularly in social work.

INFORMATION TECHNOLOGY: CONCEPTS AND TERMS

Thoughts about information initially lead to thoughts about computer applications as developed in commerce, industry, and government. Chronologically, these applications begin with the calculation of financial or scientific quantities, and move on to keeping records (typically of relatively fixed facts first, and then transactions); then on to grouping records into unrelated sets, or files; and subsequently, organized and related collections of files (data bases) are developed and managed. More recently systems that support decision-making via the interactive exploration of data bases and/or relationships (models) among data elements emerged. Sackman (1967, pp. 23–90), Schoech and Schkade (1980), and Sprague and Carlson (1982, pp. 6–14) provide details on these developmental processes and stages.

The Computer

Upon some reflection, one comes to believe that the computer is but a tool in a larger conceptual structure—a remarkable tool, a versatile and immensely powerful tool, but a tool nonetheless. That is, the computer is a mechanism for the storage, manipulation, display, and retrieval of symbols. These symbols may take a wide variety of forms, as shown in Table 2, and these forms vary with the domain of concern. What should

Table 2 **A Sample of Symbols and Manipulation Rules**

Domain	Symbols	Objects Represented	Rules of Manipulation
Counting	Numerals	Amounts	Arithmetic
Measurement	Numerals	Distances	Geometry, arithmetic
Writing	Alphabetic characters	Words, concepts, objects, actions, feelings	Grammar, definitions
Technical Drawing	Dots, lines	Device descriptions	Drafting standards
Graphics	Dots, lines, colors	Representations, feelings	Drafting standards, aesthetics
Speech	Phonemes	Sounds, pauses	Pronunciation, rules of speech
Music	Musical staff, notes, rests, sharps, flats	Sounds, pauses	Composition, harmony
Reasoning	Words, numerals	Ideas, assertions, propositions	Logics, statistics, mathematics

become clear from the table is that to apply computers to a domain requires a specified symbol set with a structure of rules for their manipulation. The question, "What can you do with a computer?" can then be answered, "Anything for which one can devise a symbolic representation and a set of meaningful and coherent rules for the manipulation of those symbols."

This definition of the computer as a symbol manipulator is essential to disabuse us of the unfortunate connotation of the computer as simply a device for high-speed calculation or, as it has been sometimes called, a tool for "number crunching." Alan Kay (1984) views the computer as both a medium and a metamedium, rather than a tool, thus expanding the sense of what a computer is:

> The protean nature of the computer is such that it can act like a machine or like a language to be shaped and exploited. It is a medium that can dynamically simulate the details of any other medium, including media that cannot exist physically. It is not a tool, although it can act like many tools. It is the first metamedium, and as such it has degrees of freedom for representation and expression never before encountered and as yet barely investigated. (p. 59)

It is with such broader understanding of the computer as both a medium and a metamedium that its use in the helping process becomes evident. Considered as a tool, it can help to inform, help to decide, perhaps even help to act, especially as when combined with robotic or other devices for the handicapped. But, when considered as a medium, its potential roles expand further. If the therapist is understood as a medium for the client's problem-solving, for example, by acting as a mirror that "more clearly" reflects the personal attributes and values of the client, then the computer, as a medium, can aid or undertake that process as well. (The ethics of such undertaking must be dealt with, and are the subject of substantial discussion in subsequent chapters.) As a metamedium the computer can be used to simulate practice situations and to test "what if" questions of interest to practitioners engaged in helping processes.

Software

What makes the computer do anything is software — the instructions followed by machine and person. Some of it is permanently a part of the computer itself (firmware, read only memory [ROM], or cartridge software). Most of it is found on magnetic storage media (disks, diskettes, or tapes) as programs; some of it is found in the manuals (documentation); and some of it is created by the user (programming, or applications program modification). The key idea is that humans create software and to that degree control the machine, but most software is so logically complex that it is never fully tested and can consequently produce unexpected and unintended outcomes (there is a woman in California who has, on occasion, received Social Security checks in the amount of her zip code). Understanding software is the key to understanding computers.

One view of computer software is that it is analogous to cooking recipes. The operating-system (OS, DOS, etc.) software provides the underlying rules by which basic processes are accomplished; for example, space is allocated in memory (the kitchen counter is cleared and prepared for measuring, mixing, etc.), and specific information is found via its memory location or address (spices in the left cabinet, butter and milk in the refrigerator). Operating-system software, whether in cooking or in computing, is generally taken for granted and, when well designed, is transparent to the user.

Language software ranges from the low-level language amenable to execution by the hardware (machine language) to the more mnemonically oriented assembly language, to higher-level programming languages like BASIC, COBOL, FORTRAN, APL, and PASCAL (which permit humans to more easily express their problems for machine solution).

In choosing a language, one typically trades human convenience for processing speed and access to special machine attributes. The higher the level of the language, generally, the easier it is for humans to express and accomplish their tasks. In terms of a cookbook analogy, a machine-language recipe would be expressed with the most elementary cooking operations and would assume no knowledge whatever on the part of the cook (the computer), including, for example, how to get salt from a salt container. An assembly-language recipe would permit some elementary operations to be grouped and labelled with mnemonics for reference and use, for example, "pinch of salt." The general-purpose, higher-level languages permit the recipe to be expressed in more convenient forms such as blend, knead, bake, simmer, and so forth. Each complex command will be converted into the numerous elementary commands for machine execution by another set of instructions—an interpreter or compiler program.

For most of us, who are too busy doing our own work to worry about programming tasks for the computer, there are applications–software packages. These perform tasks within a specific domain of activity as illustrated in Table 3. Some require the user to plan (program) the task to be performed, but the user can express the program in a more natural way than with a more general programming language. Most programming languages require explicit definition of how a task is to be done and, consequently, are referred to as procedural languages. "Nonprocedural language" is sometimes used to denote an applications–software package that permits simpler user entries to activate programming of complex tasks—the user focuses on what is to be done, not how it is to be done.

Continuing the cooking analogy, "bake at 350° F for 1 hour" would, in a nonprocedural language, be equivalent, in a procedural language, to "turn oven on, set thermostat to 350° F, when temperature is reached open oven door and insert pan filled with dough, set timer to one hour, when timer signals end of one hour get potholder, open oven door, use potholder to remove pan, place pan on heat-resistant surface to cool."

Software and End-Users

Applications programs have brought us the era of the "end-user" in which managers, clinicians, teachers, and so on, can use computers to solve problems in their domains of interest without understanding the details of how computers accomplish the tasks.

> Computers are to computing as instruments are to music. Software is the score, whose interpretation amplifies our reach and lifts our spirits. Leonardo da Vinci called music "The shaping of the invisible," and his phrase is even more apt as a description of software. (Kay, 1984, p. 53)

A first reaction might be that software cannot be interpreted in the same manner as a musical score, yet the manner in which it is used is under the user's control. That is, it can be used literally and technically

Table 3 **Examples of Applications Software**

Applications Software	Domain of Activity	Tasks Performed or Supported
Word Processing	Communication via paper or electronic means	Composing, editing, formatting, and printing text. Form letter, envelope, and label production. Spelling checking.
File Management	Record-keeping	Entry, display, organization, and output of records with a fixed data structure within a file.
Data-Base Management	Record-keeping	Same as file management, but management with ability to relate contents of one file to that of other files, e.g., "find the treatment plans for all clients under 5," where age is in demographics file and plans are in a separate file.
Spreadsheet	Financial and other information modelling	Entry, display, manipulation, and printing of information organized in an array of rows and columns, e.g., budget, income projection, client visit patterns by month and client, etc.
Expert System Shell	Reasoning	Construction of knowledge-based systems, e.g., a treatment-planning system, guidance-counselling system, etc.

as in a mechanical rendition, or it can be interpreted liberally as when a spreadsheet program (meant for financial calculations) is used to produce multicolumn text tables or to simulate biological population dynamics. Turkle (1984, p. 22) has noted the opaque quality of computers, that is, no physical view of the computer innards helps to understand its functioning. In this sense the software shapes the opaque computer by producing visibly useful results.

Software's human interface "is recognized as being primary, because to novices and professionals alike, what is presented to one's senses *is* one's computer. The 'user illusion' ... is the simplified myth everyone builds to explain (and make guesses about) the system's actions and what should be done next" (Kay, 1984, p. 54). Various approaches can establish and maintain the illusion, and thereby permit the user to focus on the tasks with which he or she is concerned. One of the most popular and effective approaches always displays a faithful representation of the product ("what you see is what you get!"), without regard to process or command structure. This approach is evident in those word processors that always display the text as it will be printed, and spreadsheets that automatically recalculate results after any change in a cell's contents. Alan Kay (1984) directs himself to the future of these developments when he notes:

> A person exerts the greatest leverage when his illusion can be manipulated without appeal to abstract intermediaries such as the hidden programs needed to put into action even a simple word processor. What I call direct leverage is provided when the illusion acts as a "kit," or tool, with which to solve a problem. Indirect leverage will be attained when the illusion acts as an "agent": an active extension of one's purposes and goals. In both cases the software designer's control of what is essentially a theatrical context is the key to creating an illusion and enhancing its "friendliness." (p. 54)

The helping professions then must identify their problems, purposes, and goals so that together with software designers they can build the illusions, "kits," "tools," and "agents," appropriate to helping. This can be achieved only through informed, active participation in prototyping and testing of software innovations that will help define needs and opportunities. Then the helping professions can use to the fullest the metamedium, the computer.

Data, Information, and Knowledge

Information is the stuff of decision-making and problem-solving, and the raison d'être for computer applications in professional contexts. Information given or received is the central commodity of professional activity. "Data" and "information" are used interchangeably in daily expression, but they are not the same. For our purposes we choose to define data as the raw material produced by observation or measurement—that is, facts or that which the senses perceive—and that produced by thought—inferences, calculations, and speculations.

> The materials of computing are the tersest of markings, stored by the billions in computer hardware. In a musical score the tune is represented in the hardware of paper and ink; in biology the message transmitted from generation to generation by DNA is held in the arrangement of the chemical groups called nucleotides . . . . Marks on clay or paper, in DNA and in computer memories are equally powerful in their ability to represent, but the only intrinsic meaning of a mark is that it is there. "Information," Gregory Bateson noted, "is any difference that makes a difference." The first difference is the mark; the second one alludes to the need for interpretation. (Kay, 1984, p. 53)

Information results from the processing of data into its relevant, useful, and meaningful components: data may be filtered (errors and irrelevant data removed), aggregated, compared, smoothed, estimated, and cor-related. Keen and Scott Morton (1978) emphasize the need to distinguish between information and data, "data being facts and infor-mation being facts that are necessary for some purpose and that have meaning and significance. If an organization collects *information*, some-one has taken the trouble to decide which *data* are necessary" (p. 56).

Knowledge results from the processing of information into a coherent body of facts, theories, and scientific laws; it is the distillation of infor-mation into its essence. Knowledge may be viewed as a compact state-ment of a collection of information, as in the law of gravity, which can then be used to generate new data and information, as in the applica-tion of the law of gravity to predict the behavior of objects on the moon's surface.

Information Systems

Information systems can be seen to be systems that store, process, retrieve, and communicate information. These systems are now most often based upon the use of computers, but need not contain com-puters. They must contain a living entity for without life there is no use for information. For example, Mason and Mitroff (1973) say:

> An information system consists of at least one PERSON of a certain PSYCHOLOGICAL TYPE who faces a PROBLEM within some ORGANIZATIONAL CONTEXT for which he needs EVIDENCE to arrive at a solution (i.e., to select some course of action) and that the evidence is made available to him through some MODE OF PRESEN-TATION. (p. 475)

There are, now, three generally recognized forms of computer-based information systems: electronic data processing (EDP) systems; manage-ment information systems (MIS); and decision support systems (DSS). EDP refers to the earliest of these systems and is most often identified by the focus on record-keeping in separate and unrelated files.

Management information systems (MIS) are another set of ubiq-uitous entities that are difficult to define. Watson and Carroll (1976, pp. 261–263) identify a spectrum of definitions ranging from the opera-tional view—a system that processes transaction data and prepares an expanded set of scheduled reports—to the view that an MIS provides all organizational units with information for effective functioning. More recently, Sprague and Carlson (1982, pp. 6–7) have described the con-notational differences found in EDP, MIS, and DSS as shown in

Table 4. According to Sprague and Carlson, this evolutionary view has credence because it approximately represents developments in recent practice, but it suffers from the false implication that support is needed only at the top levels of organizations. Schoech and Schkade (1981) have pointed out that information needs and decision environments of social-service agencies are roughly inverse to those of business and that the front-line service workers are most in need of decision support. Further, Sprague and Carlson note that decision-making needs to be coordinated across organizational levels and, thus, communication becomes an important dimension of DSS. Lastly, this model implies that decision support is the only thing managers need from an information system, when, in fact, decision-making is only one of the managerial activities that benefit from the support of information systems.

Table 4 Connotational Differences Among EDP, MIS, and DSS

EDP

- A focus on data (storage, processing, and flows) at the operational level
- Efficient transaction processing
- Scheduled and optimized computer runs
- Integrated files for related jobs
- Summary reports for management

MIS

- An information focus, aimed at middle managers
- Structured information flows
- Integration of EDP jobs by business function (production MIS, marketing MIS, personnel MIS, etc.)
- Inquiry and report generation (usually with a data base)

DSS

- A decision focus, aimed at top managers and executive decision makers
- Emphasis on flexibility, adaptability, and quick response
- User-initiated and user-controlled
- Support for the personal decision-making styles of individual managers

SOURCE: *Building Effective Decision Support Systems,* Ralph H. Sprague, Jr. and Eric D. Carlson, 1982, pp. 6–7. Adapted by permission of Prentice-Hall, Inc., Englewood Cliffs, New Jersey.

Communications

Communication is a key activity for professionals, who are by definition knowledge or information workers, and, in particular, for those persons specializing in helping others. Communication holds people, and thus an organization, together; it is both a medium for exchange and a process for transferring data, information, and knowledge. Communication methods can be examined in two groups, as in Table 5.

One of the most distinguishing characteristics of these groups of methods is the degree of feedback that is possible between sender and receiver of the communication. In fact, use of this criterion might result in the Videotex service being included in the first group because, while both Teletext and Videotex provide textual information on a properly equipped TV set, only Videotex, with its roots in telephone or cable-TV transmission, is designed for two-way communication. Teletext, because it is a broadcast service, does not provide feedback.

Table 5 **Communication Methods**

Individual-to-Individual and Group Communication Methods:

- face-to-face
- paper
- telephony
- facsimile (e.g., image transmission via xerography)
- telephone and video conferencing
- electronic mail and computer conferencing

Mass Communication Methods:

- publications
- radio, broadcast television, cable television
- Videotex and Teletext
- bulletin boards

Office Automation

Perhaps the two most significant breakthroughs in these methods, where real two-way communication is possible, are the conquest of space by telephony, and the conquest of time by "store and forward" methods of computer-based messaging — computer-based conferencing and electronic mail. The "store and forward" method, because it stores messages until the receiver is ready to accept them, ends "telephone tag" — the iterative process required to connect by telephone. With the advent of computer-based private branch exchanges (PBX's, or switchboards) this "store and forward" technology can be applied to voice messages as well. There are some, especially in the telephone industry (see Mayo, 1982), who envision the digital PBX as the central core of office-automation systems. In their view it would provide both voice and data communications switching, electronic mail, voice message recording, word processing, document preparation and distribution, meeting and facility scheduling, and directories of names, locations, phone numbers, and departments. The office is becoming the major battleground for the computer industry and the communications industry. The office is seen as extremely attractive because both industries believe that "principals"—professionals, the suppliers and users of information—can have their productivity augmented far more than that of support personnel—those who file and transform information—since their salaries are higher, and they are not well supported now. A Booz-Allen study cited in Champine (1980) reported that principals spend 25% of their time doing clerical work "and lose even more time due to time lags in obtaining information—or not being able to get information at all" (p. 96). The time lag has come to be called "information float," that is, "the amount of time that information spends in transit in a communications medium" (Naisbitt, 1983, p. 110). Information float is typically 3 days for memos in large organizations.

Computer Networking

The combination of digital computers with communications networks, whether based upon telephone systems, cable TV, broadcast media, or communications satellites, creates a computer network. This new form of network can represent the sharing of computer resources (distributed processing), the sharing of data and augmentation of tools on the computers, and the human network of computer users. As Birnbaum (1982, p. 764) noted, the automobile needed low-cost mass production and a hierarchy of paved roads to be truly useful, and networks are the roads of computing. Naisbitt (1983) notes:

> An ongoing convergence of computer and communications technologies is providing the framework for the information society that is taking shape. At the same time this convergence is controlling the pace of change by collapsing what can be called the "information float." . . . Unlike the last societal transformation, which took probably a century to complete, this one, after less than 30 years has probably passed the halfway point. . . . The trend is clear: this world of increasingly interdependent communities, under the influence of a collapsing global information float, is becoming a global economic village. (p. 110)

These networks make a variety of services possible: remote computer access, electronic mail, bulletin boards, computer-based conferencing, file transfer, resource sharing, and embedding nontextual communications (e.g., facsimile—image transmission, and voice) (Newell & Sproull, 1982, pp. 844–845). Remote computer access makes the power of major computing resources available anywhere there is telephone access, and with the advent of cellular radio, that becomes anywhere within the covered broadcast areas or cells. Electronic mail provides the automatic store-and-forward message service, along with automatic document distribution, mail-list maintenance, and so forth, while computer-based conferencing provides an enlarged service that admits filing and retrieval of messages in complex ways, maintenance of permanent message records (conferences—restricted to defined groups, with messages organized by senders, receivers, dates, and subjects, and notebooks—organized primarily by subjects). Bulletin boards are often public or semipublic postings of inquiries, offers of services, information or resources, and public-domain software. File transfer provides for exchange of large files such as research data or the text of a document, from computer to computer. Resource sharing permits a group of computers to share a task by partitioning the task and performing the subtasks according to where general computing resources or necessary special computing resources are available. The embedding of other communications takes advantage of the burst nature of computer communications to fill gaps between bursts of computer communications with other services. A consequence of computer networks is that a variety of services become available at a low cost because of the speed of communications and full communications-resource utilization. Typically, computer-network charges are about $5 per hour, regardless of distance, as compared to interstate phone calls at $20 per hour ($7 per hour, off-peak).

Another effect of computer networks has been to encourage the distribution of computer resources to sites where they are needed. Champine (1980) indicates that the pressure for increased efficiency has reduced the amount of information float that business will tolerate with the result that "the policy of centralizing the EDP function can be contrary to the goal of availability of timely information" (p. 91). In addition, he noted that declining hardware costs and available technology are such that even if economies of scale are offered by centralization their impact is becoming less significant. The primary distinction between decentralized computing and distributed computing is that in the latter the computers communicate with one another. He indicates that the reasons for the interest in distributed processing are:

- faster and easier access to data for decision-making;
- improved reliability, security, and integrity;
- improved modularity—reduced initial investment and risk;
- improved control and reporting in a geographically dispersed organization;

- lower total organization cost;
- faster response to change of requirements or priorities;
- lower communication cost;
- lower cost than upgrading a central system;
- the possibility for local financial approval. (p. 92)

The most significant disadvantage of computer networking and distributed processing is that it opens the system to intrusion when public communications media are used for part or all of the network. The security and integrity of the system can be maintained, at a cost, through a variety of technical solutions (e.g., encryption of data communications, use of automatic call-back to validated users at approved phone numbers, complex security procedures such as voiceprint or fingerprint validation at sign-on).

Most subtly and tacitly the information-system concept has entered the picture since most every node in a computer network will have some information system residing and available on it. The synergistic combination of computers and communications with information systems technologies creates information technology.

INFORMATION TECHNOLOGY: TRENDS AND IMPACTS

Rate of Change

The significance of information technology for society and the professions is difficult to grasp; the rapid pace and magnitude of the changes that have taken place is unprecedented. It is instructive to review some salient historical events to grasp the rate of change (see Table 6). Most of the history spans only 30 to 40 years (see Augarten, 1984, for details).

The dramatic rush of events visible to the public in the last 50 years brings together computer hardware, communications hardware, and software in a new and more powerful revolution that influences not only what we do but what and how we think, on the job and about ourselves (see Turkle, 1984). This history is primarily the product of two sciences, physics and mathematics, and one profession, electrical engineering. The impact on end-users, especially nontechnical professionals, is significant in terms of direct access to the power of information technology, and in terms of the direct impact of information technology upon professional work (expert systems, for example). The technology has left the laboratory to enter the shop, the office, and the home—it permeates our society. "Despite the immense achievements

Table 6 **Salient Events in the History of Information Technology**

1800	Volta discovers chemical battery and direct electric current
1823	Charles Babbage begins first mechanical calculator, the Difference Engine, which is to be programmed by Ada Lovelace (daughter of Lord Byron)
1844	Samuel Morse demonstrates telegraph system
1854	George Boole publishes "An investigation of the laws of thought," the basis for digital computer logic (Boolean algebra)
1876	Alexander Graham Bell invents the telephone
1888	Herman Hollerith invents punched-card tabulator
1889	Strowger invents the dial telephone
1901	Marconi sends first transatlantic radio message
1907	Lee de Forest invents first vacuum tube — Audion
1927	Black invents negative-feedback amplifier central to long-distance telephony and automatic control; H. E. Ives demonstrates picture transmission over telephone lines
1931	First teletype service
1937	A. H. Reeves invents pulse or digital voice communication; G. R. Stibitz builds first electrical computer of relays
1939	Atanasoff and Berry build prototype of first electronic digital computer; M. Kelly of Bell Laboratories directs funds to build smaller, more reliable amplifying device
1945	J. Presper Eckert and John W. Mauchly build ENIAC (Electronic Numerical Integrator and Calculator), formerly believed to be first electronic digital computer
1946	John von Neumann publishes key idea of stored-program computer
1947	Bardeen, Brattain, and Schockley invent the transistor
1950's	Dataphone service began

of technology by 1900, the following seven decades witnessed more advances over a wide range of activities than the whole range of recorded history. . . invented and developed to create an unparalleled social situation, full of possibilities and dangers" (Buchanan, as cited in Coggeshall, 1984, p. 73).

Scope of Change

While the pace of change has been swift, the magnitude of change has been very large. Champine (1980, p. 87), in a review of business computing, points out that the UNIVAC I could perform 2000 instructions

Table 6 (continued)

1951	First nonmilitary computer (UNIVAC I) delivered by Remington Rand (Mauchly and Eckert) to Census Bureau
1954	First commercial computer delivered by Remington Rand to G.E.
1957	Townes and Schawlow propose first laser—leads to optical disks and fiber-optic communications
1958	Felker, et al., of Bell Laboratories build first fully transistorized computer
1961	Fairchild Semiconductor produces first circuit on a chip; integrated-circuit era begins
1962	NASA maintains communications with Mariner 2 on fly-by of Venus at 54,300,000 miles from Earth
1965	INTELSAT, first commercial satellite communications system
1967	Beginning of standard large-scale integrated-circuit era
1970	First solid-state random access memory (256 bits) on a chip
1973	INTELSAT adds digital communication methods to satellites
1974	First application of knowledge engineering (automated chemical-structure analysis)
1975	8-bit computer on a chip
1976	First expert system to diagnose infectious disease and explain reasoning
1977	First non-kit 8-bit home computer—Apple II
1978	16-bit computer on a chip
1980	First automatic interpretation of lung function in real time
1981	First 16-bit personal computers
1982	First expert system sold to commercial user (oil-drilling advice)
1984	Apple Macintosh commercially introduces mouse for pointing, icons for communication and "pointing and clicking" for commands—a 32-bit personal computer

per second, was able to store 12,000 digits, cost $750,000 and weighed in at 16,000 pounds. By comparison, the Intel 8080 microprocessor (basic 8-bit processor in many CP/M machines) that was introduced 21 years later could perform 100 times as many instructions per second, weighed 1/1000 of the UNIVAC I, stored 64,000 digits (64K bytes), and cost $175 in 1953 dollars. The ratio of price to performance had been reduced by a factor of 430,000, and the size had been reduced by a factor of 1000. He points out further that super-scale commercial systems have 100 times the performance at comparable prices, measured in 1953 dollars. This kind of change is entirely outside of our experience and, thus, we have no intuition with which to understand or integrate these data. Christopher Evans (1979), the late British psychologist, tried to give a sensible analogy as an aid to understanding in this form:

> Suppose for a moment that the automobile industry had developed at the same rate as computers and over the same period: .... Today you would be able to buy a Rolls-Royce for $2.75, it would do three million miles to the gallon, and it would deliver enough power to drive the *Queen Elizabeth II*. And if you were interested in miniaturization, you could place half a dozen of them on a pinhead. (p. 77)

Just as with computer power, the mass storage of data also has dramatically increased in capacity and at reduced cost over an inflationary period. This is summarized in Table 7, which has been adapted from Goldstein (1982, p. 865).

Table 7 **On-line Mass Storage Capacity and Costs**

			Cost (thousands) per item shown	
Year	*Device Type*	*Storage Capacity*	*per Drive*	*per 10Mb Storage*
1973	IBM 3330-11	200 Mb	$28,000	$1,430.0
1975	IBM 3350	317 Mb	43,000	1,300.0
1978	CDC 33502	635 Mb	27,000	430.0
1981	IBM 3380	2,500 Mb	98,000	392.0
1983 est.	Phillips pack	100,000 Mb	50,000	5.1

Source: Adapted from "Optical Disk Technology and Information," by C. M. Goldstein in February 12, 1982 *Science*, vol. 215, pp. 862–868. Copyright © 1982 by the AAAS.

Note: The last entry is an optical disk, all others are magnetic disks. The unit of storage is 10 megabytes or 10,000,000 bytes or characters (about 10,000 double-spaced typed pages or a 5-drawer file cabinet full of double-spaced typed pages). The costs are gross in the sense that all details have not been computed.

The reduced cost and enormously increased capacities are quite dramatic, but they are even more dramatic in light of the speed of access to any item of data. For example, Herbert (1983, p. 33) reports a new thin film disk subsystem that has a transfer rate of 3 megabytes per second (1/3 of a 5-drawer file cabinet full of double-spaced typed pages transferred from place to place in one second), and an average access time of 16 microseconds (on average, any item of data can be retrieved in 1/60 of the shortest duration exposure available on a good camera — 1/1000 sec.). The optical disk mentioned earlier can also store video and sound, as many as 54,000 frames of picture information on a 12-inch optical disk. The combination of a videodisc player with a computer opens a new world of interactive and responsive entertainment, training and educational opportunities. Lynett's paper in Chapter 5 describes the use of such a system to train staff in interpersonal skills.

In the transmission of data, optical fibers used by the Bell System between New York City and Washington, D.C., carry 90 megabits per second (about 10 megabytes, or a 5-drawer file full of information, every second). In satellite receiving equipment, the 25-foot-diameter dish antenna and related receiver electronics cost $500,000 in 1972; by 1982, the homeowner could purchase a 12-foot-diameter dish and receiver kit for $2,500 to $7,000. That dish is expected to shrink in cost to $100 and in size to 2 feet in diameter in the near future and thus make the new broadcast satellite service and a new world of communications available to the average homeowner.

An Exponential Phenomenon

In the area of computer memories, random access memory (RAM), the amount of memory that can be built on a single chip, quadruples about every 2.8 years, that is approximately as follows: 256 in 1970, 1K by 1973, 4K by 1976, 256K by 1985, and so on (Robinson, 1984). Similarly, the price of mainframe computers has dropped at the rate of 25% per year compounded (or more than half every 3 years). These behaviors — referred to as exponential behavior in mathematical modeling — are extremely counterintuitive. To make this point clearly, Evans (1979) asked how thick a sheet of paper would be created by folding an ordinary sheet in half 50 times. The incredible answer is that the result would be 17.8 million miles thick, from the Earth's surface beyond the moon, past Mars, and into an asteroid belt. This consequence of compounding is exponential behavior. Most characteristics of information technology behave exponentially over time.

The hardware is wondrous to behold, and is often treated with the same attitude as are toys, but it is the software that is of real concern.

Mastery Is in the Software

Software controls the machine and makes it do what seem like intelligent things. The hierarchical evolution of software — from arcane machine language, accessible and sensible only to the most devoted programmers, through higher-level languages that permit typical mortals to express their problems to machines, and on to end-user applications software and nonprocedural languages (word processors, some data-base managers, query languages, and spreadsheets), which permit a significant range of professional tasks to be accomplished without programming—is seemingly being repeated in artificial-intelligence software. Some would describe LISP, the basis for most artificial-intelligence (AI) work, as the machine language of AI, with such expert shells as EMYCIN as the first higher-level AI language.

Mastery of the machine is attained through understanding software. The major software elements of concern to professionals are the *productivity-enhancing* software (word-processing, data-base managers, spreadsheets, graphics and telecommunications programs); and the *practice-enhancing* software (expert systems, and telecommunications programs). The first group helps to get the job done, and the second group helps to do jobs better through consultation with artificial experts, actual peers, and literature data bases.

An expert system is software that incorporates the knowledge of a specific domain, including practice wisdom (rules of thumb, good guessing, etc.), and a mechanism for reasoning about that domain in order to arrive at conclusions that are not necessarily obvious to a human. The term "knowledge base" is often used to distinguish an expert system from a data-base manager, which helps to organize, view, extract, and report or display data from a collection of related files, but which does not contain rules for reasoning about the contents of those files. They are, however, related and can be joined in a larger system. Hayes-Roth (1984) points out that data-base systems extend the power and reach of the professional by augmenting human memory, but he also notes that just as technology now gives the professional access to the vast experience of others, it will one day confer that on laypersons. "More, and more, machines will give consumers not only raw information, but also the ideas and decisions that an able human professional might build upon it. At least this is the hope of those engaged in knowledge engineering" (pp. 28–29).

"Knowledge engineering" describes the activities of those who work with the domain experts to extract and codify the domain knowledge for expert-system construction. The particularly attractive machine attributes—infinite-duration memory, stress-free, always performs at peak of ability, immune to boredom, utterly trustworthy, and immortal, with proper maintenance—make expert systems valuable for many tasks. Hayes-Roth sees the human qualities of flexibility, individualism, and intuitiveness as difficult to build into expert systems. But there is still much professional intellectual work that may be suitable for the machine. A serious problem remains in that most knowledge engineering is accomplished in a labor-intensive way that lasts 7 months to 15 years from conception to implementation (Hayes-Roth, 1983, p. 80). It has been estimated that 50 person-years of effort went into building MYCIN, the infectious-disease-diagnosis expert system. Hayes-Roth's estimates for the future are that we will need computing engines of 10,000 times the current size, and considerable new knowledge about knowledge representation, along with a 10-fold increase in the knowledge encoding rate and a 100-fold increase in the number of knowledge engineers to avoid exponential growth in the cost of building and operating such knowledge systems. Guterl (1983, p. 111) reports forecasts that knowledge engineering will become another engineering specialty, and that expert systems will provide advice to people who could otherwise not afford a human expert.

The developments in artificial intelligence and the needs of robotics converge in computer-based vision systems, and speech-recognition and speech-synthesis systems. In general, computer-based vision systems are primitive compared to human vision; they lack depth sense when only a single image is presented (but it can be derived from shadings), and interpretation of the image requires a very large body of knowledge; shape can be perceived, but recognition or identification of objects is more difficult (Kanade & Reddy, 1983, p. 88). Vision systems can contribute to the vision-limited and to extending data-collection capabilities to nonverbal materials. In the area of computer-based speech recognition, more has been accomplished in isolated-word recognition. Up to 200-word vocabularies, with limited syntax and speaker dependence, have been demonstrated on moderate-speed computers (1 to 10 million instructions per second — 1 to 10 MIPS). In continuous speech with speaker independence, recognition of a 1000-word vocabulary, with limited syntax, requires a fast computing speed of about 100 MIPS. IBM has demonstrated a laboratory model for isolated words, speaker-dependent, with unlimited syntax, which recognizes a 5000-word vocabulary, but requires a 300-MIPS machine, and it does not run in real time (Reddy & Zue, 1983, p. 85). These developments will help make information technology available to an even broader segment of the public, especially to those who cannot or will not type or point, but will speak. This wider accessibility is made even more probable by the work in natural language processing, described by Waltz (1983), which extends information technology to those who do not know a formal language.

The obverse of a computer-based vision system is a computer-based imaging system, that is, a computer-based system that helps humans to assimilate and interpret complex data by presenting it in the form of computed images, for example, computerized axial tomography (CAT), nuclear magnetic resonance (NMR), and positron emission tomography

(PET) scans. The first uses a sequence of x-ray images to form a cross-section of an object (usually a human part); the second uses a magnetic field to form a soft-tissue, cross-sectional image (particularly useful in tumor detection); and the PET uses radiation from within to form images that help follow and understand biological, especially metabolic, processes (Fischetti, 1983; Durden-Smith, 1982). PET scans have been shown dramatically useful in diagnosing mental disorders — Alzheimer's disease, bipolar (manic) depression, and schizophrenia (Jaffe, 1982). Perhaps someone will develop an evocative use of imaging technology — a technical analog to the Rorschach test.

Another developing area of information technology that has helping potential is the computer-based game. The sketchy evidence available indicates that computer-based video games are addictive because of the reinforcement received. The games demand the continued development of skill and the ability to manage stress (Smith, 1984; Loftus & Loftus, 1983). These qualities could offer some value in behavioral modification, particularly with male adolescents (females take little interest in video games). Schoech (personal communication) has suggested that video games be placed in youth agencies (e.g., probation offices) to encourage regular visiting, trust, and information-giving, and thereby save professional time spent tracking youth for services and counselling. Computer-based video games have previously been solitary adventures against a fantasy world, but an article in *Link:Up* (Ware, 1984) reports an interactive video game, Mega III, to be played over a computer network by as many as 100 players. Thus, computer networks offer another form of shared problem-solving and another fun way of learning from one another.

INFORMATION TECHNOLOGY AND HELPING PEOPLE

The connection of these wondrous products of the human mind to helping people, and to social work in particular, exists in two veins — threats and opportunities — and on a number of levels. The levels include the personal — self, individual clients and groups of clients — the professional, the organizational, and the societal. Information technology offers opportunities to help, to help better, and to help in new ways, and these will be explored further (that is the substance of this volume). Information technology threatens as well in a variety of ways. Both the opportunities and the threats must become the concern of the helping professions.

In an editorial introducing the special issue of *IEEE Spectrum,* "Beyond 1984: Technology and The Individual," Donald Christiansen (1984), the journal's editor, reported briefly on a Harris poll of the membership of the Institute of Electrical and Electronic Engineers as follows:

> It is much easier to design a new microprocessor or even a fiber-optic communications system than to deal with their ultimate application in a bureaucratic or international context. In practice, greater knowledge often helps freeze our inaction: the more we learn about the societal or institutional aspects of an issue, the less likely we are to know where to start in finding an answer. . . .
>
> One might conclude that we engineers are concerned about important sociotechnical issues and perhaps better informed on these issues than ever before, but that aside from casting our votes in a ballot box, we are not likely to become very involved in these issues. . . .(p. 25)

If the creators and builders will not act to examine and regulate their inventions and constructions, then the "user public" must!

Christopher Evans (1979, pp. 256–262), among others, has tried to examine the potential impact of technology upon individuals. He reports the likelihood of changes in work patterns with more need for education, consequent later start at work, shorter work life due to change, and a shorter work week. Communications technology will allow a reduction in business travel, and a consequent focus on the home as the center of work and leisure. There will be enormous advances in home-entertainment devices, machines to perform our work, education in the home, and the social turbulence will encourage staying in the home. There will, Evans believed, be a continuing emphasis on physical fitness and a return of mysticism and religion to "explain" the increasingly complex world. What is particularly remarkable is that in his forecast for the "middle term" — 1983 to 1990 — he foresaw the decline of the professions: "The erosion of the power of the established professions will be a striking feature of the second phase of the Computer Revolution. . . . The vulnerability of the professions is tied up with their special strength — the fact that they act as exclusive repositories and disseminators of specialist knowledge." In this he clearly agrees with Feigenbaum (1983): "We will have a form of knowledge that we have not seen represented before, the heuristic knowledge, the experiential knowledge of good practice — in short, the 'art of good guessing.' In the long-term service of humanity it is the knowledge that is important. It may make little difference whether this knowledge is processed by machines or not" (p. 78).

Hayes-Roth (1984, p. 31) presents a much more optimistic view in which the proportion of the service-delivery aspect of professional work expands dramatically beyond 1980, the proportion of the judgement aspect remaining roughly constant, and learning, studying, internship, and physical activity declining to less than 10% of professional work time. When he examines the proportions of the various factors comprising professional judgement, he finds that the proportions of intuition and perception will increase, while memory, data-gathering, analysis, and reasoning will each decline to roughly less than 5% of the total. He points out that the amount of judgement will not vary substantially, but its constituent components will change toward perception and intuition.

In Guterl's (1983) report of a panel discussion among leaders in the development of information technology, especially artificial intelligence and robotics, numerous social problems were recognized:

- the substantial dislocations arising from automated production;
- slavish conformity to decision-making machines;
- the lack of availability of information resources to middle-income, working class, and the poor because of a lack of discretionary income to pay the costs—the benefits will trickle down from the wealthy;
- there may be a loss of diversity in thought that is due to expert systems;
- the "chilling effect" of believing you may be observed;
- the confusion of know-how with knowledge;
- cross-indexing of records to invade privacy.

At least some of the panelists called for public-policy initiatives and broad public discussions of the issues. In the words of one, "Adopting the technology and dealing in a humane and appropriate way with the human and other social effects are not likely to occur without some sort of public-policy intervention. I do not necessarily mean single centralized government programs. But we need something that transcends simple individual-level market choices" (Morgan, as cited in Guterl, 1983, p. 117).

Thus we see a mere sampling of the potential and actual impacts classified by differing perceptions as threats or opportunities, and affecting various levels differently; for example, an expert system that threatens a profession may be an opportunity for individuals or groups of individuals to access information. What is clear is that we face a period of continued and striking change, and in that is opportunity. Naisbitt (1983) closes his article: "In stable eras, everything has settled in its place and little can be leveraged. In times of transition between eras, individuals and institutions have extraordinary leverage and influence — if they can keep a clear vision of the road ahead" (p. 111). This search for leverage and influence via a clear vision is what the remainder of this volume is about.

PART TWO

VIEWS OF PRESENT AND FUTURE

edited by
Gunther R. Geiss
and
Narayan Viswanathan

CHAPTER 3

EXTERNAL VIEWS
OF OPPORTUNITIES
AND THREATS:
THE KEYNOTES

> Johnny von Neumann was in love with the
> aristocracy of intellect. And that is a belief which
> can only destroy the civilisation that we know. If
> we are anything, we must be a democracy of the
> intellect. We must not perish by the distance
> between people and government, between people
> and power, by which Babylon and Egypt and Rome
> failed. And that distance can only be conflated, can
> only be closed, if knowledge sits in the homes and
> heads of people with no ambition to control others,
> and not up in the isolated seats of power.
> —J. Bronowski (1973, p.435)

EDITORS' INTRODUCTION

Today's digital computer was born in the United States in the 1930's and developed in Great Britain and the United States during World War II, in the frenzy of technological innovation that war spawns. At Iowa State College, John Vincent Atanasoff and Clifford E. Berry developed the ABC (Atanasoff Berry Computer) to compute solutions to partial differential equations (Atanasoff, 1984). Only recently the courts and the computing community recognized Atanasoff's ground-breaking contributions. In Great Britain, in 1943, mathematician Alan Turing helped design an electronic computer named Colossus. At about the same time and quite independently, the United States designers John W. Mauchly and J. Presper Eckert were working at the University of Pennsylvania on the ENIAC (Electronic Numerical Integrator and Calculator), the first publicly well-known general-purpose electronic computer. Since the Atanasoff Berry Computer, Colossus, and ENIAC, computers have moved through a continuing series of improvements: vacuum tubes, transistors, integrated circuits, the microprocessor on a chip, and other advances in memory and storage devices.

The computer's performance improved with its hardware and its software, moving it beyond simple numerical calculations to the complex manipulations of symbols representing quantities, patterns, images, sounds, concepts, and logics. Computers transformed tasks that can be expressed symbolically—design, manufacture, and information manipulation and communication in general.

The transfer of this technological innovation to medicine, education, social work, and other human-service professions is comparatively recent. Social work, as a field of professional activity in human-service organizations, is a convenient microcosm in which the transfer of computer and information technology can be observed. Computer-automated billing, payroll, and agency record-keeping are already in common use. Communication networks are slowly being set up for the rapid transfer of information. Computer-assisted generation of statistics, summarized by location, by service, by age, or by other characteristics, are used for planning, service delivery, and program evaluation. Such gathering and sorting of data by computer is already familiar to many, and additional developments are anticipated in the near future. The predictions are that every human-service professional will soon use computer work stations. Clients will become accustomed to the technology and perhaps demand that the technology be used in providing services.

An important intellectual concept that has emerged from the technology is the notion of expert systems, based on the work of Edward Feigenbaum, Joshua Lederberg, Bruce Buchanan, and their colleagues (see McCorduck, 1979, for a history of artificial intelligence). An expert system is a program that models the reasoning and decision-making behavior of experts in a narrowly defined field. The field of medicine has already begun the extensive use of expert systems. At the Stanford

Medical Center, for example, an expert system called Oncocin helps physicians choose the right types of chemotherapy for patients with certain forms of cancer. And the notion of the ultimate expert system — a program that can learn as people do, from experience — is at the center of Japan's Fifth Generation Project. This project has been underway for 3 years; its purpose is to produce computers specifically for artificial-intelligence applications in the 1990's (Feigenbaum & McCorduck, 1983).

Another useful idea is Sherry Turkle's (1984) notion of the "second self," a sociological phenomenon in which human cognition, in particular the human self-image, is influenced by technical ideas that enter the common language — in this instance, computer logic and communication.

These and other possible effects and consequences point to one of the most important changes wrought by the computer, the "order-of-magnitude" effect, where a large change brings about not only changes in quantity (cost, speed, etc.) but also a change in quality (expectations, attitudes, belief systems, etc.). Turkle contemplates these qualitative transformations in her trailblazing study of computers and the human mind.

To probe the issues of technology transfer and to provide the broadest context for the exploration of this terrain, three individuals with different backgrounds were invited to present their views of information technology. Jacques Vallee is a computer scientist and author of French science-fiction novels who is engaged in international high-tech venture-capital investments; Kathleen Christensen is a philosopher/geographer involved in research and teaching in environmental psychology; and John Henderson is a management scientist engaged in research and teaching about information systems. What unites these three individuals is a penetrating concern about the appropriate role of information technology in society at large.

Vallee presents a striking view of the synergistic power of computers, information systems, and communications which, he demonstrates, can have enormous impact on society, for either good or bad. He states it most succinctly in his opening paragraph: "Computer technology is the most powerful force changing human society today." Networks, the new computer structures, provide a new level of access to facts, to organizations and, most importantly, to each other. Together with low-cost personal computers and appropriate software, they make the formation of a new social structure a realistic possibility. Following his analysis, Vallee presents two contrasting future scenarios: an extrapolated future of drift propelling us toward a *digital society*, and a guided future that will help us move toward the *grapevine alternative*. In a digital society, data are mistaken for information and numbers take the places of values. It is a society in which hierarchical structures determine the future for us and in which individuals are reduced to numbers. In the grapevine alternative, people are empowered and are given ready access to information and to other people.

The trigger, according to Vallee, is there for either form to emerge. The grapevine alternative is the desired goal, but its achievement requires planning and guidance. Vallee believes that the grapevine alternative is not merely a utopian vision but one that is realistic and attainable. Its achievement is made possible by the distribution of computer power and the power of information brought by the personal computer, the recognition that mastery is achieved by understanding the software, not the hardware, and most significantly, by applying the equifinality principle of general systems theory, that is, the recognition that traditional formal systems design is not the only way to a successful system. Vallee's alternative to traditional design is *organic development*, the process of beginning small and growing steadily through adaptation, purposeful guidance, and learning. Inherent in this notion is the concept of natural evolution, and it is most apparent in his suggestion that a *marketplace of information* may replace formally planned and controlled information systems. This marketplace or *informational agora* is discussed by Nora and Minc (1980, pp. 136–141).

While much of Vallee's discourse is positive, he is deeply concerned by the thoughtless replacement of values by numbers and information by data. He is convinced that the technology is out of control, out of its creators' control and, especially, out of society's control. The motivations of the "techies," he says, are not only difficult to discern, but the effects are almost ungovernable. His suggestion is that we give our energies to directing the inevitable blast in the least damaging direction. Our difficulties with grasping the issues are grounded in the proposition that the nature and power of computers are alien to any of the other tools of humanity. Yet, he points to the historical relationship of the development of architectural structures and social structures and suggests that, today, communications systems are reflections of social structures. In this context, he offers the hope that computer communications and the organic development of systems will lead us to the social analog of the geodesic dome, a structure knit together by creative tension, and away from today's hierarchical structure—architecture's antiquated column-and-slab structure.

Vallee seems to leave us hanging in mid-air, but the interactive discussion that follows demonstrates that participants quickly realized the opportunities for the discovery of new roles for group work and community organization. The discussion reveals more problems and opportunities and broadens the context to include another quietly exploding technology—*cellular radio*. While much stimulating thought and specific experiences are provided, the discussion ends with the major concern of appropriate use unresolved.

Christensen dovetails with Vallee in highlighting the immense impact of technology on society. In her presentation, she confronts the underlying ethical issues implied by asking whether a particular information-technology application should be implemented. It is her assertion that technology, bound as it is to human decision-making, is not value-free, as some technologists would have us believe, but that technology is both an expression of and a shaper of human values. It has the power to transform how we think about ourselves. To ignore this power is to be morally naive.

Christensen's analysis suggests two fundamental approaches to forming the American attitude toward computers: one founded upon playfulness and fun, and the other upon work and achievement. She asserts that in the latter approach feasibility is facilely substituted for appropriateness, that both ignore the morally evocative nature of technology, and that conflicts over technology may be understood as conflicts in ethical priorities as, for example, when a manager asserts a design for reasons of efficiency and the workers oppose it because it invades their autonomy.

Christensen then introduces a framework for ethical analysis that requires thoughtful responses to five questions, and she demonstrates the process on a case example from public social services. She uses the framework to explore the moral aspects and implications of information technology in a human-service situation. While, as promised at the outset, she provides no easy answers, she does provide an insightful framework for thinking about and communicating what may be the most fundamental issues in relating information technology and the helping professions. The importance of Christensen's framework lies in moving latent issues to active discussion and its ability to generate the necessary information for resolving these value-laden issues of social work practice. The challenge facing the social work profession is to examine how technology can be best utilized in the delivery of social services. Not only must we examine technology's capabilities but we must also preserve a critical consciousness of how to form judgments about it. It is not enough, Christensen concludes, to make technological decisions on technological grounds alone: *Technological decisions are moral decisions.*

Recognizing that social work, as a helping profession, provides most of its services in institutional or organizational settings, we asked John Henderson to identify and examine the emerging issues for organizasions and professionals in organizations. Henderson begins by demonstrating the lines of reasoning that led from the old images of automation and replacement by computers to the current image of computers supporting professionals in their decision-making. He traces a path that identifies the ill-structured nature of decisions as the boundary between traditional management information systems (MIS) and decision support systems (DSS). He goes on to identify the many actors and the roles they play in the development of DSS, and the implementation processes that utilize change and innovation strategies, recognize the political character of data, and are founded in the use of iterative design and active learning processes. The use of active learning and iteration in system design is a major hallmark of the newer support systems that sets them apart from traditional MIS, which assume no learning, with their static information structures and reports.

Henderson explores the developments that make the actual implementation possible. He condenses these developments into interface management (the control of the touch screen, the light pen, the mouse, the sketch tablet, etc.), data management, model management, and communications management (internal data communications within the system, external communications to other systems, and communications to humans, e.g., graphics). It is in model management that the relationships between data elements are established, maintained, and utilized. He points to expert systems as a means for dealing with the increasing complexity of data. By imposing context and forming a *knowledge base* from the data base, and by applying *inference engines* that can produce value-added decisions and can explain the why of the decisions, he asserts that expert systems have significantly increased or extended the human capacity to manage complex data sets.

While he recognizes the tendency of individuals to develop DSS on their own and for them to remain isolated for a while, Henderson is not willing to take the laissez-faire position of Vallee. Instead, Henderson explores the strategic-planning issues and methodology available to organizations with a view toward achieving greater control over the development and the application of resources to DSS. He identifies promising pathways for institutionalizing the more valuable DSS developments.

At the same time, he recognizes the problem of networking DSS, and the hidden problem of controlling data in the end-user computing environment. The benefits of DSS and the end-user computing environment are only partially identified because of the lack of complete knowledge and experience. Nevertheless, he projects the promising prospects for increased access to decision-making, opportunities for innovation in task accomplishment, better use of professional time and other resources, and a shift of human attention to higher mental and organizational functions. As a concluding remark, Henderson notes that organizations may not have the luxury of deciding not to pursue the technology since it will likely be developed by virtue of its own momentum, or be enforced by the need to remain competitive in the marketplace. Hence, the challenge to professionals is to exert leadership in understanding the technology and its implications so that they can direct developments toward their valued goals and objectives.

These three people, experts in different fields, begin with different approaches but share a deep concern for the appropriate uses of information technology. They bring us to understand the opportunities and threats, and systematic methods for thinking and communicating about them. *They call for helping professionals to take leadership roles, on behalf of their professions, their clients, and their organizations, in understanding the technology and its implications. And, perhaps more importantly, that these professionals take proactive leadership roles in directing developments toward desired ends.*

Each of these contributors challenges us to think more broadly and more deeply about information technology and social work practice. In their suggestion that human-service professionals should exert greater control of their own destinies, they seem to echo Bronowski's recurring theme, reflected in this excerpt from his celebrated work:

> Knowledge is not a loose-leaf notebook of facts. Above all, it is a responsibility for the integrity of what we are, primarily of what we are as ethical creatures. You cannot possibly maintain that informed integrity if you let other people run the world for you while you yourself continue to live out of a ragbag of morals that come from past beliefs. That is really crucial today. You can see it is pointless to advise people to learn differential equations, or to do a course in electronics or in computer programming. And yet, fifty years from now, if an understanding of a man's origins, his evolution, his history, his progress is not the commonplace of the schoolbooks, we shall not exist. The commonplace of the schoolbooks of tomorrow is the adventure of today, and that is what we are engaged in. (Bronowski, 1973, pp. 436–7)

THE NETWORK REVOLUTION: PROMISES AND PITFALLS IN THE USE OF INFORMATION TECHNOLOGY
by Jacques Vallee

Computer technology is the most powerful force changing human society today. Over the next generation, every man, woman, and child will have the ability to use computers for access to facts, to organizations, and—most importantly—to other human beings. A new type of structure makes this access possible: the *network*.

Computer networks can be used by a government to repress its citizens, but they can also be used by individuals to share thoughts and facts, novel ideas, and visions of humanity's future. Networks constitute a communications medium unparalleled in human history.

Information Technology as the Trigger

Computer networks will soon force us to choose between two types of society: I call them the "Digital Society" and the "Grapevine Alternative."

In the Digital Society massive amounts of computer technology are used to control people by reducing them to statistics. In the Digital Society computers are tools of repression. Private communication through computer networks is discouraged.

In the Grapevine Alternative computers are used by people to build networks. The networks allow many people to access information and communicate with others easily. This use of computer networks for group communications is a dynamic force that began in obscure research organizations 10 years ago. It is now ready to explode into public view. The explosion will be helped by the growing demand for home computers, for new television services, and for access to data bases and information sources. The populace will go beyond such applications when it discovers these networks are gateways to other minds, windows to unsuspected vistas, bridges across loneliness and precious understanding.

How can we make the choice between these two societies that utilize essentially the same advanced technology for radically different purposes? First we must demystify computers. We must strip them of the

This section is based in part on Vallee's book, *The Network Revolution: Confessions of a Computer Scientist*, Berkeley, CA: And/Or Press, 1982.

aura of complexity. For this reason, I will not talk about bits and bytes, addresses, and operating systems, because such knowledge is not relevant here. We also need to understand the computer's history; it is only through such an understanding that we can learn to influence the technology.

Promises and Pitfalls

In the future, we may not be able to preserve that most cherished illusion of academia: the appearance that the human race, good or evil, has some measure of control over its creations.

I do not believe that we are in control of this exploding technology. But we can still hope to influence the general direction of the blast.

In the world of information networks, visionaries have produced enthusiastic speculations and experiments. In Redondo Beach, there is a "Consciousness Synthesis Clearing House" that is said to be "evolving a general understanding of the networking process and the development of an overarching perspective from which to view this vital phenomenon." In Pittsburgh, Rolf von Eckartsberg has set up a network for the exchange of information about psychedelics. In Washington, Barbara Hubbard has created a "Committee for the Future" that promotes the exchange of ideas about world problems. Carol Rosin directs an "International Association of Educators for World Peace" working for a "peaceful and permanent manned occupation of space." Some of these networks are nothing more than mimeographed lists of addresses and phone numbers. Others are built around CB radios and improvised channels. Still others, the most interesting ones, are constructed around computer links that give their users access to data bases and sophisticated programs.

In Table 8 I have tried to summarize the characteristics of two approaches to building information systems: I contrast the traditional centralized design and the network design approach. The table illustrates the possibilities that networking has to offer in the field of social work, not only in economic terms but in terms of ethics, of "empowerment" of the users, and of access to information. Networking also provides the opportunity to start with low-cost prototypes and allows the user group to expand as necessary.

Advocates of networking believe that the new technology can solve social problems, that "the Information Network is aware of current research being done by all aspects of science. The Information Network is also aware of political decisions and their global implications. This network shares in the ideologies and philosophies of those people that

Table 8 **Comparing Two Approaches to an Information System**

	Traditional Information Systems—Centralized Design	*Novel Information Systems—Network Design*
Hardware Characteristics	Central computer	Microcomputers
Economics	High initial investment	Low initial investment Incremental growth (but final cost may exceed that of traditional systems)
Communication Environment	Hard-wired terminals Constrained in time and space	Access by phone lines Not constrained in time or space
Design	Top-down, rigid	Bottom-up, adaptive, self-correcting
Software Environment	Integrated data base	Distributed data, possibly conflicting, overlapping, and redundant Downloading
Ethical/Moral Characteristics	A single value system is that of the management Productivity measured by volume of output	Value system controlled by the end-user Different value systems may coexist
Consequences	The system does not tolerate ambiguity High efficiency for transactions Vulnerable to changes in the environment Power is centralized at a level above the users; control of the data base is political power The generation of administrative reports is a primary task	The system adapts to ambiguity Efficiency sometimes is low System adapts to changes in terminology, law, rules, etc. Power is distributed among users, and the network acts as a marketplace Administrative reports are only a by-product of a service to the users

have integrated universal operating principles." These are heady ideals. But the technical reality is more complex.

One of the founders of cybernetics, the late Norbert Wiener (1949), called it "The Science of Communication and Control in the Animal and the Machine." This definition, as Stafford Beer (1959, p. 18) has since pointed out, suggests two ideas. The first is that distinctions between the animate and the inanimate, inherited from the Greeks, do not apply to the laws of regulation. The second idea is that communication is control, and, therefore, that information is control. Anyone concerned with computers must begin with this fact.

It is impossible to obtain information without obtaining a measure of control over the objects or persons which the information describes.

But the meaning of Wiener's observation goes deeper still: Fascination with computers is symptomatic of the quest for power. Often disguised as a scholarly pursuit of information or as the mere compilation of passive data, the true motivations of computer architects are difficult to discern, and their impact is almost ungovernable.

The dangers inherent in the use of computer power, however, must be balanced against the present reality and the future promise. The computer industry is a major contributor to progress in our society. Computers have changed every aspect of life with which they have come in contact; they have become an important national resource. The computer industry is about to collide with, and compete with, the older and bigger telecommunications industry—an industry that wields tremendous economic power and influence. The telecommunications industry is responsible for more than 20% of all corporate debt, and takes in revenue twice as large as the gross national product of the United States. In 1978, the information-technology areas employed 51% of our work force and earned 47% of our GNP. (It is also useful to keep in mind that it would take an investment of $50 billion, over the next 30 years, to bring the rest of the world up the the level of communication now found in North America.) This is the plum which the computer industry hopes to pluck.

The immense economic power of the telecommunications industry constitutes the "base camp" from which computer power will assault the old structures. For example, in the area of computer-based conferencing (the use of computers to link people together), some scientists have envisioned the rapid obsolescence of many educational techniques, the electronic replacement of 80% of business mail, and a significant alteration of transportation and settlement patterns. When these effects were first suggested in a *Futurist* article (Baran, 1973), there were approximately 100 persons worldwide who engaged in computer-based conferencing. By the end of the decade they numbered in the thousands, and Dr. Michael Arbib (1977, pp. 418–437) suggested that the building of a "global brain for mankind" was an urgent necessity. Can we build such a brain? Is it desirable to build it?

After considering these facts, the "global brain" may seem more feasible. Radio Shack maintains a chain of 6000 stores in the United States and 1600 stores abroad that have sold more than 150,000 personal computers. Total retail sales of home computers reached $100 million in 1977, climbed to $500 million in 1979, and rose to $950 million, or 235,000 units in 1980, according to International Data Co. Another market-analysis firm, Vantage Research, has different but equally impressive figures: Their data show 450,000 home computers were sold in 1979, 575,000 in 1980. Only 20,000 units were sold in 1975, the year the home-computer industry began. Spending on "office automation" equipment in the U.S. reached $3 billion in 1981 and is expected to grow beyond $12 billion in 1986, mostly for word processors.

The Digital Society

How will this proliferation of computer hardware change the way we live, the way human organizations work, and the way we relate to each other? A fact that remains hidden from scientific studies, and that is even more removed from the conversation of programmers, is that the nature and power of computers differ from the nature and power of any tools ever before available to humanity. When the community of programmers — who are a fairly dull but extraordinarily busy and productive lot — has completed its transition, there may not be very much left of the old structures. The corporate buildings and the cathedrals of the old order will still be there, but the human organizations will have crumbled under the pressure of the new subtle and complex networks through which the new power will exert itself.

The central issue I invite you to explore is a simple one: In a world invaded by machines that dissolve reality to digitize it, how are we going to recognize truth and preserve quality? How are we going to relate to each other?

An example of the digital society computers are creating can be explored by looking at the lives, hopes, and frustrations of those who work with computers. Will you choose to join that kind of society?

When you buy a personal computer, connect your television set to a home information network, or install a terminal in your office cubicle, you enter the digital society in which programmers live. The gadgets themselves are immaterial. The software — the programmed logic inside the machine — contains the control. It is the software you will need to master.

This new technology is sold to businesses and to individuals as a tool that provides better control of their world. But that same technology currently illustrates a world out of control, a world where data are constantly mistaken for information and where numbers have taken the place of values. Is this the world you want? And if the answer is "no," can you change it? The problem is as vast as the whole future.

Although the prospects for the computer industry to experience a crisis are increasing, the experts are charging ahead with bigger and better systems. They will link together not only major companies but every household in the world. In the early 1970's, the "wired nation" was announced in the pages of *Science* magazine (Parker and Dunn, 1972; Massy, 1974; Greenberger, Aronofsky, McKenny, Massy, 1973). One article hailed it as *an information utility for the purpose of fostering equal social opportunity in the United States.* More recently forecasts presenting the "Network Nation" as the most desirable future form of social development have been made. The Wired Nation would use cable television as its technical infrastructure; the Network Nation would probably start from computer nets. The two concepts could be combined to form a true Digital Society. Futurists have announced the imminent development of "neighborhood office centers" that would replace most downtown office buildings and eliminate the need to commute, thus presumably easing the energy burden. These centers, which appeal to those who like a free lifestyle, would allow people to live anywhere and work in nearby multipurpose buildings shared by many companies. These buildings would be linked together by communications satellite channels or advanced fiber optics. One positive result would be the more flexible work arrangements possible under such a plan, which would allow parents to more easily combine jobs with child-rearing. Yet some of the basic human questions have never been addressed by the engineers proposing such developments.

In the words of Harold Gilliam (1977), writing in the *San Francisco Chronicle:*

> Shopping by computer, for example, sounds amazingly easy. It will save innumerable trips to the supermarket, the department store, the shopping center. . . but it doesn't get you out of the house for a change of scene, for a chat with the neighbors and the clerks, for a look at all the enticing goods you don't necessarily want to buy but enjoy seeing. (p. 6)

In the home-computer revolution that would be precipitated by the Digital Society, it would be possible to attend school, obtain reading materials, and send and receive electronic mail without leaving one's bedroom. But what happens to the normal patterns of human interaction? Are we going to be marketing loneliness and boredom at the ends of those thousands of miles of cables? What will happen to human trust and to good old-fashioned face-to-face conflict?

Britain, Japan, and Sweden are far ahead of the United States in the testing and development of these new media (which are appearing now in America under names like Viewdata or Prestel, Teletext, and Videotex). Some of the reactions have been negative, as in the following quote from Kerstin Anér (1979) in a Swedish report (by the Commission on New Information Technology, Stockholm):

> It is necessary to bear in mind many side effects. One is that different groups have different means for making use of the new facility and that usually those previously well endowed in information now acquire more,

unless special measures are taken. Secondly that the computer technology can always be silently used to check who learns what. Thirdly that an immense power accumulates among those who decide what shall be put into such a system and what shall be left outside. (p. 28)

Other experts and amateurs, among them the computer buffs buying thousands of Apple computers and Radio Shack TRS-80's every month, argue convincingly that we will not know the real social effects of the technology until we try it. They enthusiastically state that computer terminals are now cheap enough to be installed in millions of homes, and that the price of computer time is dropping fast enough to make an amazing type of society an almost instant reality in advanced countries like the United States.

"Think about it, man," said a young enthusiast at the San Francisco home-computer fair last year, "you could have the entire Library of Congress at your fingertips."

"What would you do if you had the entire Library of Congress at your fingertips?" I asked him.

I am still waiting for an answer.

The "Organic" Alternative: The Grapevine Society

Imagine the following scene: You are in charge of emergency services for a part of Ohio that has just been hit by the worst storms and floods in years. Sixty people have died, hundreds are sick, and thousands are homeless. You need 500 Army tents, 30 bulldozers, and 2 tons of medical supplies. There's a hospital in Dayton that can provide a field emergency facility, but it must be picked up by trucks. There's a trucking company in the next state that can provide transportation, but it hasn't returned your phone messages of the last 4 hours.

It would be useful to be able to tie these people together in an around-the-clock conference and keep them posted on developments, to receive immediate and binding commitments of the assistance they will provide and the schedule to be kept, and to have your decisions and status known instantly by your teams everywhere. That ability would provide the accurate, timely information you have always dreamed of. The communications medium that would make this possible exists now, and it's called computer-based conferencing. It is easy to use, and it gives us a way to escape the closed, authoritarian structures computers seem to precipitate. If we use computer-based conferencing well, and not as the toy that the "techies" would make of it, we may find an alternative to the Digital Society.

Communication systems reflect the structure of society to the same extent that architectural concepts reflect that structure. The first system that builders used for load-bearing and stress distribution consisted of two vertical slabs capped by a third, horizontal one. The technique was revolutionized by the arch and later by the keystone. By the time the ogive arch appeared, always threatening to explode into pieces because of its taut construction, engineers had devised flying buttresses that projected the entire structure upwards. The modern stage of the builder's art is represented by the geodesic dome — each polygonal segment is a source of both support and tension for its neighbors.

With each new step in architectural technique, Man has been able to make larger structures with greater span and integrity. [EDITORS' NOTE: See, for example, Bronowski, 1973, pp. 94–120.] Societal structures that approach the beautiful distribution of tension realized in the dome have yet to evolve. These social structures have remained at the hierarchic stage, with only an occasional advance. A geodesic organization would require an information system that could instantly tie together its segments for collective decisions. This system would differ from a broadcast or a mass rally, where masses of people are at the receiving end of a giant, one-way channel. It would also differ from telephone- or television-based conferencing, which demand the simultaneous presence of the parties at a few designated sites. Instead, the geodesic structure requires an information medium in which participants can join the dialogue at any time, and in which past statements are not lost as the interaction progresses. Computer-based conferencing, electronic mail, and bulletin boards represent first steps toward the creation of such a medium: It would be a revolutionary network, where each node is equal in power to all the others, a structure that could begin inexpensively around a small nucleus, and which could grow organically, with new nodes added, not in response to executive mandate or to technical demand, but in response to a human need. It is in the growth of such grapevines that information technology will provide its greatest benefits as a communication tool.

In the field of social work, I would recommend, as a first step, a clearinghouse that would be based on a free exchange of information among practitioners. This exchange might first be an open review of choices that succeed and choices that fail as new technology is introduced into the field. The discussion would probably soon diverge from this initial topic as users began to trust the new tool. It could soon inspire more cooperation to solve problems faster and with greater confidence.

For computer-based conferencing systems to succeed, certain conditions are necessary. Conferences among large, amorphous groups usually fail. So do communications involving people who do not already know each other, or people who lack clear motivation to work together on a particular project. Such requirements, though, would only further promote cooperation.

The following is an edited transcript of the discussion that followed Vallee's presentation. It exhibits aspects of the clearinghouse or information exchange he recommends, and it simulates an electronic conference transcript just as well as it documents the actual face-to-face discussion. Only elapsed time would differ—a half hour in person versus as much as a day to a few days with computer-based conference methods. The elongation of time occurs because everyone will not be present concurrently in the electronic process. This latter quality extends access to those with meeting conflicts and thereby provides more equality in participation.

CHAIRMAN: Dr. Vallee has raised the issue of user involvement—an issue that we very much hoped would arise. The past history of the social services leads one to observe that practitioners and other involved parties have shunned technology. They seemingly have hoped that technology would not appear in their domain; that by turning their backs to technology they could ensure that it would not enter. It seems that exactly the reverse should have been the case: Professionals should have pursued an active and informed involvement with technology if only to protect their professional values and their clients.

The concept of empowerment that Jacques has raised, the facilitation of grassroots action, is a very powerful one. To me it represents one of the great opportunities to use technology to help others. At the same time it represents a great challenge to the profession because it exacerbates the tension between concern for protecting the professional "turf" and concern for betterment of the client's welfare. This occurs as empowerment provides clients with access to information that was previously the sole province of the professional, for example, the open sale of the *Physician's Desk Reference*. More public access to information can seemingly create less need for professional services, and more client challenges to professional decisions and recommendations.

Parallel to this situation in computer science and computer engineering is the creation of program-generating and artificial-

intelligence software, which may lead to less demand for programmers. As programmers create more user-oriented
software—user-friendly systems, iconic systems (Apple Macin-
tosh), touch-driven systems, voice-driven systems, report
generators, data-base management systems, decision-support
system generators, the demand for programmers will decline.
This decline in demand must occur unless the programmers shift
to more complex tasks. One wonders what will happen to the
droves of youngsters preparing for careers in computer programming, especially those being prepared for yesterday's—or even today's—world.

Anyone who has been in the engineering profession for 10
years or more knows that there are painful cycles in the demand
for engineers. The cycle begins with an industry- and
government-supported media drive to develop interest in
engineering careers. This drive is followed by a rush of students
into the engineering schools, and a subsequent collapse of
engineering employment as the surplus supply of engineers and
a decreasing demand for projects collide. The cycle is completed
when enrollments decline, and project demand increases.

Dr. Vallee has drawn our attention to a number of opportunities and threats, and has given us a stimulating presentation
about which I am sure we have many comments and questions.

PARTICIPANT: I've been using computer-based conferencing and
electronic mail for about 5 years. I use it now for project
management, but I also use it to get user feedback to help in the
further development of software. I've discovered that with the
system we use—one that permits anyone, client or staff member,
at any time, or any point in the display, to send a comment
directly to the programmers, or to any of us (they say, "This
stinks!" "I can't read this." "It's upside down!" "It's garbage!" "It's
sexist!" We get thousands of these comments.)—staff members
systematically screen clients' comments. Time and time again we
train agencies about this feature, and a few weeks later the only
comments we get are from the staff. While the staff agrees that
feedback from clients is important, essentially comments are still
screened out. This alarms me, and I don't know why it happens.

One of my questions is, "Who doesn't communicate?" We find
in agencies where the staff communicates regularly through case
notes and a conferencing system, or through private mail, that
there is a high dropout rate. There is a selective process
operating. Even when the three criteria you specified are met,
after the novelty wears off, there is a selective process that deter-

mines who continues to communicate. We have formed theories about that, and all have been proven wrong. One theory was that if top management uses these communication features, and thereby sets a role model, that all personnel will follow. This works except where the staff hates top management and everyone quits when management joins in. Our second theory was that communicating electronically means writing things down, and that seems dangerous to some people. What can you add from your experience and research to help us understand why technology does not, in fact, empower some people, but does empower others?

VALLEE: We are constantly bewildered by the social reactions to network systems and how they are used in organizations. In order to study them, sociologist Robert Johansen and I (Johansen, Vallee, & Spangler, 1979, App. A) looked for a methodology that was already in place for the evaluation of other media, and applied it to computer-based conferencing instead of developing methodology specific to the computer.

We found a group in England, the Communications Studies Group in London, that had been set up at the British Post Office at the end of World War II. There was a real possibility that London would be destroyed by German rockets and that the British Government might have to operate with a teleconferencing method from remote locations. They very seriously looked at how a large organization in jeopardy might continue to operate when face-to-face communication is impossible. After the war they continued that kind of research, mainly using the medium of audio-conferencing. They tried to find the best technology for different types of meeting. We used their methodology to study computer-based communication.

We observed that teleconferencing was not good for getting to know somebody. For example, you wouldn't want to interview someone for a job over a computer network. The network is useful for communicating positions, for relaying immediate decisions, and for recording facts.

In terms of who uses those systems effectively, we compared the same group using audio-conferencing, face-to-face meetings, and computer-based conferencing for the same tasks. When we looked at the frequency, or the ranking, of participation, we found that typically there would be only two people who would dominate the conversation by making more than 50% of the statements. The same people would not necessarily dominate each medium. The way power was exercised was different in each case. We found that the conferences that were successful typically had two leaders, one leader who was high in public communication and low in private communication. In other words, that leader sent a lot of group messages, but few personal messages. The other leader focused more on private messages, and helped people with the technology and with putting their views on the record. These observations have some serious consequences. They may cause a leveling of organizational hierarchies—a clash of the formal structure with the informal structure that is revealed by the network.

PARTICIPANT: We have found that generally people reject computer-based conferencing in favor of private messages. That is, over time it seems that people become much more comfortable if they send notes just to you. As a consequence I'll have a stack of personal notes on my screen, about 80% of which could comfortably be put into a public file. I copy them over to the public file and by the next morning I will have received another group of private messages. We don't understand what the process is, and it seems very hard to stabilize a group over time on a computer-based system.

VALLEE: Let me mention a computer-based system called "Notepad" that we have developed and in which the leaders set the style of the communications. In other words, the leaders could run a conference that was entirely public, so there would be a group in which anybody can talk to everybody else; or they can opt to send messages in conferences that admit only private messages with no public file. We found that differences in leadership style were critical to many applications. You can design a system that will support a dictatorship, or you can design a system that will be completely democratic.

PARTICIPANT: One of the things that struck me as I listened to your discussion was what you said about people deciding which information to control and which to make accessible. When I was director of the staff of a legislative committee, I realized that when my committee chairman became officially aware of a piece of information, that act was in itself an expression of policy, and that many times the actual problem-solving activity that went on between legislature and agency had to occur in an environment in which formal communication could not exist.

My major role as staff director was to let the chairman and key people know what was going on without their "knowing what was going on." I had to be very sensitive to when I had power and when I didn't have power in relation to when the information was public or not. For example, the Auditor General told me that people thought he was a powerful person, but that the day an audit was published he was the least powerful person in the state. So it seems the holder of information has power until it is public and this must bear on the question of public messaging versus private messaging.

I would speculate that people are beginning to recognize that public access to information creates issues and, especially, policy issues, and they are not yet convinced that they are not losing some degree of freedom by making their information public. It depends on the participants, but I know from personal experience that teleconferencing and office automation can easily be seen as negative. But I have to say that it will radically change our view of problem-solving mechanisms because of the visibility of policy positions and key policymakers. I think that we are just coming to grips with that interaction.

PARTICIPANT: Having reviewed some of the experiences that people talk about and have written about in the scenarios, I see a struggle for existence and a considerable restriction on the access to communications equipment. One of the developments that will revolutionize this is the provision of networked terminals or work stations connected to service providers. Few systems support that now, but once that is planned and developed there will be new insights into what can be accomplished.

VALLEE: I think we're at the beginning of that change right now. Modems, for the first time, are outselling personal computers. There are more people going to computer stores to buy modems than there are going in to buy personal computers. The people who bought computers last year have now realized that there is not very much to do with the home computer, other than to play Space Invaders, unless you start communicating. I think that in another year or so we're going to see a lot of people using personal computers for communication. A technology built to enhance productivity may not necessarily be important in a field like social work, where other qualities are more highly valued. But networking brings a new system of ethics and new communications opportunities as well, as I indicated in Table 8.

PARTICIPANT: I've been using telecommunications for a number of years now, and I wanted to address one technical area, and then give a couple of brief examples of how I've made use of it.

Few people here are likely to be familiar with *cellular radio technology*, but we all should be. It is an update of the mobile telephone, and is gaining popularity in industrial services and metropolitan areas. There are cellular units that you carry — originally the car telephone, now reduced to beeper size and ultimately to the Dick Tracy wrist radio — which transmit over distances of about ¼-mile but with a large bandwidth. Thus they can transmit and receive large amounts of information — not just voices but digital data and even video signals. If you're in a cellular field, there is a rebroadcasting device within a ¼-mile of any mobile receiver/transmitter. This can broadcast you information to another field, or to a satellite and then to another distant cellular field anywhere in the world. So if two people have cellular units and are located in any two cellular fields (no matter how distant), they can be in direct communication with each other.

The system also works in reverse; that is, any person carrying a cellular unit can be located to within 3 square feet in any cellular field on Earth. To gain anonymity, you must turn your cellular unit off. There has been "1984-type" talk of tracking the chronic-schizophrenic population this way, and also monitoring "house confinement" of nonviolent criminals. As in the early days of commercial broadcasting, most people don't know what is going on, but fortunes are being made in acquiring the franchises for the cellular fields. Each will have two operators, one a public radio/TV station and the other open to any qualified competitor. Soon the entire country will be "cellularized."

With regard to my own professional experience, I got involved in a forensic matter as a practitioner in my community, which is in a very rural area with a very small professional community. I needed quick access to a competent academic neural psychologist to answer some questions and help me to prepare court testimony. I belong to The Source — an information utility with about 40,000 subscribers. I signed on to The Source, and asked for a scan of the membership data base in order to identify members who were interested in computers and who were psychologists or psychiatrists. The Source produced a list of about 45 people in a matter of seconds. I composed a query letter on my word processor and electronically mailed it to all 45 on the list. I later found numerous responses in my "mailbox" and weeded those down to one or two that I thought would be helpful. I began a correspondence with one gentleman located across the country who solved my problem for me. While I never met him, he transmitted his data over the network and then we linked through the system for direct dialogue.

The second example relates to a colleague who had worked 20 years on projective psychological testing and wanted to publish his work in a book but didn't know how to do it. I have a small "out-of-my-garage" publishing operation. He prepared a manuscript that was entered into my computer, and then I was able to send that manuscript, electronically, to a number of typesetters in the United States who provide telecommunications access to their shops. My computer could communicate the typesetter's control codes and thereby get the manuscript ready for the printing press. My colleague's handwritten notes were transcribed onto my computer, reorganized with word processing, and then sent to three or four typesetters for immediate quotations. We took the lowest bid, had the manuscript printed, and the first time it saw paper it was coming off the press. The only additional manual work was preparation of the color graphics for the color "ink blots."

These are two examples of how telecommunications keeps rural practitioners from being quite so isolated.

PARTICIPANT: My example is not quite as technical but relates more to a social work-oriented example. In 1979, I spent a year at the University of Stockholm School of Social Work. They were developing a program in community organization and were attempting to form groups in different neighborhoods that could lobby for services. We used the telephone to form a library of conversations with different people that could be shared with other people in the neighborhood and thereby develop the groups. Using only the telephone worked very well, and I can imagine what it would be like today using teleconferencing.

PARTICIPANT: Dr. Vallee has stressed "empowerment" which, historically in social work, has been most successful when the clients "own" the agency. For example, the National Maritime Union set up its own social services which were amenable to change because the clients were able to come in and instruct the staff in what needed to be done. You're suggesting the possibility of these communications techniques empowering clients, but in what way can that be done if the clients do not "own" the agency?

VALLEE: I speak from a position of ignorance of the structure of your field, but I hear that a lot of power resides in the

knowledge of regulations. Whoever has access to those regulations and the structure behind them has the opportunity to exercise that power. If that's your case, that knowledge can in fact be
distributed through networking. That knowledge can be put into
personal computers.

I'm sure that you have seen ads that read, "Learn about important services that are available to you from the government.
Send $10 for our informative brochure." What you receive for
your $10 is a free report from the Library of Congress, a report
you could have gotten from Washington for the price of a stamp.
These phony "services" simply feed the gap in the public's
knowledge of what is public information. Most citizens don't
know what is available from the Government Printing Office, so
there is a market for that information. This knowledge gap is a
function of the information overload in our society. Anyone with
access to a personal computer and the bulletin board listing such
services could get that knowledge and exercise the power that
comes with it.

PARTICIPANT: Do I understand correctly that you are speaking of
providing individuals with more access to knowledge?

VALLEE: Yes, and more access to each other.

PARTICIPANT: What you mean by empowerment is that is opens up,
for individuals, resources that might not be available otherwise.
That is not the ordinary way in which we have spoken of empowerment in the profession.

VALLEE: There is nothing to prevent an organization that wants to
provide those benefits to its members from actually setting up
that system. A bulletin-board system is easily initiated.
Thousands of teenagers around the country have already done it.
It would enable you to stay in touch with the recipients and to
encourage them.

One benefit of a system like this is horizontal communication:
people solving other people's problems. The more you can promote that, the less would be the workload on the central office.
It also gives people more feeling of control over their own situations. An individual can help another individual who has the
same problem. There is more credibility and more trust in that
form of exchange. The role of the caseworker might be to
monitor that kind of communication and help to facilitate it.
And that's only one model of how that ability might be used.

Another possibility is that important data bases might become
separated from irrelevant ones. We may even find data bases

spontaneously created by a user community to meet its needs. In the traditional information system, there may be a 5-year or longer delay from need assessment through design to implementation and coding. The resulting data bases are often obsolete or irrelevant by the time they become available on-line.

There is also a notion that through networking you can form groups for a special purpose and find people with common interests so that you are no longer the isolated individual, or the exceptional individual. You're now a member of a much larger group that can speak forcefully for the needs of its members.

PARTICIPANT: The comments about the National Maritime Union, which owns its own social-service agency, were comments about social structure. They had to do with the structure of the social worker's organization, and I think that to assume that technology is going to alter any social structure is wrong. The correct adoption of the technology is perhaps 20% technical; the remaining 80% has to do with social organization and social structure. Before networks can really work there must be agreement that we want to collaborate, that we want to communicate, and that we're going to use this information. I think that, more than any other kind of technology in recent history, this particular technology provides real hope for social transformation. I think a lot of activists from the sixties are joining the personal-computer era because they see the potential of the technology. A potential, not to change society, but to create the conditions, the information exchange, and the social connections that will lead to social change. To think that the technology by itself will change the structure is to delude ourselves.

I don't think any of us here believe them, but there are two myths about computers that occur in nonprofit groups. One is that the technology is necessarily evil—that computers are instruments of institutional control—and therefore they want nothing to do with these tools. When microcomputers came along I saw for the first time the potential of empowerment on an individual basis, and empowerment on a small-organization basis. But all those people who ran nonprofit groups in the sixties and seventies and who believed the "myth of evil technology" have reversed their opinions and are now so enamored of the technology that they think it will solve all their problems—the second myth.

We need to debunk that myth and deliver some warnings that computers won't change the social structure. They can only lead to the conditions for change.

VALLEE: Let me cite one example of an organization that has recognized both of these myths and has used technology to achieve something similar to what you're talking about. It was a major communications company in the process of setting up maintenance programs for its telephone service. The company was recruiting people who had never been exposed to telephone systems and, therefore, had to train them in a very short time. There were racial, social, and language differences between the new recruits and the old managers who were already in place.

The company recognized that these trainees typically would not take problems to their supervisors, and that problems would not be revealed until there was a major crisis and then management action was required to solve them. The organization used computer-based conferencing to alleviate that condition.

The company instituted a network that allowed the trainees to talk to other people at their own level, people who had taken the training with them. In many cases problems were then resolved at that level. Solutions at that level reinforced the training the people had received, created an environment of trust, and provided access to people who were at the same level.

PARTICIPANT: That's what is so exciting about the technology. I think it is, as Dr. Vallee said, out of control, but this loss of control has created a tension from which many new ideas can flow. New solutions will be forced upon the technology as a larger base of people gains access to it. We will be confronted with the necessity to make some creative decisions, and to take creative steps towards new kinds of systems and organizations.

PARTICIPANT: The criteria of success that Dr. Vallee defined for teleconferencing can be applied to self-help groups or social-support networks. They have three features in common: They are composed of individuals who have essentially similar kinds of problems (for example, substance-abusers, alcoholics, or people recently divorced or separated); they often confront crisis-management issues; and they derive the support they need from frequent communication.

I don't think we have applied this technology to that situation yet. That would be a major step toward empowerment. If you take AA as an example, they rely essentially on the telephone for crisis management. The problem with the telephone is that you can reach only one person. That is, if you're really "in the dumps," and you need help, you dial a number given to you because there's supposed to be somebody there. But with teleconferencing there could be many people available to give

support. By this means we could create an infrastructure of helping networks.

We spend a great deal of energy trying to develop those
human networks. Much of the cost is communications cost—the
cost to provide access to others—because we have tried to initiate the networks in such physical terms. We try to bring people together in a certain place. In each place we realize that we
do not have the infrastucture that teleconferencing could provide. Such groups could be one of the most immediate low-cost
applications of the new technology.

PARTICIPANT: I agree. I think that social-support networks will
benefit greatly from the new technology. But one of the purposes of social-support groups is to increase coping abilities, and
professionals are usually excluded from their development. Second, how these people use computers is going to be an important question. Many social-support groups are organized as
resistance movements to technology. Or they address problems
where the only solution these people recognize is to sit down,
face to face, and talk emotionally with each other about what's
bothering them.

The computer can help, particularly in your example, by
enabling the user to send an electronic message to everybody to
ask for help. This increases the probability that somebody will
come to help. Also, for example, if you have a strange disorder
that you know nothing about, the computer can help you learn
about it by connecting you to others who have that same
disorder. There are many things information techology can do: It
can help form this constituency by doing the mailings, it can
help people get together, and it can do a lot of structured tasks
that people now have to do. It will cost extra money—money
that most self-help groups do not have. One of their
characteristics is that they're supported by fees from their
memberships, not by grants or gifts for operation. People either
pay fees or they participate as volunteers to do work in return
for group membership.

So I think it's true that technology can help, but I think that we
must understand which uses of the technology are appropriate,
and how the technology can alleviate the problems that people
are experiencing.

CHAIRMAN: I must, unfortunately, terminate this discussion now so
we can keep to our schedule.

If you haven't enough challenges for discussion, let me point
out that while Dr. Vallee reported the benefits of bulletin

boards, surveys indicate that some bulletin boards operate with perverse and destructive purposes. Some are pornographically oriented, some are oriented toward fostering sexual perversions, some communicate means to subvert telephone systems and breach computer security, and many bulletin-board operators report that they cannot keep them clean and focused.

There is some concern in the mental-health community that the bulletin board and electronic worldwide communication facilitate the support of bizarre behavior and ideation. In typical social communities, exceptional behavior and ideation are moderated by the need to remain part of the group. Now these exceptional individuals can find each other wherever they may be geographically located, and thereby gain support for their exceptional and bizarre notions. There is potential for the reinforcement of both negative behavior and positive behavior, and this may identify another professional role—the moderator of discussions, identifier of clients, and outreach worker via computer-based conferencing.

ETHICS OF
INFORMATION TECHNOLOGY
by Kathleen E. Christensen

The computer constitutes a technological cornerstone of the "Information Society." It, along with advanced telecommunications technology, provides fast, efficient, and accurate means for collecting, analyzing, and communicating vast amounts of information.

Since the introduction of the personal computer in 1975, information technology has exercised an increasing hold on the American psyche. By 1982, *Time* magazine named the computer its "Man of the Year"; and now, barely 2 years later, over 200 publications that deal solely with computer topics exist. Much of this recent surge in public fascination focuses on the technology itself—its hardware and software, its capacities and applications. Discussions center on bits and bytes, ROM and RAM, hard or soft disks, modems and printers, CompuServe and The Source.

But I do not want to examine this technology per se. I am not an engineer, nor am I sufficiently well versed to provide the technical insights to many of the technical problems it raises. But, as a social scientist and philosopher, I want to look at technology as an expression and shaper of human values.

Most significantly, this paper challenges what I take to be the morally bankrupt view that technology is value-free. Information technology, like all technology, is entirely value-laden. It must be seen as a process in which values have shaped the creation, design, and application of the device, product, or service. These outputs can never be divorced from this process of human decision-making. Consequently, any technological decision—from developing hardware to designing software to implementing a decision support system—is a value-based decision that not only reflects a particular vision of society but also gives concrete form to it.

The longer we avoid explicating the value dimensions of computer technology the greater will be our risk of serious political and moral consequences. We could find ourselves living in a society shaped by the value-free instrumentality of technology, rather than one directed by a critically reflective consciousness.

I would like to thank Richard Christensen and Rasul Murray for their valuable contributions to an earlier draft of this paper.

That may sound overly dramatic. But we are dealing with a technology that is profoundly powerful in its potential to transform how we think about ourselves as human beings (Turkle, 1984), how we make decisions in the military, in medicine, architecture, and engineering (McCorduck, 1979; Perrolle, 1983; Reinhold, 1984), how we communicate with one another (Vallee, 1982), and how we record history, pass on knowledge, and learn.

To the extent that we ignore the transformative powers of this information technology, we are morally naive, for we fail to ask the morally based question, "Should . . . ?" Should children be taught through the use of CAI? Should the military use expert systems in certain types of decision-making? Should people copy software? Legally our responses are ambiguous, technically they are easy. But what about morally?

Like other institutions and professions, social work possesses numerous opportunities to introduce information technology into the delivery of social services. The technology to automate data bases, develop decision support systems, provide centralized client referrals, and offer computer-based counseling does exist. Yet each of these technological applications poses serious questions that fall outside the realm of the technological. These questions have to do with how the technology, when introduced into the practices of the profession, will challenge or enhance the duties and rights of social workers, as well as the rights of clients.

Technology is driven by efficiency, whereas social work is defined by a professional code of ethics that specifies particular relationships among the agency, the professional, and the client. As information technology is introduced into the delivery of services, it raises the following types of questions: Should the administrator of a public agency transfer intake responsibility from a caseworker to a data-entry clerk? Should a caseworker agree to use a standardized algorithm in allocating benefits when he or she doesn't understand how the algorithm was developed and doesn't feel the resulting allocation is fair to a particular client? Should an overworked therapist rely on a therapy software program for his or her clients? Should clients be asked for their informed consents prior to their records being entered into the agency's automated data base, which can be accessed via remote terminals by a number of agencies?

These are real questions that administrators, caseworkers, and therapists will face more frequently as information technology becomes more available, affordable, and "user-friendly." What is needed at this time is not a pat answer to any one of these questions but rather a way to answer all of them that takes into explicit consideration the value structure of the profession and the moral dimensions of each question.

My objective in this paper is to present a series of five ethical questions that, when taken collectively, will form an ethical framework from which the moral questions can be answered. By responding to all five, an administrator, caseworker, therapist, or client would have an adequate moral justification relating to a particular problem, even though each question posed possesses several possible and plausible answers.

Although these questions are presented in the abstract, one cannot respond to them fully in the abstract. They must be addressed to concrete real-life situations, for an ethical analysis cannot be done outside of a context. It becomes real only when the situation is real. So although I present the framework, and an illustrative case study, the profession is required to think through the questions in light of its own case studies of real-life ethical dilemmas. The need for ethical analysis is critical in light of the dominant value-free orientation that most Americans have toward technology in general, and computer technology in particular.

At the risk of oversimplification, I would say that most Americans perceive computer technology in two ways, neither of which includes an explicit value assessment: First, in the sense of *gee whiz*, "this is a really fun machine"; and second, in the sense of *can-do*, "look at all the things it can do to make my work easier."

The Notion of Gee Whiz

The *gee-whiz* attitude sees the computer as an absolutely fascinating toy. The "toy" evokes a childlike wonder and playfulness, yet it exercises a seductive hold. It is always present, it is infinitely patient, it can do many things, and it constitutes a perennial challenge. For example, there is always the challenge to stop getting error messages, to finally get a program to run right.

One New Yorker, named Paul, illustrates this *gee-whiz* orientation when he talks about his relationship with his personal computer:

> When I wanted to be creative, I used to cook, play the guitar, and do graphics. Now I can make the computer play music and produce fantastic pictures. Unfortunately, it doesn't know how to cook . . . yet. That's one of the problems of this machine. It's seductive. It practically grabs you by the shirt and says, "Look at all this neat stuff I'm capable of doing. Spend more time with me. I'll give you anything you want." (cited in Morrisroe, 1984, p. 28)

According to Paul, the computer exercises this hold because of its constancy and patience. He goes on to say that a computer is not Machiavellian. . . . It's not scheming. It doesn't try to get the best of you, like most New Yorkers. It's flawless and patient. If you do something wrong ten times, it won't get mad at you. It doesn't quarrel with you irrationally. It doesn't mind being awakened at 3 a.m. . . . It's always there. (cited in Morrisroe, 1984, p. 29)

The computer is capable of creating and provoking a real sense of wonder, fantasy, and attachment.[1] In so doing, it seduces us into making technological decisions primarily on technological terms.

In some instances, the notion of *gee whiz* filters into work, propelling people to work longer and harder than they would if the machine were not so compelling, challenging, and demanding.

The Notion of Can-Do

Often the notion that affects how people see the computer in work is not the sense of *gee whiz* but rather the sense of *can-do*. This attitude perceives the computer as a valuable tool, a significant piece of equipment that can do many work tasks—and can often do them faster, better, and less expensively than humans would. In this context the machine becomes a money-getting and time-saving piece of equipment.[2]

The *can-do* attitude is premised on efficiency—where economy of time, of effort, and of cost is prized. Efficiency is the orientation that drives the work ethic in America.

The computer is used as a planning, budgeting, forecasting, and tracking tool; it is used as a word processor, facilitating writing and editing; it is used as a method of accumulating and accessing data bases; and it is even used as an on-line data entry, editing, and inquiry method. Coupled with communications technology, it can be used for telecon-

---

1. See McCorduck's book, *Machines Who Think* (1979) for a discussion of the history of how humans have created things in their images and likenesses in order to explore their own qualities of humanness.

2. In 1868, Charles Francis Adams, Jr., made a very similar claim about the railroad when he commented, as follows, on the near completion of the first transcontinental railroad: "Here is an enormous, an incalculable force . . . let loose suddenly upon mankind, exercising all sorts of influences, social, moral, and political; precipitating upon us novel problems which demand immediate solution; banishing the old, before the new is half-matured to replace it. Yet with the curious hardness of a material age, we rarely regard this new power otherwise than as a money-getting and time-saving machine . . . not many of those . . . who fondly believe they control it, ever stop to think of it as . . . the most tremendous and far-reaching engine of social change which has either blessed or cursed mankind." (Cited in D. Boorstein (1974), *The Americans: The Democratic Experience*, p. ix.)

ferencing and electronic mail. And, the recent and dramatic advances in artificial intelligence have created diagnostic programs that allow the computer to be teacher, architect, chemical engineer, medical doctor (McCorduck, 1979; Reinhold, 1984)—all at a bottom-line cost savings over human power.

Limitations of Gee Whiz and Can-Do

The notions of *gee whiz* and *can-do* are based on the fundamental desires for playfulness and productivity. These desires are deeply ingrained in the human psyche. To the extent that the computer serves as a toy or a tool, it not only triggers these desires, it also fulfills them.

The major problem of limiting our experiences to *gee whiz* and *can-do* has to do with how these notions limit our technological decision-making. Neither *gee whiz* nor *can-do* involves explicit value considerations.

The notion of *gee whiz* encourages decisions to be made on the basis of the potential playfulness of the act. For example, teenagers who crack the information systems of schools, hospitals, or government agencies frequently do so for the fun, the challenge, or the intrigue, and have been quoted as indicating they mean no malice by their acts. Acts of cracking security codes and entering systems represent to them adolescent versions of their childhood game of "cops and robbers."

The notion of *can-do* leads to decisions that are made on the basis of the workability of the technology. This *can-do* orientation makes technological decisions primarily, if not solely, on technological grounds: If the technology works, use it. The focus of the *can-do* orientation is on the technology as a tool, and the attention is on the nature of the tool rather than on the problem to which the tool is brought to bear. The emphasis on the workability or feasibility of the tool frequently presupposes the appropriateness of the tool to be applied to the problem when, in fact, the appropriateness has not been examined. Such an examination is a reflection on goals and values, rather than simply on technology.

What is needed is the amplification of the notions of *gee whiz* and *can-do*. We must cultivate another relationship to the computer. Just as we have allowed it to evoke the wondering children and the practical adults in us, we must now allow it to provoke our moral sensibilities. We must allow it to become *morally evocative*,[3] to compel us to ask, "What

---

3. See Turkle's (1984) book, *The Second Self: Computers and the Human Spirit*, for an ethnographic examination of the psychological evocativeness of the computer. Her argument is that the computer pervades how we think about ourselves.

are the morally right actions to take with this technology?"

Conjointly the notions of *gee whiz, can-do,* and moral evocativeness allow us to ask of the technology: Will it be fun? Will it work? Will it be right?

Notion of Moral Evocativeness

Frequently, it is argued that technology is value-free and that humans are biased and value-bound. The polarized notions of objective and subjective imply this relationship: Things, including technological objects, are objective and value-free, whereas people are subjective and value-laden. This separation of technology from people is inappropriate.

Technology never exists outside of a human context; it reflects and shapes human choice. Choices are made regarding its design, operation, utilization, application, and implementation. Each of these choices is laden with values. Since technology can never be separated from human choices, it can, therefore, never be separated from the values embedded in these choices. Any decision about technology constitutes a decision on values. When seen from this perspective, decisions about information technology — whether to use it, when to use it, where to use it, and under what conditions to do so — become ethical decisions. Conflicts over the decisions may in fact reflect conflicts in ethical priorities.

In accepting the value-laden nature of technology and technological decision-making, the need for an explicit ethical analysis becomes apparent. To make a technological decision solely on the basis of the workability, costs, or politics of the technology ceases to be sufficient.

Ethical Analysis

An ethical analysis requires the decision-maker or ethicist assisting the decision-maker to ask a series of questions, each of which has several plausible answers. According to leading bioethicist Robert Veatch (1977), there are five questions in ethics that, when taken collectively, form a general framework from which moral dilemmas can be addressed and morally justified.

The questions that must be asked in order to assume a complete and adequate ethical position on a problem or situation are:

1. What makes right acts right?
2. To whom is moral duty owed?
3. What kinds of acts are right?
4. How do rules apply to specific situations?
5. What ought to be done in specific cases? (Veatch, 1977, p. 2)

What Makes Right Acts Right?

When a person claims that he has made the right decision or that his actions are right, what makes those decisions or acts right? On what basis
is the rightness of a right act decided?

First, one must examine the language of the statement to determine
whether the rightness is normative or nonnormative. A normative statement is one that establishes a standard against which behaviors or decisions can be gauged and includes terms such as "ought," "must,"
"should," or "prefer." Such language implies that specific norms are being established as the basis for deciding the rightness of an act.

But then the question becomes whether these norms are moral or
nonmoral in nature. To say that the administrator should not transfer
the responsibility for intake from the caseworker to the data-entry clerk
might mean that it is immoral because it alters the client-professional
relationship, or that simply it is a breach of contract because collective-
bargaining agreements forbid these activities to the clerk. It is necessary
to discern whether the "should" or "ought" is premised on moral or nonmoral norms.

Decisions on the normative versus nonnormative and moral versus
nonmoral statuses of statements imply the existence of a decision-
maker. Someone must make decisions, raising the question of who that
person should be. Decision-makers may differ in their standards for
assessing moral rightness, and that should be taken into consideration
when ascribing responsibility for a decision. For example, a priest would
likely use a different standard than a scientist on the issue of abortion.

In general, three bases exist for assessing moral rightness—the personal, the social, and the universal.

The individual who uses a personal basis for adjudicating the moral
rightness of an act claims that it is right because "I say so." This personal
relativism "reduces ethical meaning to personal preference" (Veatch,
1977, p. 3). Personal relativism is highly problematic because of its solip-
sistic nature. It leaves little room for shared discourse and critical
reflection on how different facts were used to form different moral
judgments.

The social relativist claims societal norms as the basis for determining
whether an action is right. For example, in a capitalistic society where
doing good is defined in terms of efficiency, an act that increases or sus-
tains efficiency would be seen as morally right. In a religious society
where doing good is defined in terms of acts of charity, an efficiency-
inducing act would not so readily be seen as right.

Social relativism leads to different moral codes in different societies. Such relativism provides no transcendent norms for evaluating the morality of a particular society's code, and it does not allow for the possible rightness of an act that runs counter to the dominant norms of the society.

These two ethically relativistic standards could be translated, in common parlance, to "Do your own thing," and "When in Rome, do as the Romans do." They are not satisfactory for those who seek universal moral codes that transcend the individual or the society. Universal standards include the theological, the empirical, and the intuitive (Veatch, 1977, pp. 4–5).

According to the theological standard, a right act is right because of God's approval. The approval could be based on sacred writings such as the Bible, Torah, or Koran, or on practices. The Ten Commandments constitute a classic example of a theologically grounded universal standard that applies to Christians, regardless of whether their societies are aboriginal, American, or Bantu.

For the empirically minded, a right act is right because empirical observation of the laws of nature reveal it. "Empirical absolutism, as the view is sometimes called, sees the problem of knowing right and wrong as analogous to knowing scientific facts" (Veatch, 1977, p. 5). This position holds that right and wrong are empirically knowable, and that careful observation of what does and does not accord with nature constitutes the basis for moral judgments.

The third universal standard is intuition. Those who hold this view argue that rightness and wrongness are not empirically knowable or verifiable but rather can be known only through intuition. They also argue that all people, if intuiting properly, should, in principle, hold the same intuitions as to the rightness or wrongness of an act.

These personal, social, and universal standards are the dominant metatheories for defining right and wrong. They form the *a priori* basis for more specific ethical standards such as the social work profession's code of ethics. When social workers claim that they should do something because of their professional code of ethics, they are presupposing a more fundamental metatheory of rightness that has informed their code. When conflicts arise over the rightness of a particular act, it is important to discern whether individuals are drawing on different metatheories of rightness and wrongness. Such discernment gives insight into how different individuals or groups can be so thoroughly convinced of the rightness of their own claims and the wrongness of others.

This exploration of what makes right acts right leads to the second fundamental question.

To Whom Is Moral Duty Owed?

The root of this question is the issue of loyalty and allegiance. In making a moral judgment, to whom must the decision-maker be loyal? In the social work profession, primary loyalty is given to the client.

But the issue of loyalty is not always so simple. Who is the client? Is the client the client of a particular therapist or caseworker, or is the client the collectivity of all clients, present and future? How does a social worker decide a conflict among clients? For example, when an overworked therapist decides to use computer-based therapy with some clients, to whom is he or she being loyal, the current clients or the potential clients who would otherwise not be served, given existing case loads? Is there a conflict of loyalty between the two? This type of dilemma takes us into concrete situations where the social worker must decide what specific kinds of acts are right.

What Kinds of Acts Are Right?

This question constitutes the core of what is generally referred to as normative ethics. It focuses on the kinds of acts that are right or wrong and examines whether there are general principles or norms that describe right or wrong acts. This question presupposes the first question by asking, "What kinds of acts does God, society, or the person approve? What kinds of acts are in accord with nature or are intuited to be right?" (Veatch, 1977, p. 6) The answers to these questions depend on whether one measures rightness on the consequences of the act or on the inherent rightness of the act independent of consequences.

According to Western normative ethics, two major theories account for whether an act is good or right. The first claims that an act is good if its consequences are good; the second claims that an act is right because it possesses an inherent rightness, regardless of its consequences.

Consequentialism or utilitarianism, as the first theory is referred to, maintains that "acts are right to the extent that they produce good consequences and wrong to the extent that they produce bad consequences" (Veatch, 1977, p. 6). In principle consequentialism is quite simple. It assesses the rightness of an act (or a rule)[4] on the basis of its good consequences minus its bad. Analyses using cost-benefit or cost-effectiveness measures are popular examples of the consequentialist ap-

---

4. See Frankena's (1973) book, *Ethics*, for a further discussion of utilitarianism, particularly the distinction between rule utilitarianism (RU) and act utilitarianism (AU).

proach. In practice, however, this accounting formula is not so simple. The precise assessment of good and bad—benefits and costs—is not always easy, which leads to difficulties in subtracting bad from good and costs from benefits. And, most importantly to many, consequentialism is indifferent to the distributive effects of the equation. It does not examine who bears the benefits and who bears the burdens.

In contrast to consequentialism, deontologism declares that the rightness or wrongness of an act is inherent to principles of the act itself and not based on its consequences. The deontological approach argues that such principles define certain rights and obligations. For example, one could argue that social-service agencies have an obligation to ensure that professional caseworkers do client intakes because of their professional duty to promote the welfare of the clients, even though the consequence will be that fewer people can be served than would be if a data-entry clerk assumed those responsibilities.

Different deontologists list different principles that they hold as right-making principles regardless of consequences. But the lists of Western deontologists generally include *beneficence,* to do good and avoid harm; *justice,* to be fair; *autonomy,* to respect the rights of others; and *promise-keeping.*

Probably the dominant ethical principle in the delivery of social services is *beneficence*—to promote the welfare of clients or, at a minimum, not to diminish it. But, this principle can be specified in different ways. One could argue that by acting efficiently, with an acceptable cost-benefit ratio, the greatest good for the greatest number in need would be achieved and would best promote the welfare of clients. Another argument could be made that the welfare of the client is best promoted by protecting the human dignity of the client.

Another principle critical to the profession is *promise-keeping,* specified as the maintenance of confidentiality between client and caseworker. The caseworker has a duty to keep his or her professional promises to his or her clients.

A third general principle embedded in the professional ethics of social work is *autonomy,* which maintains that people have certain rights such as life, liberty, and the pursuit of happiness, and that these rights must be protected. The principle of autonomy can be formulated as "Insofar as an autonomous agent's actions do not infringe on the autonomous actions of others, that person should be free to perform whatever action he or she wishes (presumably even if it involves considerable risk to himself or herself and even if others consider the action to be foolish)" (Beauchamp & Walters, 1982, p. 27). Because of the unique nature of social work, the profession delegates the protection of client rights to both social-service agencies and to social workers. Most American social workers work for agencies, and clients seek services from those agencies, not from particular social workers. Even though the professional code of ethics in social work addresses individual social workers, the profession expects the agencies to protect the clients' rights and to foster an atmosphere in which the workers do the same. Therefore, in social work, the agencies and the social workers share the duty to protect the client.[5]

Another right-making principle is *justice*. According to many ethicists, the principle of justice is the most significant principle, even when the consequences of a decision based on justice are not the best for the greatest number. In the credo of the social work profession, this concern has to do with the equity of distribution of benefits to the clients, and the equity of access to opportunities.

One need not be either a strict consequentialist or deontologist. The mixed deontological position is one which holds that "both consequences and right-making characteristics are relevant in deciding what kinds of acts are right" (Veatch, 1977, p. 10).

Any deontologist, even one who is partially a consequentialist, must possess, however, a way of resolving conflicts among principles. The most common method is the lexical ordering of principles, which involves rank-ordering them from the most important to the least, with the first given the highest priority. Ordering principles is not an easy task.

Tensions in social work over the introduction of information technology into the delivery of services could reflect differences in the specifications and implicit ordering of ethical principles.

I suggested earlier that, left unchecked, technology tends to be driven by the value of efficiency. If we accept that social work is driven by the multiple values of beneficence, promise-keeping, autonomy, and justice, and that efficiency is only one way to specify beneficence, then conflicts could ensue if other definitions of beneficence are held, or if other principles are accorded higher priority. This point will be elaborated later in the case study.

---

5. I would like to thank Dr. Harold Lewis, of the School of Social Work at Hunter College, for bringing this point of shared responsibility to my attention. As Dr. Lewis points out, this shared responsibility can sometimes be strained if the caseworkers and the agency administration differ on how to protect client rights.

How Do Rules Apply to Specific Situations?

The fourth question of the framework recognizes that each situation is unique. The principles of doing good, keeping promises, ensuring fairness, and respecting rights are general. Thus the challenge is to formulate rules from these principles and to apply these rules to specific situations. "Moral rules are general guides governing actions of a certain kind; they assert what ought (or ought not) to be done in a range of particular cases" (Beauchamp & Walters, 1982, p. 12). For example, the principle of promise-keeping requires staff to maintain confidentiality of client records. Rules derived from that principle could include: It is wrong to release client information; and, it is wrong to deceive clients. But how binding would these rules be? Moral rules may serve either as guidelines for action or as strict rules governing practice.

As guidelines, rules inform but do not dictate action. For example, a rule for informed consent may not require the client to sign a statement but rather may serve as a guide to the worker in determining how and what the client should be told about the agency's record-keeping.

As rules of practice, however, the rules have a more binding effect. In the previous example the rule would require that an explicit consent form be signed by the client.

Conflicts arise when decision-makers have different interpretations of the functions of rules. The worker who sees a moral rule as a rule of practice will see another who treats it as a guideline as violator of the rule.

Having thought through metatheories of rightness, codes of allegiance, and normative ethics, the fifth question becomes very concrete.

What Ought to Be Done in Specific Cases?

How does one finally make the judgment of what to do in a particular situation? The answer requires an integration of the other questions:

Do you use personal, social, professional, or universal standards for defining rightness?

Given that standard, to whom do you owe loyalty and allegiance? How do you order your loyalties? If allegiances change with situations, how does the ordering change?

Given the standard, what kinds of acts are right: those that have more good consequences than bad, or those that possess certain principles that are inherently right, regardless of consequences such as acts of avoiding harm, or being just, keeping promises, respecting the rights of others? And which has the highest priority?

Given these standards, principles, and norms, how do you formulate and apply rules to specific situations? Are the rules general guides to action or are they more stringent rules of practice?

These five questions form the nucleus of an ethical framework of analysis. But, as indicated earlier, such an analysis cannot be done in a vacuum. It requires application to a concrete study. I will briefly outline a situation and a series of ethical questions it raises. The details of this case study will not be relevant to all or even most social work situations, but the structure of the ethical analysis will be appropriate.

Case Study

A public agency has received a state grant to automate its income-maintenance program. This would include the development of a client-record data base and automated intake system, which would result in improved management reporting, improved record-matching, improved ability to match applicants to the full range of benefits, the creation of a common data base for provider agencies, reduced costs through the elimination of professionals from the intake process and a reduction in the number of clerical workers, and faster turn-around time for reimbursement reporting.

An ethical analysis of this case study must involve the questions that follow.

What Makes Right Acts Right?

The social workers' professional code of ethics is arguably the final standard for assessing the rightness of automating the system. According to this code, the social-service agency and the workers are responsible for promoting the welfare of the clients (beneficence), maintaining the clients' confidentiality (promise-keeping), ensuring that the rights of the clients are protected (autonomy), and preserving the equitable distribution of benefits, burdens, and opportunities to clients (justice).

To Whom Is Moral Duty Owed?

According to this professional code, the primary allegiance is to the clients. What is not clear is whether it's only to existing clients, or future clients too.

What Kinds of Acts Are Right?

The answer depends on whether the decision-maker is a consequentialist, deontologist, or mixed deontologist, and how the principles of beneficence, promise-keeping, autonomy, and justice are specified and ordered. These factors can be revealed if we look at how different players might view the situation.

According to the agency administrator, who employs a consequential framework, beneficence is specified as efficiency. His or her primary moral question becomes, "What is the most efficient way to benefit our clients?" Such efficiency could be brought about by reducing costs, time, and labor, and by increasing the number of people served. An automated system would save money by reducing clerical staff, eliminating the cost of having professionals do intake and the cost of transcribing professionals' intake forms. It would save time in matching records, in matching clients to appropriate programs, and it would increase the number served through these savings (see Table 9).

These benefits would far exceed the dollar costs of this project, which would involve large capital outlays, increased costs for staff trained in the technology, and increased data security. Therefore, according to a

Table 9 **Cost-Benefit Analysis of Proposed Automation Plan, in Accord with Beneficence Specified as Efficiency**

Benefits	*Costs*
Time savings through • improved management reporting • faster record-matching • standardized computation of benefits • faster turn-around time for reimbursement reporting • better match of applicants to full range of benefit eligibility	Large capital outlays Increased personnel costs for high-tech staff (programmers and analysts) Data-security costs
Common data base for provider agencies	
Cost reductions through • decreased fraud • elimination of professionals from intake processes • reduction of clerical staff • standardized, equitable assessments of needs • elimination of clerical transcriptions of professional intake reports	

Table 10 **Ethical Analysis—Beneficence Specified as Human Dignity**

Actors	Impacts upon Human Dignity (Rights Threatened)
Managers	Decisions subordinated to computerized model
Caseworkers	Decisions regarding assessment of and allocation for client need subordinated to computerized model
Clerks	Pace of work set and measured by computer
Clients	Right to be treated in humane way by caseworker threatened Caseworker removed from intake procedures and distanced from client Data-entry clerk does intake, resulting in client being approached as data source. Clerks do interview training Client needs assessed by standardized algorithm Data collected may be unnecessary or inappropriate

cost-benefit analysis, the welfare of the clients would best be promoted through the consequent efficiency brought about by the automation of the system.

Caseworkers also abide by the principle of beneficence in that they seek to promote the welfare of all the clients or, at a minimum, not to diminish it. But caseworkers might specify beneficence in the sense of human dignity, rather than on the basis of efficiency. If this occurs, caseworkers and administrators would share concerns for promoting the welfare of the clients, but they would differ in how that would be achieved.

The caseworker could argue that transferring the intake procedures from a caseworker to a data-entry clerk and providing for client needs on the basis of standardized decision rules in a computer program would diminish the welfare of the client by depersonalizing the caseworker-client relationship (see Table 10).

The dignity of managers, caseworkers, and clerks could also be diminished by this introduction of decision support systems, thereby limiting their decision-making powers (see Table 10).

The fact that the principle of beneficence can be specified in terms of efficiency *or* human dignity indicates the potential for conflicts within the same principle. Moreover, because of the personal nature of the professional-client relationship, there could also be conflicts between principles. The ethical principle of beneficence, specified as efficiency, might come into conflict with the principles of promise-keeping, autonomy, or justice.

For a caseworker, the ethical consideration of confidentiality is specified under the principle of promise-keeping. Caseworkers might be concerned that the automation of client records could lead to a critical breach of this confidential relationship (see Table 11). In a nonautomated system, confidentiality may be more adequately secured because records are stored in a variety of forms and different locations and, hence, are not generally accessible. By storing clients' records on a centralized system, there can be access to personal data from remote terminals by any person who knows the procedures and the access code. Some people may have legitimate rights to this information, but others may not. Yet because of the computerized system's efficiency, violation of a client's confidentiality may be easier. Automation also increases the amount of information that can be recorded about a particular client and the ease with which connections can be made among data about the client.[6] The damage incurred by the client due to a breach, therefore, could be proportionately greater.

For a caseworker the principle of beneficence, as specified by efficiency, may also conflict with the principles of autonomy and justice. Under the principle of autonomy, the client possesses rights to property and privacy; the caseworker has the correlative duty to protect these client rights. Because of the legal ambiguity of the computerized data, it is unclear what constitutes property: Is it the data, or the disk on which the data are stored? Even without an adequate answer to this question, the caseworker, because of the obligatory nature of the professional-

Table 11 **Ethical Analysis—Promise-keeping Specified as Confidentiality and Informed Consent**

Actors	Confidentiality	Informed Consent
Caseworkers	Have obligation to fulfill promises implied by professional–client relationship (e.g., maintaining confidentiality, disclosing all relevant information to client)	*Agreement when to release data* Obligation threatened by increased accessibility to client's records by others *Agreement that data are complete and accurate* Obligation threatened by decreased accessibility by client due to complexity of technology
Clients	Correlative rights threatened	Correlative rights threatened

6. I want to thank Dr. Gunther Geiss, School of Social Work, Adelphi University, for the insight that not only can more data be collected by one individual agency, but connections among data from various agencies can be more easily made, thereby threatening confidentiality further.

Table 12 **Ethical Analysis—Autonomy Specified as Property Rights and Privacy Rights**

Actors	Property Rights	Privacy Rights
Managers	Right to retain data for purposes of reimbursement, evaluation, and accreditation threatened by technological innovations	
Clients	Raises questions as to whether contents of records are property and who owns them, and hence who has the rights to change and dispose of record contents	Threatened by— record-matching remote access to data greater content of records ability, via relationships among data items in a record, to identify individuals who were unidentifiable prior to automation

client relationship, may feel that the automation of the system will threaten the client's property and privacy rights, since so many people will have access to the data. Even though current technology provides an efficient means to promote the well-being of clients, it may threaten their autonomy (see Table 12). Advances in technology could alter this tension between efficiency and property rights.

Efforts to develop small portable *smart cards,* one of which would contain all of the client's information and would be given to the client could resolve this ambiguous issue of property. The client would own the card. Smart cards could enhance the autonomy of the clients. Such a technological innovation could simultaneously promote the client's well-being and autonomy. But, it could pose problems for agencies and servers who need to retain client data for reimbursement and practice evaluations.

Table 13 **Ethical Analysis—Justice Specified as Equality of Access to Information**

Actors	Client Records	Client Entitlements
Managers	Have access to client records	
Caseworkers	Have access to client records	
Clerks	Have limited access to client records	
Clients	Have no access to own records, physically and/or intellectually	Access to information on benefits greatly enhanced, but under staff's control

NOTE: Justice, here, means equality in distribution of benefits and of opportunity.

Whereas the caseworkers may feel that the efficiency of the proposed system might conflict with the human dignity of the clients, and with their own professional ability to protect the clients' rights to confidentiality and property, they might argue that, overall, a more efficient system would be a more just system (see Table 13). Although the clients' access to records, as currently stored on disks, would be unequal to the access afforded to agency staff members, their access to other information and benefits could be greatly enhanced. Using the data bases on agency programs, the caseworkers would be able to determine more completely the full extent of clients' eligibilities for various programs, and give the clients more opportunities to receive benefits. The automated decision support system would ensure that all clients in similar circumstances would receive equal benefits for equal needs. In principle, the standardization of decision-making would be efficient and just, assuming that the process used to develop the allocation algorithms was fair and just.

How Do Rules Apply to the Situation?

The question, "Should the agency's information system and intake procedures be automated?" cannot be answered simply. It depends on whether one adjudicates the rightness of the automation on its consequences or the inherent principles in the system, including its capacity to promote human dignity, keep promises, protect property and be just (see Table 14).

Table 14 **Summary of Ethical Principles**

Beneficence	Autonomy
• Efficiency	• Right to property
• Human dignity	• Right to privacy
Promise-keeping	**Justice**
• Confidentiality	• Equal distribution of benefits and burdens
• Informed consent	• Equality of opportunity

But, even within the principles, there are intra- and inter-principle conflicts which require that the decision-maker rank-order the principles. For example, a ranking of beneficence, specified as efficiency, then justice, then promise-keeping could lead to a different decision than if the order were beneficence, specified as human dignity, promise-keeping, and justice.

But the principles themselves are general and, in this situation, specific rules that offer guidelines for action are needed. The rules for efficiency might be characterized as "Minimize costs relative to benefits," or "The greatest good for the greatest number." The rule for promise-keeping might be that the caseworker must inform the client of the data-storage procedures and obtain his or her consent.

What Ought to Be Done in This Case?

The answer to this question, in effect the final judgment, requires an integration of the answers to the other questions. In integrating the answers, the decision-maker provides a moral justification for the decision. This justification moves through successively more general terms from the particular judgment to its justification by rule, then by principle, and then by theory (see Table 15) (Beauchamp & Walters, 1982, p. 12). If the decision-making power rests ultimately in the hands of administrators, they bear major responsibility to ensure that their primary moral duty—efficiency—does not dominate unjustly over the caseworkers' moral obligations to promote human dignity and to protect the privacy, confidentiality, and property rights of the clients.

Table 15 **Levels of Moral Justification**

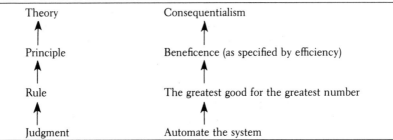

Theory	Consequentialism
↑	↑
Principle	Beneficence (as specified by efficiency)
↑	↑
Rule	The greatest good for the greatest number
↑	↑
Judgment	Automate the system

SOURCE: From *Contemporary Issues in Bioethics*, by Tom L. Beauchamp and LeRoy Walters, © 1982 by Wadsworth, Inc. Reprinted by permission of the publisher.

Technology as a Solution

So far I have focused on ways that technology can be a source of moral tensions and conflicts, but I think that we must also think about the ways technology can provide answers to moral problems.

For example, the homebound, like all Americans, have inalienable rights to life, liberty, and the pursuit of happiness. For many people, work is the means to both liberty and happiness. Yet the handicapped are too frequently denied that right. Advanced microelectronic technology is creating new home-based work possibilities in data entry, word processing, and programming, and providing technological answers to the work needs of the homebound.[7] Shearson American Express and Control Data Corporation have recently developed programs for these workers.

Another example can be found in a pending New York City experimental Crisis Intervention program. Employees will take microcomputers into disaster situations to immediately register victims for relief benefits. Again, a technological solution to the moral needs of people.

Challenge

I began this paper by saying that I wanted to articulate some of the ethical issues raised by information technology. As promised, I offer no answers. But the ethical framework of analysis provides a systematic set of questions that interrogate the moral aspects and ethical implications of introducing information technology into a human situation.

The challenge facing the social work profession is to examine how information technology can best be utilized in the delivery of social services. Not only must the profession examine what the technology can do, it must preserve a critical consciousness of how to form judgments about it. It is not enough to make technological decisions solely on technological grounds. **Technological decisions must be recognized for what they are: moral decisions.**

---

7. Home-based work for the handicapped is not without controversy, however. It has been brought to my attention by Arlene Gordon of the New York Association for the Blind that the unquestioned promotion of home-based work for the handicapped could isolate them.

EMERGING TRENDS AND ISSUES IN DECISION SUPPORT SYSTEMS AND RELATED TECHNOLOGIES: IMPLICATIONS FOR ORGANIZATIONS
by John C. Henderson

The concept of decision support systems (DSS) was first articulated by Michael Scott Morton in the early '70s. It is a concept that emphasizes the need for a supportive or enhancing role for computers. Scott Morton argued that decision processes are so ill-structured that the traditional concepts of computer automation and replacement did not offer an appropriate applications framework. Gorry and Scott Morton (1971) differentiated the concepts of management information systems (MIS) and DSS through the use of Simon's (1960) model of human decision-making. Simon proposed a simple decision model involving the phases of intelligence, design, and choice: Intelligence corresponds to building an appropriate data base for decision-making definition, design creates a set of alternatives, and choice addresses the evaluation and judgment process. Simon defined a programmable decision as one in which each of these activities could be fully defined and programmed. Gorry and Scott Morton (1971) elaborated on this concept by defining the notion of a semistructured decision (Table 16). A semistructured decision is one in which at least one of the phases is programmable but not all three. Hence the programmable phase is open to support through automation, but the human decision-maker must still address the ill-structured phase(s). Table 16 shows that the notion of semistructured processes became the basic concept for differentiating traditional information systems and decision support systems.

Table 16 **A DSS Framework**

Type of Decision	Operational Control	Management Control	Strategic Planning	Support System
Structured	Inventory reorder	Schedule loading	Warehouse location	EDP or MS
Semi-structured	Purchasing	Budgeting Master scheduling	Acquisition analysis	DSS
Unstructured	Cash management	Hiring managers Work force leveling	R & D	Intuition

SOURCE: Adapted from *Decision Support Systems: An Organizational Perspective,* by Peter G. W. Keen and Michael S. Scott Morton, 1980. Reading, MA: Addison-Wesley.

Sprague and Carlson (1982) extended the definition of DSS to reflect the technologies used to build and implement DSS. Figure 2 shows that their definition addresses both the various levels of DSS technology and the different roles of users of this technology. At the lowest level the technology includes tools such as graphics, statistical and modeling routines, and data-base management. The developers of these tools — termed toolsmiths — are highly skilled technical analysts. Generally these professionals have little direct involvement in the decision processes of an organization.

The middle level defines the DSS generator technology. This technology provides integrated, user-friendly access to the basic DSS tools. Theoretically a DSS generator links data management, modeling, graphics, and other technologies in a way that allows nontechnical users to exercise the capabilities of these tools. For example, one does not have to worry about the required data structures associated with a particular graphics package or how a data retrieval was actually executed. Instead the user concentrates on what is to be accomplished through manipulation (a model), retrieval (data), or communication (graphics). At this level the key user role is that of model-builder. This role provides the focus for translating a need into a fairly well-defined specification of

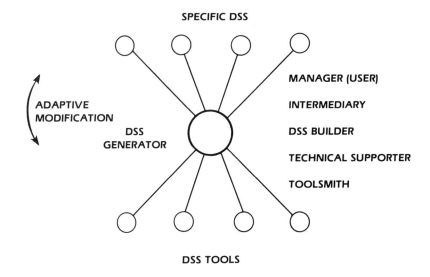

Figure 2. **Levels of DSS**

Source: Ralph H. Sprague, Jr., Eric D. Carlson, *Building Effective Decision Support Systems*, ©1982, p. 14. Englewood Cliffs, NJ: Prentice-Hall, Inc.

what tasks, that is, data retrieval, modeling, communication, need to be performed. Definitions of tasks imply creating a structure—building models, defining display-screen formats, and so on. The essence of the DSS generator is the capability to carry out the builder role rapidly and with little in-depth knowledge of the specific tools. A link between toolsmiths and builders is the technical-support person. This role recognizes that DSS generators of today have not achieved their theoretical goals. The technical-support person must understand the technologies—both DSS software and the hardware environment—so that the tool set can be adapted to serve the particular needs of individual builders.

The highest level of DSS technology is called specific DSS. At this level, the DSS incorporates the specific knowledge and structure of a decision environment. At this level the DSS provides the user with enhanced support to execute "what if" questions, to easily manipulate model structures, or to query data bases. The key user role at this level is the DSS manager or user. This individual utilizes the customized or specific DSS to support his or her decision-making. An intermediary links the manager and builder. The intermediary role recognizes the difficulty of defining the tasks and processes associated with actual decision processes. It is the goal of the intermediary to help define and communicate to the builder the specific functional requirements of the manager.

An interesting trend in DSS is the distribution of these roles among individuals. Although the early discussion of DSS envisioned a single individual carrying out the roles of manager, intermediary, and builder, experience has shown at least two individuals are normally involved: the manager and a combination intermediary and builder. However, improved microcomputer-based technology offers the potential of combining these roles and also substantially reducing the role of the technical-support person.

A third viewpoint for DSS focuses on the design-methodology and implementation issues associated with computer-based support. Keen and Scott Morton (1979), Alavi and Henderson (1981), and others argue that the design methodology for DSS must differ from that used for traditional information systems. The theoretical foundation for most DSS design methodologies is the management of change. Building on the Lewin-Schein (Lewin, 1947, pp. 330–344; Schein, 1961) change-process model, DSS design recognizes the need to create a climate for change, develop a solution or design, and then institutionalize the resulting system. Prototyping, or adaptive design (Alavi & Henderson, 1981; Keen & Gambino, 1982), has become a standard DSS methodology. This approach explicitly addresses the need to incorporate an active learning process in the design methodology. Prototyping is an iterative concept that calls for rapid development of an initial system, often based on vague definitions of requirements. The DSS manager actively uses the prototype to identify and define needed changes for the DSS builder. In this way needs are defined iteratively based on usage rather than on a predefined exhaustive set of user requirements obtained through interviews. Obviously, the iterative, learning approach is quite consistent with a semistructured decision environment. The trend toward DSS generators was motivated in large part by the technological requirements for prototyping.

Closely linked to the concept of iterative design are the issues surrounding successful implementation of a DSS. Again, research on learning, issues of end-user management, the politics of data, and related concepts of goal-setting and creating momentum for change have been studied in the context of gaining acceptance for DSS technology. A major source for many of these concepts is the research on innovation and the diffusion of innovations in large organizations (Allen, 1977).

Each of these perspectives has contributed to the definition of a DSS, and each provides a framework for introducing this type of computer-based support into organizations. The Trends and Issues section of this paper will highlight emerging critical issues that must be addressed if the success of DSS is to be continued. Finally, to close this discussion, I provide a framework for assessing the impact of DSS on organizations.

EMERGING TRENDS AND ISSUES IN DSS

Before drawing the implications of DSS, this section will review emerging trends and issues that are critical to successful introduction and ongoing use of DSS. These fall into four broad categories: technological trends, the relationship between expert systems and DSS, strategic DSS planning, and organizational issues. There are others that I could discuss, but these four are critical to DSS and have specific relevance to the use of DSS within the field of social work.

Trends in DSS Technology

The trends in technology can be viewed many ways. Here I present a general architecture for the DSS work station and use it to illustrate directions in DSS technology. Sprague and Carlson (1982) have provided frameworks for DSS technology. They recognize the need to link data with analytic tools through some user-friendly interface. Figure 3 builds upon these concepts by defining the technology or architecture of DSS as having four components: interface management, model management, data management, and communications management. Interface management refers to management of the mode of interaction and the environmental characteristics surrounding the use of DSS technology. Historically, DSS technology has been at the forefront of interface management. The use of nonprocedural languages, menus, and command-oriented systems has long been accepted as a standard feature of DSS. More recently, the advent of major physical interface technology, for example, "the mouse," the touch screen, and voice input and output, has made computer use even easier. Environmentally, the ergonomics of the technology and its portability have had major impacts on both the physical ease of use and where the technology can be used.

The most exciting impact on the interface-management area has been that of microcomputer-based technology. Microcomputer-based systems pioneered the hybrid interface, for example, menu and command structures combined and linked to the concept of "what you see is what you get." VisiCalc provides a good example of such a feature. By traditional DSS standards it is difficult to use: Variable names are quite limited, the language is very procedural, and advanced features require surprising sophistication. Yet most nontechnical users rave about the

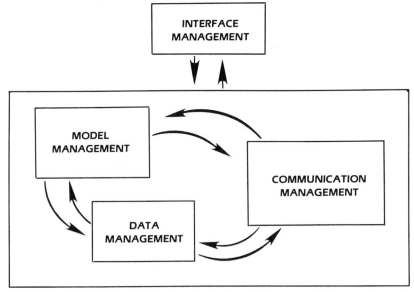

Figure 3. **A DSS Technology Model**

"friendly" interface of VisiCalc. Closer examination reveals a hybrid interface, menu and commands, command alternatives that are constantly in view, a system forgiving of mistakes, and the notion that the screen always portrays the entire realm of consequences, that is, the spreadsheet. This last point is particularly important. VisiCalc moved away from line-oriented commands (that must subsequently be executed) to a visual display of results from commands. The actual command is displayed as a necessary by-product but is not the focus of the system. Thus, the concept of *what you see is what you get*. This approach is also consistent with the rapid-feedback notion associated with learning theory. The users immediately view the consequences of actions rather than the structures of the systems, that is, commands, programs, data bases, and so on. This trend is also appearing in technologies such as word processing: The image on the screen corresponds directly to that which would be produced on paper.

A second major component of DSS is model management. As discussed by Elam and Henderson (1983), model management refers to the process of building, executing, and manipulating models. These models could be descriptive (the world as it is); they could be exploratory (simulations, models allowing "what if" questions, etc.); or they could be normative (models with explicit value functions that can be optimized). The model-management component of DSS permits the user to build or modify specific models, link required data bases to the model, and execute the models. A key notion is that the model structures become part of a knowledge base that is accessible to a wide range of users. The models themselves can then become a shared resource. These categories of modeling capability are often used together. For example, if one wishes to study the impact of adding more servers to a service organization, a queuing model that simulates the service could be used. Policies could be evaluated by using a "what if" approach to systemically alter the model. There is also likely to be a need to describe the demand function or study empirical relationships. Here, classical descriptive statistical modeling approaches are required. If the results of the model are to be used to allocate resources rather than explore the consequences of changes or policies, one is required to provide a value function that explicitly trades off cost versus benefits. If such a value function is provided, one can seek a "best" or optimal policy using modeling techniques that systematically evaluate alternatives in light of such a value function.

A third component is data management. This component provides the means to create, store, and utilize data bases. The key notion is that the management of the data is independent of the applications of the data. There are three major reasons why this component is vital, particularly for public-sector service organizations. First, a significant amount of time in public-sector organizations is spent on descriptive analysis. The user requires a powerful inquiry capability but cannot predetermine the specific data requests. Data management provides this ad hoc data-query capability.

Second, the criticality of data security and integrity often increases with successful applications of DSS. The data-management capability will provide the local user with full security and data-administration functionality associated with the more traditional applications of data processing. Data-base technology can be used to provide a control system that is consistent with the organizational control policies. For example, if the organization wishes to decentralize control, a component of the local system can ensure that each local unit adequately addresses security.

Finally, as will be discussed in the section on expert systems, the complexity of the data domain is rapidly increasing. Unless the builders and users are given significant capability to contend with this complexity, the realities of information overload may dominate the decision process. That is, the structure of knowledge bases that are necessary to support ill-structured processes is deep and complex. Simple data-management approaches, like a client file, will not be adequate to efficiently support complex inquiries.

The fourth component is communication management. This component must address three fundamental communication-problem areas: the user, linkages internal to the system, and linkages between systems. Communication with the user is an issue of presentation. At a minimum, the system must provide textual, tabular, and graphical modes of presentation. As the technology in videotex and image-processing develop, these modes of presentation should also become available.

A second area relates to the interconnections between packages and modules within the work station or host computer. For example, the system should allow the user to move data from a spreadsheet package to a graphics package. One trend in the industry is to provide a single fully integrated DSS software package as the means to cope with module interconnection. For example, Symphony is an attempt to integrate spreadsheet capability with graphics, data management, and word processing. Integration, however, has always implied a trade-off with functional power. A general capability to manage the interconnection among software modules offers the opportunity to provide both functional power and an acceptable level of integration. In addition, a generalized software interconnection provides a means to easily incorporate innovative products into the DSS work environment.

The third aspect focuses on the notion of mainframe/micro linkage, networked or distributed DSS and ultimately incorporates DSS into the larger office-automation issue. The capability to utilize and share resources while protecting proprietary interests of a given user is a general driving force of computer-based technology and should be part of the architecture for DSS technology.

Each of these components can be very functional for the DSS user. The power and price/performance of the technology for each component is rapidly improving. Hence a key issue is how to translate the concept of each component into specific hardware and software. The view of technology presented herein suggests the range of functions that must be addressed and emphasizes the evolving nature of the technology. To insure a good investment in DSS technology, one must seek an architecture that meets the needs of current users but can still evolve.

Expert Systems and DSS

The improved price-to-performance ratio of technology increases the likelihood that artificial-intelligence concepts will have practical value. The area of artificial-intelligence research that is associated with DSS is called *expert systems*. The concept of expert systems addresses architectural issues and performance, that is, a knowledge base coupled with an inference capability that should perform as well as an expert. The measure of value of an expert system is its ability to generate a problem solution that is not obvious. That is, the system adds value. It does more than just use a decision rule to compare and select from a total enumeration of possibilities.

Expert-systems research has provided several functional models of an expert system (Elam & Henderson, 1983). Two notions are central to a DSS: the knowledge base, and the inference engine. A *knowledge base* is an augmented data base that includes specific task-domain data. Alternative means to structure the knowledge base range from simple production rules — "if-then" rules — to network structures that attempt to represent multilevel conceptual relationships (Elam & Henderson, 1983). Each representation mode has strengths and weaknesses. The underlying objective, however, is to store both structure and process relationships. For example, a traditional data base may contain facts about a client and a service provider. The knowledge base would expand this domain to include a range of relationships a client could have with a provider, and likely consequences occuring from interaction between a client and service provider. One could process the knowledge base not only to retrieve facts but also to produce a range of possible outcomes. Since problem domains often have implied relationships with other problem or task domains, the expert system can aid the user in exploring unanticipated consequences of actions or in seeking viable alternative solutions to a problem.

The *inference engine* is a processing concept that relates to the ability to manipulate the knowledge base. An aspect of the inference engine that is particularly important to DSS is the ability to provide a clear *line of reasoning*. That is, in processing the knowledge base, the specific heuristic used by the inference engine may select among alternative paths or relationships. The knowledge base normally reflects the uncertainty of these relationships as well as overlapping domains. The inference engine must be able to clarify how a particular solution was reached. For instance, if one begins with the fact that a client had a "breakdown," there are a large number of events that might have caused this event. The selection of a particular line of reasoning may exclude from consideration competing explanatory sets of events and relationships. The engine must not only execute a line of reasoning, it must also be capable of communicating the process used.

The impact of expert-system concepts on DSS will be at least threefold. First, the utility of the data base will be greatly enhanced when it is converted to a knowledge base. Second, the model-management component becomes much more practical—models can be viewed as special relationships. The powerful representational schema used in expert systems can be adapted to store models. Finally, expert systems can provide a fundamental new exploratory capability. The line-of-reasoning concept could lead one to an implementation of the "why" command rather than a "what if" command. When the complexity of the problem domain is high, the ability to perform a "why" analysis is critical. Since one trend in DSS is toward more complex systems, this capability will be increasingly important.

Strategic DSS Planning

Given that organizations will have limited resources to invest in DSS, another key issue is related to the identification and selection of strategic DSS opportunities. Further, experience shows that successful DSS implementation often requires access to or support of other organizational information systems. The strategic-planning model in Figure 4 provides a means for identifying and evaluating opportunities

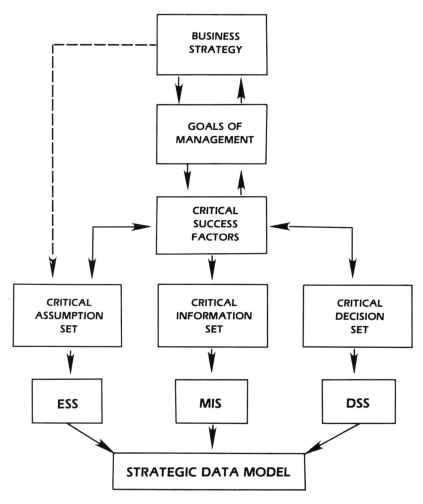

Figure 4. **A Strategic Planning Methodology**

for DSS and understanding the implications for other system-development efforts created by a DSS project. This planning model identifies three dimensions of the issue of the strategic selection and, ultimately, the integration of DSS with other organizational systems. The first is the contextual frame used in the planning process. The framing concept is related to the research in requirements analysis that indicates that an individual's responses to the query, "What information do you need?" is sensitive to the contextual environment implied by the question. For example, Mason and Mitroff (1980) provide a frame for strategic planning based on key stakeholders. This research suggests alternative frames that range from a social analysis—key stakeholders— to a contingency analysis—organizational process. A major issue in selection involves the utilization of a contextual frame that is appropriate for the goals of the users and consistent with the task environment.

A second dimension addresses the need to generate alternative views from a given frame. The planning model shown in Figure 4 provides three domain views: critical assumptions, critical information, and critical decisions. The assumption set reflects fundamental beliefs about the environments. The information view relates to a DSS as part of an organizational information set. This view provides a procedural focus that helps to specify the data resources necessary to implement a DSS. The decision view provides a focus on the process of decision-making. It examines the structure of the decision and attempts to recognize the interactions between individuals associated with most decision processes.

Each view highlights key information needs. The assumption-set view tends to emphasize data resources external to the organization. [EDITORS' NOTE: ESS refers to Executive Support System, a sophisticated analog to DSS focused on assumptions, goals, and strategies.] The information view emphasizes the need to utilize data resources captured by organizational transaction-processing systems. The decision view addresses the need to enhance processing through the use of models.

The third dimension of the planning model attempts to coordinate these views. Termed a *strategic data model*, this component provides a high-level statement that conveys how information resources must interrelate in order to support a decision process. The data model becomes a policy statement for the accomplishment of strategic DSS. This policy framework permits the development of implementation guidelines that can be put to special use across DSS applications. Such an approach increases the likelihood that a strategic DSS application can be implemented effectively.

Each of these dimensions must be addressed in a planning methodology if one wants to effectively augment or enhance the development outside the planning framework (as would be necessary with end-user systems). The issue is not to stop such innovative behavior but to channel a portion of the DSS investment directly into strategic domains.

Organizational Issues

As defined by Rockart and Flannery (1981), end-user computing addresses the emerging independent use of computer technology by nontechnical users. When DSS are also viewed as a design methodology that altered the role of users in the development life cycle, DSS are an early forerunner of end-user computing. The advent of the microcomputer, with its very appealing price/performance ratio, changed the economics of DSS and created a surge of end-user computing. It provided the opportunity for each individual to build a wholly owned DSS. Two issues arise from this circumstance: the need to provide an appropriate level of organizational support, and the implications and trade-offs for control. There are many mechanisms, both internal and external to the organization, to provide educational support and to support the acquisition of the software and hardware. Another is the need to support the development process over time. If one views end-user computing as an exercise in mass prototyping, that is, thousands of end-users developing prototyped systems, most organizations lack the capability to support the resulting systems. If every individual owns his/her prototype and remains isolated, there will be no major problem. Experience with DSS, however, suggests that a significant portion of these end-user systems will become so important to the organization that others will want to share access to those systems and their data. And yet the design and maintenance requirements of such shared systems are significant for both the performance of the system and the human resource. Since the traditional site for support of shared computer resources is the data-processing department, there may be increasing demand to transfer portions of design and maintenance responsibilities to this group.

The control issue also has several dimensions. Most control policies center around the technology. But the technology is a rapidly changing dimension of end-user computing, and the one for which an external solution—increased standardization, the most common form of control—can be provided. A more difficult problem will be the increasing demand to control data. The security and privacy perspectives, and a desire for improvement in both efficiency and effectiveness through shared data will create serious conflicts. The strategy for managing the data resource will have a significant impact on how organizations function. The control of data is the hidden issue in end-user computing, particularly for service organizations.

IMPACTS UPON AND
IMPLICATIONS FOR ORGANIZATIONS

As the technology and design methodology for DSS have improved, the impacts of the different types of computer-based systems have increased. The advent of microcomputers has created a huge potential for both positive and negative impacts on the providers of social services. Figure 5 provides a framework that can clarify the range of DSS impact and draw implications of DSS for organizations and the professionals working in those organizations.

The framework recognizes both the structural and process dimensions of the impacts. The structural dimension addresses the relation-

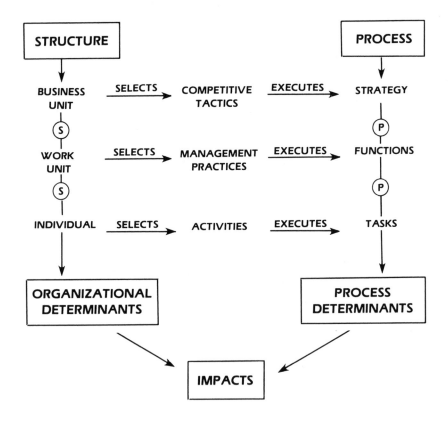

Figure 5. **Impacts Framework**

ships between individuals and work groups, and work groups and the organization as a whole. The clarity and rigidity of these structural relationships have long been subjects of study. The impact of computers in relation to these structural relationships has also been studied (Allen, 1977). One finds that there is little explicit correlation between issues of centralization or decentralization, or other measures of structure, and the use of computers. Computer technology can be used to enact both formal and informal structural relationships.

In the context of DSS, most research has examined the impact of DSS on the individual decision-maker (Keen & Scott Morton, 1979). There has been some work on the use of DSS concepts and tools to support group decision-making (Huber, 1984), but little of this work considers the impact of DSS on the work group outside of the context of a specific decision process. Henderson and Schilling (1985), however, point out that a major impact of DSS can be increased access to the decision process. The capability to network DSS work stations could affect the composition and stability of the work group, the work environment, and how the work group relates to the organization as a whole.

The process dimension views the task domain at increasing levels of abstraction. At the lowest level is the task. Tasks combine to generate functions; functions combine to generate strategy or mission. Computer-based technology can have a significant impact on the relationships of task to function and function to strategy. Automation may result in the exclusion of tasks or the creation of new tasks. One interesting trend has been the changing criticality of function with regard to strategy. For example, increased specialization of service providers, perhaps based on technology available to the providers, has increased the importance of the referral function.

DSS have had major impact on the relationship of task to function. This is not surprising since decision support has traditionally been an individual-based concept. The nature of this impact can be described in two ways. The first relates to the efficiency or effectiveness with which individuals, work groups, or organizations execute their respective tasks, functions, or strategies. DSS have generally been viewed as having a major impact on the effectiveness of individuals with respect to tasks (Keen & Scott Morton, 1979). More recently, DSS have been viewed in the larger context of office automation and, thus, as having impact on work groups' efficiency or effectiveness in executing functions (Huber, 1984). There has been little study of the impacts of DSS on the execution of competitive tactics to achieve strategies.

The other part of the impact is on the selection of activities, management practices, or strategic tactics. This is a type of innovation impact. Henderson and Schilling (1985), Keen (1980) and others have pointed out that a major benefit of DSS is that an individual will often select a different means (activities) to accomplish a task. Likewise a work-group manager may select a new control practice for a specific function. Organizations are beginning to consider new competitive tactics for accomplishing strategies.

For DSS, the innovative impact may also center around distribution of resources rather than creation of new activities or mechanisms. The impact of a DSS may be to transfer time spent on evaluation to time spent on problem formulation. If an analyst can now conduct a "what if" analysis in 1 hour instead of 8 hours, he/she can do 8 times the number of "what if's" or use the time to consider new problem formulations or address other aspects of the decision process.

At a work-group level the introduction of a DSS may create new access to a decision process. This access may be due to the externalization of the decision process: for example, access may be gained because one must identify sources of information to be used, or because the DSS allows for redistribution of work resources within the decision process. Henderson and Schilling (1985) note that changes in access to a decision process and organizational distribution of resources within that decision process appeared to be a major impact of their DSS implementation.

At a strategic level, the impact of DSS is unclear. It is difficult to attribute strategic impact to a given DSS. For classes of organizations, however, particularly service organizations that rely on highly skilled professionals as the providers of services, a strategic dimension of DSS becomes more apparent. Here, strategic impact could be formulated in terms of the capability to leverage or coordinate key human resources. If this is the case, then effective impact of the individual or work group translates into strategic impact. This view of strategic impact as a summation of individual impacts may be appropriate for small or medium-size organizations. Since the advent of microcomputer-based DSS technology creates an economic and technical environment that permits investment opportunities for small organizations and the potential for widespread individual leveraging (end-user computing), the opportunities for strategic impact should be explored.

It is my opinion that most organizations, particularly service organizations, do not have the luxury of asking whether these implications are good or bad. The conclusion that the DSS impact will be negative and therefore the organization should not pursue the use of this technology is impractical. Such a conclusion is likely to result in, at best, ad hoc development and implementation of this technology. One has only to observe the increasing impacts of information technology on the competitive positioning of organizations and the access to and quality of services to recognize that a major transition is occurring. The price/performance of this technology will make ownership of a DSS analogous to ownership of a telephone or television. **The challenge for the professional is to exert leadership in understanding the technology and its implications. It is up to professionals to ensure that the consequences of this widespread technological change are predominantly positive.**

CHAPTER 4

INTERNAL VIEWS OF OPPORTUNITIES AND THREATS: SCENARIOS

EDITORS' INTRODUCTION

A rational technique of recent vintage is the writing of scenarios to guide and inform the search for future alternatives. In spite of its brief history, scenario-writing is perhaps one of the best-known methods of generating possible alternatives for the future. Scenario-writing has been defined as a "technique which attempts to set up a logical sequence of events in order to show how, starting from the present (or any other given) situation, a future state may evolve step by step" (Tydeman & Mitchell, 1977, p. 12). Scenario-writing is a subjective activity that may involve no more than the imagination of sequences of events by some individual. Scenario-writing is open to criticisms of bias, prejudice, value judgment (often hidden), and even theatricality. It can have no more function than to sensitize others to the possibility of alternative futures. Frequently, however, acts of imagination may be anchored in or intercalated with reality. At its best, a scenario is a careful examination or creative introspection of the crucial issues in society in the hope of grasping the nature of any paradigm shifts that may occur. Hence the scenario is more than a figment of the imagination or a narration of a fictitious episode, event, problem, or issue: It is an evocative stream of consciousness.

The problem scenarios that follow were written prior to the conference by participants in that conference. The purpose of the scenarios was threefold: to stimulate thinking about the subject prior to the conference; to provide a grounding in reality and a springboard for a discussion of issues, barriers, threats, and opportunities; and to provide participants with an intellectual introduction to the concerns and thoughts of fellow participants. The Planning Committee requested that these problem scenarios be grounded in some reality: They could be actual case examples, amalgams of cases, or extrapolations of one or more cases. They could focus on opportunities, threats, barriers, or issues related to information-technology applications in social work practice. Each scenario reflects the author's view of the situation— his/her perception of it—but, in professional fashion, the identities have been masked to preserve individual and organizational privacy. Therefore, while names of people and places are used, they are only a literary convenience, unless the matter described is public information.

These scenarios show a remarkable breadth of issues, areas of application, questions, problems, and opportunities to improve upon or develop innovative services and staff supports. Many of the scenarios present current problems, some of which are problems of long standing but suggest or begin to identify opportunities for novel solutions via information technology. These scenarios may identify the innovations of the next few years.

Several of the scenarios present a litany of human pain—people in need and in crisis. They also reveal the frustrations of the professional: to see the huge amount of work to be done, and the inadequacies of time, knowledge, and the system to deliver. Each vignette hopes for an answer. One moral question posed again and again is not concerned with technology per se but with the status quo—the imperfect and incomplete state of the human-service system.

The scenarios cover a wide variety of fields of practice: mental health, family problems, adoption, child welfare, policymaking, medical social work, school social work. They range over such institutions as public social services, veterans' hospitals, voluntary agencies, and schools of social work. The problems concern staff, client, agency, and government. There are issues of resource development, information and referral, support groups, policy impacts, organizational conflict, information quality, fault and liability, ethical behavior, interorganizational cooperation and coordination, early warning, practice evaluation, assessment of progress in treatment, supervision, case management, and paperwork reduction—a long but incomplete list. The scenarios provide a wide-angled or macroscopic view of practice and of the potential applications of information technology.

Keywords are provided with each scenario and are listed in an index to help the reader classify scenarios. The index may also help readers identify scenarios that deal with a particular aspect of information technology or social work practice. Reading these scenarios provides a wide vista of opportunities and issues relating information technology and social work practice. Taken together with Chapters 3 and 5, one has a more holistic, and perhaps more realistic, view of the opportunities, issues, and barriers. The scenarios also remind us of the richness, breadth, and complexity of issues faced in social work practice.

The outlook for social work practice combined with information technology is quite promising. It offers the hope that technology will, through cautious reflection and consequent appropriate use, supplement and even enhance the role of professionals in their complex work with people who are in difficulty. If technology can truly be made to complement professionalism, clients will be helped immensely because the way in which services are delivered will be altered for the better.

PROBLEM SCENARIO
by William Butterfield

KEYWORDS: medical social work, marital counseling, marital problems, problem assessment, measurement, instruments.

Mr. and Mrs. Harris were referred to the university medical center family counseling unit because of their long-standing marital conflicts.

They have been married for 35 years, have 3 children, ages 13, 9, and 8. They report that their problems center around money management, time management, the discipline of their children and, most importantly, the lack of communication between them. She complains that he rarely talks to her and that he never expresses emotions or shares feelings. He agrees with her assessment but, he says, as a professor at the university, he spends his days talking to students and to colleagues and that by the time he gets home he is exhausted and has no desire to talk to anyone. He feels that the topics she wants to discuss are trivial and irrelevant. He feels she is insensitive to his needs and that she should understand his need for peace and quiet.

Mrs. Harris has a master's degree in art history. She met her husband while he was a doctoral student in musicology. After he received his Ph.D., he worked at several universities before he accepted his current position.

During the early years of their marriage, he spent long hours writing papers for publication. In more recent years he has written less but has been away from home 2 days each week, on average. His trips away from home are, for the most part, for the purpose of making guest appearances with major orchestras in various parts of the country. He is also involved in the governance of his professional organization at the state and national levels.

The therapist who has been assigned to work with the couple uses several paper-and-pencil assessment devices. The clients fill out the forms prior to each treatment session. The therapist would like to use the information during the following treatment session but is not able to make complete use of the information because of the limited time available for review. He also finds that it takes more time to analyze the clients' data than to see the clients. Thus it is difficult to do a thorough analysis of each client's data, even though without the analyses it is difficult to spot trends or patterns that may be developing as the treatment of the clients moves forward.

His clients also report that filling out the forms is burdensome. They complain that having to report an hour or more earlier to fill out the forms is aversive.

When the therapist is able to take the time to do an analysis of the clients' responses, he plots graphs of changes of the clients' answers to individual questions as well as marks those answers that seem to have special significance for treatment. He also uses statistical computations to summarize the data.

The therapist is dissatisfied with the measurements he is able to make using the present instruments. The current measures are generally short, asking the clients to report frequencies, intensities, or durations of feelings or events. The clients respond by completing a 5-point Likert scale questionnaire or, less often, by answering "yes" or "no" to questions.

The therapist is aware that more sophisticated methods of measuring feelings, attitudes, and estimates of event frequencies or durations are being reported in the literature, but he feels that such measures would make the analysis job even more difficult. Such measures include the use of hand-held dynamometers to report measures of intensity and the need to ask clients to give raw frequencies or raw durations when recording behaviors or events. The time it takes a client to respond to specific questions is also being evaluated as a measure of the reliability of the client's answers.

The therapist wonders whether these kinds of measures would give him and the clients a better understanding of the clients' weekly changes and whether the information would be useful in treatment. At present, he can only conjecture because of the limited time available for assessment and evaluation.

PROBLEM SCENARIO
by Al Cavalier

KEYWORDS: mental retardation, case management, accreditation, reduced records burden, reporting flexibility.

Mark is a 32-year-old man identified as one of approximately 6 million persons with mental retardation in the country. He lives in the "exit" dormitory of a large state institution for the mentally retarded, where he is involved in training programs to prepare him for trial placement in a small group home in the community.

Mark has been a resident of the state facility since he was 7, at which time his parents placed him there because they felt increasingly unable to provide the level of care and training they felt he needed. They have remained concerned and interested throughout his development. Over the years Mark has learned how to feed, bathe, groom, and dress himself, and he can also prepare some simple foods for himself. He can carry on basic conversations, but he has some trouble reading with full comprehension. He enjoys interacting with others and can work cooperatively but tends to be very sensitive to criticism. Mark can initiate most of his own activities and enjoys feeling that he can take care of himself.

Since Mark was classified as "moderately" mentally retarded most of his life, his living in the community had, for a long time, not been considered appropriate. Over the past 10 years, however, major ideological changes and supporting evidence showed that earlier assumptions had grossly underestimated retarded persons' potentials.

Since Mark was transferred to the exit dormitory, a state community-services case manager became involved in his program planning at the facility and in identifying a number of potential placement settings. Because of federal Title XIX regulations, an interdisciplinary team of professionals and lay persons was required to address a postinstitutional plan, prior to Mark's community placement, that would provide a focus for the array of services needed to continue his development and a means by which his progress could be documented.

Title XIX of the Social Security Act has provided strong impetus to large residential facilities to upgrade and maintain their services at the level specified by a comprehensive set of accreditation standards. The impetus to achieve accreditation as an Intermediate Care Facility for the Mentally Retarded (ICF/MR) is a substantial amount of federal funds provided to the facility for each resident. Since 1971 ICF/MR standards and Title XIX funds have been the dominant forces behind residential facilities for persons with mental retardation. Over 40 states participate in Title XIX, and in 1983 over $300 billion were disbursed. In 1984 a proposed bill, which would provide a major redirection in the flow of these funds, in line with the newer beliefs and ideologies about appropriate service settings and human potential, was placed before the United States Senate. If approved, Senate Bill 2053 would gradually shift the Title XIX funds and the development of quality services that these funds can stimulate from large institutions to more homelike community-based alternatives.

One of the heaviest and most time-consuming burdens dictated by the ICF/MR standards is a "comprehensive evaluation and individual program plan" that must be continually maintained and updated. This plan, however, is also the most valuable tool for program planning and monitoring. If S.2053 becomes law, the paperwork requirements for a case manager to maintain an active and useful individual program plan would become extremely problematic as increasing numbers of clients are placed in community settings and receive services from a large number of separate and distinct agencies. Even without S.2053, the increasing number of persons like Mark being placed in the community and the postinstitutional plans required necessitate increases in the efficiency and effectiveness of the information-management capabilities of case managers.

To fulfill the spirit and the letter of the regulations, Mark's case manager will need to record and update his social history, record periodic assessments and evaluations across vocational, medical, social, recreational and other domains, maintain a listing of Mark's particular strengths and needs, record all goals and objectives that were agreed upon by his interdisciplinary team, identify the person primarily responsible for each objective, identify the time spent each week on the objective plus the starting date and the completion date, monitor time lines for all specified services towards the objectives, provide periodic progress reports, and maintain a current daily activity schedule.

Since services are provided to Mark by diverse agencies, the individual program plan needs to be updated periodically, and a number of reports based on the information contained in the plan need to be generated, Mark's case manager finds himself spending a disproportionate amount of time on Mark's paperwork. When this time is multiplied by the number of clients with similar monitoring and documentation needs, the case manager becomes overwhelmed.

Can information technology reduce the burden that the Title XIX requirements place on Mark's case manager and thereby shift the cost-benefit ratio of the system back in Mark's favor? Can the documentation system be structured so that the kernels of periodic reports will be automatically generated for Mark's case manager to customize? Can information technology be configured so that important team meetings, objective due-dates, and other time-dependent events are automatically signalled ahead of time? Can information technology be used to assist the team in its decision-making as opposed to being used just as a bookkeeper?

PROBLEM SCENARIO
by Kenric W. Hammond

KEYWORDS: complex organization, coordinator of units, legal responsibility, access to records distributed nationally, risk identification, risk flags, confidentiality, alerting.

Any sizable care delivery system deals with the problems of behavioral disturbances manifested by a minority of patients or clients. Large systems typically have complex staffing, and employee turnover is inevitable. Consequently the institution's ability to deal effectively with the needs of patients with behavioral-disturbance potential is limited by the ability to recognize the problems and appropriately communicate them to those who may deal with them. A system like the Veterans Administration is even more complex because it serves people who may be geographically transient. Here are some typical situations:

Suicide risk   The veteran requests care in the middle of the night. A psychiatric resident sees him, determines that he has suicidal ideation and some depressive symptomatology but decides that he can be treated as an outpatient. The veteran fails to come to the mental-health clinic the next day. Two days later, in the medical walk-in clinic, he is seen for chest pain. The pain is determined to be of musculoskeletal origin. The internist does not have the chart with the psychiatrist's note and prescribes a 2-week supply of Tylenol with codeine. One day later the patient overdoses.

Assault risk   The veteran is well known to the inpatient psychiatric service and has had to be restrained and involuntarily committed for dangerousness to others. He has a paranoid delusional system involving his VA compensation. When longer-term arrangements for guardianship were sought in court, the veteran successfully avoided them and lives on his own. Recently a letter came from the regional office advising him that his compensation was reduced from a 70% rating to a 50% service-connected rating. He went to the Benefits clerk and was asked to take a number and wait. Moments later Security needed to intervene because he had begun screaming about communists and making verbal threats to the staff. Security Police subdued the veteran but dislocated his shoulder. He became calm when his therapist from the mental-health clinic appeared on the scene.

Failure to warn victim   The veteran has recently moved to the area. A worried aunt brings him in saying he's been restless and seems "about to blow up." She volunteers that he had been treated at the Chicago VA last year. The patient is interviewed and is found to be somewhat paranoid and hostile but expresses no plan to harm anyone and shows no signs of psychosis. The physician calls Chicago's records room. Yes, they treated the patient last year, but his record has been sent to Florida. The patient, meanwhile, requests the freedom to leave. The physician discusses the option of hospitalization, but the patient declines. The aunt is advised that the patient cannot be committed against his will. She is urged to be cautious with the patient and to bring him in again if there is further difficulty. He is given a prescription for Mellaril and leaves, after accepting a follow-up appointment for 2 days later. That evening he rapes and strangles his aunt.

Survivors of the aunt successfully sue the VA. Records from Chicago, finally located in Miami, reveal that the veteran had been jailed twice for rape, that he had a pattern of making death threats and following women, and that he had been treated in a state hospital in Oregon from 1973 to 1975 as a dangerous sex offender.

The court finds that the doctor had a "reasonable opportunity" to obtain VA records that would have altered the decision not to use involuntary committal and was negligent in not making a specific warning to the aunt that she was in danger.

Medical audit   The chief of staff has decided that an audit of treatment given suicidal patients is in order. Four cases of suicidal attempts, gleaned from incident reports, were identified for 1983. The average age of the patients was 52. Two were medical patients never seen by psychiatrists, two had been found making suicidal gestures on the psychiatric ward. No meaningful pattern of treatment was ascertained.

Two staff psychiatrists shook their heads at this report. "Sixty percent of my depressed outpatients have felt suicidal this past year," said one. The other replied, "We had four brought in on holds as dangerous to themselves last month alone. Our emergency staff usually sees one or two people with suicidal ideation per night. This report is meaningless!" The Quality Assurance officer replied, "You're right, but tell us how to even begin to find the cases without going through every record."

Approaches to solutions (and new problems)   Large institutions must develop methods for identifying patients considered to be behavioral risks and for transmitting critical information to the location where it is needed. The paper medical record, even if available, is inadequate for the retrieval of buried or dated information. An automated hospital information system could support risk-monitoring. Successful implementation would require cooperation for data-gathering and data entry. Multisite institutions would need to develop protocols for sharing data and methods for channeling information to service providers.

Most importantly, any risk-flagging system must be designed to ensure confidentiality and prevent misuse of critical information. The accuracy of alerting messages must be monitored. Implementation should not even be considered if the on-line staff and clinic clerks do not have access to such data.

PROBLEM SCENARIO
by Wandal W. Winn

KEYWORDS: computers, emergency services, telecommunications, rural services, networking, information utility.

Mark Baxter is the Chief of Social Services in a small (50 beds) general medical hospital in rural Wisconsin. He is well trained (MSW), underpaid, and liked by clients and fellow employees. A general problem he faces is a sense of relative isolation that he tries to offset through activities in his state professional society and a regular journal reading plan. He has worked 12 years at the facility and is committed to it in terms of retirement planning. He likes the fringe benefits, which include 30 days of leave per year and a $1,000,000 per occurrence malpractice policy.

Last year's site visit by a medical-facility accrediting team resulted in provisional accreditation of the hospital with re-evaluation in one year. Internal "politics" caused the administration, with the board's support, to find it convenient to blame social services in general, and specifically to identify the lack of 24-hour social work coverage of the emergency room, as one of the major problems. Mr. Baxter reviewed the criticisms as objectively as possible and concluded that the present coverage was more than adequate. In a recent meeting with the hospital chief administrator, there were overtones of "do it our way or ship out." A final meeting on the matter was scheduled for 2 weeks later. In a private conversation, the medical director told Mr. Baxter that the hospital's attorney had been consulted and the key issue seemed to be one of "prevailing community standard of care" as it is applied to the provision of social services in an emergency setting. By this time Mr. Baxter felt trapped, threatened, and especially isolated.

A few months ago, the Baxter family purchased a home computer for games and word processing, but Mr. Baxter has enjoyed exploring the telecommunications capabilities of the machine. One evening, while ruminating about his plight at work, he had an idea: Using the free subscription to an information utility (The Source) that came with the machine, he invoked the DISEARCH command and asked for a selective search of The Source's membership data base (40,000 + members) for members interested in "social work" and/or "emergency medical care." Within 5 minutes he had a list of the names and electronic-mail addresses of 68 individuals meeting those criteria.

He composed (with the word processor) a short query letter outlining his dilemma and asking for information and advice on emergency-room social services, accreditation, and the "prevailing standard." With a few key strokes, Mr. Baxter was able to electronically mail his letter to all those identified, and over the next 10 days he received 32 replies. Although some just "wished him well," there were a number of responses of substance, including one from a Dr. C. on the faculty of one of the Northeast's largest and most prestigious schools of social work. Dr. C. was well acquainted with the ethics issues involved in Mr. Baxter's predicament, as well as with the literature in the area, and offered to send references and to talk to the hospital administrator by phone if necessary.

Another reply was from a young woman, in a private-practice setting in Chicago, who had written a chapter in a book entitled *The Community Criterion As Applied To Acute Care Settings*. She also happened to know an attorney in Milwaukee whom she described as "knowledgeable about medical politics" and "very aggressive."

With the new information at hand, Mr. Baxter, feeling much less isolated, was able to prepare for the upcoming administrative meeting. Three days prior to the meeting he submitted to the administrator a written detailed analysis of the situation, with references and a cover letter outlining possible courses of action. A month later, over coffee, the medical director told Mr. Baxter how the administration had been "amazed" and "caught off guard" by Mr. Baxter's expertise and degree of preparation.

PROBLEM SCENARIO
by Gunther R. Geiss

KEYWORDS: medical social work, rare disease, complex interactions, support group, networking, information access, information and referral, information retrieval.

Angela B.'s problems began some 20 years ago with the occurrence of severe upper-back pain while she sat at her desk. The employer's medical department provided an examination and a diagnosis of pneumonitis. Her severe weight loss required treatment with antibiotics. She returned to work after 5 or 6 weeks. Angela had difficulty breathing, and often felt she would lose control of her bladder. Her husband observed her difficulty in breathing while she slept. A cold was diagnosed as bronchitis and treated with antibiotics. Continued symptoms prompted a chest X-ray, which the radiologist read to be tuberculosis, but the family's physician suspected sarcoidosis. Sarcoidosis is rare (2 or less per 100,000), seems related to pine pollen or peanut dust, is more common in rural areas and among Blacks, can affect most organs, and is characterized by tubercular-like inflammation. Most patients get well without treatment, but, for some, sarcoidosis may be chronic and permanently disabling. Angela's former employer refused to release the medical records of her case.

A search for a second opinion led to a special diagnostic test by a dermatologist in a major medical facility. The dermatologist confirmed the sarcoidosis diagnosis, but saw that it was in remission. The doctor recommended X-rays at 6-month intervals, or yearly if no changes occurred. On one occasion the X-rays showed additional lung-tissue scarring, but no further scarring was seen over the next 10 or 12 years. Her treatment regimen consisted of steroids for the sarcoidosis, a diuretic to counter water retention, and use of the IPB breathing machine 5 times per day. The frequent headaches often became severe enough to require prescription drugs.

After her second child Angela worked harder and tried to be physically active to stimulate her breathing, but she had to pace herself. About 5 years later Angela was hospitalized for gallbladder surgery. For the next 5 years, she had occasional hospitalizations for sarcoidosis, usually complicated by colds. On one occasion she fainted on leaving her car and broke her ankle.

As her children became self-sufficient, Angela looked for appropriate outlets for her energies and abilities. She studied and became a certified nurses' aide. Working in a local nursing home provided needed outlets and satisfaction until she was hospitalized for a modified-radical mastectomy of one breast. The surgeon opted to remove many lymph nodes to make sure the cancer had not spread. This added stress put Angela back on inhalation therapy—an IPB breathing machine 4 times per day, and occasional oxygen. Despite the prescribed arm exercises, she never regained full use of the affected arm. A biopsy showed the malignancy to be localized.

On her first day of normal functioning at home, Angela went out to shop and fainted on leaving the car. She fell on her arm and cracked two ribs. They could not be taped because of the surgical scars. She recuperated in 6 weeks, but her activities were limited. Three months later Angela accidentally sliced her leg to the shin bone. Apparently the steroids caused her skin to become very brittle below the knees. Stitching of each layer of flesh was required to close the wound which then required 6 months for healing.

Pain, edema, and a rash occurred a year later in the arm affected by the mastectomy. She was treated for severe cellulitis but could not take penicillin because of an allergy. She also had pain, like "an exposed dental nerve," in the neck, extending to the collarbone and shoulder. The next year Angela was hospitalized 5 times for severe cellulitis and the pain was worse on each occasion. Some of the antibiotics led to infections of her mouth and vagina. A year later Angela suffered excruciating pain and saw a dermatologist about her skin eruptions—to rule out active sarcoidosis. He recommended a neurosurgeon who suggested a nerve block for the pain. The anesthesiologist at the university hospital rejected the procedure because of complications related to her lung problems. She was again hospitalized for cellulitis and splitting the skin on her other leg in a household accident, with the same resulting complications and recovery problems. Her neck pains continue and, with the approval of her physician, she has sought help from a chiropractor.

While generally an exceptionally strong and resilient person, her problems are taking a toll on Angela as well as on her family. She has even come to question the value of her religious beliefs. Her family physician (friend and neighbor) has provided most of her care over the last 20 years, but he may not have the breadth of knowledge and ability to treat such a complex problem alone. How can she, as the victim of a very rare disease, find the support and aid of others like herself? Where and how can she learn more about her disease and its relationship to medications, the side effects of medications, the complications induced by surgery, and the roles of physical exercise and mental outlook in her well-being? Could better choices have been made if more complete information had been made available to her and her family? If so, and the information was withheld, who would be responsible?

By coincidence, Angela became acquainted with a medical social worker. Even with professional expertise, it has taken much time to find any resources since they are scattered and relatively rare. She tried an emphysema group but was told it would be inappropriate for her. Could the available resources be identified via search and retrieval? Are there means for connecting exceptional people with each other and/or exceptional professionals? How can advocates become more aware of these problems? What mechanisms would foster research into special problems? Angela and her social worker wonder, wait, and continue trying.

PROBLEM SCENARIO
by Joseph Palombo

KEYWORDS: battered women, private practice, currency of knowledge, expertise-access, networking, literature, laws.

Susan L. is a 36-year-old clinical social worker who graduated from social work school 8 years ago. She works full time in a mental-health center, and has a small private practice of 8 hours a week. In her practice she has specialized in the problems of battered women. She sees some of them in both the agency and her private practice. She attempts to keep up with the burgeoning literature on the topic, attends seminars, whenever possible, to continue her education, and is a member of a small study group that shares case materials on similar cases.

Susan has access to supervision and consultation, but neither her supervisor nor the agency consultant knows much about the problems of the clients she treats. While she is considered by her colleagues an expert in this area of practice, she feels deficient in her knowledge and competence. She keeps a card file of all the resources in her community that she has heard of, but she is not sure that her list is complete. She wishes there could be a way to keep track of these resources and make the lists available to her colleagues who might wish to use them. She would value the capability to communicate with other professionals about the specific types of services offered without having to make endless phone calls. She also wishes she could stay current with the legislative changes that occur and that legal counsel could be available to help her evaluate the relevance of these changes for her patients.

Susan feels frustrated because she has no easy access to the literature and the contributions being made by other disciplines. None of the libraries that she can reach carry the professional journals or recent publications that would be relevant to her interests. In addition, she would very much value consultation on some of her more difficult cases with some of the national experts she has heard speak at conferences she has attended. She is sure that given an opportunity she could make excellent use of such consultation. That type of contact would immeasurably enhance her capacity to help many of her patients.

Her colleagues have encouraged Susan to write a paper on one of her cases in which she used a creative approach to deal successfully with a difficult problem. She feels too unsure of herself, however, and wishes she could discuss with someone knowledgeable how to begin to structure her ideas in order to produce such a contribution.

How can Susan obtain easier access to the legislative materials, legal assistance, the literature, and national experts in her field?

PROBLEM SCENARIO
by Jacques Vallee

KEYWORDS: centralized records system, data quality, data validation, communications, injury, fault.

On Friday, 9 November 1979, at 10 P.M., three young men stopped at a gas station in Etampes, near Paris. Twenty-year-old Claude Francois was at the wheel. With him were Baptistin Lamont and Marcel Seltier. They were on their way to a dance in Salbris.

"Fill it up!" said Francois.

Mr. Nicolas, the service station operator, took a dim view of the tattered blue jeans, the leather jackets, the license number which did not look right because it was patched up with bits of black tape (3383 FM 13, indicating the car was not from the local area). Francois paid with a check on which his signature was hurriedly scrawled. Nicolas took it, reluctantly, but called the police to report the "suspicious" car and its

This section is from Vallee's book, *The Network Revolution: Confessions of a Computer Scientist,* Berkeley, CA: And/Or Press, 1982.

even more disreputable occupants.

In Etampes, police officers went to the computer terminal linking them with the central file of the Interior Ministry, in Paris, a file whose very existence had recently been denied by a Cabinet member. In response to a brief flurry of commands, the police entered the car's license number into the computer's memory for checking against its data bank. The system soon flashed its verdict: The vehicle was stolen.

Etampes called Orleans. A special night brigade was dispatched. The white and black police Renault intercepted the Peugeot, driven by Francois, at a red light. Then everything happened very fast. The only police officer in uniform stayed inside the Renault. The other two, in civilian clothes, got out. One of them covered the Peugeot with his machine gun at the ready. The other stood in front of the suspect's car and armed his .357 Magnum. One of the young men, Marcel Seltier, reported:

> We didn't understand anything. We saw the one with the gun aim at Claude. A moment later, a shot rang out. The bullet went through the windshield and hit Claude's face just under the nose. We thought they were gangsters. The one with the machine gun yelled: "Why did you shoot?"
>
> We got out of the car. Claude collapsed on the road. Right away they handcuffed us and told us they were the police. They called an ambulance. Claude was taken to a hospital. We went to the police station. They searched us and took our papers.

Subsequent investigation disclosed that the car belonged to Francois, who had bought it, legally, 10 days before. It had indeed been stolen in 1976, but it was soon recovered by the insurance company, which sold it to the garage where Francois bought it. The computer file had never been updated to reflect the change in the status of the car. The central police records still regarded it as stolen property.

The trigger-happy policeman was not arrested. Claude Francois remained between life and death for many days.

PROBLEM SCENARIO
by John P. Flynn

KEYWORDS: integration of practicums, policy content, policy process, experiments, simulation, modeling, data base, theory and empirical reality, choices, education.

Professional social work education is heavily field-based, with

practicums integrated with classroom instruction, but there is inadequate opportunity to expose students to a sufficient number and variety
of policy-development and -formulation experiences. While key learning experiences may be individualized for students through such means
as field-learning contracts and carefully designed classroom assignments, many ethical and practical considerations preclude the student
and instructors from generating policy-process experiments or experiences constructed for the sake of learning. Yet adequate professional
preparation must include exposure to, if not skill development in, the
many policy-process situations that confront a social worker in routine
practice. The social work educator must provide a range of realistic
learning experiences in policy processes, grounded in theory and empirical reality, while being constrained by what can be expected of
students and what can be perpetrated upon the practice environment.

In such a practice environment, consider the situation of the director
of the County Office of Substance Abuse Services. The office has existed for years as an independent human-services agency reporting
directly to the County Board of Commissioners, through the county executive. Over the years the principle that independence from the rest of
the county's human-services structures was necessary has been maintained. The unique requirements of the maintenance of confidentiality
in records and management information systems and the unique bases
of financial support are reasons given for independence. The ability to
provide independent advocacy for client services and system support is
also cited as a major rationale.

In my scenario the county administrator has recommended to the
County Board of Commissioners that the office be subsumed ad-
ministratively under the County Community Mental Health Board and
that the two policy boards be merged. The local and state mental-health
associations are opposed to the merger, while key county commissioners appear to favor the proposal.

There will be many demands for decisions placed upon the director
of the County Office of Substance Abuse Services. The director will
need to conduct an analysis of the content implications and project the
alternative policy-process events that are likely to ensue as a result of
the policy proposal.

Students, practitioners, and educators struggle with the need to project outcomes based on large sets of information in a way that does not
do violence to the real human situation. What guidance is available to
provide explanatory or predictive theory guiding purposive social action
in such learning situations and in these policy processes? What empirical evidence is there in other communities that may be used to
predict the outcomes of the proposed merger of services? What are

some of the ethical choices that should be anticipated early in the policy process? How can some of these theoretical alternatives be modeled? What data bases are available to shed some light on the prior successes or failures of such arrangements in other communities? What resources that might give direction for responsible action based upon theory, experience, and proper ethical considerations are available to the director?

PROBLEM SCENARIO
by Mark Vermilion

KEYWORDS: family violence, information and referral, interorganizational coordination, special services, networking, information system, support of policy and legislation.

On October 26, 1982, the Surgeon General declared that family violence is the primary health problem in the country. Recent research has determined that family violence accounts for a large portion of the violent crimes in our cities. For example, 41% of all assaults and weapon-related calls to the San Francisco Police Department are family-violence-related, totaling approximately 400 calls a week. And the most frequent reasons for homicides in San Francisco in 1981 were family- and relationship-related.

Victims of domestic violence and their families turn in large numbers to private, nonprofit service providers for help and assistance. In 1981 three organizations in San Francisco and Sacramento assisted over 4,000 victims and their families. In 1983, they began a computer network project that holds the promise of making their activities more efficient through computer-based information-sharing.

Family violence is a devastating problem that affects all aspects of each family member's life. No agency or discipline can address alone the needs of even one of those family members. The computer-linked agencies feel that only a multidisciplinary services network can address the needs of families suffering from domestic violence.

Currently participants in each of the San Francisco/Sacramento domestic-violence programs must research and maintain extensive information on the resources available to victims and their families. These resources—which include information on agency contact persons, trained service providers, and specialized services—change frequently.

Over the past 4 years, these agencies have trained service providers in practice fields such as children's services, medicine, law, elderly services, and criminal-justice services to deal with family violence as part of their efforts to increase services for violent families. The agencies provide monthly intensive training to other service providers who come in contact with victims and their families.

Daily, service providers consult with these agencies about available services. An information system appropriate to the needs and resources of the three agencies enables them to offer any service provider updated information on available resources. For example, service providers and policymakers request information on state regulations, changes in the law and current legislation, and available funding sources. This information is critical to the immediate delivery of services and to the long-term survival of many community programs.

With a computer network in place, information on client population and available services is being collected in a complete, up-to-date, and accessible format. Who is seeking assistance? Where is child counseling available? What is available for Vietnamese children? For deaf children? Where are the gaps? These and other questions can be answered once the raw data are collected and programmed for use. The networked agencies feel that providers, armed with more current information, will be able to make more rational decisions and recommendations to local and state authorities regarding future funding, training, and program development.

The computer network will also include a calendar of local, regional, and statewide conferences and training seminars for service providers and policymakers. The tragedy of family violence, as with many other social concerns, can only be addressed if large numbers of people are willing to discuss, learn about, and support efforts to develop immediate and long-range solutions. Thus the calendar of events will allow family-violence experts to maximize the opportunities for public discussions on local, regional, and statewide bases. It will continually list meetings of providers, law enforcers, educators, and church groups, and reach out to them for participation and support.

PROBLEM SCENARIO
by Walter Hudson

KEYWORDS: adoption, adoption agency, placement, child welfare, birth defect, private adoption, child-welfare agency, coordination, cooperation.

Mr. and Mrs. L. have been married for 11 years. They tried repeatedly to have children after the third year of their marriage but with no success. Three years ago they discovered that Mrs. L. cannot have children because of an undetected birth defect caused by a specific tranquilizer used by her mother during pregnancy. Last year they decided that they really did want a family and that adoption of an infant was their preference.

Mr. and Mrs. L. are a middle-class Black couple. Mr. L. is a successful accountant who recently obtained his CPA license in Illinois. Mr. and Mrs. L. live in a suburban community about 28 miles south of Chicago, and Mr. L. commutes daily to Chicago. Mrs. L. works occasionally as a substitute teacher in a private Lutheran school in their home community, although she and Mr. L. are not Lutheran.

Because Mr. and Mrs. L. have many friends in the Lutheran church as a consequence of Mrs. L.'s part-time employment, they chose to pursue adoption through a Lutheran child-welfare agency in Chicago. They want a Black child and, because of Mrs. L.'s birth defect, they have decided that they would like a child that may have a similar problem. They are willing to adopt a male or female infant who has a minor congenital disorder.

Mr. and Mrs. L. have had no success with the Lutheran agency. Although a child was not available when they applied for adoption, they had been encouraged to wait, in the hope that a child would become available. After 8 months of no success, Mr. and Mrs. L. decided to investigate other adoption agencies in the metropolitan area. They were surprised to learn that no less than 22 separate public and private agencies handle adoptions in the larger Chicago metropolitan area.

Mr. and Mrs. L. are very distressed. They have learned that none of the adoption agencies work together. It is, therefore, impossible for them to pursue a child through other agencies by collaborating with the Lutheran Child Welfare League. Because of their experience with one agency, they are also acutely aware of the enormous amounts of time and work that are required for completing the adoption-application process before they can learn whether the type of child they want is even available. The prospect of contacting and working with 7 or 8 different agencies (much less all 22) is utterly disheartening. It appears that it could take years before they can begin raising a family.

PROBLEM SCENARIO
by Wendell Ramey

KEYWORDS: centralized and common intake, client follow-up and tracking, management information system, referral methodology, interagency coordination, politics.

In 1971 the Mon Valley Community Health Center in Monessen, Pennsylvania, was constructed to house ten public and private social-welfare and health agencies to serve the 110,000 residents of an identifiable geographic "community" in southwestern Pennsylvania, approximately 25 miles south of Pittsburgh. At about the same time the building was being occupied, the Mon Valley Health & Welfare Council, Inc., a private, nonprofit agency devoted to research and planning, received a demonstration grant from the Department of Health, Education, and Welfare to develop and implement an integrated service-delivery system involving the services provided by the ten aforementioned agencies.

The Council and the DHEW intended to determine whether agencies would relinquish some of their autonomy and work cooperatively in a client-focused atmosphere that would facilitate, for the client with many problems, movement through the service system. They also wanted to be able to process clients without losing them in bureaucratic tangles. By centralizing the intake under the jurisdiction of the Council, an agency that provides no direct services, it was hypothesized that the clients would avoid unwarranted and redundant intake interviews with the many agencies that provided the services. Throughout the process, pertinent socio-demographic and utilization data would be analyzed and shared with the participating agencies. Another feature of the program would be an intake process that utilized our in-house computer to relate client socio-demographic data, problems, eligibility matrices, and a referral directory. The central intake worker would then be able to instantaneously identify resources to address a client's needs and develop a treatment plan that would encourage client follow-up.

As a preliminary step to the above tasks, the Council expended an inordinate amount of time soliciting the cooperation of the agencies and their staffs. The regulatory impingements around categorical funding also made it necessary to seek the support and endorsement of many of the bureaucrats at the state level. Because of the political ramifications and the threatening uniqueness of the program, these preparatory steps proved most beneficial to the initiation and continuance of the project.

When the components of the delivery system were in place and the system became operational, new clients were directed to centralized intake. An intake worker, with the aid of a terminal, was able to determine whether a client had previously used any of the agencies. This information could help the worker address the client's current problems. Also the worker used the program's data interface to design a treatment plan specifically for the client's present situation. Notification of referrals was dispatched, and specified report deadlines were entered to assure the evolvement of an organized tracking methodology for later follow-up. Such data were filed to be compiled with data entered by the receiving agency. Together they provided the base for individual agency and

Center management. Such analyses of data were discussed with the program directors at regular meetings so that they could be appropriately used in such activities as staff assignment, staff evaluation, cost-accounting, and utilization review. In addition, periodic reports of a similar nature were shared with the board of directors of the Council, which was composed of the presidents or regional officers of the co-operating agencies. It was thought that a board composed of such authority figures would assure the success of the venture and provide an instrumentality to influence the agencies to move toward greater program responsiveness, influence improvements in the quality of care, encourage cost-efficiency, and generally improve management.

For approximately 3 years the addition of new agencies and services, modifications in the system, evidence of decreasing commitment to the program by administrators and staff, more rigid enforcement of regulatory requirements by public agencies, the increasing insistence by many of the agencies that they conduct their own duplicative intakes, and the continued exorbitant investment of dollars led to adjustments to appease the agencies and ultimately compromised the project.

Those early efforts by the Mon Valley Health & Welfare Council, Inc., were successful. Such a program, however, could have become institutionalized and would have become a model for interorganizational management if the Council had been assured long-term funding for periodic redesign of the system to fulfill ever-changing community needs and agency attitudes. In addition, the Council, with the support of its board of directors and an ongoing community organization effort, might have been able to garner more wholehearted commitments from the public and private agencies and their staffs, with the design of a methodology that would lessen the anxieties about the disclosure of data that many agency executives perceived as discrediting their organizations. It is my conviction that an automated system similar to that discussed above is rational, feasible, and appropriate for reasonably priced quality care for multiproblem individuals or families.

PROBLEM SCENARIO
by Leonard Miller

KEYWORDS: decision-making, allocation decisions, standard language, precise language, change, statistics, modeling, education.

It may seem as if a paradox exists in the way society provides human services. Professionals—those closest to knowing the true relationships between resources and their consequences—have the least influence on the distribution of social resources. Ideally one would like the knowledge that is present at the professional-client interface to be present when decisions are made by each level of the human-service enterprise.

One reason this situation does not exist is that practitioners do not speak with a single voice. There are enough variations in prescribed programmatic actions to make it difficult to determine who has reliable knowledge.

Consider some of the fundamental allocation problems associated with a long-term-care program: Who are the proper clients for a program to prevent premature institutionalization, attenuate the expected rate of decline in client functioning, and reduce costs? Is there a particular group of services that will best lead to these results? Can it be identified? Professional opinions differ in regard to the answers to these questions.

Consider a program that operates within a capacity constraint. A queue to get into the program naturally develops. What considerations are given to whether program objectives could be furthered if some existing clients were terminated so that waiting clients could have access to resources? What about the preferred-service awards? The responses to these questions are as surprisingly diverse as if you asked a group of case managers who have just watched a videotape of a client-assessment process to make a care plan for the interviewed subject.

Clients and their circumstances are different, but not in every way. It is difficult for professionals to understand and communicate precisely which of the dimensions of any situation have meaningful similarities and which have meaningful differences. Professionals agree to their differences, to the difficulty of resolution, to not interfere with another's actions, and to not be bound by another's opinions.

Thus a problem exists at the core of social-service work. The language used in professional practice may be insufficiently precise, given the complexity of the human condition, to allow human-service personnel to ever be of one mind. Languages and methods that can further a solution to this problem do exist. Modern multivariate statistical models analyze similarities and differences, and information technology creates the possibility for these analyses to be made available to all the parties concerned. These tools provide the opportunity for professional dialogue and clarification.

The history of ideas shows that dialogues in many disciplines have changed over the last 30 years as multivariate, simultaneous considerations and dynamic methods have been incorporated into curricula and into the thought processes of the practitioners of these fields. Personnel differences, though, make the speed of changes in thought different in each field. The present rate of change in ideas is probably a good measure of the ability of any field's personnel to change its perspectives.

It is easy to reject methodological challenges. People find reasons and social supports to do so. There is a weakness, however, in the mentality that accepts the status quo. There is an accepted need for accountability and management in human-service programs. These needs are addressable with today's computers and today's — or tomorrow's — software. It is not a question of whether there will be a computer revolution in human services — we can expect an acceptance of information technology in response to the present demand for it. It is instead a question of what will be done with this technology. I suggest that the price to the field for entering the information-technology revolution will be alterations in the interests and sensitivities of its members. There will be anxiety and frustration for those defining a nonexistent golden age. There will be those who understand and respond to the intellectual challenges by focusing on a generation of research and practice. The discussion will advance from questions of existence to questions of quality. Tools — like stochastically simulated demand models — complementary to simulated expert agencies will develop as precursors to field work, and they will be more easily incorporated into the academic training of practitioners and managers. I also believe that neither the professional nor the client will get lost in this incorporation. Their needs and responses will become the basis of a more humane and efficient caring system. But new challenges and insolvable problems will emerge, and anxiety and frustration will be experienced as well by those attempting to create the golden age.

PROBLEM SCENARIO
by Walter Hudson

KEYWORDS: evaluation, monitoring, measurement, assessment, graphing, practice assessment, client-problem assessment, practice evaluation, improving practice, client change.

Jaimie C. received her MSW from a well-respected Midwestern university in June 1983. After an unsuccessful search for employment in her home community, she moved to Chicago and lived with relatives until she could find work. In November 1983, she was hired as a Caseworker I in a prominent private family-service agency that serves the north-side metropolitan area and several affluent suburban communities. Jaimie works on a fee schedule, carries 27 cases, and is primarily engaged as a therapist, with close supervision during her first year of employment. She is assured of a first-year salary of approximately $17,000.

After 8 months of experience, Jaimie is well respected by her colleagues, has a close working relationship (which includes much mutual respect) with her supervisor, and is seen by her peers as a bright and capable therapist. Jaimie appears to have a promising future with the agency, and she is being considered for an increase in salary.

In spite of Jaimie's success in her job as a therapist, she privately struggles with a number of issues about which none of her colleagues seem concerned. Because of their apparent lack of concern, she is unable to obtain help. She is not even very sure she knows how to describe her problems.

Jaimie's sense of professional discomfort began to emerge around April, while she was working with one of her clients. Mrs. J. was referred to the agency by a psychiatrist from a local hospital, and Jaimie was assigned to the case during early December. Mrs. J.'s major initial complaints were dejection, unexplained sadness, a sense of unfulfillment, and irritability on her job. Mr. J. is a very successful partner of a major Chicago law firm, and he is a doting husband.

Mrs J. is periodically severely depressed, but Jaimie has no sense of her client's level of depression unless the problem is in an acute phase. There are times when Jaimie is convinced that some progress is being made. She is able to describe such change, however, in terms that she feels are vague or general. She has an uneasy feeling that she really does not understand the case. Jaimie is a self-assured young woman who exudes self-confidence, but she privately wonders whether she and her colleagues are truly able to deal with problems such as Mrs. J.'s. Her major problem is that she doesn't have a reliable gauge to assess progress or deterioration.

Tim K. is a bright and capable 13-year-old male who has been threatened with expulsion from school for disrupting classes and failing to do his work. Jaimie has been working with Tim for about 3 months. She has discovered that there are severe problems between Tim and his father and that Tim is bored with school, which he describes as a "trivial waste of time." Although Jaimie is convinced that Tim's problems with his father may influence his attitude toward school, she is uneasy because she feels that she cannot accurately assess the degree of severity of that problem. She feels she understands the problem only in general and imprecise terms. She is frustrated because she cannot determine whether the problem is getting worse, better, or remaining unchanged.

Jaimie's concerns about case management and assessment were exacerbated when she presented two cases at a meeting in which a local psychiatrist provided consultation. Her case presentations were well received. Her major problem was her difficulty in describing the precise degree of progress (or lack of it) with each of the cases she presented. The lack of precision did not seem to bother the consulting psychiatrist or Jaimie's colleagues. Jaimie, however, felt that the discussion was vague and required too much time. She felt that the ability to describe her clients' problems with greater clarity and certainty would have markedly changed the nature of the consultation. Jaimie is convinced that these problems will continue to characterize her professional practice.

PROBLEM SCENARIO
by Richard Calica

KEYWORDS: foster care, placement, child-protection services.

Mrs. Anderson was born in Chicago. Her earliest memory is of rocking herself at night, in the dark, to try to fall asleep. She does not remember her natural parents, but she says she was abandoned, "left in the alley in a trash can." At age 3 or 4 she was placed in a foster home.

Mrs. Anderson sarcastically reported to her worker that she "did not adjust" to placement. She describes her younger sister, June, who had been with the same foster parents since infancy, as the favorite and the one who did everything right. School was an unpleasant experience, both because Mrs. Anderson had learning disabilities and because she was severely punished for not getting top grades.

Mrs. Anderson remembers that her foster mother forced her to sit on a stove burner for wetting her pants, knocked out her front teeth with a cast-iron frying pan for talking back, locked her in a closet for what Mrs. Anderson remembers as 3 or 4 days, locked Mrs. Anderson and her sister in a dark cellar, and deliberately broke Mrs. Anderson's arm when she was 7 or 8. Mrs. Anderson also reported that she was raped by a foster brother. She recalls that someone came to the house periodically to talk with her and her sisters, but says she was not aware that the person was a placement worker until much later in her life. She only knew that her foster mother instructed her on what to tell this visitor, and threatened her with punishment if she revealed the ongoing physical abuse.

At age 10 or 11, Mrs. Anderson ran away from her foster home. She was hospitalized, unable to remember who she was or to recognize people she knew. It is difficult to construct an exact history from Mrs. Anderson's recollections. She remembers being hospitalized for psychiatric treatment for about a year and being on a ward with violent older patients whose behavior terrified her. She also recalls violent episodes in which she threw furniture at attendants. She stopped eating and was fed intravenously. She also remembers being in restraints on numerous occasions.

Mrs. Anderson says her foster mother was charged with abuse. She is unsure of the outcome, but she does remember a juvenile-court hearing. She recalls the judge saying he would not allow Mrs. Anderson to be returned to the foster home and her foster mother screaming at the judge, calling him a "son of a bitch." Until this time Mrs. Anderson believed that her foster parents were her real mother and father.

Mrs. Anderson received extensive psychiatric treatment from then on. She remembers, among other things, seeing her best friend commit suicide by breaking glass out of a window and jumping through it.

Mrs. Anderson first became pregnant when she was 17; the child, a boy, was stillborn. She married the father of this child and later gave birth to a girl. When her daughter was 18 months old, Mrs. Anderson lost her job at a fast-food store and lost her apartment. She went to an agency for help and workers convinced her to put her daughter up for adoption. Her husband, from whom she was divorced, was notified about his daughter being put up for adoption. He refused to allow it and gained custody of the child, although he had not assisted Mrs. Anderson in caring for her and had abandoned his daughter and wife to live with another woman.

Mrs. Anderson soon met her second husband. She said that he had recently been released from prison, where he served time for armed robbery. She felt sorry for him because he was so alone. This husband physically abused her and, according to Mrs. Anderson, broke her jaw and cracked her ribs. She says that when he learned she was pregnant he kicked her in the stomach repeatedly and left.

Mrs. Anderson gave birth to a baby girl. In August of 1980 she was referred to the Juvenile Protective Association by the child-protection-services unit of the Illinois Department of Children and Family Services. A report came to this department from a local hospital and was based largely on Mrs. Anderson's behavior prior to her daughter's admission and during her stay in the hospital. In a rage Mrs. Anderson threw a bottle at a male nurse in the emergency room because she wanted her daughter admitted. She made statements, within earshot of the staff, that she could kill her daughter and no one could do anything about it because the baby was her's. Because of Mrs. Anderson's behavior, the hospital staff was concerned that the child's multiple depressed skull fractures were a result of deliberate injury by Mrs. Anderson, rather than the consequences of an automobile accident as Mrs. Anderson had stated.

PROBLEM SCENARIO
by Risha W. Levinson

KEYWORDS: access systems, information and referral, education, social services, competition, resource development.

One of the unique features of this school of social work is its full-time operation of a social-services center within the school and on university premises. Under the administration of the director and associate director, both of whom are members of the school's faculty, the center functions as a social-service agency to the community, and as a training center for 75 social work students. Selected faculty members supervise the students. Funding is provided by various grants, client fees for services, and contributory funding from the school and the university.

During the past 7 years, the center has developed new and innovative social-service programs that include a refugee-assistance program, hotlines for rape victims and for women who have had mastectomies, and counseling services for learning-disabled adults. In addition to inquiries generated by the center's own information needs regarding available resources, requests for such information are also received from students in other field-instruction settings, interested faculty, members of the university community, and service providers in other human-service agencies.

To respond more effectively to requests for information, and to provide client referrals with appropriate follow-up and accountability, it was suggested that the center establish an information and referral (I&R) system to compile, store, and retrieve information on available resources. This system would function as a central data base on human services that directly serves clients, and as a repository for research, policy, and planning information.

A faculty member, who has extensive knowledge and experience in I&R program development and I&R operations, directed the center-based I&R system. A second faculty member provided expertise in information systems and the application of information technology within the field of human services.

In addition to faculty expertise, the availability of a service-classification system, developed by the county community council, provided a functioning system, on microfiche, for organizing the resource file. This microfiche system fit well into the limited space avaliable, and offered economy of operation as well. The prospect of transforming the microfiche system into a computerized operation has been enhanced by the increased interest in the university library's new automated system, and the university's growing emphasis on "computer literacy."

Restricted space, limited equipment, and lack of funds and personnel contributed to the slow beginning of the I&R system. And members of the social work faculty withheld their endorsement because they saw I&R as a clerical task rather than as a professional service. Since the timing of calls was random and often sporadic, students' time on the I&R service was not optimally utilized. Students also seemed reluctant to use the microfiche system. They relied on the familiar, though often incomplete and outdated, card files. In spite of the council's efforts to issue updated sets of microfiche cards twice a year, the microfiche system also was often inaccurate and incomplete. Additionally, the school's relocation to the main campus disrupted whatever initial efforts were made to organize an I&R system.

A major problem in implementing I&R was the competition of other agencies in the county—the county public library system, the public-health department, the mental-health association, the public-welfare department, and the county office for the aging—that operated their own unique I&R programs.

To establish a viable I&R system, adequate space for the physical location of the files, microfiche readers, and supplementary materials is essential. To promote effective service delivery, the microfiche system should be converted to a computerized system, with terminals in the main library and other strategic locations. The resource file can be developed incrementally, in accordance with the nature and volume of service requests. Initially the file will relate to the range of social services offered by the center. Over time, however, the I&R system will be expanded to include more generic and specialized funds of information.

A training program will be organized to teach students and interested faculty members about the information system and the technology involved. As an educational institution the school of social work can also offer training programs for I&R program developers and I&R operators in other agencies. These programs would promote improved access to information within the community's social-services network.

In networking with other social agencies, the center-based I&R system will provide valuable data on service needs and will have the capability to identify service deficiencies. Adequate resources to implement the I&R system are of utmost importance.

PROBLEM SCENARIO
by Margaret Gibelman

KEYWORDS: research, education, grants, data base, centralized resources, information system.

To respond to an identified need within the social work profession, the Council on Social Work Education is placing a high priority on its initiation of a National Institute for the Advancement of Social Work Research. The Institute hopes to improve research utilization, to improve comprehension and production of professional social work research, to improve resource potential, and to facilitate the pursuit of resources in support of social work research. The Council views information technology as an important tool to use for the achievement of these goals.

The application of information technology will affect educational programs in social work and related disciplines, individual faculty members and other social work practitioners with interest in research, and social work students, particularly doctoral students. The needs of these groups, to be met by information technology, can be expressed as the following program objectives: to improve the data base for social work research in areas such as research expertise, research interests, inquiries in progress, and funding bodies and criteria; to improve the availability of social work research reports and findings; to make available annual statistics and other data related to social work research; to serve as a clearinghouse for information on current and past research in order to add to the building-block nature of research and to encourage the coordination of research activities.

Information technology can facilitate the work of the National Institute. Computer technology, for example, can be used to store and retrieve past and present research by academics and social work practitioners, analyze trends and gaps in existing research (thus encourage research activity in specific areas), compile a list of curricular and bibliographic materials for teaching research, and maintain information regarding the funding and publishing of studies.

Some constituencies are concerned about the costs of such a system, and the potential for duplicating existing systems. But a national survey of social work education program participants revealed that 57% (N = 64) of the respondents noted that the functions of an information system are not adequately present within their programs. Of particular concern was the lack of focus on social work in existing systems and the failure to adequately address data-base searches. The clearinghouse was seen as providing useful services in a number of areas, including developing a network of agencies and schools to identify faculty members and students to collaborate on research projects, providing information on others doing similar research, helping to identify funding sources, helping to find obscure and unpublished manuscripts, and promoting software exchanges for computer use. The need for a national social work research information clearinghouse is thus variously perceived, in part depending upon the sizes, locations, and resources of particular educational institutions.

Apparently there is not a university facility or agency facility with the capacity to store and retrieve the comprehensive variety of data needed by social work researchers. There are also concerns about system cost and maintenance. Some of the systems in operation concentrate in specific areas such as aging, or are interdisciplinary in nature. A growing problem is the discontinuation of systems, including the system maintained by the National Institute of Mental Health. The discontinuance issue is also of concern to the Council, which must obtain or allocate funds for ongoing system maintenance.

A major issue then is whether or not the opportunities and benefits outweigh the potential obstacles and liabilities. The attainment of many of the goals of the Institute can be facilitated by the application of information technology. But will the Council be able to maintain the system longitudinally and continually update its resources? Will individual researchers and social work students and faculty cooperate to make the system a success? These people and institutions will have to provide a continual flow of information to ensure a successful system.

[EDITORS' NOTE: The National Association of Social Workers now provides on-line access to *Social Work Abstracts* via BRS, Inc. The Computer Users in Social Services Network maintains a Skills Bank (data base of information-technology expertise), Curricular Data Base, and Software Exchange, and publishes the CUSS Newsletter which acts as a clearinghouse. The *Journal of Computers in Human Services* provides archival, peer-reviewed papers and software reviews. Clearly, interorganizational cooperation will be a key issue in this arena.]

PROBLEM SCENARIO
by Arlene R. Gordon

KEYWORDS: case management, supervision, data quality, training, case notes, information system, use of reports, report content and format flexibility.

Miss Jones, social-services unit supervisor in a multiservice rehabilitation agency, had received the monthly reports on workers in her unit. These included summary case-load reports and staff-utilization reports that describe each worker's activities, and provide summaries including the numbers of clients seen and the types of services provided. In addition Miss Jones had access to copies of individual case-management reports which were also available to all workers. Case-management reports show units of service to the clients by the social workers and by other disciplines providing services.

Miss Jones was looking for information to enable her to answer questions posed by the director of the department. Cutbacks in staff and the prolonged absence of one ill worker made the director concerned about the staff's ability to cope with much larger case loads and to adhere to a departmental policy of immediate assignment and no waiting list. The director wondered if the case loads met the department's standard of 45 to 50 cases per worker. To evaluate the case loads, Miss Jones needed to examine the distribution of new assignments, ongoing counseling cases, and multiproblem clients served by multiple services that required case-management coordination.

Miss Jones had been overwhelmed by the many reports produced by the agency's new computerized Client Information System. After many months, she had begun to be able to use the information to identify practice issues and to answer questions posed by management. She began her review with the case-load reports. This report showed her each worker's case load, with the new additions for the month, cases closed, and end-of-month registers. Miss Jones noted that all of the workers had case loads that exceeded the standard set when the staff was larger: The smallest case load was 58, the largest was 92. She then looked at the staff-utilization report to examine the relationships between the sizes of the case loads and the numbers of clients who received services. Worker "D" had given services to 57 out of 58 on her case load. Worker "A," who had 81 clients, had provided services to only 42 clients. Worker "B," with a

case load of 92, showed activity on only 46 cases. Worker "H" had a case
load of 72 and showed activity on 67. Worker "J" had activity on 50 of her
case load of 60 clients.

Miss Jones looked next at the number of hours recorded for client-
related activities to see how many were for personal contacts with
clients. Worker "D" had recorded 72-½ hours of service units; 41 hours
(56.5%) were personal counseling sessions with clients. Worker "A" had
given only 34-½ hours of service this month. Miss Jones knew that
worker "A" had been on vacation for 2 weeks, but she wondered if the
42% of her time for personal contacts was normal. Miss Jones noted
that worker "B," who carried a specialized case load of infants and
young children, most of whom had multiple handicaps, had the highest
percentage of personal contacts — 64% of 76-½ hours of service given.
Worker "H" recorded a total of 105-¾ hours of which 54 (51%) were personal contacts. Worker "J," also on vacation for 2 weeks, recorded a total
of 57-¼ hours of which 19-¼ (33%) were personal contacts. Miss Jones
decided to check worker "J's" and worker "A's" percentages of time
recorded for personal contacts over the past 6 months to see if the patterns were consistent or if they reflected vacation time.

Miss Jones thought of questions for each of the workers about those
clients who had not received service in the month. She reviewed the
prior staff-utilization reports to see if the same clients had not received
services during the last 3 months. She planned to raise questions in
supervisory conference with the workers about why these cases remained open.

In other cases the types of activities led Miss Jones to review case-
management reports. She reviewed two cases in depth because of indicators in the case-management reports that there were clinical problems. In one case the case-management report indicated a significant
number of cancellations/no-shows, not only with the social worker, but
also with other service providers. Miss Jones felt that the social worker
was not sufficiently aware of the evidence that the client was deteri-
orating rapidly and was unable to sustain the program.

Miss Jones began to appreciate the management opportunities that the
reports offered for quickly assessing a large case load, for identifying case-
management problems, and for selecting cases that required more intensive casework review and supervision. She dictated a memorandum to
the director to say that the reports were helpful but did not relate the
hours of direct service to the hours worked by each worker during the
month. Although this information was available from the administrative
supervisor on a manual basis, Miss Jones hoped that future computerization of personnel-department records would make this information

available as part of an overall monthly report. She added that as soon as she received a quarterly report on the demography of the new and continuing clients, she would be better able to assess her workers' abilities to manage large case loads without reducing the quality of service.

In a separate memorandum to the director, Miss Jones questioned the staff's understanding and acceptance of the constraints imposed on case notes by computerization. Her questions focused on the need to define precisely the information to be recorded in case notes.

Miss Jones had noticed much information missing and that, even where information was properly reported, it was often repetitiously stated in case notes. She felt that the present staff needed to be retrained in recording information and in using case notes only for brief assessments and/or updates on progress or problems.

The director of the department had requested that the Information Analysis Office prepare a study for those cases closed with the disposition code "not interested in further services," and another study for those closed with the code of "registered but did not follow through." The issues included whether or not the agency services were responsive to client requests, whether the clients did not wish to pursue services because of emotional problems or some environmental situation, and whether the agency developed criteria to identify such clients more quickly. Miss Jones had been asked to develop definitions for a content analysis of case notes entered on such closed cases in preparation for a meeting with the department director and other unit supervisors.

PROBLEM SCENARIO
by Joan DiLeonardi

KEYWORDS: child welfare, abandonment, foster care, mental health, family identification, individual-tracking.

A middle-aged woman was sitting on a park bench in a lower-middle-income neighborhood of Chicago when a younger woman, Jenny, sat beside her and began to talk in a distracted manner. Jenny asked the woman to hold her baby for an hour while she went to get some food, because her "milk had all dried up." The older woman agreed. But when Jenny had not reappeared within 2 hours, and the baby began to cry because he needed food and a diaper change, she called the police. With the police she searched the neighborhood, but they could not find Jenny.

The baby, whom doctors pronounced to be a healthy 6-month-old Caucasian male, was placed in the custody of the State Department of

Children and Family Services. He was placed in temporary foster care and named Foster Peterson for two streets near the area in which he was found. There were no reports of a missing baby fitting that description filed in the city in the next few weeks, and the baby was referred to a private child-welfare agency that had developed special-needs adoptive homes. Although there was a search for his mother, she was not found.

Because Foster had been abandoned, he had no available medical history. There was a possibility that he had been born to a mother who was an alcoholic or a drug addict, that he was the product of incest, that he had some level of retardation, or a genetic predisposition, or any of a range of physical problems. Since his parents had never been seen, they had not voluntarily relinquished their rights to him, nor had those rights been terminated by the courts. Although he was apparently healthy and normal, a family that could understand and accept the medical and legal uncertainties of his situation was needed.

Three weeks after his placement in a legal-risk adoptive family, the private agency received a call from a woman inquiring if the agency had custody of her nephew. Her sister, Jenny, had been picked up by the police several weeks earlier in such an emotionally disturbed condition that she was rambling, incoherent, and sporadically violent. She was taken to a state inpatient mental-health facility. For 2 weeks the staff there was unable to identify her. Finally, in some of her disconnected speech, she mentioned her sister's name. When the social worker from the mental-health facility contacted members of the family, they said they had been worried about her since she had disappeared. They related that she had had several previous psychotic breaks, prior hospitalizations, and years of outpatient treatment. They were relieved to know that she was safe, but they wondered about her son, Nathan, a 4-month-old Black male infant. When the police picked her up she was alone, and she had not mentioned a baby during the first few weeks of hospitalization. The family had called police and hospital sources for more than a week in an attempt to discover if a baby had been found near the time of her hospitalization. The call to the child-welfare agency was the result of information from a local police station and the State Department, and even though the physical description did not match her nephew, it could be him, because he was large for his age, well-nourished and light-skinned like his mother.

Could the family have received assistance in locating Jenny? Or in locating Nathan? Could the public agency have had more information on this abandoned child? Are there ways for the public child-welfare agency, the private child-welfare agency, and the mental-health system to share information? What can be done to help the biological parents, the adoptive parents, and Nathan and Jenny? Are there good ways to locate the best available family for Foster/Nathan through the resources available?

PROBLEM SCENARIO
by Connie Cobb

KEYWORDS: adoption, facilitating professional work, reorganization, automation.

The adoptions unit in a state agency that supervises but does not directly administer other social-service programs appeared to be mired in unnecessary work and forms. The staff was frustrated and top management was confused. A third party was asked to examine and report on the situation.

The study was initiated with several questions in mind: Is there too much paperwork? Is the process overly complicated? Can counties assume a greater role in adoption? Can processes be automated? Is the staffing pattern appropriate?

The response to the first question regarding paperwork was vague. Staff members feel that adoption is a complicated issue and that outsiders want to oversimplify it. They maintain that adoption is not one program but a series of programs under one umbrella. Procedures differ, depending on the program. It is relatively easy to see the difference between a subsidized adoption and an infant adoption, but lines tend to blur on Indian adoptions, stepparent adoptions, child-over-14 adoptions, and such.

To track clients, match children with potential parents, monitor state wards, maintain permanent records, and keep track of statistical reports due, the unit maintains 12 separate card files. Much of this work falls to a professional social worker who is unable to train and advise county personnel on adoption procedures because she has been relegated to the position of a royal paper-pusher. In one instance data from one paper are copied onto another paper so that research and statistics people can aggregate them. This process is repeated several times for various reasons. This same professional social worker does the court reports on all adoptions statewide. Counties are responsible for the actual adoption work, but there are always errors in the county reports.

The court trusts the state agency and likes accuracy. Counties submitting adoption information need to supply approximately 15 pages of data. Because of this paperwork, staff members feel they are not able to provide requested services on postadoption, provide necessary supervision to the staff, train county adoption workers, or maintain the 12 card files. The system is overly complicated, both legally and because of the historical continuation of work regardless of its current relevance. The Commissioner of Public Welfare approves all adoptions. The work of getting that approval also falls to the adoptions unit.

Private adoption agencies consider such action unnecessary. Also antiquated or unnecessary are legal requirements for the commissioner to petition the court, to consent to the adoption in the absence of parent or guardian, to supply background information from the investigation, to write a full report to the court with recommendation on petition, to make subsidy payments statewide, to recommend subsidy amount and review it annually, to handle appeals by adoptive parents, and to run the state adoption exchange. Most of this work, with the exception of the statewide adoption exchange, could be transferred to the counties if statutes were revised to permit it.

Statutory responsibility has been given to Minnesota's three largest counties to do nearly all adoption work. If better training was available, other counties could do the same. No time is available to train these people because the state staff is too busy correcting their numerous errors and maintaining 12 card files.

The possibility of automation generated excitement in most of the staff members. Although they had no experience with computers, they could identify numerous timesaving applications including automation of report and statistics requirements, creation of files, automation of record retrieval, simplification of record-keeping, monitoring of state wards, and running the adoption exchange.

The adoptions unit is not overstaffed considering that much work goes undone, and that periodically it must contract with private agencies that do the extra work. Private agencies agree that the unit is not overstaffed but point to problems such as gross inaccuracies in state-ward data, duplicative legalistic forms, lack of clear manual material, and overcontrol of the process at the state level. How can technology and improved procedures save this unit?

PROBLEM SCENARIO
by Al Cavalier

KEYWORDS: developmental disability, mental retardation, effect of aids, ethics.

It was difficult for Maria's mother and the family's social worker to know how deeply the derisive comments of the other children in her class affected Maria, but they were sure she was aware of them. She had been ridiculed in school since second grade because of her slowness in learning and her awkward gait.

Maria's father would not acknowledge or permit any talk of "her problems," but after he deserted the family at the end of Maria's second school year Maria's mother requested comprehensive educational and medical examinations. Her teachers were ready to make a similar recommendation. Behavioral and intellectual measures placed Maria in the lower ranges of mild mental retardation; behavioral and physical measures indicated she had mild cerebral palsy, affecting primarily her legs and fingers.

Maria continued to fall behind her peers in school. As she now qualified for special services in the school system, a comprehensive Individualized Educational Plan as specified by Public Law 94-142 — the Education for All Handicapped Children Act — was developed by an interdisciplinary team of professionals and lay persons. The plan identified her educational needs and objectives, ordered them according to their importance, specified the educational programs to serve those needs, and established time limits for accomplishing the objectives. The team included her regular classroom teacher, the special-education resource teacher, the school psychologist, her mother, her family social worker, and others.

Through third grade, despite a number of remedial strategies, Maria continued to fail to achieve the educational objectives that were considered appropriate for her. Primary reasons for this failure were some additional deterioration of fine motor control in her fingers that made writing extremely slow and difficult for her, the failure of her mother to work with her at home as much as had been agreed to during the team meetings, and increased emotional upset aroused by her schoolwork.

At the end of the school year, the team considered having Maria repeat third grade. The special-education teacher opposed this idea and recommended that Maria be provided with a specially adapted notebook-type computer similar to one that another special-needs student was using. With the computer Maria would be able to write letters or numbers by touching the appropriate keys and could thereby do her classwork at her desk. Maria could also use the computer at home to complete her homework and then print it prior to class on a printer in the resource room. The special-education teacher indicated that she could provide a program that would give Maria drill and practice at home. This teacher felt that the novelty of a computer-based aid would improve Maria's motivation to learn, increase the speed with which she learned, and might improve her general affect and self-concept.

The regular classroom teacher strongly disagreed with this proposal, and stated that with the proper behavioral techniques Maria could slowly learn her academic materials unaided. This teacher also felt that with more focused attention on finger and hand manipulations, particularly at home, she could improve her fine motor control and thereby improve her writing skills. This teacher maintained that since federal law mandates "the least restrictive environment" necessary for successful progress by handicapped students, they are obligated to use no special aids to educate someone like Maria.

The regular classroom teacher also stated that Maria's use of a computer-based aid would make her dependent on the device and that when the device was unavailable she would be even more handicapped than she is now. Maria's mother was more concerned about the extra attention that Maria might draw from her peers because of this aid. She was fearful that this device would make Maria seem "even more different" from her peers and stigmatize her as retarded or handicapped. She also worried about the effect this would have on Maria's self-concept. Under the direction of the social worker, the interdisciplinary team must come to a decision on whether or not a computer-based aid would be appropriate for Maria.

What principles and what factors affect this decision? Is an unadapted, natural environment the least restrictive environment for a handicapped child, or is an environment that incorporates some assistant features to reduce the handicap less restrictive? Is the natural environment unadapted, or are there technological aids for nonhandicapped persons embedded in the natural environment and taken for granted? Do assisting devices create dependency? If so, does this dependency outweigh the independence that their use affords? Should professionals refrain from introducing a person to a technological aid if he/she can acquire some, but not all, of a skill without the aid? Is the use of an assisting device contrary to the basic tenets of the principle of normalization? Can normalization rightly be interpreted in terms of function rather than form?

PROBLEM SCENARIO
by William Garrett

KEYWORDS: information and referral, resource identification, resource development, medical social work.

Carol Jones is a 20-year-old college junior living in a small town in Bergen County, New Jersey. She was experiencing persistent problems with her left leg. Carol was unable to put sustained pressure on the leg and frequently could not sleep at night because of the pain.

This problem caused Carol to miss numerous days of classes and led to her dismissal from her part-time job because of frequent absences. Carol's parents became increasingly worried about her condition and insisted that she see a specialist. Carol's examination and diagnosis indicated that she would require an immediate bone-marrow transplant to retain use of her left leg. The family did not have adequate insurance or funds to cover the cost of this operation. To make matters worse the doctor insisted that the treatment be performed in Seattle, Washington, at the country's best facility. The treatment and recovery period would last a minimum of 3 months, during which time Carol would have to stay in the Seattle area.

The first task was to locate a suitable donor. Carol's younger brother, Jim, was identified as an appropriate donor, but he was unwilling to cooperate with his parents and Carol. Jim had experienced difficulty in high school and had many arguments with his family. When Jim turned 18, he had left home and informed his family that he did not wish to see any of them again.

At this point Carol's father, Tom, was approached by the United Way for his annual contribution. Tom was a pressman for the New York *Daily News* in Manhattan. He was a member of the local union. Tom went to his shop steward and noted that he had contributed to the United Way for years and now needed assistance. His wife, Mary, who worked for Automatic Data Processing in New Jersey, also had been contributing. Tom demanded that the shop steward work with the United Way to solve his dilemma.

The shop steward called the United Way of New York City and presented Tom's situation. The United Way had an information and referral division that was designed to help link clients in need of services with organizations capable of providing the required services.

The United Way and the shop steward agreed to work on these problems:

- counseling for Jim to aid him in agreeing to be a bone-marrow donor;
- transportation to Seattle for Carol, Jim, and Mary (Mary insisted on being with Carol during the operation and the recovery period);
- housing in Seattle for the family during the 3-month period;
- transportation in Seattle for the family;
- securing adequate funds to cover costs of treatment not covered by the insurance carrier.

PROBLEM SCENARIO
by Theodore Stein

KEYWORDS: information system, decision support, data base, confidentiality, ethics, problem assessment.

The United Child Welfare Agency has a computerized information system. Line workers can use the system via terminals located throughout the agency. Their access is limited to two data-base management programs, one of which contains case records. Each worker may access her own records by using a code number. All case records are updated on the computer. The second program used by the line staff is a decision-making system (DMS). Access is unlimited since there is no case-identifying information in this system.

The DMS is comprised of actual protective-service cases that are deemed exemplary for purposes of teaching and ongoing consultation. Cases are selected for the DMS by a committee of supervisors and line workers. They consider whether the problem presented by a case is common among agency clients, whether the case was open long enough to determine if abuse or neglect had occurred, and whether the worker on the case documented the actions taken, the basis for each decision, and the outcome of each decision.

The line staff uses DMS to help in deciding what action to take with a case. Workers use the system mainly for help in making decisions in cases where there is no clear evidence of maltreatment — for example, in cases where nonsupervision is alleged or where the causes of injuries cannot be determined.

A search of the DMS data base may begin when a staff member asks for cases that involve one specific allegation (educational neglect, for instance). Cases called up may be sorted by additional variables such as family composition, sex of the head of household in a single-parent family, age and sex of the child, and so forth. The worker receives a printout of cases that fit the profile. Each case report includes background information, actions, decisions, and outcomes. By comparing their cases to those printed out, workers can hypothesize which courses of action will be most fruitful with their clients.

Anita G., a protective-service worker, had completed an investigation of a case of alleged nonsupervision of a 6-year-old. Her investigation did not yield conclusive data to sustain the allegation; for example, the single-parent father had been with his daughter when Ms. G. arrived at the home. He acknowledged the importance of child supervision and said that he always left his daughter with his sister when he was away from home. The sister confirmed her brother's statement. Ms. G. was not comfortable with the father's explanation, but she could not state exact reasons for her discomfort.

Unclear about the alternatives available, the worker searched the DMS for similar cases. One of the cases showed a prior report of a similar nature against her client. Ms. G. knew that the family name should not have been logged in the system. The existence, however, of a prior report reinforced her concern that the case should be opened. A prior report would help sustain an allegation of neglect. She thought the father would not know that case-identifying information should have been expunged from the system. Should Ms. G. report that the system contained a client's name? Should she call this situation and the dilemma that it created to her supervisor's attention? Should she try to make use of the information produced by the DMS? If not, she would probably have to dismiss the case on the basis of the other evidence from her investigation. Although use of this particular information from the computer is unethical, is it more or less so than leaving the child in an unsafe environment?

PROBLEM SCENARIO
by William Koerber

KEYWORDS: child abuse, medical social work, management information systems, tracking systems, networking.

Maisie Katz is a social worker for the Office of Special Services for Children in Brooklyn. She is one of several workers who specialize in child-abuse cases. Although she can reasonably manage 5 new cases a month, she has recently been forced because of staff shortages to respond to as many as 10 new cases a month. This overload seriously strains her ability to fulfill professional obligations to her clients.

One of Ms. Katz's cases became the subject of an investigation by the Inspector General of the City Human Resources Administration. In February 1984, a social worker at a Brooklyn hospital referred Mr. and Mrs. Evans to Ms. Katz. The Evans' child was treated at the hospital for internal hemorrhaging after a reported fall down the stairs at his parents' home. Other bruises and scars led the hospital social worker to suspect that the 7-year-old child was a victim of child abuse. Interviews with the child's parents revealed that they had recently arrived in Brooklyn from Atlanta, Georgia, and that they were unemployed and seeking public assistance. The parents were vague about their reasons for leaving Atlanta, but they supplied the address of a previous residence in that city, and the name of a previous employer of Mr. Evans.

The hospital social worker suspected that Mr. and Mrs. Evans were substance abusers and, additionally, that they may have had previous contacts with social agencies because of child abuse. The worker based these suppositions upon the physical appearances of the parents and their evasive but savvy responses to questions about their treatment of the child.

Ms. Katz suspected that the medical social worker's analysis was correct and that the case merited further scrutiny. Ms. Katz contacted the parents; they were unwilling to meet with her or to discuss the child's situation. Scrutiny of the family's history in Atlanta revealed that the previous employer and residence were fictitious. Contact with the child's New York school revealed a sporadic attendance record, and that the teacher was concerned because the child seemed inattentive, withdrawn, and suspicious of adults. A subsequent visit to the child's home reinforced Ms. Katz's suspicion that the Evans' son was a victim of child abuse and that the parents had had previous contacts with authorities about it.

Hampered by a lack of solid evidence, a lack of knowledge of the history of the Evans family, and an overwhelming case load, Ms. Katz made an implicit and unarticulated decision to "wait and see" what developed in the Evans case. In April of 1984 the child was battered to death.

The death of the Evans child drew attention to the problem of child abuse in New York City and led to the Human Resources Administration investigation. The report of the Inspector General cited 17 cases of child abuse in Brooklyn in which 9 children died. The report cited a rapid increase in reports of child abuse in the city (to an estimated 55,000 in 1984 from 31,000 in 1980) along with insufficient staff and overwhelming case loads as primary causes of the city's failure to manage the problem of child abuse.

The report proposed six actions on the part of the city:

- substantial increase in the city's child-protection-services staff (specifically social workers specializing in child-abuse cases);
- additional training programs to improve protective services;
- improved record-keeping in child-abuse cases;
- strengthened supervision of social workers;
- division of large boroughs into smaller zones that would allow social workers to know well the communities they serve;
- reduced case loads.

In response to the report, the mayor of New York City proposed to hire 100 more social workers within the next year to handle child-abuse cases, a 20% increase. Many of these would have expertise in the area of child abuse. News of these developments appeared on the front page of *The New York Times* on May 13, 1984.

How could computerized information systems have prevented the death of the Evans child? How can they be employed to effect a more efficient delivery of services in the area of child abuse? More specifically, how can the computer contribute to

- tracking parents known to be child abusers?
- managing case loads for social workers?
- identifying characteristics of potential child abusers?
- aiding the supervisory process?
- improving record-keeping?
- training social workers in particular problem areas?
- rationalizing dividing large geographic areas into smaller communities?
- networking social work agencies and educational institutions to maximize the efficiency of personnel recruitment in specific practice areas?

PROBLEM SCENARIO
by Yeheskel Hasenfeld

KEYWORDS: reporting, evaluation, information-system design, integrated system.

Midway Children's Society is a well-established agency that provides residential care for about 50 children with behavioral problems. It also provides a day treatment program for 120 children, and a small adoption and foster-care program. The agency is located on a 25-acre campus, and has an annual budget of more than $2 million. The governing board includes some of the wealthiest citizens in the region.

In recent years the agency has received most of its referrals from the State Department of Social Services and has come to rely on state reimbursements as a major source of income. Contract negotiations with the department are difficult because of the state's extensive reporting requirements and requests for cost-effectiveness data. The executive of the agency has felt hampered in such negotiations because he could not readily generate the necessary information.

There has also been pressure from the board to demonstrate the agency's efficiency. The average length of institutionalization at Midway Children's Village is appreciably longer than at other agencies. Some board members and the staff justify this on the basis of the "bouncing ball" syndrome: The children admitted to Midway have moved from agency to agency and thus arrive with problems compounded by their transience. Nonetheless, with the rising costs of child care and declining referrals from the Department of Social Services, board members feel that the agency's programs and allocation of resources need a better evaluation.

Several consulting firms studied the agency upon the request of the board and noted that the agency lacked an adequate information system, particularly for fiscal matters. Some board members from the business community urged the agency to purchase a computerized accounting system. The staff members of the agency felt, however, that such a system would do little to meet their needs to evaluate the effectiveness of their services. The executive was also concerned that such a system would be useless if it could not link fiscal data with service and client data.

A subcommittee of the Board on Research and Evaluation was formed under the leadership of a university professor in social work. Through her initiative, the committee asked several university faculty members—experts in information technology—to advise it on implementing an information system for the agency.

After an initial study the advisors realized that such a system would have to fulfill several distinct but related purposes: It should keep track of all the accounts and update the agency budget; it should keep track of the children, their statuses, and the services they obtain; and, it should enable the agency to determine the cost of each of its various programs and supply the necessary data for negotiations with those who want to contract for its services.

The clinical-staff members were least interested in a fiscal information system. They wanted to see an information system that would help them in their clinical decisions and in program evaluations. The executive preferred to place the emphasis on accounting and budgeting, with a capacity to engage in cost-benefit analysis. The agency decided to contract with the university to design the system so a team was organized. The team recognized early that the agency would need to have an integrated system that could satisfy budgetary and clinical needs. Yet the members faced several obstacles: A model of such an integrated system did not exist, each group in the agency wanted something different, and there were limited resources.

As a resolution to these dilemmas, the team adopted the concept of a relational data-base system to guide it in the design of the information system. The members felt that if they could identify the key data sets needed for each sphere of activity in the agency and devise a scheme to logically link them together, they could achieve the multiple objectives expected of the system.

The actual design process proved to be quite difficult. The agency staff members were quite unsophisticated in their knowledge of computer technology. They could not articulate their information needs, nor could they express them in realistic terms. The clinicians first wanted the system to simply give them a list of their clients and their scheduled appointments. Later they wanted the system to tell them which treatment techniques were successful. The executive wanted to have up-to-date budget data, but he also wanted to automate the maintenance schedules of all the buildings. The team felt bombarded with disparate and unrealistic requests. How was the team to respond to staff concerns and, at the same time, teach the staff the capabilities and limitations of the new technology?

PROBLEM SCENARIO
by Patricia Lynett

KEYWORDS: public social services, training, managing the rules.

Unit Two of the Santa Rosa County Economic Services Program is frequently a hectic place. Four AFDC Eligibility Specialists work there with a supervisor, Regina Jernigan.

Lisa Smith, the veteran specialist, has been on the job for 9 months. She is fairly accurate with the required eligibility and budget forms. But, the retrospective budgeting procedures are a problem for her. Ms.

Jernigan received a call from the Client Relations Office this morning about an AFDC recipient whose check had been delayed by Lisa's error.

Lisa had read the revisions to the policy manual and thought she knew how to interpret them.

Lisa's telephone rings for the twentieth time this morning. She glares at the empty desk across the room as she reaches for the receiver. Undoubtedly it's not one of her clients but rather one of Joe Black's old clients. He's been gone for a month and Lisa is beginning to resent the extra work. At the coffee break this morning, she heard that the next AFDC training class would not begin for another 3 weeks. She says, "Hello," in a cool voice.

Maria Ramirez finished her training 6 weeks ago. Maria reaches for the dictionary on her desk; the policy manual is open to the section on Technical Eligibility. Ms. Jernigan has noticed that Maria asks about fairly basic rules—rules that most workers learn during training. Fortunately Maria checks her work carefully; unfortunately her slowness has caused many delays.

Clara Rogers, recently separated from her husband, waits in the lobby. She's never been here before and is more than a little uneasy. No one looks very happy, employees or clients. She wishes that she did not need this money to feed and clothe her four children. What if they tell her that they can't help her? There are so many rules.

How can the accurate delivery of services to clients be ensured? Should the basic survival needs of clients be jeopardized by unsophisticated information systems?

KEYWORD INDEX TO SCENARIOS

CHAPTER 5

THE STATE OF THE ART: CONCEPTS, APPLICATIONS, AND CASE STUDIES

EDITORS' INTRODUCTION

Within the context of technology transfer, the papers of Chapter 3, External Views of Opportunities and Threats: The Keynotes, provide a broad view of the technology and philosophy upon which the field can draw to define its own appropriate use of information technology. The scenarios of Chapter 4 inform us about the *a priori* visions that their authors held regarding the technology and the field of practice. Those visions identify opportunities in some cases, constraints in others, and obstacles in yet others. These papers provide a measure of the state of the art within the field and form the basis for the identification of the issues involved in the relationship of information technology to social work practice. The word relationship is chosen here to emphasize the potential for a bi-directional transfer of technology between fields as opposed to the typical assumption that the transfer is simple and unidirectional, for example, that information technology only transfers into social work practice. The nature and content of the transfer from social work practice into information technology is an issue that will require exploration.

These papers and their authors were carefully chosen, using the following criteria: The system described must have been in operation long enough to provide meaningful operating experience; the system must be novel in conception and implementation; the system must be clearly related to practice and practitioners; and the system must be replicable (implying both transferable and affordable technology). These criteria were designed to identify exemplars that would provide a foundation of state-of-the-art operating experience from which key issues could be identified. It was expected that these exemplars would serve, together with the scenarios, to provide a springboard from which the discussion of options could be launched and which, we hoped, would then lead us to identification of directions for the future.

After much consideration we recognized the following categories of information-technology applications in social work practice:

- applications that facilitate professional work;
- applications that provide education and/or training to the servers or those served;
- applications that support the delivery of services;
- applications that directly deliver services.

In the first group of applications are those that reduce paperwork (both the collection and reporting of data), ease retrieval of information, coordinate services, help servers to prepare to serve (e.g., present a quick review of the case record), help servers to manage their resources (especially time), maintain obligations lists (especially calendars and tickler files), and so on. By doing so, they help the professional to make more time available for specifically professional activities. These preferred activities include: client contact, continuing education, case-conferencing, and research. These applications are only slowly arriving on the practice scene, most likely because of the focus in current system design on directing, measuring, and controlling. The applications currently and typically produced are very aptly described by the term management information systems (MIS). This term not only identifies those whom the system serves, but it may equally well have come to identify those whom the system does not serve—the clients and the service-givers. The latter groups are those whose privacy and whose ability to serve are invaded by the information demands that are inherent, and assumed appropriate, in most management information systems.

The applications that are identified as providing education and/or training are those that use information technology to better prepare servers and clients for service through the dissemination of information and the development of skills and insights. It is important to recognize the dual foci of server and served, as well as information, and skills and insights. While usually first seen in professional training or continuing education, these applications are equally well suited to directly serving the client in an educational, training, or preparatory matter. Further, these applications can provide not only information, that is, be fact givers, fact verifiers, and fact testers, but they can also help in the development of concrete skills and abilities, and awareness or sensitivity. We are tempted to say they can aid both the cognitive and the affective domains. To date these applications are seen in their simplest and most obvious embodiments, as they are in other areas of educational technology — such as automated "page turners," and drill and practice programs. We are only beginning to grasp their true potential as people-changing devices.

If information technology can help to inform the server by making well-established knowledge and information readily available, can it contribute to better service in other ways? It can, and it is in the applications that are designed to support the delivery of service. These applications tend toward greater sophistication because they become more directly involved in the decision-making inherent in the delivery of services. In fact, these applications are often known as decision support systems (DSS). They can help servers make decisions by informing them of options or alternatives, by helping them to select among the alternatives, and by helping them to understand their decision-making processes and how they relate to those of others. These applications are particularly helpful when they relate to the ill-structured problems so common in the practice of social work (LaMendola, 1981, pp. 51–52) and when they help the professional to learn from the collected experience.

Perhaps the most striking, and the most threatening, applications are those that propose to directly deliver services to clients without intervention by professionals. These may be as simple as applications that provide resource information to clients, or as complex as those that provide counseling or therapy to clients who have specific concrete problems or identified emotional or mental disturbances. In any event, these applications raise substantial questions about the role of the professional in these forms of service, the quality of service, and the appropriateness of such service forms.

This chapter focuses attention on each of four fundamental categories in which information technology engages those who are served and/or those who serve by helping to meet the human needs of others:

- facilitation of service;
- preparation for service;
- support of service delivery;
- direct delivery of service.

The order is purposeful, and it is chosen to reflect the ordering of these categories along a number of dimensions, namely the nature of the innovation involved, the focus of the application, the level of existing ex-

Table 17 **Ordering of the Categories of Information-Technology Applications**

Application Category	Nature of Innovation	Focus	Level of Existing Experience	Degree of System Interaction with User
Facilitation of professional service	Shift of focus from management support to staff support; significant staff participation in design decisions; flexibility of functioning	Organizational and server needs	Much with MIS, little with the innovation	Some interaction with staff and management
Preparation for service	New technology applied to established methods	Server and/or served	Much with concepts, little with the technology	Some with the learner
Support of service delivery	New approach to learning from practice and developing consensus on procedures	Server and decisions	Little in general	Much with the staff using it
Direct delivery of service	New methods of serving, new sites for services, and new services	Served	Little practice in the U.S., some experience in Europe and Canada	Much with client user

perience with such applications, and the degree of human interaction with the technology. This ordering is detailed in Table 17.

Table 17 shows that as we move from the facilitation of service at one end of the scale to the direct delivery of service at the other, we have moved in the dimension of innovation from a modification of approach to a wholly new structure; it is a wholly new conception of service, which is not bound to a human service-giver or to the agency as the service site. In the dimension of focus, we move from the concern for organizational needs and service-giver needs to the focus solely on the needs of the client. In the dimension of experience, we move from considerable related experience to little experience. Finally, in the dimension of degree of interaction, we move from some interaction of staff and managers with the technology to substantial interaction between the client and the technology. On these dimensions, the progression from category to category is natural and orderly.

Each of the first three papers in this chapter presents an exemplar practice-related system in a particular application category, and each was written in a specified format for ease of comparison. In the case of direct service delivery, no one exemplar that would represent the richness of that category could be provided. The paper in that case provides more of a survey of the state of the art. Each paper is followed by a discussion of that paper. Each discussion begins with an opening statement by the discussion leader responsible for that application category. The opening statement provides connections to the scenarios and extensions of the concepts upon which the exemplar was built. Each discussion is then completed with a summary of an open discussion. Any sense of repetition that may occur to the reader ought to be examined as an indication that commonalities do occur in otherwise disparate settings and systems.

The first paper, by Newkham, presents a staff/management information system (S/MIS) as developed in a substantial community mental-health center. This is a system that offers much operating experience with essentially well-established minicomputer-based technology. The innovation was the level of involvement of the staff in the design, implementation, and operation of the system, which resulted in a system whose focus is staff support, service quality, accountability and, most importantly, flexibility and adaptability. Rarely do we see truly simple ideas in such an environment but, as one example, the use of the computer to print a form as needed provides the opportunity to modify the form's design as required by staff members in a changing environment. This kind of adaptability increases staff members' confidence that the system is there to serve them and their clients. On the other hand, the hardware selected many years ago could now be replaced by a super microcomputer. The agency recognizes this and is moving toward a less centralized design. The most important aspect of this paper is its description of the philosophy and process that led to a system supportive of the treatment staff. This design process is one for which we need a term to denote its importance.

Systems analysts use *top-down* (Geiss, 1981) to denote their approach, which maintains their focus on the global problem while dealing with the details in subproblems. *Top-down* is what differentiates the architect's approach to building (purpose, function, space, form) from the bricklayer's (brick upon brick) *bottom-up* approach. While tempting, *bottom-up* conveys a loss of overall problem focus, which is not the case. Similarly, one may be tempted to think of this as simply a well-designed transaction system, but it is more than that. The distinguishing characteristic is the focus on the support of the person providing the service, in order to facilitate and improve the service and the sincere involvement or representation of those users in the design process. The process is much like the participative decision-making notion inherent in Japanese management methods (Ouchi, 1981), which admits each affected party to a role in the decision. This is very much in keeping with social work values. For the moment, let us refer to the result of such a design process as a Service Facilitation Information System and thereby avoid denoting whom the system serves. Ultimately, it must serve the client.

In the discussion summary, LaMendola places this exemplar into a context that includes the tensions between management and professional staff over information-system goals and objectives, the notions of centralized information systems serving management and personal computers serving their users, and the reality of life in a political economy. He makes connections to scenarios that identify the difficulties of changing organizations, the often conflicting data demands of funding organizations, the inability of staff members to use some systems, and the need for understanding information-systems technology so that intelligent staff participation in design is possible. The discussion provides extensions to our understanding of facilitation of service that carry the notion very close to decision support systems and direct service delivery. It also raises a number of key issues, many of which have substantial histories of prior concern and exploration in social work.

The exemplar system described by Lynett introduces us to the latest in educational technology—computer-controlled videodisc training systems. These systems combine the technology of programmed instruction, curriculum-building, computer control for customized instruction and management of instruction, and the enormous capability for storage and random-access retrieval of image, sound, and textual information inherent in the videodisc. While the current development costs are still very high, these systems offer enormous potential for keeping service staffs current with the explosion in rules, regulations, practices, and knowledge, and for preparing clients for service by providing background information, sensitization to issues, and such.

Lynett also describes the problems incurred because of staff resistance, lack of managerial support, lack of agreement on interpretation of rules, market demand for particular videodisc players, incompatibility of newer videodisc players with this system's design, and contracting regulations demanding return of development equipment. The outcomes of the training are very positive: Trainees prefer this mode because of its responsiveness to their individual needs, and they seem to do better with this form of training. Nonetheless, there is substantial professional concern regarding participation by a school of social work in what is clearly a governmental move to declassify professional jobs. The identification of these issues helps to relate this promising technology to its unfortunate but real organizational and professional contexts. It remains to be seen whether the profession or individual entrepreneurs will control and direct the development of this powerful technology and potential service-giver.

Vogel places the Lynett paper into the historical context of earlier educational-technology developments to inform us of the extraordinary inertia of education and educators. He identifies the roles of the computer in education (learning about, learning through, and learning with), points to *learning with* — exploratory learning with the aid of the computer — as the most promising, and identifies data to suggest the field of education has not really accommodated to these opportunities in a planful way. An impromptu survey of computer use in schools of social work is reported, and the discussion closes with an extension of Lynett's exemplar to direct-service opportunities.

The exemplar presented by Pruger is also the product of a university team but differs in its thrust — to assist the staff in making equitable allocations of limited resources that maintain clients in their own homes — and in the degree to which it was dependent upon sophisticated research methodology. The outcome is a decision support system that assists the staff in making equitable decisions but, more importantly, the outcome demonstrates a wholly new technological method for:

- producing more ethical public-social-service awards;
- arriving at a consensus about a complex process;
- learning from practice experience.

That is, this exemplar demonstrates that appropriately conceived applications of information technology can humanize and personalize what has become a dehumanized and depersonalized activity — public-social-service awards — and it can reestablish order and human sense to what is an overregulated and seemingly uncontrollable bureaucratic system. Much like the first exemplar, the philosophical focus is on understanding the servers, helping them to understand themselves, and supporting them in their tasks and decisions. It returns control, discretion, and information to those most familiar with the task. It demonstrates an effective approach to reducing information overload.

Despite the positives, this system, like Lynett's, did not get the political and organizational support to continue and to expand as a viable system. Pruger identifies the political and bureaucratic hurdles with clarity and a very real sense of frustration. He also makes the importance of the focus on the needs of the server crystal clear. Perhaps this is a major contribution that social work can make to information technology.

Calica opens his discussion with the assertion that Newkham's system is still very much management-oriented and management-motivated when compared to Pruger's exemplar. In reviewing some of the scenarios, he raises questions about the roles of technology in what he refers to as *people-to-people issues* — areas demanding human contact — and he goes on to expand that to the question of establishing priorities for determining which areas of activity should get technological support. He also cautions us not to be deceived by the implementation, on microcomputers, of algorithms that required major research data analysis on large computers—a reminder that software and people are the major cost elements of any system. The closing question, "What would be lost if information technology were not used?" may be the key question. If it is so difficult to gain political, organizational, and staff commitment, and resources aren't readily available, perhaps the field cannot afford this technology.

Garrett not only introduces us to *access systems*—a class of which are information and referral (I&R) systems—but he expands our technical horizons to include communications, the newest (for social work) and most rapidly developing aspect of information technology, and he expands our cultural view to the international arena, where more work has been done with communications in serving people. While access systems generally inform users about existing services, fewer of them inform the user about the availability of a service, and even fewer, if any, include information about the quality of a service. He identifies cable television and the telephone system as new media for the provision of these services.

In his discussion of case-tracking, Garrett reminds us of the social-services exchanges that existed at earlier times and identifies their problems of confidentiality and maintenance costs. This concept is being revived in new technological garb, with the same ethical issues inherent in the designs. He also identifies electronic mail, bulletin boards, and teleconferencing as potentially valuable tools. These systems raise many issues that Garrett presents compactly. A few that seem central are the ethical issues of equity, privacy, confidentiality and access to information; compatibility of various devices and systems; human affective consequences, that is, dehumanization, depersonalization, and fear of change; and philosophical thrusts, that is, monitor/control/punish versus facilitate/enable/reward, and support versus replace.

Schoech opens his discussion with a recognition that the technology will induce us to ask old questions: Where should service take place? What is meant by efficiency and effectiveness of service in this new context of communications technology? Our problem-solving philosophy and its value base, he says, play a key role here. In his review of the scenarios, in the context of Garrett's technology categories, Schoech identifies service-integration possibilities, and raises concerns about the impacts of expert systems and self-help software on the client and the profession.

The open discussion that he summarizes identified important questions to be considered: Who owns the data produced by human-service activities? To whom should access extend? How will quality of service be established in the new service contexts? What new issues of liability arise? How can we assure equality of access? What new roles will the professional be required to assume? And, to what degree should clients be involved in the design of new systems of service? Schoech closes with two tentative principles that arose in the discussion:

- Systems design should incorporate adaptive or self-correcting features that permit learning from experience and improvement over time.
- Service to clients should be the overriding concern in the design of information-technology applications.

There seems to be no doubt that direct service to clients via information technology is bound to be one of the most exciting and most challenging of these applications categories.

Following the conference, Hammond offered to prepare a paper on the development of information-technology applications in the Veterans Administration. In the paper that closes this chapter, he introduces us to the VA's experience, philosophy, and its available software. This is most valuable as the systems are comprehensive, well-developed, transportable, and in the public domain. They are ready and available for transfer.

Hammond's contribution is not only to provide us with the conceptualization of a large and multifunctional system, but also to provide vital development experience, some background on the MUMPS language, a philosophy of system design and equipment selection and, most importantly, a reminder of the importance of, and opportunities in, technology transfer and public-domain software. (See LaMendola, 1984, for examples of transfers that have already been accomplished.)

Hammond's paper is a most fitting capstone for this state-of-the-art presentation. It underscores and supports the importance of our theme of technology transfer and illuminates the potential value of a technology clearinghouse; it reiterates the importance of designing to support the service-giver and the service; it recognizes the viability and value of deriving management data from service data, and the failure of the reverse; it relates the value of decentralized systems and their evolution; and, it illustrates the contribution of information technology to the world's largest medical-service system.

INFORMATION TECHNOLOGY APPLIED TO FACILITATING PRACTICE
by Jim Newkham

The Heart of Texas Region Mental Health Mental Retardation (HOTRMHMR) Center is one of 31 community mental-health centers in Texas. The Center provides treatment and preventive services to persons within its catchment area who have mental-health and/or mental-retardation problems. The Center's administrative structure — Finance, Public Information, Personnel, Planning/Quality Assurance, and Clinical Records/Data Systems departments — provides the underpinning to strongly support client services. Direct-service programming is divided into four major program areas. Developmental/vocational services for developmentally delayed or mentally retarded clients include outpatient diagnosis, evaluation, and treatment, home-training/day-programming for children, and vocational and residential services. Community-maintenance/crisis services include screening, referral and admissions services, inpatient services, continuity-of-care services, halfway houses and 24-hour emergency services. Mental-health services provide outpatient services that include specialty units for drug abuse, alcohol abuse, and protective services to children and the elderly. Regional services provide outpatient mental-health services through satellite offices in five rural counties.

The HOTRMHMR Center staff of 144 full-time employees includes one half-time and two full-time psychiatrists, two certified public accountants, a programmer/analyst, four doctoral-level psychologists, 25 masters-level social workers/psychologists, technicians, registered nurses, occupational and speech therapists, and a variety of bachelors-level professional staff members, secretaries and the clerical staff.[1] The Center uses consultants in fields such as pharmacy, child psychiatry, physical therapy, and pediatrics. The catchment area is composed of six counties. The largest, McLennan County, has a population of approximately 200,000, of whom 140,000 are in metropolitan Waco. The surrounding five counties have a population of approximately 50,000.

This section is adapted from J. Newkham and L. Bawcom, "Computerizing an Integrated Clinical and Financial Record System in a CMHC: A Pilot Project," in *Administration in Social Work*, 5,(3/4), 1981, New York: The Haworth Press.

1. The author wishes to thank the members of the HOTRMHMR staff for their work in the development and use of our S/MIS system, and for being so supportive of the program efforts to provide better service delivery for our center's clients.

Table 18 **Registered-Client Demographics for Fiscal Year 1983**

		Percentage (N = 2,587)
Sex:	Males	48
	Females	52
Race:	Anglo	67
	Black	25
	Hispanic	8
	Other	Less than 1
Age:	12 or younger	18
	13 to 17	5
	18 to 44	51
	45 to 64	20
	65 and older	6
Annual Gross Family Income:	Less than $7,500	81
	$7,500 to $15,999	14
	$16,000 and more	5
Mental-Health Status:	Chronic dysfunctional	21
	Crisis dysfunctional	15
	Chronic marginally dysfunctional	43
	Crisis moderately dysfunctional	16
	At-risk functional	5

In fiscal year 1983 (September 1, 1982 through August 31, 1983), the HOTRMHMR Center served 2,587 registered clients. Table 18 exhibits their characteristics.

In addition, the staff screened 4,593 unregistered clients, some of whom did not need the Center's services and were referred to other agencies or were in need of only those services performed in screening. This description of the Center's client load demonstrates the priority of the public client, especially those who have been hospitalized, who are at risk of being hospitalized, or who are unable to obtain services elsewhere. The Center is well integrated with other human-service agencies within the community — 33% of its clients are referred from other agencies. Eighteen percent of the Center's clients required emergency hospitalization in the local psychiatric unit; only 7% of the Center's clients went to the state hospital for further services. Halfway-house services, vocational programming, and outpatient and screening-for-emergency services complete the array of services to the community. The Center has 11 intake points to maximize its accessibility to the community and the high-priority chronically or acutely disturbed public client. There are not enough services to meet all of the demands, but careful attention has been given to the needs of the targeted clientele. The Center's treatment philosophy emphasizes individualized treatment planning and active case management. The emphasis ensures optimum client care by the Center and all the community services needed.

The Information Problem

The Center's administrative staff examined the agency's clinical and financial operations in early 1976 as part of the new executive director's management review. The review listed the following problems: Reliable, current information about active and inactive case loads, and staff and client service data was unavailable to the direct-service staff and management; case records were nonstandardized and disorganized, and the staff could not easily obtain summary clinical information; the state MHMR office took 4 to 6 months to transmit needed data, and the staff did not trust its accuracy; manual tracking and reporting systems, which included revenue and expenditure data, were time-consuming and did not provide the information necessary for accountability to funding sources; it was difficult to maintain clinical and fiscal audit standards because the needed data were inaccessible; and cost-versus-outcome analysis was essentially nonexistent.

The first step taken to solve these problems was a manual cleanup of the data system for required state reports. The Center restructured the collection methodology and began to monitor the reporting data before it was forwarded to the state office in Austin. The second step was to standardize the manual clinical records to comply with state audit requirements. It was a critical time to improve the financial system because the agency had a deficit of $247,000. Because the Center significantly reduced errors in the manual reporting system, the Texas Department of Human Resources selected it to develop and test an automated data system. The state agency wanted to develop a system to provide a viable audit trail for services and reimbursement; and the Center wanted to examine the feasibility of operating a comprehensive data system in a community mental-health center that could transmit its summarized reporting data on computer tapes.

All levels of staff had specific responsibilities in the process of defining and solving the problem. The director of support services was charged with the development of forms to provide hard copies for clinical records and for computer input documents. The director of finance was responsible for the automation of the newly developed direct manual financial system. The Problem Oriented Record (POR) Committee, composed of clerical, clinical, supervisory, and administrative staff members, was to develop the automated clinical information system. The executive director helped settle issues, answer questions, and negotiate among the groups.

The Center's goal was to develop an automated information system that would assist in improving and maintaining the quality of services while it resolved the standards-compliance issues involved in accountability. To reach those goals the Center had to develop a problem-oriented record (POR), an effective data-collection process, an automated fiscal reporting system, and a computer hardware and software system. The Texas Department of Human Resources agreed to fund the software development and the Center agreed to purchase the hardware, fund the maintenance of the hardware, and commit itself to the development of an automated information system.

The Information-Technology Application

The Center staff felt several key management principles were central to the successful development of this system. The staff felt that the current management style was the best because it involved a philosophy of enabling, rather than one of controlling. This style relies on involvement of all levels of staff in the decision-making process, the idea that the combined action of a group of people produces more effective decisions than an individual—synergy—and the belief that people want to do the best job they can, and will do so when they have the necessary information and resources. [EDITORS' NOTE: This relates to MacGregor's Theory Y; see Ouchi, 1981, p. 69, and Peters & Waterman, Jr., 1982, pp. 94-96.]

All levels of staff would be involved in the design of the system from the very beginning and would be given real decision-making authority rather than just token involvement. This would minimize concern and confusion when the impersonal communication tool—the computer—became part of the human-service delivery system and it would keep lines of communication open.

Also at issue was whether the information system would serve the management or the staff. A staff information system is any system with which staff members gather, store, process, evaluate, and present information about a particular client or group of clients and then use the data to monitor, evaluate, and make decisions that concern the client or group of clients. Past experience with an imposed data system led the HOTRMHMR Center to plan for a staff information system that would first support front-line staff and give immediate feedback to all levels of staff that put data into the system. The input data would meet clinical and service needs and management-information and external-reporting needs. The term staff/management information system (S/MIS) was coined to describe the system.

The staff also wanted the S/MIS to provide accurate, cohesive, and timely information, not just unrelated data. Data are simply facts, whereas information is derived from facts—compiled and related in ways that have meaning to staff members—and communicates knowledge for effective decision-making. Thus all reports and printouts would use commonly understood terminology and a format that makes them easier to use.

Simplicity was the final feature considered important to the system's success. The amount of data available for computerization in a medium-sized community mental-health facility such as the HOTRMHMR Center can be overwhelming. A seductive feature of an automated system is the assumed capability to obtain information about everything in several different ways. The staff, however, chose a simple, practical approach, with as little paperwork as possible for data collection, in developing the system—an implementation of the old adage *keep it sweet and simple.*

Implementation began with the management staff determining the four major components to be considered in designing the automated system. These components were the software development, the state mental-health data system, the hardware system, and the local community mental-health-center system. The first step was to select a software consultation group. The Center chose the software company because of its past experience with other mental-health information systems. The agreement with the software group called for it to work with the Center staff in the design, development, and debugging of the automated system. The software group would receive $154,000 for its services.

A review of the literature for models of integrated automated information systems provided little assistance. There were a few sources helpful in providing guidelines, specifically the work of Newman, Burwell, and Underhill (1978), and Meldman, McFarland, and Johnson (1976). The system had to be designed to meet a number of criteria: It had to support client flow through the Center's treatment process with a minimum of paperwork, yet it had to capture accurate data to document services; it had to help the direct-service provider with immediate feedback regarding clients and help to keep records current; it had to meet the reporting needs for client and service data; it had to meet the financial reporting requirements for the Center's funding sources and provide an audit trail for fiscal review; it had to provide summary information for client and system management; and, it had to be useful in cost-outcome analysis.

To work with the state mental-health data system, the Center had to change from sending paper forms, which were batched and mailed in bulk, to sending a magnetic tape with summarized service data. Negotiations focused on deciding what data were to be sent, and which format would allow the state computer to receive the Center's data and incorporate them into the state data-collection process. This phase was lengthy, complicated, and involved the Center, the software group, and state MHMR data staff. For the last 6 years, all information has been sent to the state on magnetic tape, and the system has worked smoothly.

The original hardware configuration selected in 1978, with consultation by the software company, was a Wang VS 80 with a random access memory of 256K and 75MB of disk storage, one 600-line-per-minute printer, one 9-track tape drive, and four CRT work stations. The staff and consultants felt this system was the most cost-effective on the market and the most appropriate for the amount of data a midsized center would process.

In the fall of 1982, the Center added a second 75MB disk drive, two data-processing work stations, and Wang Word Processing (two additional work stations and a daisy-wheel printer), and doubled the system's memory to 512K. In 1984, the Center added a 288MB disk drive (which replaced one of the 75MB drives) to allow on-line access to more than 3 years' information and to utilize more of Wang's utilities. The Center has spent approximately $100,000 for hardware during the 7-year project. Upgrading the hardware over time has allowed the Center to benefit from falling prices in the industry (the price of the 288MB drive had recently been reduced by half).

The current system is designed to provide the Center with a tool that is modifiable and manageable, yet takes advantage of the hardware's inherent utilities and the operating system's strengths. The system's software design allows access to files through alternative key fields that revolve around the client's demographic information. Examples of this information set include Problems and Goals, Medications, Diagnostic Information (DSM III, Level of Functioning), Admission and Discharge History, Case Management History, Referrals, Service-Provided Activity, and Planned Events. While this method may not be as pure as the Center's prior data-dictionary approach to a data-base system, it has offered many advantages. Information in a category can be found as it is needed, not on a basis of how the data were originally established. For example, the medication file can be scanned based on Medication Code without first searching for which clients have that medication.

Second, the support of the alternative key paths within files allows on-line name searches, displays by client or staff, and so on, without a search of the entire information set. The overhead memory requirements of a data-base system are greatly reduced, which improves the system's responsiveness.

Also, the Report and Inquiry utilities provided with the hardware have enabled the staff to scan the information set without additional software from outside software vendors. Last, as in any community mental-health center, there are continuous changes in funding requirements. While some of these requirements establish a new code, or an additional element of data, some also require redefinition of the information set (e.g., DSM II to DSM III). The system's architecture enables the staff to accommodate these revisions with a minimum of software changes. In most cases revisions only require a change in the proper table.

In the last 2 years, the Center changed the programming language from BASIC to COBOL, which improves input and output speeds, and allows the use of the Wang's Report Utility. The system includes functions that edit the input against user-modified code tables and also test it on a field-relationship basis (e.g., the system will only accept a reason for unemployment if the unemployment-status question indicated that the client was unemployed). This feature has greatly reduced output errors. The user can request output of detailed or summary information at the desired level from an individual client or staff member up through units, programs, or center-wide levels. Also, the previously mentioned utility, REPORT, provides the capability to generate custom reports without programmer intervention.   .

The forms for the clinical record include computer input documents and supplemental manual forms. All forms are designed to follow the client flow through the system from the initial contact through assessment, case-management assignment, review, and discharge. Manual forms, not used for input to the computer, include a treatment plan, 90- and 180-day summary outlines, consent to treatment, and releases of information. Input documents use a limited number of forms, most of which are generated by the computer printer. This enables the staff to modify forms without wasting a stock of preprinted forms. The computer-generated input forms include a one-page registration form (SHARE, for its usage — Screening, Hospital, Admission, Readmission, Emergency), three service-delivery documents — individual Direct Service Records (DSR), group DSR's, and attendance logs. These forms are produced with preprinted client information when requested by the input of a planned event, or as blanks for walk-ins or emergencies. Two other input documents include the Case Management Change Form and a Discharge Form. Three additional forms, non-computer-generated, include the Diagnostic Assessment Form (which includes the 9-point, clinician-rated Level of Functioning Scale, the DSM III, the Adaptive Behavior Scale, and the TDMHMR "Service Category" level), the Financial Assessment Form, which captures level of income, insurance, and fee percentage, and the State Hospital Tracking Form used to track clients from entry through hospitalization and follow-up at the Center or other community services. All of the input forms are self-carboning with the top copies, the "originals," filed in the clients' charts as hard copies. The second sheets, which are yellow and carry the same form numbers as the originals (for audit purposes) go to support services for input of the data.

On the forms the clinician generally has only to circle the correct responses or fill in blanks. Changes suggested by the staff have been incorporated into the system. They reduced the amount of coding that needed to be done on the forms, thus reducing the completion time and the clerical support needed to keep lists and codes current. For example, an employer's name is simply filled in, not coded from a code list as had been done previously. Staff time is separated from client time to simplify the recording of single-client/multiple-staff events or single-staff/multiple-client events. Pseudo case numbers were developed in 1982. The "number" is an abbreviation of the client's name that consists of the first four letters of the last name, the first two letters of the first name, and the middle initial. All screenings and emergency calls on nonregistered clients are coded with pseudo case numbers to track prior calls by the same or related individuals, provide background information at the time of intake, analyze the large number of screenings for need, follow-up, accessibility, and such. A Service Setting Code to indicate where services were provided — a nursing home, hospital, home visit — was also added at the suggestion of the staff.

Concurrent with the development of the clinical system, the financial system was automated by the director of finance and the software consultants. It is a comprehensive financial system that meets applicable standards of accountability including the ability to track expenditures by source of funds linked to specific cost centers called reporting units (RU). The designers of the financial accounting system developed programs that provided integrated flexibility to allow the comparison of client/staff service data and the cost of providing that service, timely and regular revenue/expenditure reports, and detailed documentation for audit trails. The financial component of the automated system includes a user's guide to describe the system and instruct staff members on its use. The system provides audit trails on all revenues and expenditures and has been extremely helpful in providing both detailed and summarized data for funding-source auditors. Internally, the automated financial system provides each unit director with a regularly scheduled detailed analysis of revenues and expenditures for the current month and year-to-date. The revenue portion of the report provides actual and budgeted revenues, by source of funds, with a budget variance amount, percentage for the past month, and fiscal year-to-date. The total annual budget is also shown with a percentage of year-to-date actual revenues compared to total budget. For expenditures the report provides a detailed listing of expenses by the line item for the current month and year-to-date. Variance amounts and percentages are again shown by comparisons of actual expenditures versus budget. These reports routinely provide supervisory management staff with current information with which to plan and make decisions.

Cost-outcome evaluation of the HOTRMHMR Center is done in a variety of ways. For example, the Client Detail Report summarizes the services that a particular client has received over a given period of time by type of service and provider. These data, with the cost figures by service and provider type, allow calculation of the cost of services provided to any particular client. The cost can then be compared to any change in the client Level of Functioning (LOF) Scale. This capability allows evaluation of clients receiving expensive services for whom less expensive services with similar outcomes might be available. Other examples include using the cost of service with various service summary reports to evaluate the need for additional groups versus individual treatment, use of other more efficient types of services, the uses and costs of billable versus non-billable services such as telephone counseling, and the loss of revenue if services are provided by a clinician who does not qualify for third-party reimbursement.

Associated with the development of the demographic, clinical, and fiscal data input forms was the vital requirement that the staff be able to summarize the data into concise information reports. Again all levels of staff were involved in the design of these reports, which helped to ensure each report's meaningfulness to the Center staff while fulfilling external reporting requirements.

The first of these reports is the preprinted DSR (Direct Service Record), which contains a visual array of current client/staff data. The DSR goes directly to the clinician for each individual, family, marital, or parent-child service encounter and includes on one page current problems, objectives, status of case, treatment for each problem area (including medication), initial and current level of functioning, case-manager identification, and up to three future, planned service events. Preprinted group DSR's and attendance logs are provided for psychotherapy groups and larger day-activity groups. After each service the clinician concisely records the service provided, time involved, service provider, recipient codes (including client or collaterals involved), appointment codes (including scheduled, nonscheduled, cancelled, no-show, or emergency), client billing information, and additional planned service events. Blank DSR's are available for walk-in and emergency situations. The individual DSR is unique among the forms in that it is both an input and an output form, and it is the preprinted form that reminds the staff of duties and obligations (service events, summaries due, follow-up calls, fee reassessments, etc.). The planned-event capability allows staff members to plan future events (from weekly therapy sessions to 180-day follow-ups) by simply entering the dates and event types on a DSR.

The Case Management Listing Report is provided monthly to individual clinicians. It is a list of their active clients, with the dates and types of their last services, the statuses of the cases, diagnoses, service groups, and a schedule of the next service events. This report helps direct-service providers manage their case loads. At the unit or program level, this report helps balance case loads, monitors workloads between units, and guarantees that every open case is assigned a case manager.

The Staff Event Listing Report is a monthly printout that lists each service activity by clinician, date, type of service, and length of time the service was provided. Activity is then summarized by the total time the clinician spent in each service activity for each service unit. This provides the clinicians with information to monitor how their time and talents are expended.

Other standard reports include the Service Summary by Unit Report, which provides monthly summary service and client information on unit, program, and center-wide bases; the Client Detail Report, which lists summarized services received by clients; and the Client Profile Report, which summarizes demographic information on any of the 40 profile elements captured, and which is made available by clinician, unit, and so forth, upon request. There are also reports that profile, for example, diagnostic groups or service groups.

As the clinical system was developed, it was implemented on a unit-by-unit basis. The in-house developers provided training. Center-wide formal training was accomplished with the use of the CHARTS (Community Health and Record Treatment Systems) Manual (Gifford, Shaw, & Newkham, 1979) and the CHARTS Training Manual. These two manuals have been condensed into the user's manual, FACTS (Financial Administrative Clinical Tracking System). FACTS incorporates the changes made in the forms over the years and is in a three-ring binder to accommodate the anticipated future changes. As changes and modifications have been made in the system, the staff has been trained on a unit-by-unit basis, as many of the changes affected one unit or program more than others.

The continual involvement of the staff in the modifications has resulted in minimal resistance to the constant changes. Turnover and eventual withdrawal of the software consultants from the project allowed Center staff control over changes without concern for voiding the development agreement. A settlement with the software consultants and the hiring of an in-house programmer/analyst allowed full control and provided a skilled operator who was readily available and who could implement changes. The capacity, whether through staff or consultants, to modify the programs, reports, input forms, and such is a basic resource that must be readily available. Hardware maintenance has worked smoothly through a contract with Wang and downtime has amounted to only 3 days in the last 5 years. A manual system to parallel the computer's financial side was maintained for 2 years but the Center discontinued its use after the automated system was audited and re-audited and found to be excellent. The clinical side has an equally trackable audit trail, with the duplicate forms providing actual documents for the clinical record. The whole system has been reviewed and audited many times and has received high marks.

The design-and-development phase consumed much staff energy but was exciting; contract negotiation with the software consultants, which culminated in their abandonment of the project, frustrated the staff; however, the completion, modification, and utilization of a working integrated automated system was extremely satisfying and rewarding.

The Next Steps: Plans for the System's Development

The Center is currently converting the language of the financial side to COBOL. Also underway is the site-and-development work needed to finalize the design for an automated client fee system. This will involve reports on client income, percentage of fee paid, collection rate, and fee balance by clinician, by unit, and by program. These specifics are being determined from the input of direct-service providers, and data, finance, and administrative personnel.

Data are entered in the computer and reports are generated at a central location. The Center is decentralizing portions of the system by, for example, placing a Wang personal computer in one or two of the regional offices for local generation of DSR's, fee analysis, inventory, client and staff activities, and word processing.

The Center plans also to place CRT's and small printers at points of intake and screening where the intake workers and/or clerical persons can search for prior contacts with any person who seeks services. The staff can then directly review the files for any history of services. If there is a history, it can be called up immediately and printed for use in assessment and screening.

Other ideas for the future development and use of the system are directed towards clinical analysis. For example, some clients could avoid hospital admissions if immediate warnings were provided when clinical patterns such as sudden drops in levels of functioning occurred, or if particular stressors surfaced in certain diagnostic groups. The Center would like to be able to study patterns of problems and the effectiveness of treatment modalities, the constellation of problems on the LOF that indicate a high risk of deterioration, and the indicators of crises in clients' lives that suggest the need for special attention.

Even with the excitement of creative development, design, and analysis, extensive commitments of time, money, and energy are required to accomplish these ideas. These commitments have to be balanced against the day-to-day demands of meeting the basic needs found in any human-service delivery system.

Similar or Related Systems in Other Organizations

The staff at the HOTRMHMR Center has been involved over the last 7 years with other information systems at other CMHC's, hospitals, and governmental entities at the city, county, state, and federal levels. The systems generally have in common the accomplishment of much routine work — counting, summarizing, and displaying information gathered. The differences between the HOTRMHMR Center Automated Data System and the others lie in two broad areas: the specific design, implementation and purpose; and, the ease of data entry balanced against the capability to provide timely and relevant output.

Historically, information systems have been designed from the top and imposed on portions of the system down the ladder. This methodology was a way to meet the needs of the times, since these systems were most often designed to monitor and control operations. The philosophy surrounding the development of the HOTRMHMR Center's system, however, was to involve all staff members in the design and implementation processes so that the system would meet their needs, as well as management and reporting needs. The Direct Service Record (DSR), for example, is both an input and an output document and the most frequently used form in the system. It displays summarized clinical information for use in working with clients and is a major direct-service support. The system is *user-friendly*, which means that most of the output reports are prepared for and used by front-line staff. The summarized data are used by supervisors and management personnel to support the service process, while meeting the management, administrative, and reporting requirements. The result of this approach to a staff/management information system is that all levels of staff are involved in making the system work and they view it as a major tool, rather than as another demand on their time.

There are many similarities in other systems with regard to the ease of data entry, but major differences occur in the output area. The HOTRMHMR Center system is now approximately 10 times faster than the original system because of modifications in the hardware/software configuration and design. This reduction in report-preparation time significantly increases the accessibility and usability of the system. The programmer/analyst reduced input time by 40% through program redesign. Another difference is in the relevancy of the output reports and information. Even though the reports are generated regularly—the DSR on a daily basis and the Case Management Listing on a monthly basis—they can be requested and, in most instances, obtained immediately. This function gives timely information as compared to a state agency that issued a report in February 1984, summarizing services provided in October 1983. The output of timely and relevant information appropriate to the users at all levels of the organization makes the big difference between the HOTRMHMR Staff/Management Information System and other systems.

Issues Raised by Our Experience and the Experiences of Others

The issues raised by automation itself were unclear in the Center's experience because it corrected agency management problems while automating and revising the clinical records and the financial system. However, the four major issues that we addressed throughout the process were quality of care, accountability, information needs, and communication needs. Experience has validated the Center's view that automation is an effective method for dealing with these critical professional issues. The clinical information entered into the system, and its quick return to the staff in scheduled or on-demand reports, encourages and supports the high quality of care by supplying accurate and timely information and facilitating communication. Operating procedures for the system and the record forms themselves encourage face-to-face communication—a staff member must first talk directly with the other staff member before case-management responsibilities can be transferred and documented. A second example is that the DSR focuses communication between staff members and their clients on the course of the treatment.

Automation's effect on confidentiality became an issue in the staff's acceptance of the system. Administrative procedures on confidentiality of client records and information were expanded to guide the staff in protecting the documents and various output reports that contain client-identifying information. The concern over dehumanization by the computer was managed by emphasizing personal communication. Staff members—whether they were direct-service providers or managers—soon became aware that the information the computer produced aided them in improving clinical services by increasing the individualization of clients and by increasing the efficiency of service delivery and program evaluation. Concern about increased time used for paperwork or for learning a new system diminished as the staff found that appropriate automation saves time.

Management philosophy—control and monitoring versus enabling and autonomy—was a large issue for most staff members. Enabling rather than controlling was implemented to deal with this. All levels of staff were involved in the process rather than having the system imposed on them from the top, down. The record format allows for a variety of treatment approaches and the output reports were designed and are used primarily to provide information to the direct-service provider. Many of the enhancements in the system have been at staff suggestion. Also, the system was not designed and implemented to capture 100% of a staff-member's time (i.e., control), but rather to capture time in major activities—direct-service time, case-management time, report-writing time—thus enabling the staff members to review how their time is spent. This supports staff autonomy and improved professional practice by providing more effective tools with which to do good jobs.

The question of whether the system is unique to this agency or one which could be replicated elsewhere was recently resolved. Beginning in 1983 the Center installed the system in four other Texas Community Mental Health Mental Retardation centers. The installations began by involving staff members from all levels within each center, and as they became familiar with their own systems, their acceptance and use of them grew. These staff members became the trainers in their respective centers. The installations went smoothly, and the systems were operational within a few months. The training materials, essentially the FACTS Manual, were generated by the integrated word processor and became the users' manuals at the four centers.

Staff members have begun to find the system supportive. It frees them from many routine tasks, and allows them the time to concentrate on solving clinical and other professional problems rather than data-gathering and reporting. They have also begun to generate ideas for additional uses of the system.

Conclusions and Summary

Professionals in the social-service fields work in a complex and complicated system. We are often asked to do more with less, do it yesterday if possible, be concerned with quality as well as quantity, and work under the watchful eyes of the community, local, state, and federal bureaucracies and auditors. The collection, manipulation, and application of information to accomplish our goals is a central theme of our work.

When the Heart of Texas Region Mental Health and Mental Retardation Center analyzed the situation in 1976, the Center staff members found serious gaps in their information about Center clients, services, and finances. The process of automation, through its design, development, implementation, and operation phases forced the staff to look at each aspect of the Center's operation. This process alone was positive and beneficial. The design and development of the Staff/Management Information System was a lengthy, often frustrating, but valuable experience, and was well worth the effort. Automated information systems are tools that do not solve problems by themselves, but they do greatly enhance the ability to define and solve problems. There have been continual changes, modifications, and improvements to the system as experience has shown how to further its support of service delivery.

Use of the automated data system has improved service delivery by enhancing the staff's ability to collect, analyze, use and report information; by encouraging more effective communication; by increasing clinical and fiscal accountability; and by providing reliable information for service planning, design, and management. The Staff/Management Information System has proven to be a major asset in facilitating professional work. However, the Center feels that it is only on the threshold of the system's potential to meet the challenges of service delivery in the future.

DISCUSSION OF
INFORMATION TECHNOLOGY APPLIED
TO FACILITATING PRACTICE
by Walter LaMendola

Opening Statement

The theme of this application area is facilitating professional work via information technology, and our task is to explore the state of the art. The description of the Staff/Management Information System (S/MIS) at the Heart of Texas Region Mental Health Mental Retardation Center provides one view of a computer-based information system that can be examined for its promise to help the worker collect and review report data, schedule appointments, manage work time, be aware of items due and pending, and reduce paperwork requirements.

The description of the S/MIS system highlights one of the contemporary tensions between the tradition of management information systems and personal-computer-based information systems. An MIS, by definition, serves the needs of the organization's management. A personal-computer-based system serves its user. The S/MIS system attempts to do all of the first task and some of the second task. For example, the S/MIS system is centralized; its use is dedicated to the organization and its outposts; a single data base is maintained. The system meets internal and external accountability needs through financial and service-based data capture and reporting. Examples in Newkham's paper of meeting the second task, that of serving the professional, include a reduction of paperwork by use of forms that require only circling appropriate items and which contain less coding, an awareness of items due and pending through Case Management Listing reports, the management of work time with the Staff Event Listing reports, and the collection, review, and reporting of data through the Direct Service Record. The Center also plans to install CRT's and printers in work areas where, presumably, staff members could request and receive data. The duality of serving both management and service-delivery professionals is one that is reported to be successfully evolving at the Heart of Texas. This is not the case in the field of information technology in general, nor is it a problem the profession of social work has resolved. There are continuing and persistent conflicts between social work direct-service practitioners and managers.

In social work, it is also true that the question of whether or not the worker is acting as an autonomous professional or as an agent of the organization for which he/she works continues to be at issue. Another manner of approaching this question may be to ask, "Who benefits?" Is it the person receiving service? the professional? the organization? society? The field of information technology has been dramatically altered by changes in the "beneficiary" made possible by changes in the technology. The most significant example is the introduction of personal computers with the capability of networking. The use of personal computers has several democratizing effects. For example, the concentration of power associated with data being in a single centralized data base is diminished by the existence of multiple, decentralized data bases. The political implications of data control passing to multiple members, each with his/her own data bases and networks, alters fundamental concepts of organizational control and social innovation.

Organizational control and social innovation in the conduct of social work have often been determined by the political and economic forces in the environment. The Cobb and Ramey scenarios are contrasts of such influences in a public and an experimental public agency. In the Cobb scenario, the adoptions unit in a state agency is unable to free itself of paperwork requirements, of the 12 card files of the client-record system, and of antiquated rules and jurisdictions. By-products of this system are inaccuracy of data and poor worker training. The information technology in use is obviously outdated. What contributions can updated information technology make to resolve the problem? First, the political economy in which services exist will not allow information-technology improvements to alter existing power relationships without struggles. In so much as improvements in information technology can serve the purposes of the dominant elite, they probably will be adopted. A major dilemma in the scenario is that staff members readily identified such areas where information-technology improvements could be both timesaving and helpful. While this is an opportunity to introduce staff-supported data processing, will it serve the interests of the staff or of the controlling jurisdictions? If the needs of state and counties are served first, the staff will certainly be discouraged. It is also true that if the computer system is designed in a traditional manner by traditional system developers, the situation of the staff may not be improved despite the improved information technology. The Ramey scenario addresses a situation in which an improved information technology was implemented at the start of the project. Forces in the environment in 1971 had provided support for service integration as a solution to service problems. The information technology used to support the project agency, Mon Valley Community Health Center, was visionary in concept and implementation. However, the innovation that the project represented could not be maintained in a changing political economy—regardless of either the elegance of information technology or the improved service to the clients.

Information technology can be used by social workers to enhance their organizational control. Gordon provides a rich description of a social worker struggling to make sense of a data system not designed for her use. Even under those circumstances, the worker translates the data into information. How? Since the worker knew what questions to ask, some part of the data became information that could then contribute to improved services. But finding that information occupies a great deal of her time: Why was this person excluded from the design of the system?

The use of information technology, in Gordon's example, fails to capture the worker's attention. And attention is a limited resource to which improvements in information technology must respond. The application of information technology must capture the attention of the workers: It must surprise them. It surprises them and captures their attention when it presents possible answers to questions they feel are relevant to the work that they perform. This type of application appears in Winn's scenario. In an example of the power of information technology to allow people access to each other through networks, the hospital social-service administrator uses a computer network to ask questions and exchange materials with other hospital social-service administrators across the country. Their contributions provide him with the necessary professional support to maintain his position in a controversy with the hospital administration regarding the delivery of social work services by his department.

The Cavalier and Hasenfeld scenarios provide a final contrast of interest to the topic of the facilitation of professional work. Cavalier writes of the paperwork burden of Title XIX: Can information technology assist? The answer is "yes": Contemporary information technology can assist the professional in meeting accountability needs. This will indirectly facilitate professional work by releasing time, supporting the judicious use of time, or providing timely information. Hasenfeld's scenario presents a common dilemma, but it is not, as Hasenfeld states, a dual dilemma; it is a triple one: How do you meet accountability needs, facilitate professional work, and allow the system to evolve with the growing understanding and sophistication of organizational members? Systems developers and theorists have not resolved these problems. The personal-computer-based data-processing system has new potentials for resolving old dilemmas, but it creates new ones. For example, it provides new opportunities for professional autonomy, for changing the content of professional work, and for social support. An evolutionary dialectic, not resolution, results from the use of improved information-technology capabilities.

Conference Discussion: Summary

The people involved in the system development must know information technology, even if they are primarily social workers. A system that involved many disciplines was developed at the New York Association for the Blind a number of years ago. Ethical issues surfaced immediately and persisted throughout the experience. For example, there were questions of client participation and client access to case records. The computer system seemed to take on a life of its own. It illuminated and magnified social work practice problems. The computer needs to be demystified with systematic thinking about its use. Services to clients must come first, accountability, second. What is most needed is a system that supports practice to demonstrate that the support of management is not the only major issue. But whether or not new applications of information technology to support clinical work can be developed now is another issue.

We have a serious need for an integrating concept or vision. The life model of social work practice is one example of an integrating vision that addresses the dual focus, person and environment, of social work practice. To reason by analogy, if social work could be considered an industry, what would be at the production end? In other words, who benefits? For example, in the airline industry there was a great deal of disagreement about that question, but once the passenger-data concept took hold, the industry was able to act in concert and move ahead. There were variations in ideas about the data base. But the industry was able to use the concept as a foundation upon which all other applications were developed. In health, the consensus reached is that the patient is the integrating concept. The student data base has become the integrating concept for the education industry. People working in that area began with financial and administrative applications, but they came to realize that the student data base is very valuable. As universities increase their competition for students, the concept of the student data base has continued to gain value. In social work, who is the client? If it is the person receiving services, information technology should evolve to support the production of services to people. If it is a funding body or a governmental instrumentality, then the information technology should evolve to support these institutions. Once the integrating vision, or the definition of the beneficiary of social work services is clarified, there can be a structuring and development of the appropriate data base. At that point, new information technology could be infused into social work organizations and practice. Social work organizations have seemed to follow the same path as other types of organizations in the incorporation of new forms of information technology. Accounting systems have come first, followed by a variety of management systems. Yet the critical interactions for social work are at a transactional level, and we need to develop a data system that is useful to the worker at that level.

The same point can be made by the human-service manager. The manager needs data for organizational and survival reasons. Even though managerial data needs are different in quality and derived meaning, they originate from the production of services. There is some congruency between management and practitioner issues, but they require different complex knowledge bases.

Practitioners need to facilitate their work not through time management or accountability alone, but through access to expert systems, through the development and use of information technology that helps them evaluate client progress and their own work, and through *nonutilitarian* systems where workers do not have clear outcome goals. Such practice-based issues cannot easily be the subject of deliberation if human-service organizations continue to receive conflicting, imposed data requirements and societal demands.

Exploring the more straightforward practice-based issues — such as a modest client system — may allow us to introduce these examples from practice into the university curriculum. Some interesting things are now available, including very limited forms of direct treatment in the areas of phobias and depression. In an anxiety-disorders clinic at the University of Wisconsin at Madison, each of the clinicians uses a computerized administration of the FDL-90 as a form of monitoring progress and treatment. Every 10 days to 2 weeks the therapist and the patient meet to look at the results of the most recent FDL-90, and they compare the results to prior results in the course of therapy. It has been acceptable to clinicians and patients, in part because the technology is being used by the clinician and the client as a team. In the area of clinical consultation, the technology provides a data base in a format that a busy, struggling clinician as well as his/her client could use. For example, the clinician can have access to the data base of all references to a particular disorder that have been made in the international literature. A client can telephone a place that has a communications capability and scan that data, look for a key word that applies to him- or herself, and get a printout of references sorted by publication dates. With the printout directing him or her to the appropriate literature, the client examines the abstracts and can also use the data base to read the work itself on-line.

Another example of an area of direct clinical application of technology would be personal bibliographical retrieval. Practicing clinicians are bombarded with tremendous amounts of information. They try to read as much as possible, but they have limited time for that activity. There are journals now that make their tables of contents or their indexes available in computerized format. Clinicians can also enter and maintain their own personal bibliographic records on computers. This might quickly resolve the problem of trying to find the articles that they read in the past but need right now. They can also annotate the literature or direct it to the attention of other network participants.

The problems of improving our information technology have been with us at least since the 1920's. The questions we have so far considered were considered and discussed then. They focus upon the actors and their actions, the nature of what the social worker reports, and the service created through interaction. These are fundamental problems that we must solve together so that information technology does not become a wedge between people and their interactions. Perhaps there is an integrating concept — but we cannot resolve that question in a few days. The scenarios demonstrate that the content of social work practice to which newer forms of information technology must be addressed are not trivial and not narrow in scope. Practice serves to inform social work education in this regard. Both must work to unlock the creative potential of the practitioner. Both must enable the practitioner to grasp and develop the utilization of evolving forms of information technology in social work practice.

Discussion Issues

1. Can the profession establish direction for information-technology development by agreeing on a single description of the beneficiary of social work services? Can there be an agreement on the goals of social work practice that would allow us to suggest such an integrating concept? Are there common definitions of practice that can inform our work to develop this integrating vision?

2. Should the transactional level — the service encounter — be considered the most important level to model for the infusion of information technology? Or should we consider continuing to develop it at any level, taking care of the most structured problems first?

3. Is it possible to construct a data-processing system from one point of view? For example, can we begin to develop systems from the point of view of the person receiving the service and use that as a departure point? If we do, can this type of system development then lead to meeting worker, manager, and organizational needs?

4. The use of information technology illuminates practice problems. Then it puts them under a magnifying glass. In this sense,
the technology is threatening and becomes the scapegoat for
complaints. How do we deal with this?

5. There is generalized staff resistance to information technology.
In order to counter staff resistance, do we build the system
around the needs of the practitioners, to the extent that they
can articulate their needs; do we provide direct assistance to
practitioners, for example, through the use of automated interview or testing devices; and/or do we work to make more time
available to practitioners to spend on providing service? The
staff people who provide direct services often have no time
available to help develop systems, so how do we start with them
and involve them in the evolution of the system?

6. Should systems that are developed be seen as prototypes? Certainly, systems should be seen as evolutionary. For example, relatively little work has been done in designing systems that support clinical social work practice. Coupled with staff resistance
and lack of time this results in few clinicians who understand
and are willing to design a clinical support tool. Such a tool
designed only by systems analysts probably would be insufficient
to meet the clinician's needs. One remedy is to design a simple
model that meets some needs. The creative powers of the clinician can take hold as familiarity with the potential of improved
technology is gained through system use. But where and how do
we begin?

7. How do we foster use of the capacity of the practitioner to
create and utilize applications of information technology?

8. We have a great deal to gain by examining the history of the
development of information technology in social work. Information-technology evolvement has always been intertwined with
fundamental problems that the profession has addressed over
the past 40 years. We have yet to gain a consensus on the definition of social work practice, its objectives, its units of measure,
its definitions of success. This lack of definition is amplified and
made more visible by the necessary logical requirements of improved information-technology applications.

INFORMATION TECHNOLOGY IN PROFESSIONAL PREPARATION AND DELIVERY OF SERVICES
by Patricia Lynett

Organizational Setting

The University of West Florida (UWF) Social Work Department and the Florida State Department of Health and Rehabilitative Services have had a 10-year partnership in the education and training of social workers. In early years this cooperation took the form of a contract that supported two or more social work faculty positions at UWF. Under Title XX guidelines for the provision of long-term training services for persons who were preparing to deliver social and economic services, these contracts supported faculty members who taught in the BSW program. As these positions were absorbed into the budget of the university, the UWF Social Work Department recognized the need for in-service training of those persons already employed by the state and who were delivering services to clients. Training services included development of training curricula, presentation of training, need assessment, evaluation, development of audiovisual materials, and dissemination of training packages throughout the state. UWF is a leader and advocate for quality training services within this state agency, and so the Economic Services office consulted the Social Work Department on the development of the plan to solve their training problems.

The solution to some of the problems of the Economic Services Program was the development of an individual learning system that utilized standard training content. The Office of Interactive Technology and Training (OITT) was organized and funded by contract to do that development work over a 3-year period. Since this project required a large staff and space was not available within the Social Work Department, the OITT was located a few blocks away. The Office was, however, tied organizationally to the Social Work Department under the Director of Social Work Grants and Contracts. Also, all budget documents were approved through the social work chairperson.

The key persons directing the computer-based interactive videodisc project for Aid to Families with Dependent Children (AFDC) were not social workers. The project director was a writer and instructional designer with degrees in education, and the technical advisor to the project was an associate professor of physics with expertise in the use and programming of microcomputers. In view of the future work of the OITT, it was felt that the identity of the work group should reflect the broad application of the technology rather than the content area of social work. Therefore, the staff composed a statement of purpose that does not mention social work but emphasizes research and training, and utilizing computer and videodisc technology.

At this writing, marketing and sales efforts to develop other research and training projects have failed. It appears that efforts in these areas began too late to keep the AFDC project team together. Efforts to secure other contracts have not been focused in social work. Industrial and technical training projects seem more likely prospects because of the presently prohibitive cost of hardware and software for this type of training and delivery system.

The Problem/Service Setting

The Florida Department of Health and Rehabilitative Services (HRS) is the organizational unit under which all social and economic services are delivered to clients. Within this agency the Economic Services Program is the deliverer of AFDC payments, and the Office of Staff Development and Training is the central planning group for training employees of HRS. Aid to Families with Dependent Children is available through county offices throughout the state, and new eligibility specialists receive initial training in one of 11 district HRS offices. Economic Services employs AFDC trainers in these district offices. The Director of Staff Development and Training was the person who realized that the training problems of Economic Services could be solved with funds provided by Title IV-A of the Social Security Act. These funds are associated with the AFDC budget and are earmarked for training new employees.

The AFDC Eligibility Specialist's job is to apply many technical and sometimes nonspecific policies and guidelines in the determination of the eligibility of a client for a welfare check. This job includes correctly completing many forms, conducting countless interviews, making changes to budgets based on changing client situations, resolving crisis situations, dealing with sometimes hostile, confused, and upset applicants, absorbing new policies and frequent changes, and trying to accomplish this work despite constant interruption. While determination of the economic award is the primary task of the eligibility specialist, the worker needs good interviewing and case-management skills, and the ability to provide information, referrals, brief counseling, and crisis intervention.

The Information Problem

The new eligibility specialists were trained in 11 sites throughout
Florida. Training was based on a policy manual, which would be the
employees' "bible" on the job. The interpretations of policy varied, so
there was not a standard training curriculum. Therefore, the training
received by the new workers came in 11 versions. The method of training, however, was consistent—classroom-style presentation. This arrangement dictated that many staff vacancies exist before a class could
be assembled, and then there was a 4- to 5-week period before the new
employees arrived at the job site. Meanwhile, the extra work was absorbed by already overworked people. In some areas of the state, turnover was 300% per year, which required continual training sessions. In
these situations AFDC trainers were rarely able to do in-service training
on new policies. In other areas turnover was very low, and vacancies
could exist for lengthy periods of time before there would be enough for
a class-size group.

Because of this situation, the error rate in determining the AFDC
payments clients were eligible to receive was very high. When the error
rate exceeded the federal government's standards, Florida was not reim-
bursed for all of the AFDC monies that it distributed. Florida suffered
because of high error rates, and the state was highly motivated to identify and correct possible causes.

The Problem-Solving Philosophy

The University of West Florida had demonstrated expertise in the
design, development, and delivery of custom training packages for the
state of Florida. While the Department of Health and Rehabilitative
Services did employ persons whose roles were to assess training needs
and deliver training, it did not employ instructional designers, writers,
audiovisual specialists, and computer programmers.

During the research of the availability of funding, a technological
breakthrough occurred within a few miles of the state offices of HRS. A
small company had manufactured the first interface card to allow computer commands to be read by a videodisc player. This marriage of
videodisc player and personal computer permits the design of individualized learning materials that include audiovisual motion sequences, still-frame slides, and sound with computer text. The videodisc, which is read by a laser, is extremely durable and can store 54,000

frames of picture or print as well as digitized information. The learning carrell used for the AFDC training includes an Apple II + computer, a Zenith monitor, and a Pioneer 7820-3 videodisc player.

Federal funding was available in 1981 with the requirement that 25% of those funds be matched; in 1982, the requirement was a 50% match of funds. The University of West Florida, primarily the Social Work Department, assumed these matching responsibilities. The classroom teaching of the faculty qualified as matching activities.

Having identified the problem, the sources of funding and required matching funds, and the training delivery system, the UWF and the Office of Staff Development agreed to a contract. The decision to locate the contract management with the Office of Staff Development rather than with the Economic Services Office became a source of many problems. Problems are likely to occur when one group provides the content expertise and content approval after another group has conceived the curriculum project and, during 80% of the project, has responsibility for managing the contract. It is possible that the administrative officers of the Economic Services Program never thought the new training package and mechanism would be successful and, therefore, did not demand complete responsibility and ownership. Development of the project was significantly slowed by the lack of support from Economic Services. In that respect this major research project on information technology in training did not follow a fundamental premise of staff development and training: Top management must be supportive for an activity to be successful.

The Information-Technology Application

Description of the Design

The hardware had a great impact on what could be developed, given the assumptions, requirements, and restrictions described hereafter. The learning carrell includes a monitor, an Apple II + computer and a Pioneer 7820-3 videodisc player. The computer allows storage of missed questions during practice and test activities. During the practice activities missed competencies are stored and the learner is routed to further information about them. The computer also provides access to the videodisc. The videodisc is the truly amazing piece of this hardware constellation. It contains 54,000 frames that can be used to store slides, motion sequences, audio with or without motion, and digitized data. The computer can recall this information in random sequences to allow an infinite variety of presentations. With this combination, slide projectors, movie projectors, overhead projectors, cassette recorders, and stereo record players become unnecessary.

Initially it was believed that the need for an individual, self-paced training-delivery system meant that the training ought to be delivered in Spanish as well as English, and that a learning carrell should be located in each of the more than 100 county social-service centers in Florida. It was decided that the differences in the Spanish dialects—Haitian, Cuban, Puerto Rican—precluded definition of a single Spanish language. It was also decided that the training would continue to be delivered at the 11 district offices, which would negate the anticipated savings of travel costs of trainees.

The decision to continue the training at the central offices was connected to a larger issue. Each district employs at least two AFDC trainers. These employees felt their jobs were threatened during much of the project. Their concerns and the skepticism of the Economic Services Program administration led to a decision to include the trainer in training delivery despite the individualized, self-paced design and the hardware capabilities.

The qualifications required of the person hired as an eligibility specialist also put limits on the instructional design of the training. Since typing skills were not a requirement, trainees would be asked to make only computer-keyboard responses, with one stroke per response. This limited the kinds of interactions the trainee could have with the learning system.

Another agency requirement was the integration of the AFDC policy manual into the training. Reference books were developed to organize the policy manual into cogent, learnable facts. Economic Services reviewers feared that trainees would prefer the organized content and not gain familiarity with the existing policy manual.

A final assumption about trainee behavior that affected the way in which the content was presented was that the courseware must be very user-friendly. Therefore the character TESS (Technical Eligibility Specialist's Specialist) was created as a surrogate instructor, guide, and prompter. People are more familiar with computers than they were when this project began, so the need for "friendliness" appears to have declined. More straightforward presentation and feedback are now appropriate.

The policy content of the training was an established requirement. The policy manual served as the guide to mandated rules and interpretations. However, the precise applications of many of the manual chapters were not defined until the review of the first draft of the courseware. Much that was thought to be mandated AFDC rule was actually being applied in many different ways.

Within these assumptions and requirements, the training package was designed for 100-percent mastery, with remedial instruction available at several levels of learning. Demonstrated competence exempts a learner from materials presented to the trainee who responds erroneously. Some remedial lessons occur in a loop, which opens only with incorrect answers or a consultation with a trainer regarding problems.

The training experience is tailored to the individual's rate of learning and need for extra practice. The trainee is very much in charge of his or her own opportunity to learn. The learning process appeals to visual and auditory senses, thereby increasing the likelihood of learning. The motion sequences that portray job situations provide both models and interactive simulations. Practice of skills, therefore, occurs with as much realism as possible.

Development Process and Experience

Once the staff members of the Office of Interactive Technology and Training were assembled, they began a study of the hardware's capabilities and the best process for preparation of videodisc learning materials. The staff consulted leading authorities in this new medium, and explored various scripting strategies.

In general, the following steps are necessary in the production of computer-based interactive videodisc training:

- Identify instructional goals and objectives.
- Develop and verify, with client, the learning competencies.
- Develop instructional design.
- Write script (see sample, Figure 6).
- Shoot video portion of script and edit onto a one-inch videotape.
- Write the computer program.
- Produce master videodisc from videotape and produce videodisc copies.
- Catalog videodisc (each still-frame and motion sequence is indexed by frame number and content).
- Insert frame numbers into computer program.
- Test and correct combined computer and videodisc courseware.
- Duplicate floppy disks and videodiscs.

Every bit of information presented in dialogue, still-frame, or computer-generated text must be written in a script. This script includes not only the material the learner will see and hear but also indicates in what way the presentation is made. The script page, developed and utilized by the OITT, is printed in several colors. Pink is used for computer-generated text, white indicates video motion, blue indicates use of the second audio

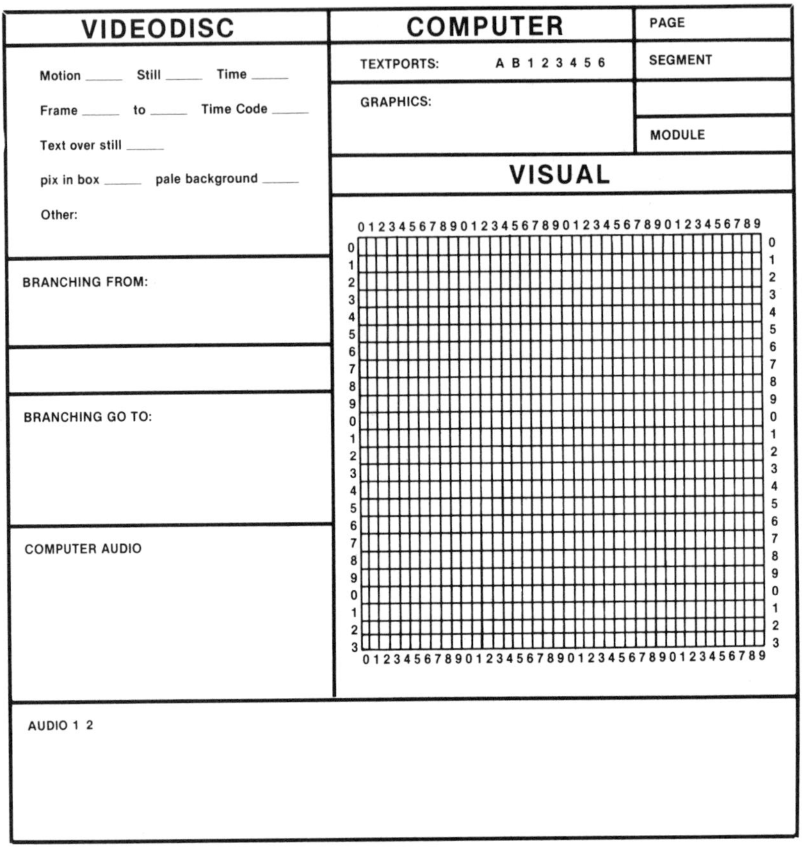

VIDEODISC	COMPUTER	PAGE
Motion _____ Still _____ Time _____	TEXTPORTS: A B 1 2 3 4 5 6	SEGMENT
Frame _____ to _____ Time Code _____	GRAPHICS:	
Text over still _____		MODULE
pix in box _____ pale background _____	**VISUAL**	
Other:		
BRANCHING FROM:		
BRANCHING GO TO:		
COMPUTER AUDIO		
AUDIO 1 2		

Figure 6. **Sample Script Page**

channel, and gold is used for still-frames. Computer programmers, video producers and directors, and the writer all work from the same script.

Note the box in Figure 6 for branching information and competency identification. The visually displayed material is written in the box, with the grid ensuring that the words will fit on the screen. One side of a disc includes 54,000 frames that play at a rate of 30 frames per second. A description of a motion sequence and its dialogue may occur on 5 script pages that use 300 frames in the disc.

The selection of authoring language (i.e., the high-level computer language) is usually made during the instructional-design phase. Style of computer text display, desired degree of storage of learner test data, use of computer graphics, and the type of learner input responses are factors that determine language choice. Pascal and Super Pilot are common selections.

In the AFDC material Pascal was used because it provided the necessary sophisticated test-data storage. Subroutines for common programming sequences were also developed.

The developmental process included extensive interaction with the subject-matter experts in the Office of Economic Services Program and the trainers across the state. It was difficult to build a relationship of confidence, partnership, and trust with the trainers because they feared the loss of their jobs. Interaction with the Office of Economic Services was hampered because its personnel did not conceive the project and, therefore, lacked initial ownership of it.

Strategies to involve individuals and gain their trust were implemented early in the project. This trust was necessary for the accurate assembly of the content and also to assure successful transfer of the training technology to the agency. A Delphi study was conducted among the trainers to ascertain the best order of presentation of the material in the training. Their input was requested several times until substantial agreement regarding the skill hierarchy of the AFDC policy existed. In addition, a workshop entitled "Teaching Technical Skills" was provided to upgrade their classroom teaching until the computer and videodisc courseware was implemented 3 years later. Demonstrations were given throughout the state to illustrate the capabilities of the computer-supported-learning carrell. Selected AFDC trainers reviewed draft scripts as did the state experts. Finally, field tests were conducted in several locations. All of these strategies were of modest success. Only the sight and demonstration of finished products, supported by publicity in national journals and press about computer-assisted training, and the acclaim accorded the videodisc seemed to elicit positive responses.

Perhaps some of the reluctance of the subject-matter experts can be attributed to their awareness of a major problem associated with the AFDC content and this delivery system: The contents of the AFDC manual change frequently and are open to interpretation. Policy changes require a training content that can readily be changed. And standardization of content requires agreement on one interpretation. These two issues were continual barriers to the development of accurate training materials.

Implementation and Operating Experience

The primary goal during the last 6 months of the project was to execute a full-scale pilot test in the work setting with newly hired AFDC Public

Assistance Eligibility Specialists. Second, recommendations were to be developed for maintenance and updating of the system. Major shortcomings of the training package discovered in the pilot test were corrected before the final delivery in February 1984. Types of data gathered from the pilot test were test scores, time on task, objective and subjective evaluations of each of the eight modules by the trainees and trainer, recorded observations of the OITT staff person at the pilot site, and the number of wrong answers associated with all test questions. These data revealed that the average completion time was 120 hours whereas classroom training routinely lasted 160 to 200 hours. Eighty-five percent of the group achieved the 70% final test score necessary for promotion to the job as compared with only 50% of a recent classroom group trained in the same location. When the scores of the interim and final tests were averaged, all of the pilot-test trainees achieved the required 70% score. The classroom group did not receive interim tests.

There was also a follow-up survey of the pilot-test personnel and their supervisors. This instrument was designed to assess job skills as well as evaluate the training, now that trainees were implementing what they had learned. Employees were asked to rate their job knowledge and comment on the effectiveness of the training in preparing them for the job and accurately simulating the job. Analysis of the response data indicated that all respondents would choose computer-based interactive videodisc training over trainer-led classroom presentation. While several learning activities were rated as accurate job simulations, the new employees also suggested an increased amount of on-the-job training. Specific strengths of the technology, noted frequently by the former trainees, included the opportunity to learn at their own paces and to review whenever they felt it necessary.

At present the agency will attempt to maintain the system in-house. All documentation was delivered to the agency so that it could hire a programmer and a writer to change the content. Competencies were indexed so that a changed policy could be located in the 15,000 script pages. The Office of Interactive Technology and Training would still be available to participate in the updating of this system—the largest computer-based interactive videodisc program in existence.

Besides maintaining the training package, the agency must also maintain the hardware. This factor was not initially considered and required the negotiation of a $100,000 contract for statewide equipment repair. This aspect of equipment ownership is complicated by new technology. An unanticipated high demand for videodisc players by the video-game industry had drained the market of the player used in this learning carrell. While all of the necessary training equipment was purchased early in the project, Coleco recently bought the remaining Pioneer 7820-3 players for use in a video game. Expansion of the system will now be difficult because newer models produced by Pioneer and other manufacturers are not compatible with the AFDC teaching software as developed.

The role of the AFDC trainer did change. The trainer was previously the primary mechanism for delivery, explanation, and testing of the content. He/she will now be primarily a manager of training and a guide to the self-instructional experience of the trainee. This change ought to allow the trainer to conduct more in-service training to alleviate special problems of experienced workers.

Overall Evaluation of the Experience

Evaluation of the development process suggests that the project might have been completed in less time if subject experts had had a greater investment in the project and a standardized content had existed throughout the state. The Office of Economic Services Program assumed contract management during the final 6 months of the project; however, the director of the Economic Services Program gave no indication of support for the innovation at any time during the project or at the time of delivery of the package.

The appropriateness of the delivery of this content with this method should be considered. Since the policies and regulations tend to be unstable, it is advisable to put practice and test questions on computer floppy disks. Only common client situations should be put on the videodisc since the information on it cannot be easily changed. This strategy was attempted imperfectly. Data show that trainees performed better with the policy manual organized into a reference book.

The primary accomplishments of the project include the standardization of the AFDC training in the state of Florida and, more importantly, the development of practice and job simulations which ensure learning. The individualized presentation of the content and the opportunity to practice with simulations of job situations are the unique strengths of this training. These aspects lead to improved performance and a reduction in training time. The integration, throughout a comprehensive training program, of computer text, printed text, audio and visual materials, and computer graphics had not occurred previously.

The most disappointing consequence of the project, from the OITT point of view, was the state's demand for return of all the hardware purchased with "university match" funds. It is the interpretation of the state and federal government that this equipment cannot be used in anything but AFDC-related work. It will not be available to the OITT even for the development of other projects for the Department of Health and Rehabilitative Services.

The entire cost of the AFDC project, including the 50% matching of funds, was $2.2 million. The average time for training, based on the 13 pilot-test participants, is 120 hours. Therefore, the cost of the first use of the training program is $18,333/hour of group training (or about $1,410/student hour). This figure could then be divided by the number of trainees per year for the expected life of the package. Interactive training development can be accomplished less expensively if, for example, existing video footage and slides are used, fewer characters and scenes are portrayed, and less complex testing and reviewing are required. It is too early to determine whether this project is cost-effective. [EDITORS' NOTE: A master videodisc is very expensive to produce. Subsequent copies are quite inexpensive. If this training program could be used for 70 such groups without major changes the cost would be about $20/student hour, or roughly equal to current tuition levels.]

Related or Similar Systems in Other Organizations

Other states have tried to solve some of the problems that led to this project in another technological fashion. In Wisconsin and New York, computers directly evaluate clients' eligibilities based on the data the clients provide on written forms. This method should produce accurate assessments of those data and lower error rates, given that the input data are accurate.

A project related to the OITT-AFDC project used the same constellation of technology to teach and test interviewing skills, time management, and stress management for AFDC eligibility specialists. The instruction, as in the policy training, teaches concepts and allows evaluation of performance and modeling of effective interviewing skills. Another area of the Health and Rehabilitative Services agency that used computer-based interactive videodisc training is Children's Medical Services. Six to eight packages are available to nurses, doctors, and parents of ill children who wish to learn about such topics as court testimony, child abuse and neglect, and spina bifida. Unfortunately, there has yet to be an evaluation of the use and effectiveness of the large library of CMS training programs.

Opportunities for Development

An application of computer-controlled videodisc technology in training and education that has not yet occurred is its use for training groups of persons rather than individuals only. If case staffing is to be taught, input into the computer and subsequent branching could be in response to a group decision. The group would be able to practice the skills to be learned during the very act of learning. A ride at the Disney World EPCOT Center requires the riders (a group of 4) to collectively choose the country in which they want to take their tour. Videodiscs are used in this entertainment and allow tne experience to be tailored to each particular group. In like manner each team of trainees could have a unique learning experience designed for the degree of skills it has in working as a group.

This technology could be used in assessment centers to direct the social workers seeking or requiring skill or knowledge development to the appropriate training content. If training stations were located in all service centers, workers could use their free time for training rather than attending workshops that they often don't need, and which often occur at inconvenient times.

Clients of social-service agencies could use this technology in the form of information stations that could privately and individually answer questions about rights, services, eligibility criteria, or respond to more personal inquiries about health or needed services. Providing information and referral has been a basic function of public and private social services, but technology could make this function simpler, less expensive, and more private. The client could be given a choice of a computer or a counselor for certain interactions. Technology could also make information and referral available in any language. The expertise and empathy of social workers could then be directed specifically to situations that require more than just accurate information.

Technological Advances

Many technological advances have occurred since the inception of the AFDC project. In terms of increasing the accessibility of information through technology, developments include the touch screen, which allows interaction between a person and a computer with a touch of a finger to the display screen. The touch screen and developments in artificial intelligence allow information to be easily accessed and tailored to a wide range of reading levels, languages, et cetera.

The videodisc can also be used for data storage and can accommodate the data from thousands of floppy disks. [EDITORS' NOTE: See Chapter 2, Table 7, for more details.] This advance solves many physical storage problems and increases the ease of information distribution. The compact audiodisc, which is only 4 inches in diameter, was initially developed for more efficient storage of digital data. Recently the compact disc has gained attention as a method of storing high-fidelity stereo sound.

The DRAW (Direct Read After Write) system allows a user to buy a blank disc and write on it one time. Thus far no process allows the videodisc to be changed after mastering. Erroneous data can be eliminated only by reprogramming around incorrect or otherwise inappropriate frames on the disc or by remaking the master disc.

Utilization of telephone lines for the transfer of data can result in overnight transmission of revisions to the computer-based information files. This could eliminate errors in training delivery caused by changed policies or procedures.

Issues

The Process of Technology Transfer

The transfer-of-technology process for this project started even before the OITT work began. Only part of the client organization, and particularly not the part containing the ultimate users, was in favor of the technology. Job loss was a predominant fear. This fear was exacerbated by suspecting the outsiders of tampering with a vital part of the program. For these reasons, and others, OITT could not build a working relationship or develop a feeling of client ownership that would form the basis for the technology-transfer process. As a research organization interested in the use of technology in the human-service field, OITT would probably do this project again even knowing the reservations of the client-user. Forewarned, OITT would urge the client agency to accomplish some internal team-building prior to, or in the early stages of, the project. But, perhaps the agency needed the 3 years of development to adjust to the concept of the new technology.

Working for an Agency That Does Not Value Social Work Education

The Florida Department of Health and Rehabilitative Services has declassified many social-service positions. At present no jobs require or give preference to persons with degrees in social work. This de-emphasis has happened even though Title XX money and Florida general revenue funds continue to support five social work departments in the state. The University of West Florida became involved early in providing training in the agency because it no longer needed those funds to support the BSW program. UWF may undermine its degree program with its provision of high-quality social work training in the agency. This involvement in training has been accompanied by a great output of energy from UWF, the National Association of Social Workers and the other Florida deans and directors as they try to change the hiring qualifications. Since that effort has proven to be unsuccessful, UWF decided that its commitment to providing effective services for clients should take the form of involvement in training within the agency. By making this decision UWF assures that social work principles, values, and skills will be part of the training content. It is a difficult choice, particularly when the agency lowers allowable indirect-cost rates and requires that anything purchased for the development of the project be returned. The desire to assure quality service delivery could be replaced by a more pragmatic view of "What's in it for us as a department?"

Training Delivery versus Organized Staff Development

Training through a contract with a university should not simply be a matter of the provision of a child-abuse-and-neglect trainer in Wausau on Tuesday. Rather the university has an obligation to make sure that an environment and a support system for the acquisition of skills exist in the agency. The simple delivery of content accomplishes very little without endorsement of the training experience by the management. Social work trainers do their profession a disservice when, because of no organizational/consultative work, trainees arrive without knowledge of the topic to be addressed and with no interest in being involved in the experience. Staff development, successfully executed, includes all levels of the organization in active assessment, planning, and evaluation with the university.

Interpersonal Skills Taught without People

Can interpersonal skills be taught individually, much less with a piece of hardware as a teacher? That question has not been answered because operational definitions do not exist for many interpersonal skills. The AFDC packages on policy and interviewing have used the best strategies available. They use the hardware for the presentation of models, drill and practice, review, and test-score management. The trainer provides guidance, personal evaluations, role plays, and group exercises. The student can attain knowledge, evaluate the performance of others, and test behavior. (For example, the social worker in the motion sequences asks the learner to select the next response that the social worker should make. This response is acted out and the learner sees the resulting client response that has been programmed into the scene.) While some client problems and behaviors are more common than others, there is a danger in suggesting that a particular behavior on the part of a social worker will routinely result in a specific client response. [EDITORS' NOTE: This objection to programmed instruction can be dealt with by programming random variations into the selections of "client responses."]

Summary

A strong new learning tool is now available. However, the strengths of the technology do not eliminate the need for the human users to prepare for its implementation. Universities should continue to be involved in the research and development of this technology. Little research is available concerning the effectiveness and efficiency of the computer-based interactive videodisc as a training system. It is evident that private industry does not include research about appropriate use of technology with the development of products. The industry has done almost no research about appropriate use of the videodisc.

Therefore it is the responsibility of the UWF Office of Interactive Technology and Training to incorporate research into its activities. With admittedly small samples of employees, our research does prove effectiveness. The issue of appropriateness will be more difficult to operationalize and quantify. Therefore it is even more likely that only an entity such as a university, with research as its mission, will address the question. Until the data are available, technology should be viewed with reserve. **The question of appropriate use should most closely examine sensitivity to the learner and the rights of the social-service client.**

DISCUSSION OF INFORMATION TECHNOLOGY IN PROFESSIONAL PREPARATION AND DELIVERY OF SERVICES
by Lynn Harold Vogel

Opening Statement
A Brief Introduction to Technological Support

The use of technology to support the preparation of professionals and the delivery of services has a history that precedes the introduction of computer support into such activities, although we often think of computers as the beginning of technological support. For example, in the 1950's a number of educational institutions made use of telecommunications capabilities to share classroom instruction with homebound students. The presence of "teacher-phones" was not uncommon, even at the primary- and secondary-school levels. In the 1960's and early 1970's, television and videotape playback equipment became increasingly prominent in educational settings, and became widely used in higher-education settings as well. Lecture halls with video monitors were much in evidence to help cope with the "baby-boomers" as they entered college. Within social work, the use of videotape recording and playback equipment became prominent both in agency settings (to enhance the supervisory process and provide direct feedback to clinical staff members about their intervention activities) and in schools of social work, where role-playing of client/worker situations became more "alive" with video playback capabilities.

More recently (see Lynett's preceding paper) the use of videodisc players — both as stand-alone training-support systems and as microcomputer/videodisc systems — has become a technological possibility for supporting professional preparation and service delivery. At least one lesson from the past, however, should give us pause before we rush to embrace the latest technology. With each successive technological innovation in education, from the "teacher-phone" to video equipment to videodiscs, the cost of participation has become greater. That is, the level of capital required to acquire the technology and use it effectively has become greater. In addition, the cost of supporting and maintaining the technology has also often increased. Many schools of social work, after investing upwards of $10,000 in videotape-production facilities (or at least videotape equipment) several years ago, could not afford to continue to invest in subsequent (and higher-quality) equipment and discovered their own initial purchases increasingly expensive to maintain. As a result, the technology that once held such promise often lies dormant in a closet rather than continuing to be used to support professional preparation. Microcomputers follow on the heels of videotape, and a fully equipped microcomputer laboratory can cost as much as $30,000 to $40,000. From what we know about the videodisc as the latest technological innovation, the costs of production of the master disc can be great—often as high as $60,000 to $100,000. And, unfortunately, with any of these technological innovations, the need for maintenance and support is not likely to diminish after the initial equipment purchase has been made. [EDITORS' NOTE: As with other forms of hardware and software, development costs can be quite large but are bearable if they can be spread over many units, i.e., repeated uses or duplicate copies in use.]

Training Models Using Technological Support

Turning our attention to educational models that have supported professional preparation, we can observe at least three basic training approaches: the programmed instruction model, the individualized instruction model, and the computer-based instruction model. In the first, students are taken through a set of lesson modules on a step-by-step basis. When students provide correct answers to test questions, they are permitted to continue on to the next set of materials. Wrong answers cause students to review the set of materials again. They must answer the test questions correctly before they are allowed to proceed.

In the second model, students are led through a branching process in which wrong answers may cause them to review materials with a slightly different focus, and correct answers lead to progressively more difficult materials. The instruction is individualized in the sense that the system is able to respond to different students' learning needs rather than providing only a single path through the lesson modules. With a computer supporting the branching process and holding all lesson materials until they are needed, and providing access from a variety of directions, the instruction model is made more efficient and more effective.

The third model focuses specifically on computer use and actually has three primary components: learning about computers (how they function); learning through computers (computers as a learning support tool); and learning with computers (in which the computer plays an interactive role in the educational process). In this model, the computer is used as a learning tool and students learn about its use, use it passively as a supportive tool, or use it interactively as a supportive tool (e.g., through the individualized-instruction approach mentioned above or in exploration and discovery learning—as in simulation). Alternatively, the computer can become more of a background support to the educational process to control other aspects of learning support (e.g., videodiscs). In the latter area there is increasing agreement that the computer holds its greatest promise for professional preparation, and thus underscores the importance of Lynett's contribution.

A recent report from a conference at the New York Institute of Technology (Braun, 1983) indicated that using computers to support the learning process has been shown to have several positive aspects. Computer support often results in quicker learning of the subject matter and often gives the students more positive attitudes toward computers in general. By some measures, computer support results in better learning, as indicated by higher scores on objective tests. But the evaluation of such processes is a difficult task even in the absence of a role for the computer. And with computer-assisted learning, the evaluation becomes doubly difficult since often both the training and the use of the computer imply changes in the *status quo*.

Technological Innovation: Questions about Content and Use

Two fundamental issues arise when considering technological innovation to support professional preparation. First, we must consider questions about the technology itself. What types of technology can be used for training support? If we view it as supportive of the educational process rather than as a replacement for some portion of resources currently committed, will this alter our views of its potential (i.e., will the cost-benefit analysis of computer or videodisc use be changed)? Can we respond to the challenge raised by Vallee (1983) in his book, *The Network Revolution*, to seek ways to use the technology that we previously couldn't even conceive?

A second fundamental issue has to do with the use of any technological innovation, particularly in the arena of education. A recent study by a national association of school districts found that 95% of the nation's primary- and secondary-school districts have purchased computers, but only 87% have developed any guidelines for their use. Further, 70% have seen no change in textbook-purchase policies to reflect the different requirements for software purchases rather than book purchases, and 60% have seen no change in curriculum or course designs as a result of the purchase of computers. This raises serious questions about the capacity of educational institutions to use a new technology even when they have the means to purchase it. The experience that many schools of social work have had with videotape technology, which 15 years ago held much promise for innovation and change in curriculum content, is strikingly similar to the experience that elementary and secondary schools have had with computer technology.

Beyond questions of the technology and its use in educational settings, we come to questions about possible changes in the educational contexts that might result from the introduction of technology. For example, how would the introduction of technological support affect the human element in teaching? This is an important question in social work, a profession that is based on assumptions about the central importance of human relationships. To what extent might teaching about human relationships (which often involves experiential learning for the student) be affected by the introduction of computer support? How do (or can) computers change the way we currently teach about human relationships and thus prepare students for professional social work roles? How might computer support change the nature of the educational environment, particularly in regard to the social relationships that now are such an intricate part of that environment? What are the implications for the roles of individual teachers, with particular strengths and weaknesses? What about the cost of introducing this technology, particularly considering the "bootstrap" nature of much of the educational enterprise, including social work? Who should bear the cost of developing educational programs that will likely require investments over a multi-year period? Even if teaching or professional practice are made more effective (and not just more efficient) by the introduction of computer-technology support, what are the rewards to the educational enterprise and the educators for this enhanced effectiveness?

Technological support in the educational enterprise can take place in several arenas — instruction and administration are the primary choices. Disciplines and organizational entities larger and wealthier than the social work school are likely to see the benefits of the technology sooner, and administrative applications or research support in "number crunching" disciplines are likely to dictate acquisition and development policies. Instructional uses are likely to be last in virtually any order of priorities, since efficiency in word and number processing is more easily demonstrated.

In situations where instructional applications can be supported, the applications are likely to be what has been called the *horseless carriage* type. That is, educational practices that have been followed for years are the most likely to be candidates for computer support, usually in their most mundane aspects (e.g., drill and practice). The challenge is to use the technology to expand what we have done before, not simply to repeat it, for instance, by helping learners to build experience more rapidly than is possible with traditional instructional methods.

In another context, the introduction of technological innovation such as computer support raises important questions about values. In a profession in which equal access to resources is a fundamental goal for clients, the introduction of technology can exacerbate the lack of equal access. In the educational arena, the introduction of computer support in some institutions and not in others can become a marketing tool that displays competitive advantage to gain students or increased financial support. How quickly we embrace the computer as a technological tool may in large measure determine the speed of increasing polarization among schools of social work, social work agencies, and the clients and students they serve in society. Those of us who have access to the technology are among the elite in knowledge (and some in resources) within social work—and in many cases within the general society—but as a profession, we strive against elitism.

Finally, even well-developed, well-planned, and well-executed projects that demonstrate the feasibility and effectiveness of computer support in social work settings can fail to be implemented, even after substantial expenditures of both time and money. This is a lesson common to both the Lynett and Pruger experiences. The use of even a successfully demonstrated project falls short of the goal. We must consider how to change the likelihood that successful training and practice demonstrations will become viable full-scale systems.

Conference Discussion: Summary

Brief Review of Experiences at Schools of Social Work

Many of the schools of social work represented at the conference had made commitments to the introduction of computer support and computer instruction within the social work curriculum. For the most part, these activities were at early stages of development, and none used or had made plans to use computer support of the sophisticated nature of the videodisc/microcomputer system described in Lynett's paper. Most of the instruction was via demonstration, although some schools had sufficient resources to offer hands-on instruction. Standard computer applications in social agencies and in research were the most prominent (e.g., data-base systems, statistical applications, word processing, and spreadsheets). Microcomputers had been introduced in some settings, although they tended to be used primarily for administrative support within the schools, rather than for student instruction. Where the larger university community provided access to mainframe computers, schools of social work tended to rely on such support rather than develop their own facilities, with one or two notable exceptions. This can be blamed on both the capital investment required for the school's own computer capability (and the likelihood that the school itself will be required to provide the funds) and the fact that the statistical software packages most often used in research teaching (e.g., SPSS and SAS) are generally more productively used in a mainframe environment. Another comment from participants who had used mainframe computers for teaching support was that the task of translating programs from mainframe to microcomputers, should these micros become locally available, might be too costly and time-consuming to be justified.

The task of developing computer software to make computer support a reality in an educational setting was not an activity rewarded by educational institutions—nor one in which the expectations as to technical, computer-oriented skills versus training and subject-matter knowledge were well understood. Marilyn Flynn, a conference participant, commented on the experience with computer-assisted instruction at the University of Illinois:

> In the PLATO experience, it was initially assumed that with a higher-level language such as TUTOR [the PLATO authoring language] good teachers could both develop and program instructional materials. After several years' experience it was next believed that teachers should design the instructional software, but programmers should be hired for management of the technical aspects of software development. At this point, after 20 years, we have largely concluded that teachers and agency staff should be trained to *implement*, but few are capable of either effective design or programming. A *team* is needed. The locus of this team, who should direct it, and how it should be maintained is now the focal point for concern.

The experience at the University of Illinois underscored the need for caution in the introduction of technology into the process of professional preparation. While it is true that it is easier to use current computer software than what was available even 5 years ago, we still have not clearly identified the differential requirements of designers, programmers, implementers, and teachers.

Questions of acquisition of resources—including hardware, software, and other necessities for the introduction of technological support into the educational process—will likely continue to be problematic for social work educators. Social work continues to be viewed as an area of education in which computers are not considered by students, faculties, and educational administrators as essential to the educational enterprise (certainly not as essential as in mathematics, science, or business). The institution, therefore, often relies on a "buy your own" policy which, given the investment required even for small microcomputers, almost guarantees that a minimal level of technology will be introduced.

Beyond Professional Preparation to the Delivery of Services

Lynett's paper focused on the preparation of specific workers to carry out the tasks of service within the agency context. But it is becoming increasingly feasible to consider the possibilities of using technological support to provide clients with access to computer support without the intervention of the agency staff. In some areas, computers are already being used in client orientation to agency programs, to assist in the diagnostic process and, in some limited instances, for the treatment of specific problem areas. Agency orientation might take place in the waiting room prior to intake; a preliminary assessment of client problems might be carried out on-line with a resulting hard-copy output being used by the worker and the client in the initial encounter; the completion of specific goal-achievement instruments might be monitored by a computer with direct feedback given to the client; and data bases on community resources might be available to clients in settings other than social agencies to increase client access to resource data. These are examples of new ways to think about the agency-client relationship in which primary concerns are to assist clients in focusing their energies and attentions on their problems and needs, to widen the repertoire of possible agency and client responses, and to stimulate client progress toward the goals established for service. **Much of this is already happening in some settings, so the issue is not whether it will occur at some ill-defined future time. Rather, the issue becomes one of understanding how the technology—much of which exists already—can support our efforts to work with clients in ways that enhance the effectiveness of the service-delivery process.**

INFORMATION TECHNOLOGY IN SUPPORT OF SERVICE-DELIVERY DECISIONS
by Robert Pruger

The Organizational Setting

The activities described in this paper took place in three county welfare departments in the San Francisco Bay area. Since California has a state-supervised rather than a state-administered welfare system, these agencies operate independently of each other. Each agency is accountable to its own county board of supervisors and to the state and federal governments.

Because state and federal requirements are the same for all, the three departments have many characteristics in common: the same extensive varieties of income and service programs; similar personnel similarly trained to carry out similar tasks; and very comparable multilayered bureaucratic structures typical of welfare departments in urban-suburban counties throughout the United States. Onerous amounts of paperwork are a part of virtually every service action.

Other shared characteristics are not formally determined but are both relevant and familiar. These include: high orders of interrank and, to a lesser extent, intrarank alienation; rigid top-down command structures; widespread apathy; heavy case loads; chronic budget shortages; unfavorable public images; clients whose lives seem fixed at one or another pathetic boundary of existence; the appearance of order generated by the volumes of rules that are supposed to govern every administrative and service action; and the reality of underlying chaos created by the infinite number of means by which and instances in which those rules are circumvented.

Reforms initiated at higher staff levels are almost always regarded by those at lower levels either as ludicrous ("It can't work!") or ominous ("Whatever they say is the reason for the change, its real effect will be to make our work harder or to get rid of some of us."). Reforms that involve the computerization of anything are most likely to evoke both reactions at the same time and from the largest number of workers. By the time the activity described in this paper began, staff members in all three agencies had had experiences that, to them, justified these evaluations.

The Problem/Service Setting

County welfare departments in California are required to offer In-

Home Supportive Services (IHSS) programs. Eligibility is based on financial need and physical impairment that limits a person's ability to maintain him-/herself in his/her own home. The wide array of services performed (e.g., meal preparation, cleaning, bathing, shopping) is intended to prevent or forestall the placements of the disabled and elderly persons, to whom the program ministers, in expensive nursing homes or acute-care hospital programs.

The IHSS program has always had two related problems. It has been extraordinarily difficult to contain costs; for many years IHSS has been the most expensive social-service program in California. And there has been no effective way to ensure the equitable allocation of the service budget across the case load.

The major means for dealing with these problems are the state assessment and time/task guidelines. These identify and are intended to regulate the amount of services a worker can award to clients. More than 30 service tasks are listed, and different rules exist for each one. For example, the maximum time that could be awarded for bathroom cleaning to a client living alone in his/her own home is 20 minutes per week. If, however, the client lives alone in a one-bedroom apartment, no more than 15 minutes could be awarded; and if the client lived with anyone older than 14, only 7-½ minutes of service could be given.

The time/task guidelines and the supervisory hierarchy assigned to review worker decisions have consistently failed to solve either the cost or the equity problem. Each year's failure was met by the issuance of even more detailed time/task guidelines which, in turn, preceded the next year's failure. The frustrated legislature finally solved the cost problem by making the IHSS budget closed-ended.

State and county agencies responded by dropping certain service tasks from the time/task guidelines and those clients judged to be less severely impaired.

The equity problem was never solved, but with costs capped IHSS became much less visible to the legislature. Once the program moved from the center to the wings of the political stage, it became much easier for local welfare officials to live with, if not ignore, the equity problem.

The Information Problem

Equity requires that clients with like degrees of impairment receive like service awards, and clients with unlike degrees of impairment receive unlike awards, with the more impaired receiving more services than the less impaired. Line workers determine the equity of IHSS service distributions through the two decisions they make: first they determine each client's degree of need (the workers' assessment decision), and, second, they determine the weekly hours of service the client should receive (the workers' distribution decision). In a perfectly equitable program, any given client would be described in exactly the same way, and clients with the same assessments would receive exactly the same awards, no matter which worker made the decisions.

Both decisions require the exercise of worker discretion. Hierarchically created guidelines necessitate that exercise at least as much as they restrict it. Equity additionally demands that all workers exercise their discretion in the same way. Moreover, they must do it voluntarily, since there is no way to compel their behavior.

Analysis indicated that to improve the workers' ability to make the two decisions involved quite different problems, which required different approaches and solutions. And to advance equity both problems had to be solved.

The Assessment Problem   State guidelines presented workers with a list of impairments and disabilities and required them to indicate for each client the observed dysfunction and, on a 5-point scale, the degree of each dysfunction. The most general problem with these guidelines was that they had only limited correspondence to what workers actually observed and believed revealed the client's *true* degrees of need. For example, the guidelines forced workers to assess such things as visual capacity, mental state, and ability to climb stairs. Workers observed, however, that task-related items such as the ability to cook, shop, clean bathrooms, and do laundry varied considerably even among clients with equal degrees of visual impairment or other officially assessed conditions.

Since no credible definitions were given, each worker had to determine independently the meanings of the scale terms (i.e., no problem, moderate problem, etc.). The probability that different workers would describe the same client in the same way was low. Because of the limited credibility of the guidelines, workers felt free to interpret them loosely. Thus they regularly came to their own judgment of what a client needed based on what they observed, then made a service award in accordance with that judgment, and reported the disabilities and their magnitude in a way that would blunt any supervisory challenge of the award. Put another way, the workers' judgment of the client's need determined the assessment, rather than the other way around.

The Distribution Problem   The worker's distribution decision is a matter of converting the assessment into a service award. Equitable distribution requires that like descriptions elicit like awards.

Because workers regarded the time/task guidelines with the same skepticism as they did the assessment guidelines, they felt equally morally free to use them to justify the award they thought should be given. In addition, the workers knew that no one could use the pattern of checks that made up the official assessment and convert it into a correct award. For example, workers knew that no one could authoritatively transform a typical assessment (e.g., Client A = moderate visual impairment; slight hearing loss; severe problem climbing stairs; plus 10 other comparable statements) into the "right" number of minutes or hours per week for meal preparation, kitchen-counter cleaning, shopping, and 27 other services. Like assessments could not and did not generate like awards.

Even if none of the above were true, any worker who wanted nothing so much as to make equitable decisions could not do so because one critical piece of information was missing in the program. What no worker knew when he/she made a service-award decision was what all workers, on average, would award to that same client.

Producing this information would not be a simple matter. Each assessment is a pattern of checks along 12 or 13 axes of impairment, each of which is scored on a 5-point scale. The number of possible patterns or assessments is extremely large, well beyond the capacity of the mind to store and recall. Until this problem was solved, one could expect to find a large amount of inequity both within and across the case loads of even the most competent workers.

In an earlier study a research team from the School of Social Welfare at the University of California, Berkeley, had documented the substantial degrees of inequity in the IHSS programs of the three county welfare agencies of concern in this paper. With the concurrence of their highest-ranked administrators, a $300,000 proposal was prepared by the research team and funded by the California State Department of Social Services. It promised to design and implement a decision support system (DSS) that would increase equity by supplying line workers with the information they needed, and which would arise from the workers themselves, so that it would be sufficiently authoritative to lead them to exercise discretion in similar ways.

The Information-Technology Application

Description of the Design

The solution to the assessment problem would require guidelines credible to the workers, and scales that ranked degrees of impairment in terms workers commonly observed to reflect different levels of need. To establish the new guidelines, we first secured a waiver to enable the counties to replace the state-mandated assessment form with a locally created one.

We then surveyed the workers about the behaviors they observed and considered in making their distribution decisions. They responded with a total of 100 items. We asked them to assess clients along these dimensions and list their service awards. Our data analysis revealed that 15 items actually influenced the size of the service award.

A group of workers took on the task of describing, in physically observable terms, scale scores that report degrees of each impairment. Here, bathing is used as an example:

1. can bathe self without difficulty;
2. can bathe self with general supervision;
3. can bathe self with assistance when getting in/out of the tub;
4. cannot bathe self in tub without physical assistance;
5. must be bed bathed.

In meetings with workers, these specifications were modified further until the new assessment form could be put into use.

Throughout the project we met with workers regularly to refine the guidelines further as workers reported uncertainties in applying them to specific cases, or analysis of worker decisions indicated the need for refinement. Over time, impairment items were added, combined and/or dropped; scale terms were respecified; and the number of discriminations for each impairment on the scale was either enlarged or reduced.

The solution of the distribution problem was somewhat more complicated technologically, but it was much more difficult to negotiate with the workers.

Analysis of the workers' survey data yielded the first estimate of the average importance workers gave to different kinds and degrees of impairment. These results helped to create a crude algorithm that converted assessment information into an estimate of what workers, on average, would award in any given case.

A microcomputer (TRS-80) was placed in each IHSS district office in the three counties. After a worker made the required home visit to gather the assessment information, he/she would enter the assessment into the microcomputer, a transaction that took about 2 minutes. As it registered each score, the computer, as a check on the worker, flashed the meaning of the score. For example, the computer asked for the worker's assessment of the client's bathing capacity. The worker entered a score of 4 and the computer screen flashed the phrase "cannot bathe self in tub without physical assistance" as taken from the worker-created assessment guidelines.

After entering the assessment information, the worker almost instantaneously received a predicted award (i.e., the award all workers would, on average, make for the assessed client, based on the current algorithm). This prediction was not a mandatory award. It was merely information to guide the worker's discretionary decision.

The worker would then enter his/her distribution decision. If it was within a predetermined range around the predicted award, the computer stored the decision and the worker-computer interaction ended.

If the award was substantially higher or lower than the predetermined range, the computer informed the worker and asked him/her to enter a comment. This step helped the worker clarify either that he/she made an assessment or distribution error, or the case had one or more features not yet encompassed by the algorithm that justified a substantial variance from the predicted award. The comment captured, for the program and the DSS, new, relevant information about clients that had not been previously available for use in program decision-making. Typical comments were, "Must see doctor 3 times per week and no public transportation is available," or "Client is very independent; refuses some of the service hours offered." The comments were stored in a disk file.

After 3 months we analyzed the stored decisions and comments. On the basis of this analysis, we proposed changes in the assessment guidelines and recalculated the algorithm.

Workers and supervisors received computer-generated reports about each worker's decision-making pattern during the just-completed cycle. These reports compared each worker's assessment and distribution decisions to those of the other workers in his/her unit, district office, and county. In addition each worker received a computer-generated analysis that identified the most likely explanation of whatever error pattern the analysis revealed, and practical suggestions for improvement.

Each worker was informed about three measures of his/her decision behavior as it compared to that of the other workers. The first measure concerned the assessment decision. It told the worker if he/she reported a case load that was more, less, or equally impaired, compared to other reported case loads.

The second and third measures analyzed the pattern of the worker's distribution decisions. One measure reported the average difference between the worker's awards and the computer-generated predicted awards. (By this measure, if a worker made two decisions, one 2 hours higher and one 2 hours lower than the predicted awards, the average difference would be zero because the plus and minus signs are used in this calculation.) The final measure reported the average spread. (Here, using the same example, the average spread reported would be 2 hours, because this calculation ignores the plus and minus signs.)

For each measure the worker was told that his/her decisions were, in terms of statistical significance, higher, lower, or approximately the same as the average decisions of all workers. Three measures (assessment, average difference, and average spread), each of which could be scored in one of three ways (statistically higher, lower, or equal to all other workers' decisions) yielded 27 possible decision patterns, though some were extremely unlikely to occur. Analysis of each possible problematic pattern yielded the most likely explanations of what the worker was doing that caused the error, and the most likely corrective actions the worker could take. The computer automatically attached these analyses and suggestions, stated in the most unthreatening way possible, to the reports it generated for each worker at the end of each cycle.

Supervisors also received summaries of these reports. At training sessions for them, however, we helped them understand why they should do nothing about a decision pattern that occurred at the end of only a single cycle. In such a case the probability that some random occurrence was behind the pattern was still as high as 1 in 100, and the purpose of the system was not to expose workers so much as it was to give them the information they needed to correct themselves. A pattern that repeated itself over two cycles had only a 1-in-10,000 chance, and over 3 cycles a 1-in-1,000,000 chance of having a random origin. Then a supervisor would have more incontestable authority for intervention.

We held unit meetings with workers to review their reports, discuss their comments, and identify changes in the algorithm and assessment guidelines recommended by the analysis of their decisions over the last 3 months. Then we revised assessment forms and the computer programs; we put the refined distributive-rule formula in the computer program; and the cycle began again.

Implementation and Operating Experience

It is impossible to describe adequately in this brief paper the experience of implementing the IHSS DSS. The list of qualifying terms that would have to be justified in the telling would include exhausting, maddening, rich, infuriating, profoundly satisfying, and deeply disappointing. But I hope the following summary statements can collectively give some hint of the implementation experience.

Implementation with the Workers   As workers began to realize that their worst fears (e.g., computers would replace them; clients would be dehumanized; worker discretion would be taken away) were unjustified, acceptance, at least in the sense of peaceful coexistence with the DSS, grew substantially. Some workers became active, intelligent improvers of the system. A much smaller number remained in the permanent opposition, but they found it increasingly difficult to act effectively against the system's technological or interactional development. As one measure of success, after the project was closed down in one county agency, workers from two of the three field offices submitted petitions to their directors and boards of supervisors protesting the removal of the computers.

What success was achieved with the workers could be attributed to a variety of factors. The DSS substantially reduced paperwork for the workers. We continuously revised programs to reduce the time it took for workers to input or receive information and to correct entry mistakes. We also made the system allow workers to enter their assessments, receive predicted awards, and return at a later time to enter their decisions without having to reenter the full cases.

Because workers raised this fear, we initially decided that supervisors would neither reward nor punish any worker for decisions the computer evaluated. This precaution was necessary to free workers to give an award different from the predicted one, which they had to do if the algorithm was to improve over time.

When the project began, we programmed the computers to allow a wide range of awards so very few workers would be asked for explanations. This had two great advantages. The initial interaction between the large majority of workers and the computers was positive — the computers implicitly conveyed to these workers that their award decisions were equitable. And, the worker decisions that the computer challenged had such clearly deviant elements that it was easy to categorize the decisions as inequitable or to use them to improve the distributive formula. As worker confidence grew, the range of unquestioned deviance was made narrower.

The project staff assumed the full responsibility for capturing worker suggestions and feedback regularly; for reporting to workers about how and why their ideas were or were not used; for preparing workers for every change in the forms, policies, algorithm or other routines; and for preparing workers for anything the staff could anticipate might go wrong such as hardware and software problems, complications or frustrations arising from actions taken by those higher in the chain of command, supply shortages, communication failures, and delays affecting promised actions or events. No single element of the implementation process was especially difficult, but collectively it represents a substantial effort, the requirement for which never abated.

Some specific attempts to be responsive to workers failed. Workers said that they wanted to continue to tell the clients during the initial home visits what their service awards would be. Returning to their offices to interact with computers did not allow an immediate response. Voice synthesizers added to the computers would have enabled the workers to phone the computers to enter the assessments and receive the predicted awards. Equipping workers with calculators programmed with the latest algorithm would also have enabled them to determine the predicted awards while still in the field. For a variety of reasons, these suggestions came to naught.

Workers, sometimes out of interested curiosity and sometimes out of hostile skepticism, wanted to know how the computer converted an assessment into a predicted award. Though the project staff offered several times to explain the logic and underlying mathematics, only a small group of workers in one agency accepted the offer.

Implementation with the Hierarchy   During the project's first year we rarely approached supervisors so that our efforts could be directed to eliciting the more vital contributions needed from the workers. In the second year we held regular training sessions with the supervisors to help them understand their role in the DSS. The major task was to train them to interpret the computer reports and to clarify supportive supervisory interventions. Supervisors from all three counties met and, over time, common practices began to arise. One major problem was the consistent failure of some supervisors to participate in these sessions. Even more disappointing was the inability of many supervisors to conceive of themselves as leaders in the program with strong roles to play in adjusting program rules over time.

At the level of agency director, one of the three never got involved in the project. He only sought assurance that none of his mid-level staff had any complaints and, even more important to him, that the project had no dollar cost to his agency. The other two directors were much more positive and available for project problem-solving. Both were instrumental in arranging to continue the technology in their agencies after the project ended.

We made vigorous efforts to induce relevant state officials to plan for the implementation of project technology in other counties. The greatest disappointment in the project was the failure of these officials to move in this direction. They did not deny project accomplishments; it was just more important to them that the legislature no longer was pressuring them about the IHSS program. Their efforts went to programs that were livelier objects of political attention.

Project Results

When the project began, 60% of the variance in service awards was explained by the variance in client characteristics. When the project ended, the figure was between 85% and 90%. Thus the 120 workers in the three demonstration counties, many of whom never saw or spoke to each other, came to follow the same rules and apply them consistently. The project accomplished this while it eliminated many top-down rules and guidelines, and reduced the detailed and onerous hierarchical supervision.

The Next Steps:
Plans for the System's Development

State officials decided not to expand the use of project technology. Project staff members, particularly the principal investigator, were in a position to challenge the state decision in a politically credible way, but did not have the energy to do so. We developed strong doubts about the ability of state bureaucrats to implement the project successfully elsewhere. Following the dictum, "If you can't do any good, at least don't do any mischief," we abandoned the effort at the state level.

The project staff used its connections, however, to insert language into the state budget act that required state bureaucrats to continue to support any efforts the three demonstration counties made to continue to use the DSS. This requirement made permanent for these agencies the waivers granted by the state for the demonstration period. After the project officially ended, one of the demonstration agencies hired two former project personnel to expand its DSS to generate information to facilitate budget planning.

The most important postproject development occurred as several former staff members, using the experience gained during the 3-year demonstration, helped argue for, design, and then implement a much more ambitious DSS, summarized below.

Similar or Related Systems in
Other Organizations

The Multipurpose Senior Services Project (MSSP), with a $40 million budget, is the largest social-services experiment ever sponsored by the state of California. Its primary mission is to establish and test an alternative long-term-care system for the frail elderly. One aspect of this complex undertaking is the creation of a DSS. The DSS is needed to help case managers construct minimum-cost service bundles that would maintain each client in the most appropriate residence.

Both the IHSS and MSSP systems involve the use of computers to provide relevant, timely information to line workers to guide their discretionary service decisions. The systems also use worker deviations from prevailing decision rules to improve those rules. Both systems make possible the creation of guidelines from the bottom, up, rather than the more conventional flow of standards from the top, down.

The major difference is in the informational complexity relevant to the major decision each DSS addresses. To answer the IHSS question, "Given a budget, what is each client's fair share of undifferentiated service hours?" the DSS needs to process only two kinds of data—client characteristics, and worker awards.

To answer the MSSP question, "What works for whom and, given a budget, which client should get how much of which services?" the DSS must process four kinds of data: client characteristics; where and for how long a client remains in each of several possible residences (e.g., home, noninstitutional community facility, intermediate or skilled-nursing facility, acute-care hospital) or "absorbing states" (e.g., death, drops out of project); the quantities and kinds of services (regardless of the number of providers involved) each client received in each residence stay; and the costs of services. This information is required to create the algorithm that advises each worker on the most efficient service bundle to offer a client. To promote efficiency the full design will computerize a number of office routines, including a note pad (the basic source of demographic information), a calendar-date book, and automatic telephoning.

The prototype of the MSSP DSS was to be completed soon (1985). It then will be implemented in up to eight MSSP sites throughout California. The implementation process, in which workers and supervisors must become involved in improving the algorithms and the DSS, will probably provide many of the same experiences as the IHSS implementation experience.

In another development the School of Social Welfare applied (Spring, 1984) for a share of the $10,000,000 IBM recently contributed to the University of California at Berkeley, in part to promote the use of computers in teaching. Microcomputers will be programmed with the decision rules of perfectly functioning social-service agencies of both the maintenance—IHSS— and people-changing—MSSP—kinds. Students will learn the relevant theoretical contents with specifically prepared didactic materials and will apply that material through computer simulations of line-worker, supervisor, and manager decision problems.

Steven Segal (Baumohl & Segal, 1981), who has spent many years studying the placement of former mental-hospital patients in community care facilities, has proposed a computer-assisted brokers' market model made to help case managers deal with the complex relationship between client and facility characteristics. "Computers are often wrong, for their premises are not better than our own," he writes, "[but] they are positive wizards at keeping all the facts in mind. This is their great value, especially in conditions that inhibit reflection" (p. 60).

Periodic facility surveys and data from archival sources would yield updated analyses of placement contexts. His own research, augmented by the ongoing experience captured by the brokers' market model in operation, would yield the predicted client outcomes along dimensions of interest (e.g., client integration in facility or community) for various client-facility-community combinations. As in the IHSS and MSSP cases, the computer predictions would serve as advice to case managers for decision or discussion purposes.

Issues Raised and Lessons Learned

The IHSS experience left us with the overall conclusion that properly implemented DSS can substantially increase the amount of rational decision-making in social-service organizations (i.e., decision-making that advances the organizational mission rather than merely the organization). However, we found that it is extraordinarily difficult to realize this potential, and that raises the issue of whether or not the effort involved is worthwhile.

We cannot offer a definitive answer to that question based on the experience of a single project. All we uniquely have, however, is that experience. What follows, then, can claim only that degree of authority. It is organized as a set of issues or problems not specifically developed thus far but which we think are probably inescapable.

The Management of the Research Team Is a Substantial Exercise

The creation of a DSS involves different people with different talents trying to solve different problems in different and often conflicting time frames. Masses of data yield information at one rate; line-worker impatience with the algorithm grows at another; political opportunities and dangers arise at still another; and bureaucratic and other accountability demands accrue at even a different pace. In the absence of strong research-team management, there is little chance that a true team will ever exist. Even when they give it a good try, different kinds of specialists feel inept at grasping, let alone sympathetically carrying to their own work, the problems that arise in each other's domains. The mutual support and coordination needed by the overall objective do not occur spontaneously.

At various times, and sometimes for a protracted period, the most urgent or most interesting problem faced by the project requires a focus on one kind of expertise and a lack of attention to the others. Maintaining everyone's sense of involvement becomes difficult. And if the importance of particular varieties of expertise is transformed into perceptions of the importance of particular individuals, the possibility of an effective team effort erodes further.

All members of the team more readily admit some skill deficiencies than they will others. For example, it is one thing to accept that one does not know linear programming or regression analysis; it is quite another to admit, even tacitly, that one knows little about human relationships or what should be done about the latest threats or opportunities arising from the bureaucratic or legislative arenas.

A single demonstration of quantitative or programming expertise can be sufficient to establish leadership in that area. It is much more difficult to do so with reference to the skills based on vaguer bodies of knowledge. This can have the doubly problematic effect of the team too uncritically accepting technical conclusions, and being too tentative or argumentative about solving strategic, tactical, and human-relationship problems.

A DSS of the IHSS Type Is a Substantial Political Exercise

The core product or contribution of the IHSS DSS is an algorithm that represents the workers' collective mental process for converting an assessment into an award. The creation of a good algorithm is largely a matter of technical skill, but the work cannot proceed unless certain political problems are solved.

The first set of political problems arose early in the project. They occurred when unanticipated barriers to the development of the algorithm became clear soon after implementation began. The major barriers were the need for a waiver from all state assessment and time/task schedules, and authorization to use worker-created guidelines. State officials did not deny our argument that these requests were logically derived from the goals of the state-approved-and-funded proposal. Nevertheless they said a host of legal and administrative concerns necessitated a refusal of our requests. It took organized pressure from county agency officials and the threat of legislative action—all won at some cost in time, energy, and political credits—to overcome bureaucratic timidity.

During the long middle period of the project, there was an endless sequence of smaller political challenges. These included implied threats from the workers' union; constituency-building activities among legislative consultants, workers, selected high-ranking bureaucrats, and officials from nondemonstration counties; and efforts to neutralize excessive, sometimes mindless, and always time-consuming formal accountability demands (e.g., monthly progress reports that no one read).

The most significant political problem we faced—and failed to solve—arose out of the increasing efficiency of the algorithm. First we succeeded in creating an authoritative decision rule in each district office, albeit a necessarily different rule in each of those offices. Then we created an effective county-wide rule, though a necessarily different one for each county. The achievement of the next step—a common intercounty standard—required that the state award equitable IHSS budgets based on county case-load characteristics rather than the varying abilities of the counties to argue their cases and make political fusses.

This requirement became clear to us and was anticipated with the state at the end of the project's first year. It was more and more forcefully argued in more and more different ways. The influence of a sympathetic leading state senator was brought to bear and the project's principal investigator took a leave from his academic post to serve as a consultant to the state assemblyman who chaired the legislative committee that controlled the budget of the relevant state department. But all to no avail. As mentioned earlier, we were able to secure the use of the technology beyond the project's term for the demonstration counties. Since that extension is all that remains operational from our total effort, it is a deeply disappointing result.

A DSS of the IHSS Type Is a Substantial Technical Exercise

Excellent data-analysis, model-building, and programming skills are needed to create a successful DSS. In addition to technical competence, there must be creative ability, a term difficult to define.

Creativity in programming, which more than anything else determines the relationship of the worker to the computer, is crucial. The increasing use of the term "user-friendly" conveys the widespread acceptance of the point. However, the usual, or at least minimal meaning of the term—commands should be in everyday English—is not nearly sufficient.

A more demanding and necessary standard is reflected in a plea made by a 22-year-old programmer who worked on both the IHSS and MSSP systems. With reference to the computerization of MSSP office routines referred to earlier, he wrote:

The task for the system developer is to organize and present the (office) system in a way that is understandable to the user. To make a system understandable, a familiar paradigm must be used. As analysts and programmers, we see an information system as a program operating on a data base as specified by a user. We live in a world of relational and hierarchical systems, of keys and commands. Social workers don't, and there is no reason they should. Social workers live in a world of desktops and filing cabinets, folders and forms, mail and memos, typewriters and copiers, reports and phone calls, and not least, clients and decisions. The more closely we can stick to that paradigm, the more successful our system will be.

Using the office paradigm for the more general office information system leads to an unusual system design. First, we should try to use office reference points whenever possible for operations and data structures. Icons representing telephones, waste baskets and copiers will be more natural to workers than commands or menus for invoking the operations of automatic telephone dialing, file deletion, and printing. File cabinets, drawers, folders, and contents with separate datebooks, reminder books, and note pads will be more usable than some abstract hierarchical file directory structure. Secondly, we should attempt to provide a "modeless" environment. Programmers are quite used to modes on computers since, until just recently, doing anything on a computer depended on knowing exactly where in the operating system or program you were, what the system expected, what commands it accepted. As programmers and analysts we have all been "in" a text editor countless times. I don't know a social worker who has ever been "in" a typewriter or note pad. An office worker doesn't get out of telephone mode and go into file retrieval mode; he simply puts down the phone and opens the filing cabinet. [EDITORS' NOTE: This is another expression of what Kay calls the "user illusion." See Chapter 2.]

In the area of data manipulation, creativity is necessary to tease knowledge from the masses of data (including elements that are conflicting, and/or incomplete, and/or superfluous, and/or erroneous) that are the raw input into a DSS. The formation of an algorithm requires powerful statistical techniques not typically in the repertoire of those who most often evaluate social-service programs. For example, because Markov chains and similar techniques are relatively unknown, the analysis of decisions made in a dynamic rather than static context are rare in the field. Certainly the MSSP DSS could not be created without these complex techniques.

Otherwise highly qualified technicians (i.e., econometricians and other creators of measures and analysts of data) still need creativity to meet the challenges to their trained incapacities presented by the DSS.

A problem of this type that we had to guard against was the technician's tendency to create or select measures that eased the creation of the algorithm but that workers would neither accept nor use. As another variant of this problem, those with the greatest expertise in and patience for developing the needed scales acted as if they had never experienced very lengthy questionnaires like the ones they issued to workers. Their trained incapacities made it extremely difficult for them even to guess at the predictable frustration that caused workers to return consciously false and incomplete data. At other times, with regard to both the relatively simple measures and the unavoidably more complex ones, technicians either did not appreciate the need to explain them to practitioners, or tried to do so and failed very badly.

Conclusion

The largest issue raised, "Given the difficulties and requisites involved in creating an effective DSS, does it pay to try?" must have an affirmative answer. As I whispered to the skeptical chairman of a legislative hearing concerned with the state department's request for funds to computerize its tracking of children in foster-care placements, "It's possible to screw things up with a computer, but without them there's a zero chance that we will make better decisions tomorrow than we were able to make yesterday."

That made sense to the chairman; the department got its computers. Now it is up to them and us, in the light of our growing understanding of what it takes to win, to get on with the winning.

DISCUSSION OF
INFORMATION TECHNOLOGY IN SUPPORT
OF SERVICE-DELIVERY DECISIONS
by Richard H. Calica

Opening Statement

Pruger's paper, "Information Technology in Support of Service-Delivery Decisions," was written to address the broad area of how computers might assist the direct practitioner in his or her task of delivering of service to clients. Computers are typically utilized to solve an array of management problems from bookkeeping, financial modeling, and statistical record-keeping to monitoring social workers' unit output and billing for service. While these are necessary tasks appropriate to computerization, the more interesting questions lay in the uncharted territories of decision support systems and expert systems—namely, the use of sophisticated programming to enhance both the delivery of help to those who suffer and to enhance the care-giver's capacity to discover more about how to help those in need. If the social-welfare field is decades behind the business world in the more mundane aspects of computerization of rote tasks, it is light years behind in even conceiving of the use of computers to facilitate service provision. Pruger not only makes a tremendous contribution by reporting on a project that utilizes computers to enhance the equitable distribution of resources to clients, but as in a Bach fugue, he intricately interweaves the themes of system design, prototyping, organizational development, and the use and misuse of the user community into a statement that has significant implications for the development of decision support systems in the future.

The social work field is still more concerned with the management of numbers than it is with grappling with the issues of direct-service provision. This can be seen in the contrast between Newkham's discussion in "Information Technology Applied to Facilitating Practice" and the work of Pruger.

Newkham's paper is an example of the attempt to rationalize a legitimate management need for information into an innovative and helpful tool for on-line workers. While the information system that he describes was needed, and while careful attention was paid to the details of inviting worker participation in implementation, the information problems as originally stated by Newkham are management information

228

needs. If an individual worker requires 512K core of memory, 438MB of disk storage space, $100,000 worth of hardware and $150,000 of software to determine how many cases are currently being carried as well as which ones are active or inactive, that worker has a big problem. A large organization's management might need such peripheral equipment to collect aggregate data, but none of what was described as the purposes of the Heart of Texas system addresses itself to direct-practice issues. Pruger's paper, in contrast, is directed toward an interesting aspect of information directly relevant to direct service, that is, which psychological, social, and biological factors workers take into account when determining the levels of disability and need of elderly clients. Pruger and his project team remain acutely aware of the complex set of motivations existing at all levels of the organization within which their experiment in information technology takes place.

Both Newkham and Pruger describe initially successful and useful systems. Both are sensitive to the need to involve line workers in the development and implementation phases of system design, and both claim to support the workers in the provision of direct services to clients. Management's enthusiasm for information systems should not lead to the delusion that line workers have been directly aided by their efforts. Pruger and his team do not suffer from such a delusion.

Before examining Pruger's contribution in the context of the important issues and concerns that are emerging, I would like to direct the reader's attention to the relationship of the scenarios to Pruger's work and the theme of the conference in general. The scenarios are a grounding in reality for us (and particularly for those of us who are not currently involved in the direct practice of working with those who suffer). They give individual case examples of problems facing workers and clients so that we can attempt to creatively apply our knowledge of the capabilities of hardware and software to the provision of services to our clients. While all the scenarios provide a rich opportunity to explore the relevance of information technology to the practice of social work, I will highlight several of them to highlight practice, as opposed to management, needs.

Garrett's scenario offers a case situation that poses several problems, most of which do not require the direct use of information technology. Computers cannot assist relatives in deciding if they want to donate bone marrow, nor can cooperation between union members and their unions be aided by information technology. These are people-to-people issues and it would be inappropriate to force them into the frame of reference of computer technology. It is not our intent to replace what is uniquely a human experience with an interchange between a terminal and a person in need of human contact. [EDITORS' NOTE: Information technology could inform the decision-makers and support the cooperation of groups via communication, but there is a unique human role in both that is being emphasized here.] Problems in the areas of travel arrangements and eligibility for benefits can be aided by on-line flight information and free text-search capabilities of eligibility regulations.

The scenarios by Palombo and Geiss direct us to the exciting potential of networking by computer to share information about the availability of people and information relevant to the problems confronting both clients and workers. Search and retrieval of bibliographic information, expert consultation, or peer-group support activities are all possible and helpful aids to workers and clients.

The scenario presented by Koerber suggests that information technology can be used to train social workers in particular problem areas. It is within this general area that Pruger's paper may be categorized. The efforts of Pruger's group not only helped them discover the decision-making rules in a particular service area but served as instruction to workers to insure the validity and reliability of their decision-making behavior. As a final note on scenarios, both Vallee and Koerber address the tracking of detailed information on individual clients to identify dangerous individuals or patterns of dangerous behaviors. Information technology makes it possible to keep such detailed records and the temptation to do so is great, particularly in the areas of child abuse and neglect. If only we kept detailed records on individuals, perhaps we could predict the possibility of abuse and prevent the senseless suffering or death of a child. Vallee's sobering example of what can happen when inaccurate information is used to make critical decisions makes us wonder if the technical possibilities are more of a burden than a help and once again supports the tired phrase "garbage in, garbage out."

The Organizational Setting and the Information Problem

Our introduction to the organizational setting and information problem brings us to a major concern: How shall priorities be set for the tasks to be supported by information technology? Pruger shows us how a complex set of competing (but perhaps not mutually exclusive) demands set the stage for the introduction of computer technology. The state legislature and the management of the state welfare department were concerned with the uncontrollable rise in the costs of in-home social services (a program that serves the disabled and elderly with the goal of maintaining clients in their own homes and forestalling the use of expensive nursing homes and acute-care hospitals). The author extends the definition of the problem to include the ethical concerns of the equitable distribution of resources:

> Equity requires that clients with like degrees of impairment receive like service awards, and clients with unlike degrees of impairment receive unlike awards, with the more impaired receiving more services than the less impaired.

The problem to be solved now includes not only how much is spent but what are the rules for determining how much is spent on whom. Line workers are required to make two types of decisions that have both ethical and financial implications: What is the degree of each client's need (*the assessment decision*)? And how many hours of service per week should each client receive (*the distribution decision*)? As Pruger points out:

> Both decisions require the exercise of worker discretion. Hierarchically created guidelines necessitate that exercise at least as much as they restrict it. Equity additionally demands that all workers exercise their discretion in the same way. Moreover, they must do it voluntarily, since there is no way to compel their behavior.

Here Pruger highlights the reality that workers' discretion is beyond the control of administration and that their cooperation in exercising this discretion towards mutually agreed-upon ends must be voluntary. This is the practical argument for designing systems from the bottom, up. Pruger's expanded definition of the information problem to include the notions of worker discretion and the requirement of equity puts a new wrinkle on the issue of how decisions are made, what information is to be collected, and for what purpose. In this example the initial motivating factor for computerization was an administrative concern about cost control, but the problem was expanded to include issues of social justice and began to focus on the client-worker interaction and the worker's decision-making behaviors in that context as the area for exploration. We begin to see a system that does not view the service-giving-level concerns as mutually exclusive of the administrative-level concerns.

With his brief explanation of the public-welfare agency and legislative context within which the problem exists, Pruger also introduces us to the political aspects of information-technology implementation. Legislators, government agency administrators, line workers, and university professors all have different interests and motives for supporting or resisting the use of technology. He points to the complexity of these issues and the necessity to expend a great deal of time, thought, and effort in accounting for these variables while planning and implementing an information system.

While defining the information problem, Pruger also alerts us to other issues in the implementation of information technology. Staff members' resistance to implementation comes from the expectation that computerization makes their jobs harder, eliminates some of them from the work force, or monitors their performance for punitive reasons. In addition, there are some who maintain that "it won't work." The project staff is faced with a problem of organizational change that requires as much or more attention than the technical details of system design. The issue of staff motivation to participate in such an undertaking also has roots in the social workers' view of their role. If it is the social workers' idea to represent the service of their agency and see that people make maximum use of the resources it makes available, then they are more likely to be motivated to participate in an activity that could be seen as having a potential benefit to clients. However, if social workers view the agency as being there to help them do "their thing," motivation to participate in the use of information technology will be lacking. These issues are not unique to the social-welfare field, and those who fail to address these issues will produce disastrous results.

The Information-Technology Application

An endemic problem with the use of information is the imposition of data collection from the top, down. The service workers are continually asked to collect data that have no meaning for them. Pruger describes a project that recognizes that the service workers' cooperation is necessary to implement an information system but that the workers are the experts in explicating how decisions are made. In this project, worker input regarding what information was needed to determine the client's true degree of need was used to modify administrative rules as well as to help design the decision system.

His description of the system-design process highlights the issues of top-down versus bottom-up system design. This study illustrates the issues raised in Henderson's keynote paper and extended in discussion. Pruger gives a real-life example of the evolution of a system through successive approximations. The system designers and users learned from experience. Modifications of the system were made based on this learning, and the system was refined.

The act of designing the system directed participants to the issues of what it was exactly that the social workers were doing and what kinds of decisions they were actually making. This inquiry was done in what appeared to be an atmosphere of respect for the worker, and the project staff was sensitive to the issue of not using the system as a punitive tool. As data entry by workers was used to first establish norms for degrees of impairment and the amount of the service award, and then to monitor individual workers' decisions against group norms, the project staff attempted to preserve an atmosphere of inquiry and discovery as opposed to inquisition and destruction. The very act of designing and using the system added to the knowledge base of the individual workers and to the field as a whole.

Although the system was implemented on a microcomputer, it is dangerous to believe that advances in technology and the drop in the cost of hardware make these systems readily available. The project staff analyzed the weights workers were giving to different kinds and degrees of impairment and created a crude algorithm that converted assessment information into a prediction of what workers, on average, would award to a client in any given case. The expense for this expertise, when combined with the costs of attending to the organizational aspects of design and implementation, are not trivial. While workers may be the experts in specifying relevant elements in decision-making, they could not create algorithms or program systems. Off-the-shelf software and powerful but inexpensive hardware put certain capabilities into the hands of everyone — word processing, data-base management, financial modeling, accounting, and list management, for example. Integrated systems (if they are indeed desirable), decision support systems, and expert systems are beginning to be available on microcomputers. There is a complex difference between a spreadsheet program and a system that helps service workers decide whether or not to remove a child from his/her parents' care, or as in Pruger's project, how much a particular client should be given so that he/she receives what he/she is entitled to receive. And there is a big difference between a spreadsheet program and a system that guarantees that these decisions are being made in a reliable way by all workers.

The Next Steps

Pruger's paper leaves us to struggle with two issues: What would be lost if we did not use information technology in this case example? And, was the investment worth it? The use of information technology in this case contributed to social justice (by insuring equitable decisions regarding service awards), added knowledge to the field (by defining the relevant elements in workers' decisions and creating algorithms to predict awards), helped administrators and legislators (by creating the potential to predict future expenditures), and assisted line workers in the performance of their jobs (by providing them with feedback about their decision-making behavior and by handling some clerical tasks). Yet, the system was ultimately destroyed by the political forces and climate that made its implementation possible. **The implications are that we must not concentrate only on the problems of applying information technology to the arena of client-worker interactions to support the delivery of social services, but that we must also develop models of organizational change and system development that are consonant with the values of our profession and that adequately account for the political problems that will arise.**

INFORMATION TECHNOLOGY IN DIRECT SERVICE TO CLIENTS
by William J. Garrett

A study of 40 business organizations demonstrated that most companies initiate their data-processing operations with low-level systems in one of several functional areas—typically accounting (Nolan, 1979). Social-service agencies, which for the most part have become active with computers only during the past decade, have also commenced their use of computers through functional areas. Boyd, Hylton, and Price (1978) concluded from their survey of the literature that computer applications in social services have been generally restricted to compiling statistics, assisting in administrative and budgetary tasks, and processing routine forms. A survey by Comprehensive Community Services, Inc., in Chicago, Illinois (1981), revealed that 72% of the nonprofit agencies in Chicago using computers did so for financial operations. Only 28% of the system applications were related to services to the individual. If workers benefited from the computer, it was primarily by being relieved of time-consuming tasks that detracted from their abilities to provide direct services.

Application of computer technology in the delivery of services to clients is becoming more prevalent in the 1980's. This paper presents an overview of computerized systems design for the delivery of concrete services. It presents selected systems for retrieval of information about available resources, client case-tracking, electronic mail and bulletin board services, and teleconferencing.

Information Retrieval

One area of direct-service delivery that has seen progress in terms of computerization is information and referral (I&R).[2] These services use computers to refer clients to services and control client case-load vacancies. I&R services also use computers to store, sort, and retrieve data on agencies, their branches, and the services offered. Many I&R services have developed the capability to sort and retrieve data by alphabetical

---

This section is adapted from "Technological Advances in I & R: An American Report," by W. Garrett, in R. Levinson and K. S. Haynes (Eds.), *Accessing Human Services: International Perspectives*, 1984, Beverly Hills, CA: Sage.

2. For additional reading about computerization and information and referral, see "Special Issue on Computerization and I and R Services," *Information and Referral: The Journal of the Alliance of Information and Referral*, 5(1), 1983. For an international perspective, see Levinson & Haynes (1984).

order, service category, and location. The more sophisticated systems have software to sort and retrieve by such additional criteria as eligibility (age, sex, marital status, and income level), key words (such as "target groups"), type of service provider (governmental, private, voluntary), accessibility to the handicapped, hours of operation, languages spoken by service providers, forms of payment accepted, and affiliation (such as membership in a sectarian federation). For example, a program can be developed to retrieve a listing of agencies in a particular geographic area that offer day care for the developmentally delayed child who speaks only Spanish.

Two of the more sophisticated systems operate at the Greater New York Fund/United Way in New York City and at the Community Service Council of Broward County in Ft. Lauderdale, Florida.[3] The New York system maintains data on more than 5,000 locations that offer services. Workers use in-house terminals to retrieve data on services based on up to 15 variables — such as language restriction, income level, age, sex, ability to pay — that the client requests.

The system design for New York's computerized data service was developed with considerable input from information and referral agencies operating in New York City. Over 15 months were devoted to the process of planning a system that would meet the needs of its workers. As the system is prepared for further development — namely the provision of remote terminals — another lengthy planning process has begun. Extensive user input to the on-line system design has been sought. Training programs and a detailed user's manual were developed to aid the workers who must now convert from manual operations to a primarily computerized retrieval system.

The Broward County system, which has been functional since 1973, offers 18 community-based agencies remote access via leased lines to a data base of approximately 500 agencies. This computer system is one of the largest networks of independent agencies linked to a central data base.

Another computerized I&R system was the Computer Based Educational Opportunity Center (CBEOC). The system allowed a client to respond directly to a series of computer-generated questions to obtain relevant information on educational services. The computer was programmed to be user-friendly. The client identified the types of educational services needed, fees he or she was capable of paying, hours available for classes, and such. The computer then generated a listing of

3. Contact person for the Greater New York Fund/United Way: Ms. Bonnie Shevins, Director, Service Agency Inventory System, 99 Park Avenue, New York, New York 10016, Telephone (212) 557-1050. Contact person for Community Service Council of Broward County: Ms. Susan Buza, Executive Director, Community Service Council of Broward County, 1300 S. Andrews Avenue, Fort Lauderdale, Florida 33316.

available programs that would most directly meet the client's needs. This system was available in the late 1970's in several units of the City University of New York. Although no formal evaluation was ever completed, the CBEOC was used extensively by individuals seeking educational services. The system also helped provide clients with information on required supportive services such as day care or counseling. Federal funds for the program were withdrawn under the Reagan administration.

The second function of the computer in I&R services is to provide Vacancy Control Programs, or Service Opening Registries. This function has been computerized because of the frustration experienced by workers who spend time finding a particular service for a client only to discover that the agency has no openings and cannot assist the client. This most frequently occurs with such services as day care, nursing-home services, emergency food and shelter programs, senior meal programs, subsidized-housing and employment-training opportunities. To facilitate the efforts of I&R workers, communities have established computerized vacancy-control programs to provide current information on openings within these services.

Conceptually the computerized vacancy-control program is similar to the airline reservation system: A call is received, a search is conducted, and if the caller is satisfied, a reservation is made. Unfortunately the vacancy-control program is not as sophisticated as the airlines' system: Much of the data are gathered manually (each week local day-care centers must be called for openings). Vacancies must also be filled manually with the I&R service, or the client must call the agency to register for the service.

The Crisis Clinic in Seattle, Washington, offers vacancy information on day care and shelter bed space.[4] This vacancy system is one of the longest-standing systems in the country. The Crisis Clinic registers all centers with openings each week. At the end of the week, these centers are automatically removed from the listing unless the information is updated. The system can also accommodate midweek changes to the file.

Future Developments

In the past few years there has been rapid advancement in the communications component of the electronics industry. Two important developments include cable television and advanced telephone services. I&R services are now beginning to become involved with interactive in-

---

4. Contact person for Crisis Clinic: Jean Lee, Executive Director, Crisis Clinic, 1530 Eastlake Avenue East, Suite 301, Seattle, Washington 99102, Telephone (216) 747–3210.

formation systems using these communications systems (Videotex). Cable-television-based Videotex relies on cable-TV wires, a television set, and a keypad or keyboard to communicate. Telephone-based Videotex uses telephone lines, a Videotex terminal ($525 cost), and a keyboard. Both admit two-way interactive service, while another design based upon broadcast media allows only one-way communication.

Cable-Television-Based Videotex The Volunteer and Information Agency, Inc. (VIA), of New Orleans, Louisiana, is striving to provide human-service information on cable television.[5] In negotiating to win the franchise to provide cable television, Cox Cable agreed to dedicate a part of subscription fees to promoting community-access programming. These funds are administered by a city agency that awards grants to community organizations. A nonprofit organization was formed, Human Services on Cable, Inc. (HSOC), and has been awarded a grant to design a unique program service on Cox's two-way interactive cable-TV service, INDAX. Through a computerized retrieval system, information on local services will be available in text form to subscribers at home and at work. Provisions also have been made to establish volunteer-staffed Neighborhood Viewing Centers in low-income areas where residents cannot afford cable access. Trained workers will interact with the clients to retrieve data; the clients will not have direct access to the system.

The HSOC service will be known as KEYFACTS. Subscribers will be given small keypads to be used with their cable-connected television sets. A user of the HSOC system will be given a list of subject headings (e.g., [1] Food, [2] Clothing, [3] Housing) to choose from by pressing the number on the keypad that corresponds with the described subject heading. A second screen will then appear to break the major subject heading (e.g., Food) into discrete services (e.g., [1] Emergency Food, [2] Free Meals). By pressing the number on the keypad that is associated with the desired service, a listing of agencies that offer the service will appear. Further details about any particular agency can be viewed by pressing the number appropriate to the agency.

Primarily because of the cost, the KEYFACTS system has not yet been implemented. The system was to be operational in 1985.

Telephone-Based Videotex Videotex, which has been termed interactive television, is also a telephone-based, two-way interactive service that allows for remote banking, shopping at home, and electronic

5. Contact person for Volunteer & Information Agency, Inc. (VIA): Mr. John Campbell, Executive Director, Volunteer & Information Agency, 4747 Earhart Boulevard, Suite 105, New Orleans, Louisiana 70125, Telephone (504) 488–4636.

mail. Someone with a telephone-based Videotex system will be able to read the pages of the morning newspaper, review the current stock market activities, or make airline reservations. Videotex allows the user access to several different computerized data bases and transaction services through one terminal. Data are then displayed on the screen through the use of a combination of colored charts and other graphics.

Telephone-based Videotex was conceived in England more than a decade ago. Today, Britain's largest Videotex system has over 25,000 users. West Germany, Holland, Japan, Canada, Switzerland, and France have successful systems. The United States has only recently become involved with Videotex.

The Community Information Center of Metropolitan Toronto is the foremost I&R user of telephone-based Videotex.[6] Through grants from the Canadian Federal Department of Communications and Bell Canada, the center has produced over 2,500 pages of information on community services in metropolitan Toronto. This information is maintained on the Telidon system and is among the most popular interactive features of Telidon. Among the listings are a description of the center and its services, a map and listings of the 18 local community information centers in and around metropolitan Toronto, and a listing of emergency community services. Information appears in pictures and words that can be enlarged for the visually impaired. More than 200 terminals are available for direct use by clients in public places such as shopping malls, hotels, government information centers, libraries, and transportation terminals.

Client Case-Tracking Systems

During the 1940's, 1950's and 1960's, social workers made extensive use of social-service exhanges, particularly in large cities. The social-service exchange was a centralized clearinghouse for client data. It maintained basic information on each client receiving service. When the client went to any agency to receive service, the social worker could call the social-service exchange to get the existing data on that client.

Because of the cost of maintaining this system and legal issues of confidentiality, the social-service exchange was virtually ended in the early 1970's. With the advent of computer technology, the concept is being revived in a more sophisticated format.

The Community Service Council (CSC) of Broward County in Florida is at the forefront of this movement. The Broward County

---

6. Contact for Community Information Center of Metropolitan Toronto: Community Information Center of Metropolitan Toronto, 34 Kings Street East, Toronto, Ontario, Canada, Telephone (416) 286–0505.

District Mental Health Board (DMHB) has provided funds to establish a client-tracking system. As stated by Lisa Buckley (NASW, 1983):

> Use of a computerized tracking system is new. . . . Its potential for improved delivery of service to clients is impressive, although so is its potential for misuse. A tracking system can be used, for example, to detect clients who are going from agency to agency seeking a service that they are evidently not getting from any of them. . . . The clients may be making the rounds of a number of agencies purposefully as in the case of a drug addict deliberately seeking multiple prescriptions. . . . Or they may simply be confused and in need of a service that none of the agencies has thought of providing. The benefits of a tracking system to detect such clients—those who fall in between the cracks, as it were—are obvious. The negative side of it, however, involves the whole question of confidentiality. (p. 24)

The Broward County DMHB has given careful consideration to the issue of confidentiality and formed a committee of several executive directors active in the program, lawyers from the Legal Aid Society and DMHB, and an attorney from CSC. They established a thorough set of procedures to insure confidentiality. Access to information in the file is provided at three levels. On one level, any agency can request a client's file by name. These clients have given written permission for this level of access.

On the second level, only agencies in the mental-health field that are part of the system can view data on specific clients. These clients are informed that such sharing of data will occur. The final level of access to data makes some client files available only to the servicing agency.

Entry to each of these access levels is restricted by security codes, thereby maximizing client confidentiality. The legal issues of the sharing of data have been resolved through the use of client consent forms and by the fact that agencies involved in the network operate under state contracts and are, therefore, legally entitled to share data. [EDITORS' NOTE: While this approach limits the legal liability of the agencies, the ethical questions remain: Should clients give up their privacy so easily? Do clients fully understand what they are agreeing to, and to what degree does the need for service coerce agreement?]

Electronic Mail and Bulletin Boards

Use of electronic mail systems by social-service organizations is expanding rapidly. Many organizations, particularly those with nationwide membership bases, are finding these systems cost-effective for rapidly transmitting information to their constituent groups.

Electronic mail systems are generally established as part of a large national (or international) computer network. Subscribers to the network connect their local terminals or microcomputers to the telephone system with modems and call another computer through a local number (or WATS-line number). After appropriate clearance checks by the host computer, the users are able to receive and send messages. Many systems also have electronic bulletin boards that provide access for posting and retrieving information on topics related to the network.

Costs for these systems include the communications hardware (the terminal or microcomputer and the modem), communications software (when using a microcomputer), the local telephone charge, the connect time to the main computer (from $3 per hour to hundreds of dollars per hour), and a subscriber fee payable to the organization that maintains the particular service or data base.

One organization that uses electronic mail in direct services to clients is DeafNet.[7] This system, which was established in 1978, offers several hundred deaf users a vehicle for communicating. Subscribers include families, clubs, and service organizations involved with the deaf. They use GTE-TELEMAIL, an electronic service that offers computer conferencing, electronic mail, and bulletin board services.

Several other organizations offer electronic mail and bulletin board services; however, these services are primarily for agency use and are not yet functioning at the client level.[8]

The National Adoption Exchange is one organization that will soon be instituting an electronic mail system.[9] The first phase of development will provide a link between state or regional adoption exchanges and adoption

7. Contact for DeafNet: Deaf Communications Institute, P.O. Box 247, Fayville, Massachusetts 07145, Telephone (617) 872-9406.

8. Organizations active in electronic mail include:
SpecialNet, National Association of State Directors of Special Education, 1201 16th Street N.W., Suite 404E, Washington, D.C. 20036, Telephone (202) 822-7933. (Education)
Community Health Information Project (CHIP), Telephone (415) 968-1126, (415) 996-4957. (Disabled)
Tele-Information Network (TIN), Southeast Resource Center for Children and Youth Services 1J3, 1838 Terrace Avenue, Knoxville, Tennessee 37996-3920, Telephone (615) 974-2308. (Children and Youth)
Computer Users in Social Services Network (CUSS Net), c/o Dr. Dick Schoech, Graduate School of Social Work, P.O. Box 19129, University of Texas—Arlington, Arlington, Texas 76019, Telephone (817) 273-3964.
FIDONET, c/o Tom Jennings, 2269 Market Street, No. 118, San Francisco, California 94114, Telephone (415) 864-1418 (300/1200 baud).

9. Contact person for National Adoption Exchange: Ms. Marlene Piasecki, National Adoption Exchange, 1218 Chestnut Street, Philadelphia, Pennsylvania 19107, Telephone (215) 925-0200.

agencies. The National Adoption Exchange, which is currently maintaining a computerized resource file on waiting children and waiting parents, will electronically transfer nonconfidential data to the electronic-mail carrier (GTE-TELEMAIL). Subscribers can then retrieve data by a number of variables such as age of child, race, or disabilities.

The National Adoption Exchange planned to have the first phase of the system operational by January 1984. Future plans call for the expansion of the network to permit adoptive-partners groups to also have access to the data base.

The system, which will cost users $100–$200 per month plus access charges and equipment costs, will greatly reduce telephone costs, mailing charges, and printing expenses. This system will also provide a much faster response time for dissemination and retrieval of information.

Organizations interested in pursuing telecommunications may wish to contact Telecommunications Cooperative Network.[10] This organization provides discount rates on access to electronic mail networks, specialized databanks and an electronic bulletin board exclusively for nonprofit organizations. [EDITORS' NOTE: FIDONET, a computer-based network operated by computer enthusiasts for noncommercial purposes, provides national store-and-forward message services at a nominal cost.]

Teleconferencing

There have been few applications of teleconferencing—the use of communications media, frequently the telephone system, to provide interactive transmission of audio, visual and/or computer data among groups of users dispersed in space and/or time—within the social-service field. One current user of teleconferencing is the Iowa Department of Human Services.[11] This organization uses teleconferencing for administrative purposes, not direct services to clients.

The Iowa system is called CIDS—Central Information Delivery System. The system, begun in 1979, connects 146 local offices, institutions, prisons, and area education agencies to the main headquarters. This statewide system uses private telephone lines. It currently is used for audio transmission only. CIDS has been extensively employed by the 99

10. Contact for Telecommunications Cooperative Network: Telecommunications Cooperative Network, 370 Lexington Avenue, Suite 715, New York, New York 10017, Telephone (212) 689–1321.

11. Contact person for Iowa Department of Human Services: Mr. Michael Turney, Department of Communications, Iowa Department of Human Services, Hoover State Office Building, Des Moines, Iowa 50319, Telephone (515) 281–3147.

district supervisors in the Iowa Department of Human Services to conduct biweekly meetings. The system is also essential for emergency meetings, and staff training and development.

Frequently a meeting will be initiated from headquarters for all users. The system does, however, have the capability to allow for any combination of offices to be on the system at one time; for example, one or more counties could be using the system to address particular needs without involving headquarters. The system does have a privacy feature that allows for selected users to exclude all others when discussing confidential data.

Utilization rates vary from about 80% of work hours during budget season to 40-50% during normal periods. The yearly operating cost of the system is about $420,000. This includes the telephone-line fees, equipment costs, an operator's salary, and overhead. The department estimates that to provide the same level of meetings and training without CIDS would cost, in staff time and travel, five times its yearly operating cost.

In general the response to the system has been positive. Many managers appreciate the substantial decrease in travel time, and the flexibility the system offers. [EDITORS' NOTE: The advent of cellular radio extends teleconferencing to staff in the field and while traveling.]

Issues

Use of computer technology in direct service to clients has impact on four broad groups: management, staff, the client, and society in general. I will review the issues that affect each group.

Management

Cost   The banking industry, telephone services, the insurance field, accounting services, and so on, have demonstrated that the use of computers saves significant amounts of money. The same cannot always be said for social services. Most agencies that have computerized have seen their operating costs increase, not decrease. Staff members must continue to interact with clients to assess their problems. Staff reduction seldom occurs. Hardware, software, computer supplies, and computer staff all cost money. Frequently an agency must sacrifice a staff position to afford a computer—a difficult choice for management. [EDITORS' NOTE: Business has generally not experienced reduced total costs or staffing, but rather has been able to do much more, thus increasing revenues or reducing unit costs.]

Hardware   The lack of compatibility among hardware products of different manufacturers makes it very difficult to choose the best equipment. This problem is made more difficult when telecommunications are involved. Fortunately, the FCC has established uniform standards for electronic mail transmission, thereby reducing issues of incompatibility in this area.

Use of Consultants   Many managers hire computer consultants to design their systems. The resulting systems, while technologically good, often do not meet the needs of front-line workers. Finding computer consultants with knowledge of and training and experience in social services is becoming more critical in designing useful systems. [EDITORS' NOTE: For this reason Geiss initiated the CUSS Network Skills Bank in 1980.]

Client Access to Data   Many data bases have extensive information on agencies, their programs, and costs for services and staff. Some clients or advisory groups may desire access to such data. Management may not be willing to share such data. In New York one sectarian federation refused to list detailed information about its agencies unless the data were safeguarded from unauthorized use.

Quality of Services   With the proliferation of self-diagnosis and self-therapy computer software many professionals are concerned about the quality of computer-provided services. Questions of the establishment of standards, quality control, and evaluation of programs arise. As Joseph Weizenbaum states, "There is no way of controlling who gets the program, even though you recommend using it in conjunction with a counselor" (cited in Chin, 1983, p. 27).

Staff

Depersonalization   Many staff members express concern that the computer will lead to clients being treated as statistics and not as people. When staff members spend many hours interacting with computers and statistics and not with people, this problem may occur.

Fear of Change   Job security and fear of failure are prevalent. Many agencies do not spend adequate time or money preparing their staff members for the new technology. Widespread use of self-aid software may erode the service base for professionals.

Confidentiality Human-service professionals frequently mention confidentiality as a major issue of computerization. Through the use of well-defined systems and security codes, this concern can be minimized.

Client

Confidentiality Clients are anxious about the amounts of data that computers retain about their personal and financial situations. This is particularly true for clients receiving entitlement assistance.

Impersonalization When a major bank recently forced all customers with balances of less than $5,000 to use the automated tellers, there was a tremendous public outcry. Many people are still very uncomfortable with computers. Widespread acceptance by clients is still years away. The high-tech/high-touch principle (Naisbitt, 1984) must be followed.

Society

"Big Brother" Many computer systems are used to check for fraud. New York State is spending millions of dollars to develop a Welfare Management System (WMS) designed, in part, to catch abusers of entitlement programs. The Broward County system is designed, in part, to identify overpayments to public-housing clients. Much news focuses on using the computer to minimize fraud and assume greater direction in the client's life. This emphasis leads to increased resistance to computers.

Availability and Access A have/have-not society could easily develop. Access to computers may be afforded only by the rich. Proper training and familiarization with computers may not be offered to the poor.

Conclusions

Computerization can be a valuable asset to agencies and their clients. It cannot take the place of the therapeutic encounter, but the computer can help agencies provide better and faster services. Cost reductions, in some circumstances, can occur. As stated by Britton and Elverhoy (1981): "If designed in accord with the basic mission and purpose of the agency, an automatic [sic] information system can serve as a real tool for the front-line worker and client" (p. 6).

With greater availability of tested, proven computer software designed for social services, agencies should be able to implement effective systems at reasonable costs. Training of staff members is also becoming more available. Better long-term planning and use of consultants trained in human services will assist the field in developing its computer capability.

Cost and time will continue to be the major obstacles to computerization, particularly in the information dissemination and retrieval aspects of human services. **Funders, managers, and workers must be committed to expending the extra time and effort required to implement and develop a system (Schoech & Arangio, 1979). Adequate funding must be made available for development, implementation, and maintenance of systems.**

Computerization is here to stay. Its benefits to society and the human-service profession are enormous. Now is the time to develop greater understanding and utilization of the computer.

DISCUSSION OF INFORMATION TECHNOLOGY IN DIRECT SERVICE TO CLIENTS
by Dick Schoech

Opening Statement

The previous discussions focused on the use of information technology to help practitioners manage their work, provide education and training, and support their practice decisions. This discussion goes one step further by examining information-technology applications in which the practitioner plays a supportive role to people who receive services directly via the technology. Unlike the prior papers, Garrett's does not describe one experience but presents a variety of settings and applications of information technology.

The Setting

The most natural setting for service delivery by direct client-computer interaction is where the client lives, works, or shops, except when these settings hinder problem resolution. Our present human-services system is organized around the efficient delivery of scarce resources. Thus, a client, whose time costs an agency nothing, must travel to the place of delivery at the convenience of the practitioner, whose time is costly to an agency. The debate about whether this efficient method is the most effective way to deliver services can be reopened with the use of information technology that serves clients directly.

Services in which the practitioner is not directly involved in the delivery process, whether delivered in the home or office, also have important implications for traditional issues of accountability, service quality, and equity of access.

The Problem

Information technology can be used to directly address most problems that presently face the voluntary human-service providers. These are human problems of coping with society, peers, families, and ourselves, both physically and mentally. One only needs to read the problem scenarios to see the variety of problems addressed. Human services provided by public agencies have an additional feature in that their recipients are often the most deprived and vulnerable members of society who are typically in crisis states in their lives and beyond the scope of their usual coping mechanisms.

Problem-Solving Philosophy   Since information technology is to be used here to deal with a variety of human-service problems, the problem-solving philosophy is that derived from society's political and moral values. These values have been incorporated in legislation and in the values and ethics of the many professions that provide services.

Service delivery is often seen as an art that cannot be quantified rather than as a science that is subject to measurement and automation. The philosophy that the complexity of the person/problem/situation will always be beyond automation, or even technical support, is being challenged by the use of information technology in direct service to clients.

Information-Technology Applications

Applications: Information, Referral, Vacancy Control, and Client-Tracking   Perhaps no problem has plagued the human-service delivery system more than that of providing clients with easy access to information about the service system and easy access to the services themselves. Most communities have numerous information and referral (I&R) providers who constantly try to provide those in need with more current and accurate information. Providing one complete source of I&R has been difficult; presently, the client is responsible for finding and integrating the range of services needed, especially if the client's needs cut across agency boundaries.

The problems caused by having the client responsible for locating and integrating services can be seen in several of the problem scenarios. One example is the description of the couple who found that adoption agencies did not work together, which forced them to continually reapply to insure their needs would be met (see Hudson). Another example is the confusion that resulted in the human-service system when a woman was separated from her child, and they were subsequently helped by different agencies (see DiLeonardi).

The Ramey scenario on human-service integration illustrates a solution to this problem, especially if the central intake location in the scenario is moved to the client's home through the use of information technology. The scenario also points to issues that must be addressed when implementing some of the information technology presented in Garrett's paper; for example, service-integration concepts were successful, but they did not survive. Similarly, information technology will provide only the potential for more successful service delivery. Organizational and professional changes are needed to insure that this potential is actualized. One point that often arose in the discussion is that technological developments, although important, are only one aspect of the process of diffusion of innovation or planned change.

Technologies: Cable Television, Videotex, Electronic Mail/Bulletin Boards, and Teleconferencing The information technologies, described and illustrated by Garrett, for providing direct client services are only beginning to be used in the human services. However, they represent powerful tools that can be applied to some of the problems presented by the scenarios. For example, an electronic mutual-support network could greatly serve the emotional and informational needs of the woman with the rare disease called sarcoidosis (see Geiss). Teleconferencing could be a useful tool in finding a bone-marrow donor and funds to pay for the transplant operation (see Garrett). Such a national electronic conference could involve agencies, funding sources, and the clients, if they had access to information technology. The scenario describing the information needed on the rapidly growing problem of family violence alludes to the role that cable TV and Videotex could play in direct service to clients (see Vermilion). National educational programs for the general public and for professionals could be made available on cable TV, and more sophisticated programming could be made available in areas with two-way television capabilities. Television programs that record viewer responses could be a valuable source of research data. [EDITORS' NOTE: Some of these opportunities have been explored and developed to varying degrees. NASW has supported a presentation of simulated counseling sessions on cable TV. The American Medical Association presents continuing education for physicians in an all-day Sunday series of programs on various specialities which is broadcast over the Lifetime Medical Television cable-TV presentation system. Commercial TV networks have presented medical news as part of their general news programming and special information shows. Some special shows have taken viewer response "votes" via telephone calls. The National Science Foundation supported interactive-television experiments in education and social-service delivery in the early '70s.]

Other Applications The applications of information technology mentioned above have been provided through the traditional service-delivery system. That is, service providers played a major role in the design of the information technology and its use. However, we cannot assume that such roles will always involve human-service professionals. For example, the self-help-software movement, which is currently in its infancy, may involve human-service professionals only in the initial design phase, if at all. If self-help techniques were to be well published, software vendors could produce self-help software packages with little or no involvement of human-service professionals.

Self-help software is only one of many new ways that technology is supplementing human-service expertise. The field of artificial intelligence, and especially the development of expert systems that mimic human expertise in a limited domain, increases the likelihood of having firmware such as a behavior therapist, a Freudian therapist, or an addictions counselor on a microchip. Present expert systems function more as consultants to professionals than to clients, but artificial-intelligence research is making computers more intelligent and capable of understanding common spoken English. These new potentials are traditionally disseminated according to marketplace forces. If selling stored human-service expertise to individuals is profitable, then the marketplace may deliver the expertise, regardless of the values and ethics of the human-service professions.

Conference Discussion: Summary

The use of information technology in direct service to clients involves many issues, some traditional and some totally new.

Ownership of Personal and Service-Delivery Data and Assignment of Resulting Responsibilities

A key issue in a human-service delivery system and especially one in which clients interact directly with information technology is the ownership of the data collected and the responsibilities of both the owners and trustees of the data. Technology such as the "smart card" allows clients to own and be responsible for personal and service data. Information technology thus opens the debate on what data the client, agency, or funding source owns and what rights to service data are to be relinquished by clients when they apply for services. Clients' physical retention of data resolves the problems of misuse and confidentiality; however, it also causes problems because both agencies and clients need summary data to help document and improve service delivery.

If data are jointly owned or placed in trust, what are the responsibilities of each party when using data beyond what was stated in the initial agreement with the client? For example, who must approve the transfer of client-identifying data outside the agency, or who must assure that client names are appropriately purged from agency data bases? Also, what rights do client advocacy groups have to nonidentifying client data in agency data bases?

Quality of Service

Another issue is the control of the quality of services in a system where professionals are not involved because clients interact directly with information technology. For example, who is responsible for the quality of self-help software? Should a "buyer beware" attitude be taken, or do human-service organizations have the responsibility for evaluating and making public their evaluations of the quality of self-help programs? Should standards for information technologies that interact directly with clients be established and enforced in the marketplace? If so, who should create the standards and what criteria should they use? Should sanctions be imposed on professionals who develop and distribute unapproved products? What liabilities would developers incur by producing information-technology products that may be misleading and potentially harmful?

Our discussion pointed out that the ethics of self-help are different from those of the traditional service-delivery system, since self-help programs involve networks of peers and not the traditional professional-client relationship. What ethics apply to service delivery using information technology in direct service to clients?

Equality of Access

Equality of access is an important issue because many human-service clients cannot afford technology or do not have the physical or mental ability to use technology to help themselves. Having information does not insure its appropriate use. Or, expressed in another way, having access to information technology that provides a service does not insure problem resolution. Often additional resources are needed, resources such as personal understanding of each client's needs, an organizational structure to help provide the service, and follow-up to insure continued problem resolution. Even with sophisticated information technology available, human services will involve intensive professional involvement. However, information technology could be used as an excuse to abandon society's responsibilities to its members in need.

Professional Roles

Other issues concern the new roles of human-service professionals as a result of direct-service information technology. Should human-service professionals be trained for the new roles that accompany information technology, or should these roles be left to others? For example, the roles of evaluating self-help programs, or designing, convening, monitoring, and analyzing self-help electronic networks must be filled. How should new information-technology skills be implemented in professional-education programs? The skills associated with video programming, networking, computing, and working with technical consultants are some that must be considered.

Another role-related issue raised was service location. If practitioners will play a vital role as information brokers, should they not be located where information is disseminated, for instance, with a library or information utility?

Tentative Principles

Adaptive Systems   One principle proposed in our discussions was that we should develop self-correcting or adaptive systems. Adaptive systems would provide deviation-correcting feedback or information that facilitates self-correcting action. System designers typically do not automatically develop feedback mechanisms.

One method commonly used to develop adaptive systems is prototyping, or developing preliminary systems that are tried and subsequently modified in an iterative process that uses feedback of user experience. A limitation of prototyping stems from the lack of an overall conceptual framework. Prototyping may result in a very narrow system that cannot deal with sophisticated change. Another limitation is that prototyping requires having good initial information, a common language for describing events, and money to train people to understand and use the prototype system. Human services typically lack these requirements.

Another way to provide the feedback necessary for adaptive systems is to involve clients in the system-development process. Client involvement is necessary throughout the process, but clients seem to be most comfortable when they contribute in phases such as problem definition, testing, and evaluation. Client involvement in the design phase often results in more creativity, but the results may be more difficult to implement. Mechanisms are needed to insure that client feedback is not screened out by professionals during system development. Since clients' reactions to information technology often may not sound intelligent, staff members tend not to value them and to eliminate them.

One problem with the principle of adaptive feedback is that it is often difficult to distinguish corrective from erroneous feedback. Also, since erroneous feedback becomes amplified as a system progresses, an entity outside the system is needed to help eliminate erroneous feedback within the system.

Client Focus   Another principle stated was that service to clients should be an overriding concern in developing information-technology applications for direct service to clients. This focus is consistent with our professional ethics, which make service to clients the primary reason for the existence of human services. Thus, human-service professionals must be careful not to use charges such as dehumanization and impersonality as smoke screens to protect their professions from potential losses of jobs or status. Meeting the client's needs should be the criterion used in determining which roles are best performed by information technology and which are best performed by professionals.

Conclusion

The use of information technology in direct service to clients offers great potential but raises substantial issues for which principles are difficult to establish. The area of direct-service technology is most challenging because it involves working with new technologies, and employing professionals outside of the human services to develop products and set up mechanisms that allow clients to help themselves.

RELEVANCE OF THE VETERANS ADMINISTRATION DECENTRALIZED HOSPITAL COMPUTER PLAN TO SOCIAL WORK PRACTICE
by Kenric W. Hammond

Prior discussions have broadly addressed the problems of applying information technology to social-services delivery. Diverse views, agencies, computer languages, hardware configurations, and tasks have been described. Deep concerns about confidentiality and ethics were voiced. Silent questions may have been left unanswered. Whatever the concerns, computerized information systems in social work will become ubiquitous within a decade. This paper will examine some realistic goals for computer use in clinical work and consider key applications that may reasonably be implemented. I will draw upon my experience as a clinical-software developer in the Veterans Administration (VA), a large system that is now in the process of adopting a flexible, decentralized information system. This experience has considerable bearing on my opinions about priorities, strategy, and equipment.

In the past 5 years, I have had an opportunity to watch the VA make rapid progress with its computer information systems. In the effort to use computers to increase productivity and improve care, I have been involved in motivating and training staff members to use the new technology. As chief of a psychiatric unit, I have witnessed its impact on the multidisciplinary treatment process. In the following pages, I will discuss this experience and the implications for social work practice.

The VA Decentralized Hospital Computing Plan

Somewhat uncharacteristically in such a large, centrally run organization, VA software has taken an unusual, decentralized growth path: medical information systems are networked through hospital-based minicomputers and coordinate information-handling for a large number of employees hired for skills other than adeptness at the keyboard. The broad distribution of resources has been challenging, but it has offered an opportunity to develop applications growing from the needs of clinical users.

The history of decentralized computing in the VA began in 1978 and resulted directly from the availability, at reasonable cost, of high-speed, multi-user minicomputers with sufficient mass data storage capability to handle medical records. The fascinating story of how an older, centralized, batch-processing paradigm was replaced by a user- and communications-oriented network is summarized by McGuire and Cooper (1983). By 1982, decentralized hospital computing was officially established (Nimmo, 1982). Within a year, a plan was launched to install multi-user minicomputers at 169 sites, running core applications in scheduling, admissions, patient registration, pharmacy, and laboratory.

A high-level computer language, MUMPS (Massachusetts General Utility Multiprocessing System) was selected because it was expressly designed to handle data bases and manipulate text (Greenes, Pappalardo, Marble, & Barnett, 1969). Unlike the many dialects of BASIC, it conforms to a standard set by the American National Standards Institute (ANSI). Chosen with software portability in mind, it can run on many brands of machines ranging from microcomputers to mainframes, allowing useful independence from hardware vendors.[12]

Combining linguistic unity with File Manager, a data-base management system written in MUMPS and developed within the VA, and adhering to a standard but readily expandable data dictionary, has yielded a large and useful set of applications that are readily transferable among the 172 VA facilities (Timson, 1980). Adopting this system has required training and adjustment for thousands of employees but has offered unprecedented leveraging of the programmer and clinical talents available within the agency. Development has proceeded swiftly. An extensive mental-health package was tested for release in early 1985, and user groups were developing and planning applications for nursing, social work, personnel, and geriatrics.

The Current Status

File Manager has improved the participation of nonprogrammers in software development. Its flexible data-base-management tools allow clinicians to "flesh out" applications with their chosen content. Nonprogrammers can easily design information files. Regular use of this data-base approach has created a sophisticated user community.

Multisite development of the evolving, complex data-base applications has required careful compliance with commonly defined (but expandable) data dictionaries to avoid the unanticipated lethal effects of new programs on existing applications. Centrally, the Medical Information Resources Management Office (MIRMO) has been established to

---

12. The MUMPS Users Group, Suite 308, 4321 Hartwick Road, College Park, Maryland 20740, furnishes the public with information about microcomputer implementations of MUMPS programs, including VA software.

coordinate and support development in the field.

Telecommunications software now allows us to send electronic mail between sites. Specialized user groups, which now include medical-administration, nursing, mental-health, laboratory, pharmacy, social work, library, and dietetic services, routinely use teleconferencing.

Confidentiality and security have been major concerns. MIRMO has sponsored the development of a *security kernel*, which permits multilevel control of read, write, and delete access to every data field.

Clinical Applications in the VA

Importance of Satisfying Clinical Users

Clinicians must prepare to adapt their information-storage process to realize the advantages of information technology because learning to use information systems temporarily increases the burden of recording. Some motivation will be needed to make the change. If the computer is shared, the clinical user must accept the prevailing method of recording information. Information entry, whether by checksheet, keyboard, touch screen, or "mouse," will be different from pen-and-paper information entry.

Acceptance of an application hinges on its appeal and relevance. Users who anticipate tangible benefits from an information system will be more eager to learn it. If the benefits are absent, remote, or perceived as serving only the management, then management can expect intense resistance. Resistance may be manifested by the staff refusing to enter data because of objections to the "dehumanizing" nature of the computer, by sloppy and inaccurate data-gathering, and by "computer anxiety." Busy clinicians seldom bother with awkward, slow, or idiosyncratic software, unless they have written it themselves.

Few systems that address the needs of line clinicians exist. This is not because of the insensitivity of management or the data-processing department. Human clinical-information processing requires sophisticated integration of assessment, formulation, decision-making, and communication skills. Clinical systems supporting these tasks are difficult to design and are of doubtful commercial profitability. When the prospect of high-volume usage appears to justify the development costs, large institutions like the VA naturally lead in the development of clinical applications.

Case Example: The Mental Health Package   Developers of the VA Mental Health Applications Package quickly learned some of the limitations of rapid, decentralized software development as they welded together applications developed at separate sites. One quickly learned that the "right" way to solve a task at hospital A was different than at hospital B. Assumptions about the clinical or the administrative processes were frequently embedded in the structures of the applications.

For example, a behaviorist's problem-oriented medical records differ from those of an analyst or a psychopharmacologist. When a problem list was designed, it was necessary to allow for varying perspectives and attempt to accommodate them by preserving flexibility. Note, though, that the question of whether problem-oriented records were needed was not seriously debated. Problem-orientation offered the most practical way to classify and organize clinical phenomena. Table 19 shows the options available with the VA Mental Health Package.

Social Work Applications

Generic Applications for Social Work My clinical work and our discussions suggest a group of applications useful in clinical social work even though VA-developed social work applications relate primarily to the hospital environment. Major advances in nonhospital applications will probably not occur until there is sufficient interest within the VA or the private sector adapts the VA software. The applications overlap and blend but are sufficiently distinct to discuss separately (see Table 20). Where noted, the VA's Social Work Special Interest Users' Group has begun to develop applications.[13]

Client Demographics Identifying data is the keystone of a patient-oriented information system. Data help locate clients, determine eligibility, identify patterns of need, and control the duplication of services. Client registries imply a data base organized around client identifiers. Management may frequently organize the information it needs without knowing individual data, for example, by administrative subsection, cost, service rendered, or employee. While management data can be easily extracted from clinical data, the reverse is not true. Clumsy access to client data compromises the clinical utility of an information system.

This happened with the VA's outmoded management information system. It was possible to determine the number of discharges for depression and the number of appointments per outpatient clinic, but because patients' identities were lost in the aggregate, analyzing the

13. Information about progress in VA social work applications may be requested through Social Work Service (122), VA Central Office, 810 Vermont Avenue, Washington, D.C. 20420.

Table 19 **Version 3.05 of the VA Mental Health Package**

A: Main Menu

1 Clinical Record
2 Patient-administered Instruments
3 Vocational
4 General Management

B: Clinical Record

1 Profile of patient
2 Problem list
3 Diagnosis (Psychiatric/Medical)
4 Brief treatment plan
5 History—present illness
6 Past medical history—patient self-report
7 Family history—patient self-report
8 Social history—patient self-report
9 Review of systems—patient self-report
10 Crisis note
11 Patient message
12 Progress notes
13 Physical exam
14 Tests and interviews—results only
15 ECT tracking
16 DSMIII teaching program
17 Select another patient

C: Patient-Administered Tests and Interviews

1 Past medical history (patient reported)
2 Review of systems (patient reported)
3 Social history (patient reported)
4 Family history (patient reported)
5 Other tests and interviews—administer
6 Tests and interviews—results only
7 Select another patient

D: Vocational Rehabilitation Functions

1 Update job bank
2 Search job bank
3 Vocational interview
4 Print vocational interview

E: General Management Functions

1 Wait lists
2 Text entry and list

Table 20 **A Group of Social Work Computer Applications Feasible with Current VA-Developed Software**

• Client demographics	• Case and clinical activity-tracking
• Information and referral (community resources database)	• Communications for the provider community
• Information-gathering and interviewing	• Report preparation

number of appointments per depressed patient was impossible. Commitment to client registration reflects an outlook that clients, not procedures or DRG's, are the essence of service delivery.

Why, if the advantages of client-oriented data bases are obvious, are other methods widespread? One reason is that although multi-user systems are now practical at reasonable cost, organizations and governments still amortizing their investments in mainframe-scale equipment may be committed to batch processing for the forseeable future.

The amount of data that can be attached to the client identifier is an important consideration. Severely limiting the amount of information stored restricts the richness and expressiveness of clinical records. Cheaper mass memory storage has eased these restrictions considerably, and brought the capacity of computerized records closer to that of paper records.

Tracking Cases and Clinical Activity   Case-tracking is essential to case work. Social workers have devised personal systems to keep tabs on clients and to pace periodic contacts. The ubiquity of paper-and-pencil "data-base systems" suggests considerable potential interest in case-management applications. Records linking the recipient's identity to services provided could be used to improve client follow-up via letters or telephone reminders. A benefit for management would be a provider activity summary.

In addition to a suitably designed data base, the adequate distribution of terminals is important. The worker's access to clinical information must be adequate to allow regular updating and review. Although a work station in every office would be ideal, most budgets will not yet allow this. Interim data-entry methods, which use secretarial help and "turn-around" documents or checklists, can be effective if work stations are scarce.

In the VA, the Social Work User Group has begun to develop programs to track patients placed in nursing homes. Another system screens hospital admissions for high-risk demographic factors (age, chronic disease, geographic isolation, etc.), and identifies candidates for early social work interventions.

Information and Referral Data Bases   Along with the pencil-and-paper data base, a list of agencies and contacts is indispensable to the seasoned worker. Sometimes, when time, money, and energy are available, an agency will compile and publish a community-services directory. My most recent Riverside County directory is from 1978 and is less and less useful. Few of the self-help organizations that sprang up in the recent era of budget cutbacks are listed.

Requirements for a resource data base are fairly easy to specify. One would like to identify and locate a resource by its area, clients served, services rendered, eligibility requirements, and fees. A narrative description and notes by others who used the resource would be helpful. The ability to seek a resource by looking up several factors at once would be convenient. A method to regularly update the resource data base would help assure the currency of the listed information.

The directory itself could become a valuable community resource. Dial-in lines could support remote inquiries. Publishing a cross-indexed directory on paper or diskette would be straightforward. The Tampa VA has developed a prototype community-resources directory. There is considerable interest in improving it and verifying it for export.

Communication for the Provider Community   The telephone is an indispensable tool for the social worker. The spoken word facilitates while the written word affirms. Communication between workers is essential to solving problems and creatively using resources. Computer technology will vastly supplement, but not supplant, the telephone and the answering machine.

Electronic mail and computer bulletin boards will be useful in the office of the future. One can scan, analyze, and respond to electronic messages more quickly than to "call-me-back" messages. Electronic mail is self-documenting and can be printed, saved, or reformatted into other documents, if needed. It can be forwarded to someone else. Responding does not require person-to-person contact. Bulletins and announcements can be routed quickly.

Effective use of the electronic medium will require adequate and compatible communications equipment. Until this equipment saturates the provider community and communications-software standards are established, the most important effects of facilitated communication will not occur within agencies. Possible telecommunications applications include posting information and referral directories, bulletins, and providing access to remote data bases.

The MailMan electronic mail system was recently developed and is now widely distributed across the VA. It allows very flexible handling of messages and permits interhospital communication. The VA also developed and began frequent use of an electronic teleconferencing program this past year. It has enhanced consultation, supervision, and project development for management and remote software collaborators. Clinical applications of electronic mail and conferencing have just begun to be explored, but they show great promise.

Interviewing and Information-Gathering The computer-administered structured interviews that are part of the VA mental-health package free the clinician from some data-gathering tasks and allow more time to query responses that need follow-up. Specialized inquiries such as health, occupational, and substance-abuse histories may be covered in depth. Psychologists can conveniently administer and review psychological tests. Currently, social, childhood, medical, and substance-abuse histories are used for screening in mental-hygiene clinics and psychiatric wards. They save time and facilitate the identification of problems.

The VA has not yet explored using patient interviews on medical and surgical units, but their use could probably improve the early identification of cases likely to need services. Social workers could begin planning interventions earlier. Structured interviews for financial screening would also be useful to the Medical Administration Service. Prehistories in ambulatory care might improve patient flow in clinics.

Report Preparation Data in an electronic record can be pulled together in a referral document that accompanies the patient to a new placement or agency. In the VA, clinicians use programs that produce structured clinical narrative documents for histories, treatment plans, and progress notes. These are valuable for transmitting treatment information and strategies. Because they are available on-line, the continuity of care improves. If the treatment is evolving, updating the care plans can be less burdensome.

The Mental Health Package presently supports clinical text-processing, but it will require additional work for the full integration of reports and outputs. Using a microcomputer with a word-processing program as a "smart terminal" brings this capability to the enterprising user now.

New Directions for Computing in Social Work

An agency should consider its equipment configuration in terms of the size, organization, and distribution of its data base and the channels of information flow. In only the smallest of offices would a microcomputer be practical. Most agencies at a single site would benefit more by investing in a multi-user system that could handle a shared, updatable data base. For more than six users, minicomputers are the most cost-effective. Newer techniques for networking microcomputers may change this threshold.

The choice of a computer language and an operating system will be important. While a turnkey system with a proprietary or customized language may satisfy the user's functional specifications, the software's enhancement and evolution are tied irrevocably to the vendor. The VA committed itself to MUMPS because of its excellent data-base handling and portability.

It is important to know if software requires special equipment. VA programs were developed to be device-independent and run on a variety of printers and terminals without special modification. Displays are simple and formatted screens and embedded control characters are avoided. Differences between terminals are handled by tables that are called at the point of output or input rather than being hard-coded into the application. This has resulted in a desirable independence from equipment vendors and puts the VA in a strong bargaining position when making large equipment purchases. This design policy will promote flexibility in the future. Independence from vendors has resulted in the VA creating a large body of public-domain software that has set a standard of excellence in the MUMPS community. This required a commitment to in-house programming that once was criticized as inefficient, but experience with fickle vendor support has proved the value of the approach.

Increasingly, the clinician's first introduction to information technology will be via small computers. Interest in microcomputers is high, and there have been many inquiries about installing VA software on personal computers. Isolated systems are of limited use in the VA's shared-database strategy, but I believe that microcomputers serving as networked intelligent work stations have a very positive future in social work. Currently, isolation, not size, limits the processing power of the desktop microcomputer. Until techniques for sharing data bases are developed, I do not advise the wholesale acquisition of small computers. Important benefits will come when microcomputers can link in a network and share information. The next few years will prove whether newer, perhaps UNIX-based software, will allow micros to interconnect and transparently link data bases. Interprocessor communications standards like Kermit are in their infancy and their contribution is not yet assessed (Da Cruz, 1984).

If social-service providers decide to explore VA or other public-domain software and adapt it to their usage, vendors may play a role in the adaptation. Developing a brand-new system can be expensive. Borrowing and adapting public-domain software is a way to reduce development costs. The VA's commitment to maintaining backward-compatibility allows ongoing benefits from advances made by the original developer.

This, then, is the VA's message for social workers: A sophisticated information system with many capabilities for key social work tasks exists in the public domain. It is backed by the largest health-care delivery system in the free world. It is exceptionally flexible and portable and will involve a large user and programmer community. Anyone searching for a low-cost, well-explored set of applications and development tools would be well advised to explore using VA software in his/her setting. Breaking into automation will entail risks and change. The VA experience should be instructive for those who desire to take this plunge.

PART THREE

ISSUES
AND OPTIONS

by
Gunther R. Geiss
and
Narayan Viswanathan

This section is based on the conference discussions

CHAPTER 6

ISSUES IN INFORMATION TECHNOLOGY AND SOCIAL WORK: A SYNOPTIC OVERVIEW

Then came, at a predetermined moment, a moment in time
    and of time,
A moment not out of time, but in time, in what we call history:
    transecting, bisecting the world of time, a moment in time
    but not like a moment of time,
A moment in time but time was made through that moment:
    for without the meaning there is no time, and that moment
    of time gave the meaning.
                                                    —T.S. Eliot (1963, p. 163)

THE LEADING EDGE OF TECHNOLOGY AND THE GROWING EDGE OF SOCIAL CHANGE: PAST, PRESENT, AND FUTURE PERSPECTIVES

Unprecedented technological changes have occurred during this century. More profound changes lie ahead. The future may indeed be different from the past in many ways. To make the decisions that will be required, we must understand the nature of change itself—its dangers and possibilities. Viewing the future is an invitation to change. Nevertheless, looking at past experience can help us to avoid a narrow or myopic focus on a single element of change. A people without history is not redeemed from time. We live in a new space and hear old voices. We need new glimpses into the past and future. This is particularly important when dealing with a stream of innovations and the seamless web of interactions between technical and cultural factors that affect the enterprise of social work.

Change dominates the modern world, change driven largely by advances in science and the technologies they engender. The exponential growth of the enterprise of science marks the postmodern era. *Technology*, defined broadly as the scientific knowledge and technical know-how needed to make capital and labor work together to produce marketable goods and services, covers a wide range in complexity, in time, and in space, from the traditional through the complex frontier technologies. We name eras and upheavals after technologies: the stone, iron, steam, nuclear, and space ages; the Industrial, green, and computer revolutions also come easily to mind. Today, revolutions continue — in biology, in space, in electronics, and in communications.

Modern social revolutions share technological roots. The electronics revolution, which is now called the microelectronics revolution, has been in progress throughout the twentieth century. This revolution has been accompanied or followed by technological innovations that have penetrated and influenced the wider culture in which they were implanted. A dramatic example of the cascading effect of the technological revolution is the invention of the computer; that invention has, in turn, been accompanied or followed by a new wave of innovations in information and telecommunications technologies; that new wave has produced new changes in the popular culture. Technology molds society by affecting its values and by channeling and redefining the limits of actions and resources.

Trends in technology (and possibilities for advances within the known limits) foreshadow future developments. Chemical and biological technologies bring even greater capabilities to design and synthesize molecules. Advances in imaging technology (e.g., Nuclear Magnetic Resonance [NMR], Computer Axial Tomography [CAT], and Positron Emission Tomography [PET] scans) bring new capabilities to visualize, conceptualize and understand body processes (Fischetti, 1983; Jaffe, 1982; Durden-Smith, 1982), especially the physiological and biochemical bases of behavior and emotion. Rapid developments in space technology have created new possibilities in the commercial development of communications and weather satellites, and foreshadow human settlements in space. Meanwhile, computers and communications services continue to grow in power while shrinking in price; the pace is already swift and ultimate limits distant. Software is also improving and proliferating, and the developments in artificial intelligence continue to become more worthy of the name.

These innovations in physical and cultural artifacts have already become major tools in the advancement of scientific and professional disciplines whose central mission is the production and distribution of knowledge. Some educational institutions are working at the forefront of science and technology, while others are working hard to catch up and adapt to the new reality. Educational institutions are but one element of the culture experiencing the impact of social change. Equally important, service institutions (and service-related enterprises like financial institutions, as well as state and local governments), whose central mission is the provision and distribution of needed goods and services for consumers, have also resorted to the use of technological innovations (for example, Electronic Funds Transfer Systems in banking, and the New York State Department of Social Services Welfare Management System) in reorganizing their modes of service delivery. Thus, the multiplier effect of social change is discernible in the spheres of production, distribution, and consumption.

Social Work

Predictably, some of these technological innovations are now making inroads into the helping professions, in particular into social work education and practice. Indications are that the pace and rate of acceleration are increasing and will continue to increase in the next few years. Almost every aspect of educational, organizational, or professional activity has been affected in a relatively short time. New applications of technology have made existing procedures easier and led to innovations that were inconceivable or seemingly impossible two decades ago. These innovations continue to evolve at a quickening pace, and it is therefore important to try to understand and chart their evolution, and also to assess their impact. With such a pervasive and rapidly changing environment, trying to chart a course by looking forward becomes a practical necessity. There is no point in deploring or denigrating any of this or wishing that the technological fad or euphoria will wither away. It won't! It is a new reality that affects the way we think about matters ranging from service delivery to how the professional practitioners will attack new problems, that is, how future practitioners might change their approaches, concepts, methodologies, or techniques.

Social work, as it is practiced in a variety of public- and private-agency settings, is enjoying a period of innovation in its supporting technologies. Recent developments in the application and use of information technology in support of social work practice are exemplary of the innovation process that is our focus. The effort to use these innovations to best advantage contributes to changes in the structure of the services and in the services that an agency offers. We can postulate, based on evidence from the practice of social work in today's world, that technology is one of the forces that can motivate and facilitate change.

Through the applications of new forms of information technology, modern societies provide the public with a choice of services more diverse and differentiated than those that were available in the past. But, from another perspective, the increased complexity of the services provided, the diversity of services offered, and other effects following the introduction of technology are not amenable or acceptable to all users.

Changes in basic social institutions and organizational arrangements almost invariably raise questions for policy governance. The basic tenets of existing policy may no longer hold; or, if they do, the existing means of realizing established goals and objectives may no longer work. Relationships between and among institutions and individuals may be altered in ways that make some relatively worse off while others become relatively better off. The results of such shifts can be political pressures for new or modified policy goals and mechanisms for achieving those goals.

Formulating issues and options with regard to these changes meets with one immediate and serious challenge: changes are coming so rapidly and from so many directions that it is difficult for the institutions in which social work practice occurs to anticipate the patterns that will eventually prevail.

Technological Change

Nevertheless, it may be possible to foresee some of the broad patterns that are likely to emerge and to anticipate in a general way their likely consequences. It is important to do so now, because decisions made or avoided may have far-reaching consequences. For example, some potential benefits of new technology may not be realized, costs and benefits may not be equitably distributed, unnecessary burdens may be imposed on service providers or on consumers, and human rights and liberties may be compromised.

While significant uncertainties about the future remain, it is essential that we make an open and informed assessment of the implications of advanced technologies for social work practice. Many of the issues raised and discussed herein are not new. There are striking historical parallels between old issues and some of the "new" issues. Nevertheless, we suggest that, while the issues are not entirely new, the social, organizational, and service contexts in which these issues occur are new and changing. Thus, environmental dynamics must be considered in the issue-oriented analyses and discussions of this text.

The history of technology is replete with examples of initial misperceptions about the potential uses and abuses, and possible consequences, of new technologies. Over and over, technological innovations that were expected to provide new possibilities in a limited area or narrow field ended by having unintended and unpredicted effects in other areas. As a number of participants reminded us many times during our discussions, we need to reflect upon past experience to examine, understand, and assess the patterns of change that may result from the utilization and applications of new technologies. Some of the issues raised by the application of information technology are unresolved issues that get new emphasis. For example, an examination of the history of social work records, the underlying information of practice, is provided by Kagle (1984, Chap. 1), who concludes that no one form of record-keeping meets the varied needs of practice and that recording must be diverse, but it can and should be systematic. This need for diversity and the lack of standardization make the communication and comparison of records more difficult in general; but, the technology, especially database management systems, makes accommodating diversity more feasible. That is, the concept of a complex and complete data base with a data-base management system that provides a host of *user views* (specified subsets of variables displayed in particular ways) has been evolved expressly to allow a variety of users to utilize a common set of data files in unique ways (see Martin, 1984, 1981). However, the key requirement then is that if the data base is centralized it must be sufficiently complete to meet the diverse needs of the users. If the data base is distributed, each group of users can define the contents of its own data base, but must develop some commonality for communication with other groups.

Any judgment on the future of social work, its probable state, or the ways of achieving a particular desired state, is based on our knowledge of the past, the present, and the prevailing forces. Knowledge of the past is not univocal; its implications for judgments regarding the future need not, therefore, be the same. Individual commentators will always have at their disposal rather diverse premises pertaining to the facts and on this basis will formulate varying judgments concerning the future.

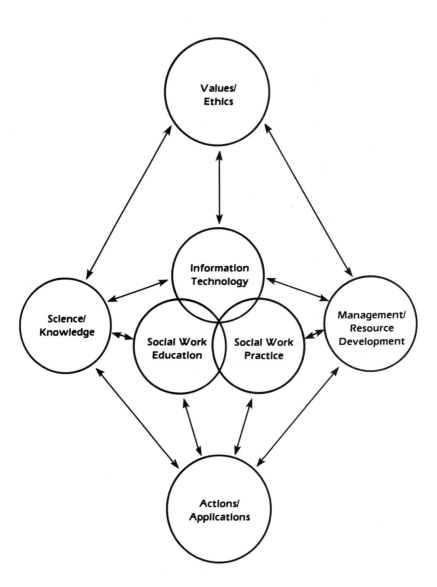

Figure 7: **A Framework for the Analysis of Information Technology and Social Work Practice and Education**

BLENDING INFORMATION TECHNOLOGY
AND SOCIAL WORK:
A CONCEPTUAL FRAMEWORK

One of the major difficulties in approaching the task of discussing the relationship between technological innovation and social work is that there are no frameworks to which we can relate — frameworks that help to define the nature of the issues and problems that we confront. What is proposed, therefore, is to create a framework and introduce it for consideration. The building blocks for this framework derive from a synoptic overview of the material that precedes this chapter. Additional elements can be incorporated into the design and development of the framework as we begin to focus upon relevant dimensions of information technology and social work. The proposed framework consists of the five interdependent and interactive components of Figure 7. Each component is the subject of one of the following chapters.

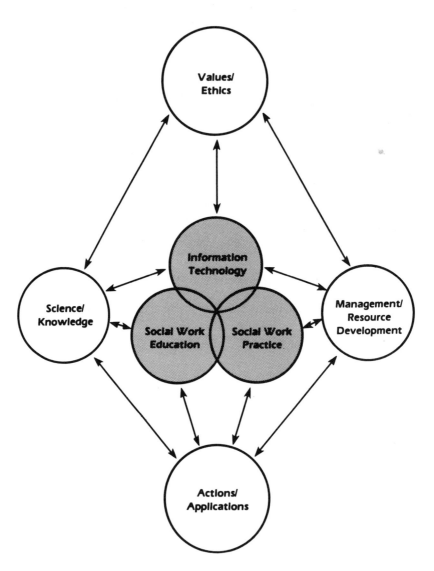

Framework for Analysis

CHAPTER 7

THE CENTRAL CORE: INFORMATION TECHNOLOGY, SOCIAL WORK PRACTICE, SOCIAL WORK EDUCATION

INTRODUCTION

At the central core of the framework, we have three interlocking circles to represent information technology, social work practice, and social work education and their intimate relationships. That part of the representation is in the form of a Venn diagram (named after John Venn, a 19th-century logician) showing the relationships between sets of items and, more particularly, the nature of their overlap or commonalities.

Information technology, as a general term, was introduced only recently, but constituent elements of information technology — for example, the telephone system — have been familiar for years. What distinguishes information technology is the way it combines a variety of communication channels with the information-handling capabilities of computers. New methods for dealing with the generation, transmission, and reception of information are proliferating rapidly. At the same time, methods of communication that have traditionally progressed separately (such as the telephone and the television) are now being drawn together — in Videotex, for instance.

A new resource of strategic importance has been developed; some refer to it as the information sciences, others as information processes, and still others as the information environment. The term employed in this volume is *information technology,* a term we think is more agreeable and more embracing than its primary competitors, *telematics* (Nora & Minc, 1980) and *compunications* (Oettinger, 1971). It is the means for the collection, storage, processing, dissemination, and use of information. Whisler (1970) defined information technology along these lines: "The technology of sensing, coding, transmitting, translating, and transforming information. . ." (p. 11). Meadows, Gordon, and Singleton (1982) provide a more recent definition of information technology as "the acquisition, processing, storage, and dissemination of vocal, pictorial, textual, and numerical information by means of *computers* and *telecommunications*" (p. 93) [italics supplied]. Trowbridge (1972) reaches out farther than Whisler and Meadows et al., and provides a sweeping view of this technology: "It is not confined to hardware and software but acknowledges the importance of man and the goals he sets for information technology, the values employed in making these choices, the assessment criteria used to decide whether he is controlling this technology and is being enriched by it" (Preface).

Information technology has been termed the Second Industrial Revolution; its later developments and widened applications in automated process controls have been called the Third Revolution. McHale (1972) observes that "the core of these revolutionary transitions and its most visible component is electronic data processing via the computer" (p. 187).

The undercurrent in most views of the technology is its relationship to the broader society and culture. "Within two decades," says Max Ways (1972) "these new information technologies have become an indispensable part of the web that holds society together. . . . The new ways of handling information have brought about fundamental changes in governmental and political processes. They have altered the psychological and cultural attitudes of hundreds of millions who have only the haziest notions of how the technology works" (p. 3). These views of information technology as an integral part of human culture and the superimposition of values and value systems on technology are consonant with the premises of our analysis.

MAPPING THE NEW HORIZONS OF SOCIAL WORK EDUCATION AND PRACTICE

The Information Technology and Social Work Practice Conference

The center-moving forces of today are the leading edge of technology and the growing edge of change. Information technology is an exemplar of a technology at the leading edge. The increasing penetration and diffusion of this technological innovation in the helping professions, through planned and sometimes unplanned transfers, is an indicator of change. Extrapolating from observed trends both past and present, we forecast that the trend will continue, and intensify, in the near future.

Since the use of information technology is a new and growing dimension of the helping professions, the professional community should critically examine and sort out the ways in which social work education and practice, for one, might respond creatively to the opportunities and perhaps even dangers spawned by this technology. To initiate such exploration and to assist us in the preparation of this volume, our sponsor, The Lois and Samuel Silberman Fund, suggested that a ground-breaking, national, by-invitation-only, working conference be organized. (The details of the conference—planning process, execution, documentation, and evaluation—are in Appendix B.) The Planning Committee (see Appendix A) chose the conference purposes to be:

- To broaden the social work profession's utilization of information technology.
  - To define information technology as it applies to the social services.
  - To explore the opportunities to apply information technology in the social-service-delivery process.
  - To examine the appropriate and necessary roles for social workers in the development and evolution of information-technology applications.
- To suggest directions for the development of information-technology applications in the practice of social work.
  - To identify opportunities for change in the education and training of social workers for direct practice.
  - To identify particularly attractive innovations and directions for research and development.
  - To identify the issues, especially ethical issues, created by adopting, or not adopting, information technology in the service-delivery process.

In simple terms, this statement recognizes the importance of enlarging the present view, and the importance of identifying directions for future development. The Planning Committee also saw the need to begin that process with a tentative identification of key issues, but with recognition that much would be contributed by the conferees. We expected that the experiences described in the papers of Chapter 5 would substantially inform this list and that the keynotes, Chapter 3, would expand our vistas. The scenario format, Chapter 4, was selected to encourage the participants to identify issues from their own experiences. Thus, by design, the following list was but a bare beginning.

- What is the state of the art in information technology vis-à-vis its utilization in the social services?
- What are the opportunities for development, and which are the preferred directions for development of the field of social work via the utilization of information technology?
- What steps are required to encourage the immediate use of information technology by the social work profession?
- What actions are required to enhance the long-term development of the utilization of information technology by the social work profession?
- What investment guidelines and project priorities would be most appropriate for The Lois and Samuel Silberman Fund?

Some Problems with the Key Terms

Some of the key terms used to designate the broad conceptual domain and specific boundaries for exploration of issues of interest to the conference were identified as information technology, applications of information technology, social work practice. Experience suggests that there is ambiguity, fuzziness, and widespread variation in the ways the professional community defines, articulates, and understands these terms. Hence, the Planning Committee felt that these key terms needed to be defined explicitly to facilitate common understanding and consistent usage. While a consensus was neither sought nor obtained, the following formulation represents a reasonable proxy of agreed-upon understanding of the connotative and denotative meanings of these terms, and it identifies some of the inherent problems.

We have already stipulated *information technology* as the synergistic combination of computers, information systems and communications. However, while the substitution of *computer* for *information technology* is seemingly common and comfortable, it is conceptually delimiting and ought to be strenuously avoided, particularly in light of the very rapid advances in communications technology, especially computer communications. Similarly, the equation of *information* with *written information* is facile and conceptually restrictive. It is particularly inappropriate within a profession that places a premium on both verbal and nonverbal communications; and it is especially inappropriate, given the advances in imaging technology, symbolic computing, computer graphics, and computer speech recognition and synthesis.

The *applications of information technology,* especially computers, in social work have been primarily to administrative, evaluative, and record-keeping problems, and also, with increasing frequency, to social work research. It is imperative for the development of the profession, its services, and technology applications that the early applications not be seen as encompassing the whole range of possibilities. Newer applications have begun to appear in service delivery and in support of service delivery. It is vitally important that we encourage the exploration and development of applications in all aspects of social work practice, and encourage participation by all the individuals involved in the delivery and use of social services. It is exactly for these reasons that the conference emphasis was chosen to be practice and not administration or research.

Social work practice is, in a similar way, often easily understood as subsuming one or another form of clinical, therapeutic, or mental-health activity, to the relative neglect or exclusion of other forms of practice (macro-practice). In some instances, the opposite viewpoint is advocated, to the neglect of clinical-practice interventions or strategies. As Alfred Kahn (1973) cautions, practice thinking based upon only one of "any type of conceptual orthodoxy, whether derived from Freudian psychiatry, behavioral modification psychology, welfare economics, neo-Marxist change strategies or organizational sociology—to cite only a few—blocks out possibilities" (p. 192). We need to be clear that *social work practice* is used here in its broadest form, which includes, but is not limited to, policy development and analysis, program development, community organization, group work, planning, concrete service delivery, clinical practice with individuals, families, and groups, research, evaluation, and administration. In a similar way, the organizational context in which social work practice occurs may include, but is not limited to, hospitals, schools, the work place, and a host of public- and voluntary-agency settings, together with private-practice offices.

Social Work Education and Practice

Technological innovations are sometimes gradual and evolutionary and, at other times, rapid and cataclysmic. The development and diffusion of these innovations often call for planned and orderly responses for their absorption and utilization. Innovations are change-oriented and negentropic; they disturb the steady state and help move systems from being closed to being open. The introduction of information technology into social work education and practice has aroused, and will continue to arouse, some disequilibrium or destabilization, at least until such time that a new equilibrium or steady state is restored.

Social work education and practice are viewed as separate but interrelated components. Significant shifts in social work practice will influence prevailing patterns or models of social work education, and vice versa.

As the wider culture in which technological innovations occur may be significantly different from the professional culture of social work, the transfer of technological innovations into social work may appropriately be viewed as the phenomenon of intercultural or intracultural transfers. Such transfers may take the form of products, processes, and the skills needed to apply technical ideas. This suggests that the process of technology transfer can be an orderly, deliberate, and planned process. The literature on technology transfer provides ample evidence of the disastrous consequences of mindless and unplanned transfers. At the same time, the literature also points to the beneficial effects of technology transfer when proper attention is paid to the process by which beneficent transfers can be effected from the host culture to the recipient culture.

Several of the conference papers and participant discussions made it clear that much is already known or is being learned about the introduction of information technology into social work education and practice. Chapter 5 boldly presents a series of experiments to implement technology in the field. The emphasis is not on the reality of technology but on the human response to its implementation and the lessons learned. Implicit is how technology can make each agency a bit better at meeting human needs and serving the client. Newkham's work in Texas allows him to conclude that information technology reduces dehumanization in the field by providing the staff the time and the ability to individualize each client's situation, to provide more resources to address them, and to shift attention from just immediate problem-solving to prevention as well. Pruger's paper about technology development in public agencies and Calica's discussion of it underline the importance of the need to build a system from the bottom, up by involving staff members in all aspects of planning and implementation. Such input allows a system to be adjusted and refined. Pruger also incorporates the equity principle in a manner that is unique to systems design and policy analysis. Lynett demonstrates how members of a staff can be better prepared to serve in a way that meets their personal learning styles and how this could be extended to prepare clients for service as well. Garrett's review of the many applications of technology in the field leads him to conclude that computers cannot replace the therapeutic encounter but can help agencies provide better, faster, and more effective social services. Hammond presents an illustration through the VA experiences and identifies the resulting public-domain-software resources.

He thereby underscores the opportunity in technology transfer. Again and again, we are led to discover technology's supportive and supplementary role vis-à-vis professional expertise. There is also a recurrence of the theme that technology can support professional efforts to work with clients to enhance the effectiveness of the service-delivery system. Thus, the developments in practice suggest the need to reexamine educational program focus, content, methods, and practice roles, and the professional stance on issues raised.

COMPILING AN ENCYCLOPEDIA OF IGNORANCE: EXPLORATIONS IN PRACTICE ROLES AND PROFESSIONAL STANCE

Does the use of information technology and its applications in various forms and fields of social work practice suggest new roles or demand new professional postures for social workers? Does form follow function or function follow form? How do forms and functions modify professional roles or postures? (See LaMendola's [1981, 1985] work for discussions of these issues.) As there is no a priori way of knowing the answers to these questions, the best we can do is to ask more questions regarding both social work roles and formal stances that the profession might adopt. Some philosophers have suggested that the path to knowledge-building might begin with admission of the areas of our ignorance.[1] This advice is most apt in this instance, and what follows, therefore, is a synopsis of ignorance together with some conjectural, visceral, and reflective viewpoints.

Social Work Roles

Does information technology offer new roles for social work, and what are they? The advent of information-technology applications in social work practice suggests new roles for the professional in the development and direction of these activities. Conversely, the need to develop an ethical component to technological decision-making and to assure the appropriateness of systems with which humans will have direct contact suggests new roles for social work outside the current definition of professional social work. Finally, the advent of infor-

---

1. Christensen brought to our attention the concept of developing the conference product as a statement of significant ignorance based upon the model developed in Duncan and Weston-Smith (1977).

mation-technology applications provides the opportunity to strengthen and reaffirm traditional, but often forgotten, social work activities — such as community organization, sponsorship of self-help groups, provision of information and referral services — where access to, and dissemination, use, and interpretation of information are the keys to successful and effective service.

What ought to be the role of the social worker if, and when, the computer or other information technology is the primary service-delivery mechanism?   Certainly, if we accept the possibility of software-based services delivered via a machine as a primary service-delivery mechanism, and we recognize the human limitations of many of the clients, then the educator, facilitator, interpreter, and supporter roles will not only remain necessary but will be even more important.

We have learned that technical staffs tend to ignore or screen out clients' evaluative comments about systems. An important role for social work then becomes assuring that systems meet client needs and assuring that client input is used in designing and maintaining systems, that is, assuring that systems truly serve the clients, and that they change with changing needs. There is no need to limit concerns of the helping professional to social-service or human-service systems; their concern ought to encompass all systems that bear upon the quality of life, and especially the lives of their clients.

Professional Posture

Is the ultimate purpose of information-technology applications to improve the service-delivery process and thereby the service delivered?   The purpose of change ought to be for the betterment of clients' life situations and thus, necessarily, change ought to be directed toward better services. Yet, most systems in place today do little more than monitor services. They contribute naught toward the services; they detract from the services because they take time away from service for tangential or indirect service activities such as data collection.

Should the profession establish standards for information-technology applications that directly involve or affect clients?   The profession's responsibility to its clients extends to all aspects of the clients' relationships with the agency and staff. It would seem appropriate then for the profession to be concerned with how clients are treated, whether by person, by person and machine, or by machine; and to be concerned with the clients' rights regarding privacy and the quality of services. How can the quality and appropriateness of technology-supported services and technology-based services be established and assessed?

Beyond the client's relationship with profession and agency is the question of the profession's concern for the client in the marketplace of services, where services may be provided via information technology but without an agency or professional auspice. This might include the public-communications-media-based phone-in help programs, and software aimed at "self help." Shall the profession attempt to influence that marketplace, and how?

How shall the profession respond to the proliferation of "self-help" software? The choice of responses was seen to be among professional regulation and standard-setting (the accreditation role), professional evaluation, review and public comment (the public-information role), and laissez faire, caveat emptor (no role). This question revolves around the protection of individuals who are probably ill-equipped to protect themselves, protection of the professional's role and responsibilities, and recognition of the rights of others to provide help.

Can technology provide solutions to moral problems and, if so, should social work take the lead in advocating such solutions? The question of how to treat client data is in part a moral one. The advent of the *smart card,* a memory chip on a "credit card" (Weinstein, 1984; Mayer, 1983; Lessin, 1982), makes it possible for clients to literally own the records of their personal data. Technology can provide a means to enhance client privacy by placing the physical record in the client's possession. Technology affects many other moral concerns such as equity, open access, truth-telling, and promise-keeping.

Since technologists seldom seem to concern themselves with the moral issues inherent in technological developments (Christiansen, 1984), another concerned group is needed to intervene in decision-making with a moral perspective—perhaps a new breed of ombudsman. Given social work's concern for the underclass, and human welfare in general, should it undertake the new role of advocate for solutions to moral problems via technology? This would, of course, demand a knowledge of technology, its implications and opportunities, beyond that with which social workers have concerned themselves in the past.

How can ethical concerns be incorporated into decision-making? Christensen's paper, Chapter 3, and the discussion of it show that there is at least a framework available for analyzing the ethical consequences of decisions about the utilization of technology. How does one get that framework adopted as part of the decision-making process? Shall social work take on the role of advocate for ethical analysis in decision-making, especially when technology is involved?

Should social work accept the role of enabling the disenfranchised to have access to and use of information technology?   There is evidence (Anderson, Welch & Harris, 1983; Anderson, 1983) of inequity in the distribution of computers in elementary-level classrooms. Where the poorer districts are on a par with wealthy districts with regard to equipment, there is inequity in how the equipment is used, that is, the wealthy districts develop mastery of the technology, and the poor districts use it to reinforce long-division processes through drill-and-rote programs. There is evident sexual bias: males predominate in the use and study of computers. (See Lockheed, Nielsen & Stone, 1983, and Zimmerman, 1983.) There is evidence that such bias does not exist at early ages (about 3). The poor are less likely to be able to afford the equipment and the use charges associated with networking and information-system access. In fact, they are less likely to be able to use the technology effectively if they are given access (Childers, 1975). Who will speak for these groups?

Should the profession take an active advocacy role in favor of electronic networking?   Networking is an inherent aspect of the information and referral activity, and of access systems in general. The professional needs to remain current, to be able to easily exchange and share information, and to provide mutual support. These are a significant part of professional supervision and interaction and can now be extended to a much broader domain than the agency.

   The opportunity also exists for the networking of clients with professionals, resources, and other clients. What is not clear is how to provide access for clients, and how to assure equality of access. Further, there is the need to support clients who may not be prepared to use electronic networking.

Should social work take responsibility for advocating and developing the "grapevine alternative"?   Vallee's discussion, Chapter 3, of the "digital society" and the "grapevine alternative" suggests that the latter is more congenial to social work objectives and would enable or facilitate the achievement of some social work goals of long standing (see Nora and Minc [1980] for an elaboration, and the French view). This aspect of information technology, if adopted, could advance both research and practice in social work and, as noted earlier, might be a key to enabling the social changes begun in the '60s. Computer communications, especially, can be without color, ethnicity, sex, or other discriminating characteristics at the discretion of the communicators.

Is it appropriate to rationalize decision-making in social work practice via information technology?   Much of the discussion, and especially Pruger's paper and LaMendola's discussion summary, in Chapter 5, pointed to the political aspects of agency life. What is the place of particularly rational systems in that context? Technologists assume that to rationalize a system is to improve it, and that is a highly valued goal for them. Discussion around the use of electronic communications, especially electronic mail, identified it as a process fraught with the common fear of "writing it down." Yet, there are also reports of disinhibition caused by the technology.

  If we agree that applying rational systems is appropriate, then how is it most easily done? Which rationality will prevail — economic, political, technical, ethical, or organizational? How are the political processes and the individuals to be changed, and by which methods?

What role should the profession take in defining appropriate data-collection, data-access, and data-reporting practices? What role should the profession take in enforcing or supervising those practices?   The history of information systems in social services is replete with examples of data-collection practices that are specified by funding agencies, usually governmental agencies, and which do not regard client rights as significant issues. Further, those data-collection practices often do not serve the data collectors or their agencies. As a profession concerned with the quality of life and human rights, social work should take responsibility for asserting the rights of individuals and groups to limit the types of data collected, and to whom, how, and under which circumstances data access is to be granted and data are to be reported.

  With regard to data-collection specifications, one could define data that are necessary to the service and its support, data that are useful but not necessary, and data that are unnecessary or intrude unnecessarily on a person's privacy. The issue of access deals with who may see the data, who may demand changes in the data, the process of data verification with the sources, and the reporting of demands for access to properly concerned parties. Data-reporting can be regulated with respect to which data are reported to whom; how those data are reported, for example, without identifying elements; and establishing a "need-to-know" justification process, that is, requiring a demonstration of appropriate need before data are reported. But the absence of identifying data elements should not be presumed to protect individual privacy. For example, Denning and Schlöler (1983) have shown that other "non-identifying" data elements may be combined to form unique identifiers.

As in areas mentioned earlier, for example, "self-help" software, the profession may choose among setting and enforcing standards, and evaluating and publishing reviews, and laissez faire/caveat emptor. Likewise, it might choose between a reactive posture—objecting to repeated occurrences of rights violations—or a proactive posture—anticipating and preventing rights violations.

Should the profession emphasize technology transfer over innovation? It was noted that much effort is utilized in developing systems that might simply have been transferred from elsewhere. There are good examples of transfers, for instance, the National Adoption Exchange's system (Wilson-Ress, 1983; "Match Made by," 1983; "Computerizing the Adoption," 1984). This system is based upon the use of a time-share vacation-home industry (Resort Condominiums International, Indianapolis) exchange and reservation system. Hammond presented, in Chapter 5, the description and advantages of one public-domain system available for transfer. Once a system has been proven, shall that become the de facto standard, so that the field's limited resources can be devoted to the development of nonexistent but desirable systems? Shall there be an agreed-upon method of rewarding the innovators so that they can continue innovating while others adopt their earlier contributions?

What ought to be the focus of systems that facilitate professional work? Newkham showed, in Chapter 5, that such systems can reduce the time and effort previously given to paperwork and thereby make more time available for the professional service-delivery tasks. Equally well, such systems can provide information for doing the job better and time for staff members to prepare themselves to do their jobs better, for example, in-service training, research, and continuing education. Unfortunately, they also provide the opportunity to do the same job with fewer staff people. Therefore, the question is properly phrased as *ought,* not *can.*

INFORMATION TECHNOLOGY AND EDUCATION FOR PRACTICE

In the treatment of the potential for technology in social work education, a common theme throughout Chapter 5 is that information technology is (or shall be) supportive of the educational process and should not threaten educators with replacement. However, as O'Reilly points out in what follows, the field is beset with the problem of the lagging diffusion of that technology. There are sophisticated users in social work education, but too many others ignore or refuse to use the technology. Further, practice seems to be in advance of education in the use of technology, and until schools catch up, successive classes will not be fully prepared for the job market. Schools should both serve and influence their clients — the agencies and the students.

In spite of the lessons learned, the leading edge of technology creates doubts, uncertainties, and ambiguities for both social work education and practice. As with practice applications, there is much we do not know about education for practice in an information society or about education with or through information technology. To cope with innovations successfully, several conceptual orthodoxies in education and practice may have to be discarded, revised, or reworked. (See Geiss [1983, 1985, & in press], Brauns & Kramer [1984], LaMendola [1985] for views on possible changes.) Because of the special position of education, that is, the preparation of future practitioners for the practice of the present and future, and because of the need to address the many educational issues, we asked the dean of a clinically oriented school to prepare the analysis that follows.

Information Technology and
Social Work Education
by Charles T. O'Reilly

After the conference, I was asked to comment on the opportunities and the problems associated with the introduction of information-systems technology in a school of social work. Although this technology encompasses more than computers, the microcomputer is its best-known and most widely used example; so I chose to focus on it from the perspective of the dean of one median-size school of social work. We have a median-size graduate program that educates for clinical practice and a median-size undergraduate program. Impressions from the conference and experience here and at other schools led me to relate primarily to master of social work (MSW) programs. Others may discuss why computers should not be ignored by undergraduate social work programs and how they already play an important role in doctoral programs. Their roles in the several practice areas and their long-term societal implications as they relate to social work are important topics that merit separate attention.

Much of my experience with computers has been in assessing them as tools for education and practice and in facilitating their use by faculty members and students. Although I am familiar with mainframes and microcomputers, my comments here are those of an academic administrator rather than a user. From that vantage point, they seem neither a panacea nor a threat to the integrity of education or practice.

The increased use of microcomputers by middle-sized and small social agencies has been an important incentive for schools to get involved with them. Schools sense that students must learn to use these new tools to cope with what will be state-of-the-art in a job market that places a premium on professionals who can use such tools.

The conference made it clear that a great deal is already known about the introduction of information technology into social work education. A nagging problem, however, is the lagging diffusion of that knowledge. Although we have a sizable cadre of social work educators who are sophisticated users of computers, too many educators seem unaware of, or resist, their use. This is disturbing because in many ways practice is considerably ahead of education in using this tool. Unless schools realize this, successive classes of students will be poorly prepared to meet the demands of a job market that understands the computer's potential. That market is the real world, and schools exist to serve as well as influence it.

Reasons for the lagging diffusion of technology are both technical and nontechnical. The former are easier to understand, having to do with machinery, or hardware, its cost, and so on; the latter are more intangible but nonetheless real. In addition to the ordinary resistance to change, they include concern about such matters as confidentiality and other ethical issues, the possible manipulation of data to the disadvantage of clients, and the possible threat to jobs. There also is the notion that as sensitive, empathetic professionals social workers may be temperamentally unsuited to use the computer. While they would not be alone in sharing "computer anxiety," it is hard to generalize about this facet of the profession's character.

Along with philosophers and musicians, many social workers have embraced the computer, perhaps not to the extent of the people in the hard sciences or business but enough to show that stereotypes do not hold universally when it comes to computers. In our school, for example, faculty members teaching clinical practice have no reluctance to use computers and neither do students interested in careers as clinical social workers.

Some academics see the computer fostering a sterile, impersonal approach to teaching and to helping those in need, and yet another step toward dehumanizing the social services. While this last area needs no help from computers, such objections ought to be faced squarely by a faculty. Ample evidence is available to inform critics of another side of the coin, if not to fully answer their objections. That other side might be that while the problems of information technology are real they may pale by comparison with the opportunities for improved services for clients that it opens. Computers already save scarce monies through more efficient administrative practices via word processing, easier fund-raising, and better case management, thus releasing resources for improved services. That contribution should not be underrated.

Instead of speculation about such matters, however, we need hard evidence to decide whether the computer is a benefit or a bane. Some answers can be obtained only through observing its use in real life. Some might even come from computer modeling. A social work faculty is uniquely qualified to provide the disinterested resources needed to do both. Social workers are expert information processors, and this is what information technology is about. Social workers have an edge on others when it comes to understanding the potential of the computer in their own practice domains. Better than many others, they know the substance of what is involved in the issues that surface with the use of computers. Many of those problems are analogous to those that surface with advances in medical technology and genetic engineering and are just as serious. They transcend familiar categories of experience, and we lack clear guidelines for dealing with them. While carefully evaluating computers and insisting that they prove themselves, we cannot ignore the ethical and more narrowly professional challenges they pose to us as caring professionals.

Efforts to induce faculty members to use microcomputers as personal tools or in teaching should distinguish between the older technology and its associated psychology of the mainframe period and today's microcomputers. High cost and the esoteric skills needed to work with the mainframe placed it off-limits for most social work faculty members. Microcomputers and their software have changed that situation radically, and today's computer systems are a far cry from yesterday's. At the same time, they should not be oversold to students or faculties as really user-friendly, although that quality seems to be improving rapidly.

From what was said at the conference (see Vogel's discussion of Lynett's contribution, in Chapter 5), many graduate schools of social work are using microcomputers mostly, it seems, in teaching research and management. But microcomputers are used also in internal administration for example, in keeping field-course data, student records and in word processing. Our faculty members use micros instead of typewriters to write articles and revise course outlines. The reduction of secretarial workload is already noticeable and welcome when new secretarial lines are virtually nonexistent. Also, once hooked, the faculty members swear by their computers. The goal would be for every faculty member to have a micro, if only for word processing. Once familiar with the machines, they will find other applications, and at their own paces, as in other matters.

Computer courses are becoming more common in graduate education, sometimes offered by specific schools and sometimes by other departments, but usually as electives. The local situation tends to dictate the important curriculum decision regarding whether the school itself provides this instruction or it is farmed out. If provided internally, someone with considerable computer expertise is needed, but the school is assured control of the content. The delights of interdisciplinary collaboration aside, we at Loyola's School of Social Work opted to do it ourselves on the assumption that the substance of the application of the computer to social work, regardless of the method involved, outweighed having students learn the refinements of computer science or of computer applications in other disciplines.

The problems encountered in gaining acceptance for the computer may be of short duration. With regard to students, consider that the average age of MSW students in 1983 was about 29, and only about 27% were under 25. For this age group, as well as those who are older, computer literacy is the exception rather than the rule. Many of today's high-school students and a considerable number of those now in college are more likely to have been exposed to computers, sometimes at advanced levels. By the time the current undergraduates enter schools of social work, much of the basic conceptual and skill-oriented teaching now related to computers may be eliminated or significantly reduced. This already happens occasionally at our school. [EDITORS' NOTE: Unfortunately, Anderson's 1983 testimony before a subcommittee of the House Science and Technology Committee does not support this hope. A national survey showed in 1981–82 that only 33% of all 17-year-olds and 23% of all 13-year-olds had any use of a computer. He also cited data (Anderson, 1983) that show, "... in about half of the schools with micros, only 1 or 2 teachers, at most, are regular users" (p. 3).]

As for faculty members, within 10 years the micro probably will be taken as much for granted as the copy machine and the overhead projector. The findings of a 1983 study of recent social work doctoral graduates (reported to the Group for the Advancement of Doctoral Education) were that 80% believed that some computer knowledge is necessary for doctoral students. About half of those surveyed already are teaching, so we can assume that most new teachers with doctorates are aware of the need to use, and are prepared to use, their knowledge of computers when teaching. Whether they do so depends upon the encouragement they receive from their colleagues, including deans.

Accustomed teaching patterns will not vanish with the introduction of computers and the entry of computer-literate students into schools any more than they did with the advent of instructional TV. Computers will be additional tools to be used as faculty members deem appropriate in their courses. And as computers become more user-friendly, perhaps voice-activated, and more software is designed specifically for social work and social work education, the tensions associated with the introduction of a novelty will lessen. All of this should allow faculty members to concentrate less on teaching about the computer and more on how to utilize it for both education and practice.

I believe that it was significant that social work and non-social work educators alike were restrained when talking about the applications of information technology to social work education. No Star Wars scenario emerged from their discussions. Although convinced of its present importance and future potential in social work practice and education, they cautioned about its limitations. A computer can assemble and analyze the facts for a diagnosis much faster than a human, but the meaning, interpretation, and communication of that diagnosis to the individual at risk is another matter. That is why a place will always be reserved for the knowledgeable professional social worker.

The participants were highly sensitive to the possible ethical problems associated with the use of computers. Some observers suggested that the presumed ethical issues have been overplayed and used as a delaying tactic by those opposed to the new technology. Whether true or not, the field ought to deal openly with something that is of genuine concern to many in social work, as well as in other disciplines. There is much to learn in this area from other disciplines such as engineering, medicine, business, and computer science, which have grappled with problems similar to the ones we face.

One need not be a science-fiction enthusiast to envision the role computers can play in society and in the social services in the next decade. Faculty members who fail to come to terms with them will be ill-prepared to teach an upcoming generation of practitioners who must learn how the computer fits into social services and what it can contribute to improved services for clients. This does not mean that every faculty member must become computer-literate. It will be enough if they are willing to understand how the computer relates to practice and, as once was done with content about dynamic psychology, social roles, and social systems, allow it to enter appropriate parts of the curriculum. That will not alter the fundamentals of social work education or violate its integrity; nor need one fear that the computer will radically reshape practice. The profession and its educators are, let us hope, too wise to allow that to happen. **But if social work does not act to shape the new technology's applications in ways social workers believe proper, for better or for worse, those applications will be shaped for us.**

O'Reilly has raised a number of issues from the perspective of an educational administrator, and he has offered some reassurance that information technology will not inappropriately change the world of education. In the following commentary, Marilyn Flynn deals with computer-based educational approaches and their relationship to the experiential component of social work education. Her views are based upon years of experience in social work education and in developing courseware and working with the PLATO system developed at the University of Illinois. (PLATO is one of the major educational systems developed for large computers — TICCET and GNOSIS are others — and there are many others for microcomputers, for example, PILOT.) It is her conclusion that the experiential dependence of social work education does not preclude computer assistance, but will require creative insights, innovative efforts, and challenging the apparent truths to enhance experiential learning.

Computer-Assisted Instruction and Experiential Learning
by Marilyn Flynn

Social work students at the MSW level bring with them a diversity of educational backgrounds and an impatience with theory and, typically, they have had comparatively little contact with the clients or organizations they hope to serve. In a domain where knowledge is uncertain and conflicting principles often apply, and where time available for professional preparation is limited, it is difficult to ensure that students have adequate experience to launch post-MSW careers. Even where students have acquired significant related experience with certain populations or programs prior to their graduate studies, most still lack breadth of vision. One might even say that the single major unanswered dilemma for social work education is how to distill the practice experience of an individual who has been in the field for 15 or 20 years and communicate this experience in a focused, systematic, cost-effective, and replicable manner.

Conveying experience in uncertain knowledge domains is a complex issue because, ideally, prototypic case examples should not be used for teaching (there are too many potential outcomes), and "drill and practice" formats are not suitable for forming the problem-solving skills that students need. Traditionally, social work has used field instruction for communicating experience. However, this method produces highly variable results, depending upon the availability of suitable sites in the students' areas of interest, the experience and qualifications of the instructor, the ability of the instructor to convey knowledge and experience, the appropriateness of the cases or problems that are referred to the students, the definitions of competencies to be achieved, and other factors.

In the classroom social work educators have tried a variety of tactics to develop the students' experience. Examples include printed case studies to be analyzed in the classroom, videotapes, films, guest lecturers, testimonials by former clients, self-help or self-analytic group sessions, field visits, and role play. Despite sometimes quite high levels of satisfaction among students, most faculty members remain convinced that much more intensive and systematic input is needed to build the wisdom and perspective that students need for effective intervention in complex community, organizational, and individual/family systems.

A more negative way of stating the issue is that current teaching practices are based on learning as a passive exercise involving the transfer of chunks of information from a "talking head" (teacher or other lecturer), or from a textbook, to the students. The dominant paradigm of the classroom includes following the rules, finding the "right" answers, and practicing lower cognitive processes. Schools of social work have been slow to accept or make use of new technologies offering the promise of interactive instruction.

Moreover, the special case of teaching students to make professional judgments does not involve the same cognitive processes as mastering formal principles in knowledge areas with clear cause-effect relations. The experienced practitioner is able to rapidly form perceptions of recognized patterns in a multivariate environment, rapidly calculate, or at least estimate, the probabilities of alternative outcomes, and efficiently recognize identifying features of client or organizational behavior. In this respect, human beings are "hard-wired" in a way that far surpasses the ability of present computer technology. Even seasoned practitioners, paradoxically, fail to learn from experience, and they themselves need means of forming new perceptions.

The computer revolution offers an opportunity to move beyond the intuitively accepted notion that experience is the best teacher. New authoring languages that are designed to build experience in the user are under development at the University of Illinois and in a few other institutions across the country. These languages should, at this point, be distinguished from work on artificial intelligence and expert systems, although the points of distinction are not always clear. The basic purpose is to use computer technology in a way that maximizes the "hardwired" capabilities of the human mind in indeterminate problem-solving environments. Computer programs built with this objective in mind combine many case histories in which different organizing principles or outcomes can be observed. The human mind puts a "face," or pattern, on these cases after being introduced to a wide range of episodes. The "correct" principle is discovered by the user, not incorporated into the software design.

Computer-assisted instruction using this approach is now confined to disciplines where cases or episodes are easily quantified—for example, stock-market analysis. In theory, however, client records and organizational histories can be adapted with relatively little difficulty.

One of the greatest obstacles to the use of computer technology for helping students and professionals to gain experience is that we are in what might be called the "horseless carriage" phase of computer implementation. By *horseless carriage,* I mean the preoccupation with number-crunching capabilities of automated systems; that is, we think of the new tool as simply a substitute for the old one. After 25 or 30 years of extensive computer use, 95% of computer power and 95% of computer time are still used to crunch numbers, either for purposes of scientific and/or engineering calculations or to keep the payroll and ledgers. At this stage, one would be hard pressed to show that computer-assisted instruction (CAI) has made substantial difference in the educational system or in social work. I would conclude that it is because most CAI systems fit the horseless-carriage description. Approaches that faculty members used with students (for example, drill and practice) were simply put on computers. That might be cost-effective, but it isn't particularly interesting. **I would submit that the single greatest challenge to social work education is the adaptation of new programming languages to intensifying experiential gains of students during their graduate educations.**

The contributions on information technology and social work education are concluded by DiLeonardi's comments on the relationship of practice to education, and the need for cooperative efforts in information-sharing. It is her belief that social work will not develop new technology, but will assume the role of adopting technology as appropriate—technology that supports service delivery. It is also her contention that social work skills can be applied to easing the introduction of technology and change; and that social work education should enable practitioners to consider the full range of implementation problems.

Information Technology and Social Work Practice: A Second Look
by Joan W. DiLeonardi

The role of information technology in social work is, much like that of social work education, a supportive one. Social work will never provide the cutting edge of technological development, nor should it attempt to, since that is not its role. While social workers, like other intelligent, educated professionals, can be informed about and take pleasure in technological development, its proper application in practice is as a tool to assist in the improvement of that practice. In this context, practice includes not only treatment of individuals, groups, and families but also the broad range of activities that take place in social work settings, including home studies for adoption and foster care, community and neighborhood organizing and planning, vocational training and rehabilitation, information and referral, discharge planning, day-hospital activities, administration of those services, and a myriad of other activities.

The most common functions for such technology are currently the collection, storage, and reporting of information used to make direct-practice and administrative decisions. And, less often, it is used in decision support systems, computerized assessment tools and diagnostic interviews, and computer-assisted instruction.

An innovative example of the use of current technology to support social work practice is the use of interactive microcomputer-videodisc programs to train AFDC Eligibility Specialists in the state of Florida (see Lynett's paper in Chapter 5).

Even this, however, is not an example of the development of new technology by social work practice or education, but the appropriate adoption of existing technology as a tool to solve a social work practice problem, the need for continuous training of workers in a job providing access to income-maintenance services in which there is a 300% staff-turnover rate annually.

Each practitioner who has found a way to make a part of the practice of social work easier, more efficient, or more effective by the use of existing technological tools has felt the same sense of discovery, of wonder, of triumph, and, perhaps, of isolation. Often, in social work settings, the implementation of technological innovation is seen as peripheral to direct-practice concerns or not truly or appropriately scholarly for educators. Sometimes these judgments have been proven correct over time as the innovation proves to be innovative but costly or ultimately useless. At other times and in other settings, computer-assisted instruction, the use of simulation models for practice or assistance in decision-making, client-information systems for tracking clients and reporting statistics, and interactive microcomputer software for testing or assessing client functioning may be eminently useful and improve the efficiency or the effectiveness of practice.

Social work is traditionally concerned with the interaction of the individual with his or her situation, family, group, or environment. Because of this, it seems that the major concern for social work education in the adaptation or adoption of information technology to social work practice is in the process by which it becomes integrated into practice. We must also clarify and discuss the value assumptions and ethical decisions that are an integral part of such implementations. If social work educators discard attempts to deal with those technological systems that are not state-of-the-art, they are abrogating their responsibilities. That some uses of technology have become common in business does not mean that they have become common in social work practice. A combination of a lack of money and a lack of technical sophistication among social work practitioners and educators has led to a lag that is only now being erased.

The experience of the profit-making sector can now combine with social work skills in working with people to make the implementation of technology less painful and more profitable to the workers and the clientele. Newkham, Chapter 5, cogently states the necessity for staff involvement in system development in a mental-health agency. His idea of turning unrelated data into useful information would provide extremely valuable training for students in schools of social work.

Mental-health and social work information systems that have failed have usually done so not because of technological flaws but because of the lack of user involvement in their development and implementation. Computer-assisted instruction has usually languished and died not because of faulty systems design and programming but because of a perceived lack of pertinence and applicability. Computer-assisted decision-making such as that reported by Pruger in Chapter 5 has encountered both technological and human problems in implementation. Social work education can help prepare practitioners to be most effective in considering the full scope of the implementation issues and using their professionally acquired skills to resolve conflicts, work with the larger system, and include in the process all who are essentially affected.

In all of the areas of technological innovation that he discusses, Garrett, in Chapter 5, stresses its impact on management, staff, clients, and the general public. He raises such crucial social work issues as client access to data, quality of computer-provided services, fear of change, confidentiality, and depersonalization. **Few, if any, schools of social work are preparing their students to integrate and adapt even current technology, let alone the cutting edge, or to consider the value implications of the necessary implementation decisions. This is their major need for the immediate future.**

Assistance to social work education with the integration of information technology into practice should come in the development and dissemination of model curricula that help students recognize and resolve the conflicts that come with the adaptation and adoption of technology into a humanistic and nontechnological field. This development must be done in cooperation with those agencies and individuals in the field who are grappling with the issues of technology implementation as a necessary part of their working lives. Information-sharing is a necessary but not sufficient first step in the process.

With these contributed commentaries as background, we present the educational issues raised in conference.

COMPILING AN ENCYCLOPEDIA OF IGNORANCE: EXPLORATIONS IN EDUCATION FOR PRACTICE

Shall information technology be integrated into the social work curriculum, at what educational levels, with what expectations and outcomes, and how? The question of whether information-technology content should be included in the curriculum is intimately related to the question of what role professionals should play in the design of technology applications within their field. A conservative or reactive stance would require preparation to aid those affected or dislocated by the technology. A proactive stance would require preparation for intelligent use, participation in the design of applications, and professional leadership.

Similarly, the questions of educational level and expectations at each level relate to the definition of differential roles for graduates at each particular degree level. But this problem is old and unresolved, in general, and particularly for technological education.

What is clear from the discussions is that, in general, the content should not be programming per se, nor simply what is referred to as *paper-and-pencil literacy*, that is, the skills analogous to the ability to make marks on paper. Alan Kay (1984), former chief scientist at Atari, Inc., and at Xerox PARC, developer of a prototype of the first personal computer, proposed the following definition of computer literacy:

> It is not learning to manipulate a word processor, a spreadsheet or a modern user interface; those are paper-and-pencil skills. Computer literacy is not even learning to program. That can always be learned, in ways no more uplifting than learning grammar instead of writing.
>
> Computer literacy is a contact with the activity of computing deep enough to make the computational equivalent of reading and writing fluent and enjoyable. As in all the arts, a romance with the material must be well under way. If we value the lifelong learning of arts and letters as a springboard for personal and societal growth, should any less effort be spent to make computing a part of our lives? (p. 59)

What is not clear is the curriculum content and how it might be allocated among fundamental understanding and conceptualization, attitudes and behavior, skills and abilities, recognition of opportunities, and analysis of consequences. Further, it is not clear how to provide space in the existing curriculum.

More specifically, what is required, educationally, for social workers to actively and effectively participate in the use and design of information-technology applications?   Sackman (1975) points out that the problem-domain experts must be involved:

> A final outcome of this effort was the realization that mission oriented computer users in a particular problem area are in the best position to systematically add to our knowledge and capability in the application of computers in the problem domains. This seeming tautology has major implications for the thrust of future work—effective leadership in the formulation and solution of social problems is the proper responsibility of those closest to the problem, *not the computer expert.* (p. 78)

Sackman's observation is further underscored by more recent work in artificial intelligence, which has led to expert systems and the new role of knowledge engineer—the person who helps domain experts organize and codify their knowledge and practice wisdom for system-building (see Feigenbaum & McCorduck, 1983; and McCorduck, 1979).

To respond to this challenge, we need to define the roles that social workers and other professionals should play in the implementation and use of technology in their field. We can identify the roles of informed observer, user, system-design participant, system-design initiator, system builder, system designer, and system architect. Given a particular choice of roles, we should be able to define the related knowledge and skill requirements.

As with all educational innovations, there will be tension between teaching what we know and know how to teach, and teaching what needs to be taught. There will also be tension and contention over that terribly limited resource called "curriculum space." What shall be displaced or done differently to make room for the new materials? Where in the educational continuum shall the new materials be placed?

In the case of social workers already at work in agencies, the concern will be over how the requisite skills and knowledge should be provided to them—through in-service training, on-the-job training, continuing education on-site, or at the university. There will be, as noted elsewhere, grave concern over taking the time required away from service delivery.

Should educators begin their applications development with the easy-to-establish and very visible applications that are obvious to them? There are obvious uses for computers and other information technology in teaching agency management, evaluation, and research, for example, in the quantitative areas of finance and statistics, but the more difficult applications would appear to be in enhancing direct practice with clients. Yet, if we begin with the easy, obvious and visible applications, our colleagues in the other areas are apt to "leave the driving to us." How can we encourage our colleagues to think broadly about applying technology in all aspects of practice teaching?

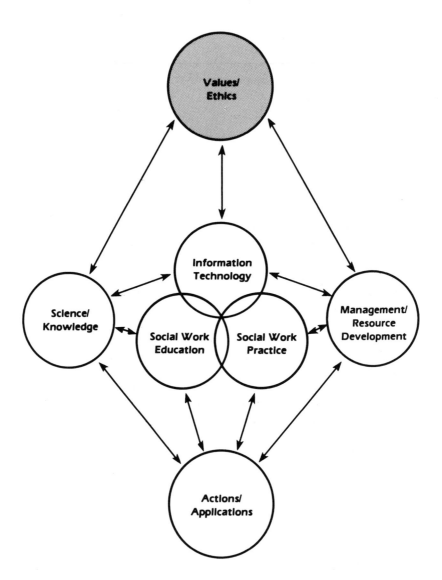

Framework for Analysis

CHAPTER 8

VALUES AND ETHICS

Rockeach (1973, pp. 3–5) observes that human values are those that derive from society and its institutions and personality. A question therefore arises as to whether human values and technology separate entities in society, in a stand-apart relationship, or are they integrally related, subsuming each other? Jacques Ellul (1964) cautioned us about the threat that technology may pose to human values when there occurs a disjunction between the two. In his view, technological progress leads to gradual dehumanization in a busy, pointless, and ultimately suicidal submission to technology in the western world.

Most informed observers today recognize that there is indeed an integral relationship between technology and human values. A particular technology chosen to have certain objectives also has values built into it, since both technology and values are products of a given society. In Goulet's (1977) terms, "there exists a value universe which is proper to modern technology" (p. 16). Heller (1985) provides an insightful probe of the relationship between technology and human values in the technology-transfer process. He comments, "The technology that is transferred is like genetic material in that it carries within itself the core of the society in which it was conceived and nurtured. . . . Thus, technology often encodes old value differences of race, class, gender, and age even when transferred into supposedly advanced systems" (p. 29).

The hallmark of a service profession is the centrality of values and ethics. Relationships between workers and clients, between providers and users, and between faculty members and students in schools of social work, are entwined in a complex web of professional values and ethics. Technological innovations compel us to articulate and realize those values and ethics. The fields of medical ethics and legal ethics have come under intense scrutiny, regulation, and reconceptualization as a result of innovations in life-extending and life-supporting technologies. Likewise, the issues of privacy, confidentiality, access, dignity, self-determination, and others have come under renewed scrutiny in social work.

Several of the authors and participants raised questions or expressed concerns about the use of technology in the complex arena of human relationships. In Chapter 5, Vogel wonders how technology can teach students about human relationships that are at the core of the profession's raison d'être. And, there, LaMendola states emphatically that, as a moral criterion, technology must never become a wedge between people and their interactions. Schoech notes specific moral issues that need to be faced and resolved: the ownership of client data stored in computers; how to monitor the quality of self-help-software development; and whether people will have equal access to technology. Schoech also advocates the cybernetic principle of self-correcting systems that would utilize the adaptive feedback of client and staff reactions and evaluations. He also observes that clients' needs should determine what is best done by technology and what is best provided by professionals. What is "best" is what allows the clients to help themselves.

Before we engage in further discussion of values or ethics, there is a fundamental question to be addressed. This question arose, with some exasperation, after repeated discussions of lack of resources, political intrigues, lack of knowledge, lack of interest, and general resistance to change.

What are the consequences of not using information technology in social work practice? There was some sense that the implementation of information technology in social work practice seemed so difficult, was so resisted, and was supported by such meager resources that we ought to ask, "Why bother?" It was suggested that the conferees might agree that the field simply can't afford the technology, that the field doesn't find it sufficiently useful, and isn't interested in using it. On the other hand, the motivation to develop applications might be increased if professionals in the field would be informed of what would be lost rather than what would be gained. Yet, Henderson concludes, in Chapter 3, that the choice *not* to use technology is not available to the field since others outside the field will impose the technology. So it is clear to him, at least, that we will lose control, and this is reminiscent of the arguments of the seventies for training agency managers from within the social work profession.

The ethical dilemma of technology development was clearly an issue for the participants, who also felt strongly that the profession has a unique contribution to make to technology development because of its focus on the relationships between people and their environments. Left unresolved, however, is the more fundamental issue of morality, and with which set of values we should judge it. Christensen addresses this issue in Chapter 3 and presents a series of five questions that, when taken collectively, form an ethical framework for analysis that we can use to interrogate the moral aspects and implications of information technology in a human situation. It is not enough, she concludes, to make technological decisions on technological grounds alone: Technological decisions are moral decisions.

COMPILING AN ENCYCLOPEDIA OF IGNORANCE: EXPLORATIONS IN VALUES AND ETHICS

Do we need to reexamine the social work code of ethics in the light of new technologies? Just as genetic engineering and medical advances force a reexamination of medical ethics, so too does information technology pose new questions for social work. Are these of sufficient concern to require a formal reexamination of the profession's Code of Ethics? (For a copy of the Code of Ethics, see Turner, Morris, Ozawa, Phillips, Schreiber & Simon, 1977.)

Who owns the data that are the basis for social work practice? It has been taken for granted in social work and other human services that clients lose control over their personal data in return for service. But the technology of the smart card, the memory microchip on a plastic card (Weinstein, 1984; Mayer, 1983; Lessin, 1982), provides the opportunity for clients to literally own and control the records of their personal data. They can present their data transiently to obtain service, and the agency need retain only that part which is necessary for agency reasons, for example, service evaluation and payment. Corollary questions are: Who has what rights to the data? Who may have access to the data? Who has a right to know what data are kept, for what purpose they are kept, and who has access to the data? Who may change the data, and who must verify the accuracy of the data? Are there data that should never be collected, especially if there is no way to truly expunge data because of *back-up procedures?* (Generally, to protect the integrity of data, a copy called a "back-up copy" is made before initiating any action that could destroy data or the integrity of the data. This is particularly true for operations meant to remove or delete data. There is then a question of when the "back-up copy" should be destroyed, and a question as to whether data are ever fully expunged or destroyed.) Should there be an *audit trail* attached to all client data accesses so that one may know who has seen the data?

Should the profession take a stance on the client's rights with regard to personal data?   The profession has seen itself as the guardian, trustee, and speaker for the "underclasses, disenfranchised, et cetera." There is, in the new information society, the potential to develop new groups whose ignorance about information technology and their rights regarding information will lead to their rights being taken for granted and abused. Sweden is one of the first countries to recognize this potential and has established an ombudsman's office together with laws that restrict the retention and exposure of information. It seems only appropriate for the profession that understands both the need for information and the abuses of information to take a public position with regard to the need for protection of rights. To do so requires that we understand the rights of each of the parties in any service transaction. It also means we must understand the potentials and processes of information technology.

For about a century—from Bismarck's first social legislation in 1883 in Germany, to the later emergence of the Fabians and the Labor Party in Britain, and still later, the Populists and Progressives in the United States—the domestic political agendas in the democracies of the industrial world have centered on one question: How can we build societies that reconcile efficiency in a world of rapidly evolving technologies with the human values in which Western culture is rooted? The question looms before us again, perhaps ever more sharply today, as we come closer to the end of the twentieth century. The inexorable march of science and technology continues unabated. The introduction of new technologies often demands new institutional structures and behavioral patterns. Traditional conceptions of time, work authority, hierarchy, loyalty, and morality face challenges from the progress of modern technology. The established codes of ethics in the helping professions may require renewed scrutiny and even revision.

It was pointed out in discussion that conflicts over technology are likely to be fundamental arguments over values and ethics. There are many who hold strongly felt convictions that they may not articulate easily because of their value foundations and feeling contents, yet we must not be so cavalier as to reject them out of hand. There was at least one member of the conference who tried repeatedly to express some of these views and concerns. He subsequently offered to write about them for this publication. We include them here because they are value-oriented, because we believe in his right to express them in this context, and because we believe they may be expressive of the concerns of many others in the field. But we do not agree with any argument that leads without question to the universal obstruction of all information-technology applications in social work practice. For example, we cannot accept the argument that if all the consequences of a technology application cannot be predicted, then the application should not be permitted, and therefore, since all consequences cannot be foreseen with certainty then all technology applications must be stopped. Still, we feel that Palombo's position and proposal warrant discussion and therefore presentation, for reasons of ethics, for reasons of values, and for a balanced and fully informed presentation.

The Relationship of Values to Information Technology and Clinical Social Work
by Joseph Palombo

One of the major difficulties in discussing the relationship between the explosion of information technology and the practice of clinical social work is that there are no true historical parallels from which one can draw and which help define the nature of the problems we confront. One parallel may be found in the period of prehistory, when the discovery that the written word could be used to record human events was made. Another parallel that has been suggested is that of the Industrial Revolution and its effect on the intellectual and social climates of the time. Yet, I find it impossible now to conjecture on the far-reaching effects that information technology will have on our economic, social, and cultural foundations. Here the concern is around one component of the possible effects that new technologies might have on the practice of clinical social work: the effect on the social and moral values to which we as a profession subscribe. The question I raise is whether it is possible to anticipate some of the moral dilemmas which will confront us, and whether it is possible to make a statement to reflect a stance we should take a vis-à-vis the developments in order not to compromise what we value most about our culture.

The evidence from other disciplines—for example, physics and medicine—has demonstrated the dangers of neglecting to address these issues as the technology is applied. The challenge to those who are concerned about the impact of the new technologies on social work is not to make the same mistakes as those disciplines. To avoid those mistakes we must develop our own conceptual framework to identify substantive ethical issues.

Such a broad framework must help us to articulate our assumptions about human nature, the ethical and professional values imbedded in clinical practice, and the effects on these values within our cultural, social, and political contexts.

The major danger that we confront is that we will approach the issues as technocrats, without addressing the more fundamental problems. The issues cannot be framed in terms that decide simply "how best to solve a given problem by making available the current information technology to the broader segment of the service-delivery system." This narrow problem definition pays little attention to the consequence that through applying information technology we create an environment in which a new culture is evolving and in which new questions and new problems confront us.

I will begin to outline an approach for practitioners whose primary concerns are the patient-therapist relationships. The Information Technology and Social Work Practice Conference did produce two statements that attempted to present such an overarching framework, but I feel both of those could be improved. [EDITORS' NOTE: These conference products are discussed here, and are reproduced in Chapter 11, Actions/Applications.]

Contribution of the Conference

In the opening address to the conference, Christensen presented a philosopher's position on the issue of values and information technology. One of her major contributions was to present a scheme through which an "ethical analysis" could be made by decision-makers to clarify the underlying ethical problems. Through a process of answering five questions, she suggested it would be possible to resolve and justify moral dilemmas. The five questions are:

- What makes right acts right?
- To whom is moral duty owed?
- What kinds of acts are right?
- How do rules apply in specific situations?
- What ought to be done in specific cases?

Miller subsequently presented the conference with a statement that purported to be sufficiently inclusive as to encompass almost all of the possible issues that could be discussed. His statement was as follows:

> The objective of information technology is to inform the production and distribution process in the social-service system for the purpose of improving the efficacy of that process/system. A set of meaningful steps toward making this occur includes:
>
> - Description of the process
> - Implementation of that description
> - Transfer of information
> - Resource development and acquisition
> - Definition and examination of the relationship to concerns of the field

As the discussion during the conference indicated, a problem with this conceptual framework is that it appears to neglect something essential to the social-service system—the value component embedded in the articulation of the system and its implementation.

In the discussion of this statement, Miller pointed to the inclusion of the term "efficacy" as suggestive of that which might be valued and might act as a guide to the profession.

This term is totally inadequate to the purpose. Aside from its vagueness, which could lead to any interpretation, it does not make explicit the specific values that are the focus of concern. The greatest deficiency is that "efficacy" could be used to further dehumanize the service-delivery system. For example, clinicians have a major concern with keeping the focus on the human relationship, which is at the core of all practice. This human relationship by its very nature contains the seed through which a healing process can take place, a healing of the wounds inflicted by society or by people upon themselves. I can easily conceive of a proposal which, for greater "efficacy," would direct that intake interviews be conducted through a computer. Decisions about case dispositions would be made from the data gathered. Such a method would be abhorrent to some practitioners who would perceive it as dehumanizing.

Viswanathan, on the other hand, presented a different perspective. In his conceptual framework (see Figure 7), there is a core of three interactive areas of concern: information technology, social work education, and social work practice. Concerns about these areas relate to the knowledge base, the values and ethics base, the applications and utilization methods, and, ultimately, the implementation or actions and decisions. This conceptual framework has much to commend it to us as a way of beginning to think about the issue. It appears less mechanistic than Miller's approach and adds richness to the fabric of what is to be considered. Furthermore, it has the advantage of directing our attention to more traditional categories through which we can begin to define the problems. As a framework, however, it seems based upon an approach to the problem which is analogous to the approach to a jigsaw puzzle in which a variety of the pieces are placed on the table and an attempt is made to make them fit into one another. It does not address the relationship that each piece has to the others. If the components are to become a skeleton onto which some flesh is to be added, we must formally define the relationships among the pieces before the frame becomes meaningful. The common values would also have to be explicated.

The third approach to the problem is one that was suggested by Geiss' list of the issues formulated in the course of the conference. [EDITORS' NOTE: The list referred to was presented near the end of the conference, and became a major element of the data base used to create this issues presentation.] One can take the fifty-odd topics and, by aggregating them, find niches under which they could fit. One possible set of niches may be elucidated in the following manner.

Educational Issues   The identification and development of uses of information technology to enhance the learning process at the undergraduate/graduate levels, to provide in-service training to agency staff or in continuing-education activities, and in educating service recipients are the foci here.

The Service-Delivery Issues   Under this category I include the formation of client data bases and the related issue of the organizing principles under which we should form such data bases. The definition of client-worker interactions, of dealing with staff reactions through the introduction of information technologies into the service-delivery streams, the coordination of services and agencies at the practitioner level in order to facilitate and enhance service delivery, and the questions of client involvement in the evaluation and the implementation of the service as well as the involvement of the providers of the services, would fit under this rubric.

Professional Issues   The major professional issue is to consider the ethical problems related to the introduction of technologies into the service-delivery systems. I do not mean that only the issue of confidentiality of records must be addressed since, as was pointed out at the conference, confidentiality may be a secondary issue. The more essential issue is to address the possible dangers of dehumanizing (fostering selected values or behaviors over all others) the delivery system through the introduction of technologies that may be unresponsive to people's needs or may violate their values. A further issue is the necessity for networking and conferencing to facilitate the flow of information. And, finally, there are the issues of control and self-monitoring to assure both the quality of services and the appropriateness of the applications of the technologies.

Legal Issues   The legal issues relate to questions of the ownership of client data, the expunging of data, confidentiality, and the protection of the rights and obligations of all participants in the service-delivery system.

Political Issues   The political realities are that local, state, and federal governments are the primary sources for funding of social services. Major social-policy issues are determined at those levels. These often affect the practitioners in dramatic ways. Affecting such large systems often is one part of the problem, yet information technology presents opportunities through which more efficient changes of these systems may be accomplished.

This organization of topics does not presume to take any position or value to which practitioners should subscribe; consequently, it too needs a more explicit statement to supplement it. This review of conceptual frameworks may lead a practitioner to prefer one framework over another. Each framework has limitations which necessitate an introductory statement that can give expression to the set of beliefs that embody the values with which we approach all problems.

Human Nature and Social Values

Embedded in any position is a view of human nature (Brian & Miller, 1971, Chap. 2) that becomes articulated in the course of addressing technical problems such as those presented by the information-technology revolution. In social work, the most familiar points of view of human nature are those chosen through adherence to a specific developmental psychology. That is, the more behaviorally inclined practitioners may tend to minimize the importance of relationships in the achievement of given ends. They will see the modification of a set of behaviors as the desirable method. Those who are inclined in a Freudian direction will place more emphasis on the significance of libidinal and aggressive motives in the expression of human behaviors. Those who adhere to a psychology of the self will set a premium on empathy and interdependence as the conditions of the human environment in which all interactions must occur. There are fundamental values that accompany each theoretical position.

The professional code of ethics may at times be insufficient to deal with novel situations. Technological advances often present new sets of problems. Perhaps the best parallel lies in the problems faced by medicine today, where the processes and capacities for the prolongation and for the conception of life have led to issues that were inconceivable half a century ago. In the physical sciences, the emergence of nuclear energy presents similar dilemmas. If we are to creatively and appropriately approach information technology, we must now attempt to anticipate the kinds of moral dilemmas that will confront us but which, at the moment, seem inconceivable. It is too easy to rush ahead with the implementation of technologies and to enthusiastically reap the benefits, which they seem to provide in the short term, without giving adequate thought to the distinctive and irretrievable modifications that they bring to our lives.

While no one can claim to be able to foresee the issues that might arise in the future, it behooves us to imaginatively conceive some of these. We might then be able to anticipate moral dilemmas. Interestingly, in *The NASW News* (1984), a headline screamed "Media Therapy Controls Asked" ("Media Therapy Controls," p. 19). The article calls for controls on radio and television counselors, who are on the increase. Such activities may be but one example of the types of problems that should be dealt with prior to their inception rather than after the emergence of public outcries.

Proposed Statement

The following is a proposed statement that can, hopefully, be fully discussed at a future conference and which articulates the values to which our profession might subscribe:

I. We, as Social Workers, are committed to the Code of Ethics of our profession and dedicated to the preservation of human dignity, and the alleviation of human suffering.

II. We are aware that the applications of technologies can significantly alter the nature of our society and the values to which our culture subscribes, often in ways that are unforeseen and unrelated to the purposes intended by the originators of the technologies.

III. We have also seen evidence that the applications of new technologies have given rise to moral dilemmas for which professions have been unprepared.

IV. We anticipate that the applications of information technology may have an impact on the welfare system, and the entire service-delivery system, in both the private and public sectors, and that it will affect all persons involved in that system from policymakers to service recipients.

V. We recognize that powerful new technologies at times give promise of immediate beneficial effects, and may create an urgent demand for their application prior to the full exploration of the impact they may have.

We, therefore, wish to affirm our commitment to the examination of the consequences of the applications of new technologies prior to their implementation, being mindful of the ethical issues that might be raised by these applications, and of the impacts such implementations might have on all people involved in the service-delivery system.

We further commit ourselves to insisting upon the widest possible discussion of the moral dilemmas that might arise, helping to articulate the choices or costs, in human terms, of the implementation of any technological instrument.

We sanction the use of new technologies prior to the fullest examination of the consequences of their applications when it appears *prima facie* that the gains to be made far outweigh any possible negative consequences, and when the risk of possible damage appears minimal.

We dedicate ourselves to actively resisting the implementation of any technology that conflicts with our Code of Ethics, and thus diminishes the worth of any individual, or detracts from the dignity of the person, whether recipient or provider.

Palombo provides a helpful review of the conceptual frameworks displayed at the conference and introduces one of his own construction. His concern is for a broad conceptual framework that admits and utilizes an appropriate set of values. Each of the frameworks, including his own, is lacking in this regard. Miller's proposal used the term "efficacy" explicitly to allow varied values to be imposed as appropriate in a given context. This lack of a clear and explicit values statement leads Palombo to a proposed statement, preamble, or values stance, which asserts:

- A need for an exhaustive examination of the consequences before an application is implemented
- Wide discussion of each moral dilemma that arises
- Sanction (in the sense of support or encouragement, we presume) of obviously "good" applications without full and exhaustive study
- Active opposition to those applications that conflict with the Social Work Code of Ethics.

In principle, this would be quite acceptable. But we wonder how, in practice, this might be carried out. Will the practice be de facto opposition or substantive impediment to any application? There is no question that reasonable restraint is needed in our relentless pursuit of "change" and "betterment," and to the degree that Palombo gives voice to that, he makes a significant contribution; but, just as he calls, most appropriately, for a foundation of values, so must we call for more details on process and procedure before judging the feasibility and merit of the proposal.

INTERNATIONAL AND GLOBAL ISSUES

International and global concerns about the impact of technological innovations on the world social order are as important as the intraprofessional or intrasocietal concerns about ethics and values. The implications of what has been called the Information Revolution have received increasing attention in recent years. As Fred Branfman (1984) observes: "We are living in the earliest stages of a transformation as profound as the Industrial Revolution: the emergence, for the first time ever, of a global civilization. New information technologies are driving economic and social growth. A new global power balance is restructuring international relations" (p. 33). In the same vein, Jean-Jacques Servan-Schreiber (1985), President of the Paris-based World Center for Microcomputer and Human Resources, points out that, "we can no longer think of the computer revolution as something that will take place in the next century. In fact, it is emerging as one of the great social and political battlegrounds of *our* time" (p. 569 [italics added]). In his thoughtful and perceptive survey of the world social scene, Servan-Schreiber goes on to observe that the high-tech enthusiasts' promise of a brighter future for the world often seems greatly exaggerated; at the same time, many of the negative consequences now associated with the new technology are not inevitable. Ultimately, whether the economic changes these technologies are fostering will improve the quality of our lives depends upon the larger political environment.

The ability to compete in high technology has become an important determinant of success in the competition between nations and regions. The shape of society—of what actually happens to people—is not wholly determined by the state of technology. All advanced countries today can use comparable technologies, yet Europe, Japan, the United States, and the Soviet Union differ both socially and politically. Despite lags, technology spreads. Countries standing aloof from technology—whether from preference, poverty, or oppression—seldom count as forces shaping social change; however, often we hear of forces reshaping them. Countries insulated from new technologies become pawns. It does appear that some of the unplanned side effects of technological innovations are the increased stratification of high-tech and low-tech societies together with the increased spatial and temporal gaps between modern and traditional societies.

Furthermore, there is an attenuation of the economic and cultural gaps between rich and poor countries, which gives rise to new forms of economic colonialism and new patterns of scientific and technological domination. Differences in the nature, quality, and degree of production and use of scientific technical knowledge tend to produce the most asymmetric relations among the nations. This presents us with a different global perspective for viewing the value dilemmas of equity, resource development, and resource allocation.

The greatest lack and the greatest need is an integrated view of the world order. The international system—if it can be called a "system"—is highly stratified, segmented, fragmented, politicized and, hence, unstable. More than a decade ago, the declaration of the Columbia Conference on International Economic Development (Ward, Runnallo, & D'Anjou, 1971) contained the following concluding remarks:

> The widening gap between the rich and poor countries of the world has become a central issue of our time. In incomes, living standards, economic and political power, one-third of the world has, in recent decades, been pulling steadily ahead, leaving the remainder of mankind in relative poverty, in many cases to live without clean water, education, basic medical facilities, or adequate housing. Yet with modern technology and existing production capacity none of this need continue if mankind would develop the will and organization to use the resources at hand. (p. 34)

This description of the international development process in the 1970's is equally applicable to the shape of the development process in the 1980's; the instability persists.

If, however, the transformation is managed successfully, the information revolution will create a new domestic economy that utilizes computer, bioscience, and information and telecommunications technologies to raise living standards, increase employment, reduce manual labor, promote freedom and democracy, and give individuals new opportunities to reach their potentials. It will also usher in a global economy in which the Third World has substantially closed the gap with the developed world and various national economies are integrated to a degree never before experienced, thus restoring stability on an international scale.

Sackman (1975) has observed: "The name of the game is not what computers are doing to society, but rather what society is doing with computers. The issue is social choice." He went on:

> There are two basic social alternatives for the grand design of individual computer services. One, already well underway, is economic exploitation of the individual market for information services via two-way CATV. **The heart and soul of this approach is simply private profit. The other, almost nowhere in sight, is deliberate social planning of individual services for maximum benefits to every citizen over the long run. The heart and soul of this approach is the supreme worth of every individual. The design of mass information utilities is no less than our design of the new individualism.** (p. 82 [emphasis supplied])

CHAPTER 9

SCIENCE AND KNOWLEDGE

The concept of the knowledge system is used in a sense analogous to the economic or political system. It refers to the structured distribution of knowledge-related activities through institutions, organizations, persons, roles, and resources. Every society, whatever the level of its development, has a knowledge system of its own. But the nature, degree, and quality of instrumental competence of the knowledge system vary from society to society, and depend on the level of institutionalization, organization, and utilization of modern science and technology. The assumption is that the higher the level, degree, and quality of institutionalization, organization, and utilization of modern science and technology in a given knowledge system, the higher is the level, degree, and quality of its instrumental competence.

Technology is a derivative of scientific knowledge. Science and technology exist in a close, synergistic relationship. It is unproductive to transfer technology without the scientific knowledge that is integral to it. The utilization of information technology in social work practice requires us to forge a more systematic link between social work and the sciences that contribute to the growth of scientific knowledge and technological know-how. Mere knowledge of the rudiments of technical operation is hardly sufficient. New knowledge must be transmitted into social work education and translated for use in social work practice. As is the nature of the profession, social work must absorb new knowledge from many other sources and professions.

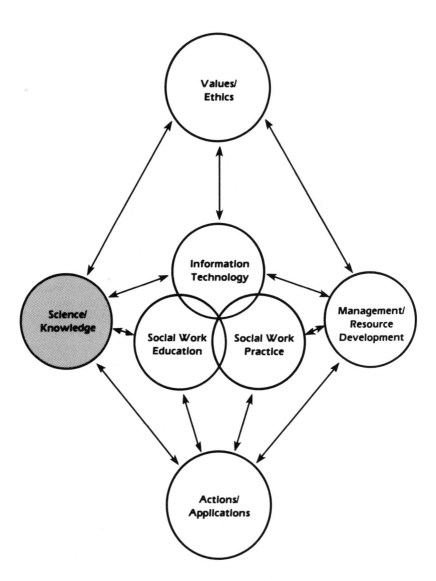

Framework for Analysis

COMPILING AN
ENCYCLOPEDIA OF IGNORANCE:
EXPLORATIONS IN KNOWLEDGE NEEDS
AND TECHNOLOGY DEVELOPMENT

Is there a concept that will integrate the information used in social work practice? What is the appropriate focus for the design of information-technology applications? Observations of other fields of activity, especially commerce, indicate that significant advances in information-technology applications occurred after an integrating concept evolved. This evolution required the definition of the elemental unit or source of information, for example, the passenger in reservation systems, the student in school systems, or the patient in hospitals. Another way of expressing this is as a focus on the base or elemental transaction to be captured and processed. For social work practice the question is whether the client-and-worker interaction is the appropriate base transaction to be captured.

Another aspect of this question arises in the discussion of the structure of decision support systems where one identifies, as separate entities, a data base and a model base (see Henderson, Chapter 3). The former relates to questions of content, form, structure, and elemental units of information, and the latter refers to the relationships among the data elements and how they are to be used, for example, hypothesis-testing, or alerting, or prediction. The issue of design focus in this context is that of emphasis on the data base versus emphasis on the model base.

Throughout the conference, and especially in the discussion of Vallee's paper (Chapter 3), there was the sense that a focus upon capturing the data that would support and inform the service-giver's activities would necessarily result in satisfying the needs of regulators, funders, managers, and evaluators as well. It was also indicated that a focus upon serving these latter needs rarely resulted in a system that would serve the worker, who must divert energies from primary service-delivery tasks to supply the required data.

In the context of decision-support-system location, the question that arises is, "Which decisions warrant support?" There is evidence to suggest that the decisions to support are those that are critical to the success of the enterprise, involve high risk, and won't demand the intervention of higher authority if properly supported at a lower level in the organization. These decisions, in social work practice, most frequently occur at the service-giver's level.

What is the proper role for information technology in the practice of social work? Many current applications focus on controlling and monitoring practice activities, yet a fundamental characteristic of professional functioning is the autonomy to exercise judgment and discretion. This would suggest a focus on enabling and facilitating via the technology. (See the dissertation of LaMendola, 1976, for findings that support these observations.) This raises the issue of support of professional work versus the replacement of humans in selected tasks. Questions were raised regarding which tasks, if any, can and ought to be automated, especially in the context of activities where human relationships are considered the key to the success of the activities. Christensen's analytic framework, in Chapter 3, begins to inform the ethical aspect (ought), but we also need more information to respond to the feasibility (can) aspect.

What are the proper roles for person and machine in social work practice and social work education? In particular, can and should interpersonal skills be taught by or with the support of machines? Joseph Weizenbaum (1976, pp. 207–227, 268–280) asserted that machines should never be permitted to substitute for "a human function that involves interpersonal respect, understanding, and love. . ." (p. 269). Yet the notion of being able to simulate human exchanges, at least for instruction in interpersonal skills, is very appealing. It is especially appealing because it offers such a rich variety of experience in an observable, controllable, realistic, and timely way. While audiotaped or videotaped client interviews and role play have been used before, the Lynett experiment (Chapter 5) opens exciting possibilities of adaptive and tailored presentation of material containing complex aural and visual images that were previously unavailable to learners and teachers. The fundamental questions remain: "What are the appropriate roles for human and machine?" and "How do we identify those functions involving respect, understanding, and love?"

Does social work have any unique needs in hardware or software? Clearly, social work is a communications-based (verbal—aural and textual—and non-verbal, as well) profession. How does this fit with the present nature of information technology, especially, for example, data-base management systems? MUMPS, the Massachusetts General Hospital Utility Multi-Programming System (Krieg & Shearer, 1981; Zimmerman, 1979; LaMendola, 1984), was created to meet the special needs of health-information systems by providing efficient handling of variable-length text-oriented records, and rapid access to the data base. Another example of special requirements, we learned, is that spreadsheet programs have been designed as two-dimensional models, while most social-service analyses are based upon at least the three dimensions of line items, calendar time, and equity. If social work were to require the use of nonverbal information, what would that imply for information technology?

What are the "communities of interest" that seem to be required for the successful use of computer conferencing? The evidence presented by Vallee (Chapter 3) clearly suggests that continued success with computer conferencing depends upon establishing a group with a common interest and specific problems. It was suggested that a major product of the conference might be continued discussion via electronic media. To do so would require the identification of such communities of interest among the conference participants and the social work community at large. Can this entire presentation of issues serve to define such common interests around which to build conferences?

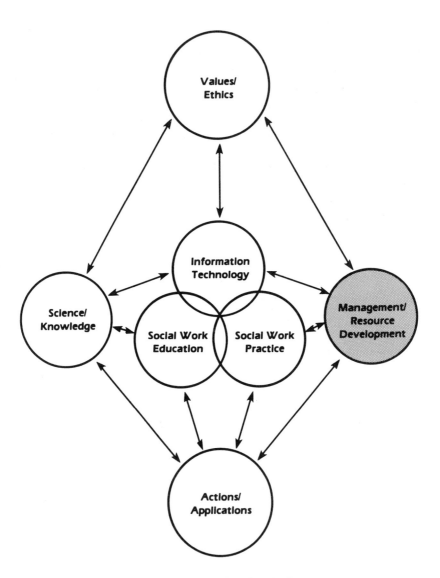

Framework for Analysis

CHAPTER 10

MANAGEMENT AND
RESOURCE DEVELOPMENT

There are at least three types of management and resource-development factors that bear on the issues of interest to social work that we can identify: conceptual, which are hard to formulate but have long-term payoffs; professional, which are easier to formulate and have near-term or shorter-term benefits; and policy, which are immediate actions that foundations, governments, and industries should be taking to support the use of information technology in social work.

The advanced technologies are characterized as knowledge-intensive, and needing substantial capital for the costs of research, product design, and development. They require a sound technical infrastructure, in particular, strong habits regarding collection and use of information.

Furthermore, these technologies are ephemeral—here today, overtaken tomorrow by newer advances. But this is no reason to delay action. Often the older technologies remain viable, productive tools. The exponential rates of change call for flexible and rapid responses that involve potentially large outlays, but creativity can produce less expensive alternatives. In this situation the objective of the human-service organization should not be merely to acquire a single technology or process but to painstakingly develop the technical capabilities to adapt a program or service design, improve it, and then innovate, in a self-reliant manner appropriate to its context and means.

Another noteworthy and correlated characteristic of the innovation process in technology development and utilization is that it requires a high order of entrepreneurial skills and support by venture capital. The structure of the high-tech industry is marked by small, newly established firms, often linked to large established corporations. Here, again, the human-service organizations are at a considerable disadvantage because they generally lack the climate for entrepreneurship or the risk capital.

COMPILING AN ENCYCLOPEDIA OF IGNORANCE: EXPLORATIONS IN ORGANIZATIONAL AND RESOURCE PROBLEMS

What is an appropriate strategy for making the changes that will be necessary? While the profession presumes to practice by helping others to change, can it itself readily change? What is the appropriate path to such change? There was some cause to believe that we, as a group, have not been very successful in changing our immediate colleagues' interest in information technology. If so, then how will we change the profession's interest?

What do we understand about the origins and dynamics of human resistance to the implementation of information technology and how to deal with it? Most instances of information-technology application produce examples of resistance, especially by directly affected staff (see, for examples, LaMendola, 1976; Hedlund, 1974; Byrnes & Johnson, 1981). Resistance may be simply passive or, in some cases, active disruption of the implementation process or interference with the system's operation, for example, providing false or incomplete data. There was some suggestion that this is a problem of organizational change in general. But there were questions regarding the special issues and problems related to social work such as concerns over protection of client rights, and ethical issues. We note, again, the observation that conflicts over technology may, in reality, be conflicts over values. There is also the question of whether, and what, social work can contribute to this change process from its knowledge base and practice wisdom.

Can resistance be classified in some way, and can we then build models for dealing with each class of resistance? To begin, one can refer to Keen and Scott Morton (1978, Chap. 7) for a review of change strategies and an analysis of resistance in the context of management information systems (MIS) and decision support systems (DSS). Resistance to change, they point out, is more constructively understood as a lack of unfreezing in the context of the Lewin-Schein model of change (Keen & Scott Morton, p. 199), than as a pathological rejection of the "truth."

Thus, it may arise from a lack of motivation to change. Similarly, they view semi-successes as failures to properly refreeze the new state—a failure to institutionalize change through the creation of a new equilibrium.

What do we know about the political aspects of implementing information-technology applications in social work? The Heart of Texas system (Newkham, Chapter 5) came about in a political way. The agency was in need of reorganization, and the state recognized the opportunity to cut costs. The California experiments (Pruger, Chapter 5) in decision support were technically and professionally successful but were never implemented statewide. Many information and referral projects can't move forward because of the lack of cooperation among agencies. Ramey's scenario (Chapter 4) describes a system that comes into being in one political era—one where services integration is favored— and cannot continue in the succeeding era. The Florida experiments (Lynnett, Chapter 5) with computer-controlled videodisc training, while quite successful as a demonstration or pilot project, also were not permanently or broadly accepted.

This all suggests that technical or professional merit may have little to do with the initiation, continued development, and full-scale implementation of successful demonstration projects. What do we know of the political and organizational aspects of system implementation and operation? Can we classify the problems and develop approaches? How can we assure the continued use of worthwhile systems? Can social work contribute its expertise to the resolution of this issue in other domains as well?

How do we provide staff members with the time to be trained in information technology and to be involved in the development of applications? It was noted many times during the conference that the staffs of agencies are overburdened. How can they be expected to take time to learn about this new technology? Similarly, in the educational area, faculties will need to be trained to teach the new processes and concepts, yet there is no space in the curriculum and faculty members, too, have little time of their own. In both cases, the organizations often claim they do not have the requisite resources. Given this constrained and impoverished state, how can the field move ahead? In the least, these questions raise issues of priorities (i.e., How are our resources being used? If not most effectively, why can they not be redistributed?), if not issues of sheer capability (i.e., Can social work and its organizations afford information technology?).

Will the field of social work, in practice and education, recognize the utilization of information technology as essential and then adjust its priorities to provide the required resources to do the job?

Will the creators of educational or professional software get appropriate credit?   For educators, especially in higher education, the question of credit for innovations is essential. If a faculty member creates educational software, is that creditable activity for decisions on tenure or promotion? It probably would not be in most institutions now. Under these conditions, many potential contributors, especially the youngest, who are more conversant with the technology, will seek other areas of expression, and even other areas of employment. Attracting capable people to the field is likely to become a critical issue for the increased utilization of information technology. There is also a question of the ownership of related and potentially very valuable copyrights. For example, agencies have never had to deal with questions of invention in the way commerce does, but now a staff member who creates saleable software poses the problem of ownership in a way that had not arisen before.

BARRIERS TO PROGRESS: A SAMPLING

What we heard at the conference were not only confessions of our own ignorance, but frustration with the many barriers to movement and, ultimately, success. It is important to underscore the lack of resources with an observation on investment ratios. If a typical computing-project budget is analyzed 10% might be for hardware, 30 to 40% for software and the remainder for personnel training, salaries, and benefits. The microcomputer and mass-marketed software will change these figures further, but personnel costs will remain the significant part of any such project expense. This will be the case until the operating-knowledge requirements are either minimal or a common part of professional education, and the software can be "taken off the shelf" and used without substantial staff effort to customize the application.

Another aspect of the resource problem that provides barriers is the "poverty-stricken" self-images held by many agencies and schools. This may arise from the failure, or the unwillingness, to set priorities and to define specific foci of activity. In this context the "flexible human" is always preferable and more valued than the "inflexible machine," no matter how productive the latter is at specific and valued tasks. Agencies seem to be confused about whether they are employers seeking to provide services to some particular groups or whether they are employers for the purpose of solving the unemployment problem via their own hiring practices. This impoverished self-image also does not permit generation or retention of income surplus for capital investment since there is always another "good purpose" for which to expend the money now, and often this self-image leads to acceptance, without question, of gifts of hardware, software, and personal services which "though free, are still not cheap enough!" These gifts, often obsolete in some respect, may produce an albatross about an agency's neck.

Without the capital to do research and development, the field depends upon, and searches for, easy transfers, most often from business (see, for example, LaMendola, 1976). These transfers have provided and emphasized the managerial models of information-technology applications, not the service models. Commerce has only begun to explore the service potential of information technology and the concept of a service or product to which value is added via information technology. An example of this is Toyota's dealer information network, which can quickly locate available vehicles, accessories, and parts in any dealer's inventory and thereby speed sales and service to the customers of any inquiring dealer.

Even in the professional schools, the first uses of computers were reported (see Vogel in Chapter 5 for the impromptu survey results) to have been in administration and not in service provision. The obvious utility of such applications, the purse-string power of administrators, and the importance of their work seem to universally merit the first applications in the organization, even if other applications are equally, and perhaps more fundamentally, meritorious.

Educators are notoriously slow to change despite evidence of the effectiveness of alternative methods. In social work, this resistance is compounded by a complex variety of schools of thought and approaches to education and practice. There is, consequently, no common model of education or single set of principles for which applications can be easily built. When computers reach social work education, the effort is usually, with some notable exceptions, focused on teaching about the computer and its applications, instead of teaching with or through the computer. This narrow focus limits the potential of the tool (see Geiss, in press, for an elaboration).

This narrow focus is further evidenced in the profession's unwillingness to see itself as a data-based profession. While Schinke (1983) reports an increase in the number of journal articles dealing with data-based practice, neither his own review of the history of the idea nor our own observations suggest that the field is changing rapidly in this regard. Until it does, serious and creative innovation with information technology will come slowly. This slow pace is evident in the difficulties that abound in trying to arrive at common definitions of services, let alone service outcomes or processes. Without such standards meaningful communications and comparisons will be difficult. It is also exemplified in the lack of unified professional objection to the inappropriate and conflicting demands for data that drive present system designs.

Finally, the failure to recognize data and the analysis that produces information as the foundation upon which professional service is built leads to unsupportable claims of uniqueness that are used to oppose standards, evaluations, and technology applications.

CHAPTER 11

ACTIONS AND APPLICATIONS

Chapter 5 provides examples of major applications of information technology in social work. Other applications exist, and many more are possible (see Chapter 4). The usefulness and feasibility of these applications suggest an agenda of future actions needed in social work education and practice. Creating an agenda for action along these lines should be the responsibility of each concerned professional and, certainly, of the Council on Social Work Education, the National Association of Social Workers, and other professional groups committed to the future of social work education and practice.

There should be some form of central planning or guidance mechanism to foster research and development (R&D) that supports the goal of technology diffusion and transfer in social work. The implication here is that R&D activity will occur at a variety of levels and in a variety of places — for example, federal government, universities, and human-service organizations. There ought to be a mechanism for coupling and dovetailing the work carried out by these groups in order to permit systematic processes of technology utilization in social work education and practice. In the least there needs to be a dissemination mechanism to keep interested parties informed of others' work so that unnecessary duplication is avoided, and the work of individuals can be cumulatively supportive of the profession's chosen directions. The advantage of planned and coordinated activity is efficiency — the elimination of waste caused by duplication — while the advantage of the "free-market" form is diversity and minimal administrative overhead — the elimination of waste caused by focus on a single "blind alley" and by nonproductive effort.

With regard to the commercial R&D area, where an efficient technology-transfer process should operate, it is desirable to keep a close

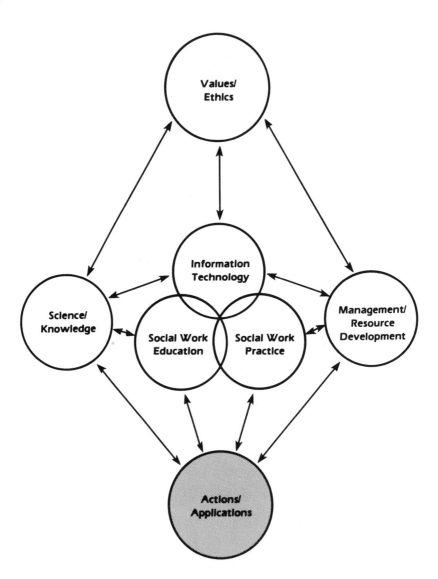

Framework for Analysis

coupling between the developers of a technology and its marketers throughout as much of the R&D process as possible.

It is imperative that we foster cooperative university-federal government-social-agency research. (For examples of opportunities, see Geiss, Schoech & Viswanathan, 1982.) The pressures on human-service organizations to make their research and service dollars cost-effective are intense, and it makes good sense for them to tap the resources of both the universities and the federal government. These institutions have specialized knowledge and capability in areas ranging from unique subject-matter content or practice fields to advanced computer-based model and data-base systems. Yet it does not make sense to make any one totally dependent upon the others. It seems especially inappropriate for the human-service sector to be wholly dependent upon the government for research support. That leaves research, a long-term investment, open to the vagaries and vicissitudes of political interests, usually short-term concerns, especially in the social-services arena. We already have a model in the aerospace and defense industry that permits accumulation of surplus (profit) from federally supported work that may be used to fund private research initiatives. This provides incentive to be efficient and effective, and since the rewards may be used in ways most attractive to the organization, for example, to improve its own knowledge base, it has long-term consequences beyond present employment.

Tripartite partnerships between federal laboratories, universities, and industrial organizations are popular today. A current example of such sharing is an effort in which the steel industries, two national laboratories of the Department of Energy, and the National Bureau of Standards are working together to develop "leapfrog" technology to help the steel industry achieve increases in productivity, meet foreign competition, and prepare for the twenty-first century. University researchers are also involved, and it is hoped that the steel industry — and the nation — will benefit from the sharing of expertise among the three types of organizations.

There are, we learned in Chapter 5, some first efforts in social work practice to establish technology transfers and cooperative efforts with industry. Newkham's agency has begun exporting its system, built with state support, to other agencies. Hammond describes in his paper the technology developed by the Veterans Administration that is available as public-domain technology ready for transfer. Lynett's state-supported development in curriculum and training process could be adapted and transferred. Finally, Pruger gave us a clear example of a product of state, county, and university cooperation. External to the conferees, the National Adoption Exchange (Wilson-Ress, 1983; "Match Made by," 1983; "Computerizing the Adoption," 1984) provides an excellent example of the advantages of transferring technology from the reservations portion of the time-share vacation-home industry to the adoption-agency problem of identifying prospective parent-and-child pairings. Social work would benefit from such a pooling of effort. The end result, we believe, of interactions of this sort will not only be beneficial to social work education and practice but will also strengthen and rejuvenate the overall system of research and development of supportive technologies.

In addition to listing the barriers to change, an analytical approach requires a careful delineation of the costs and the benefits of the proposed change. The conference process did identify some opportunities and threats that are exposed here, prior to investigating further what our next steps can be.

OPPORTUNITIES AND THREATS: A SAMPLING

We have been exposed to opportunities ranging over the spectrum from the major social change envisioned in Vallee's "grapevine alternative" (see Chapter 3) or the revitalization of the social movements of the sixties and seventies envisioned by others, to the improvement in service to selected individuals, and on to Sackman's (1975, pp. 81–83) view of a new individualism and his call for a "computer bill of human rights." Similarly we have images ranging from people helping other people to solve problems over networks, to the individual having direct access to the world's experts via expert-systems technology. We can envision the handicapped and otherwise homebound with an entirely new world of work, relationships, and leisure available to them, as well as the nightmare of the obsessively "workbound" with new opportunities to work anywhere and without respite. There is also the image of capital poverty in a capital-intensive world juxtaposed against a level of access to others and their creativity that has never existed before. This image of open access, open communications, and participatory democracy provided by information technology, is countered by the potential to know an individual's location to within 3 square feet, at all times, via cellular-radio technology.

These contrasts emphasize the need for a fundamental way of making choices. From what we have learned, that means framing questions as *should*—the ethical frame of analysis—not *can*—the feasibility or opportunistic frame of analysis. There is, then, an opportunity to reassert the need for values clarification and ethical decision-making. These contrasts suggest new emphases on alternate ways of learning, learning from peers, learning with machines, and learning (in the adult fashion) what is needed, when it is needed, wherever it is needed. This implies reconsideration of what one needs to know in order to learn what one may need to know, that is, teaching to learn, not necessarily teaching to do. It is just this consideration that may make social work well prepared to engage this new world. The field of social work has always asserted the value of a variety of learning modes, with the exception of learning with machines, and has implemented them in the field and in the classroom.

The focus in social work upon field instruction offers another opportunity to both teach the student and change the practice community by having the students bring to agencies the new practice- or service-related applications of information technology. The students in field instruction form the needed bridge between the university laboratory and the world of practice, and information technology is their link to the community at large. The opportunity to inform the community at large, via new communication techniques and media, of the importance, variety, and availability of social services has never been greater, but we must seize the opportunities and begin to use these techniques and media appropriately and effectively. (See Brawley, 1983, for details on public media, and LaMendola's work, unpublished, at the University of Denver for an exemplar in field instruction.)

One of the most difficult parts of teaching practice is to develop appropriate modes of decision-making — modes that take advantage of the varieties of information available and the varied rationalities for dealing with the content of each variety. Decision-making taught in practice is limited by the few experiences that can be obtained and examined in any time period, and the unpredictable quality of those experiences. Information technology (see Lynett in Chapter 5) now provides the opportunity to have a larger variety of very realistic experiences in a controlled and observable manner, in a relatively brief period, and wherever they are needed (e.g., classroom, home, agency, etc.). These admit adaptation to the needs of each learner and each learning situation. What has not been explored is their use in group process or group decision-making. The use of simulations to teach complex decision-making and experiential learning in the variety of areas of interest to social work, areas such as policy development, community organization, concrete service delivery, therapy, and research, has hardly been explored. For example, Pruger (Chapter 5) provides insight into a system with some exciting potentials for learning in the field and the classroom settings, and Stein and Rzepnicki (1983) provide the foundations for simulating decision-making in child welfare. What is perhaps most exciting is the potential to teach and explore decision-making via simulation, without fear of injury through error, before engaging the real world of practice. For the teacher, this offers new emphasis on the role of "enabler of discovery" rather than the role of "instructor of method, fact and belief," thereby returning the excitement to learning and to teaching.

The advent of communicating by means of personal computers opens a new world for us all, especially for those in need of the support of others, whether professionals in need of expert consultation or clients in need of simple solutions to problems of daily living. The electronic bulletin boards provide the means for supplying and obtaining information, and that opens access in a way we have never known. They also provide means for users to evaluate services and to communicate those evaluations to interested parties. This capability is a two-edged sword that can cut the ineffective and harmful from the service field, but can just as easily cut the life blood of a service that is irresponsibly maligned. Again we return to the vital need for a foundation of ethical thought and behavior to modulate our actions in the context of our newfound freedoms and opportunities.

There is no question that information technology threatens us as well in other ways: we are concerned about job loss, and job dislocations — the increasing demand for skills possessed by ever fewer people and the reduced need for people with lesser or "outmoded" skills. For this reason and others, we have developed the theme of support, and not replacement! Automation threatens the worker's freedom of action and discretionary judgment, especially when an administration forms and imposes the rules without regard to the needs and realities of service. Pruger made this point in Chapter 5, and the subsequent discussion raised the question of the value of regressing all workers toward mean decisions, that is, having the system encourage convergence to some average "good decision." Christensen clearly identified other threats in her analysis in Chapter 3, namely, violations of the obligations of professionals to clients (confidentiality), violations of clients' rights (privacy), and so forth. Palombo asserted further concerns in Chapter 8, but he seems especially troubled by the intrusion of machines into human relationships, relationships that he sees as fundamental to the provision of service. In this regard, he shares Weizenbaum's (1976) concerns. The advent of cellular radio extends our concerns from having personal information about us kept in written records to having our physical whereabouts known at all times. There is then added reason to assert the need for more questions involving ethics than questions involving technical feasibility, and that they take precedence in our valuations. In the following, we elaborate other issues raised at the conference with regard to opportunities, threats, and next steps.

COMPILING AN ENCYCLOPEDIA OF IGNORANCE: EXPLORATIONS IN OPPORTUNITIES, THREATS, AND ACTIONS

Are the loss of confidentiality, the loss of privacy, the loss of freedom, depersonalization, and dehumanization necessary consequences of information-technology applications? How can these effects be avoided or at least minimized? How are these effects to be measured? Many critics of technology assume that these effects are necessary consequences of the technology. Advocates for technology say that they are in fact consequences of thoughtlessness or simply poor designs. It is not clear that we have good definitions of these effects (see Brod, 1984; Turkle, 1984; and Weizenbaum, 1976, for some definitions and discussion) or that we have means for measuring their magnitude. Without such measurement techniques, we cannot compare competitive designs.

Can social inequities be reduced or relieved via information-technology applications? Greater access to information, to experts, to other resources, and to services seems to be possible for everyone through information technology, that is, for everyone who can have access to it, and who has the skills and knowledge to use the media, mechanisms, and information. To the degree that information represents power, people are empowered by access to information. For information technology to have such positive effects, it will be necessary to increase the public's access to, understanding of, and ability to use information. It may be necessary to furnish human supports for particular user groups. This could be a new or expanded role for properly prepared social workers. Some conferees even argued that information technology is contributing significantly to enabling the social changes advocated during the '60s and '70s. If such is true, this also renews opportunities for social work.

Can coordination of services and interagency cooperation be stimulated and achieved via information technology? The Ramey scenario in Chapter 4 gives one example of what has been attempted and achieved ın this area. There are other examples of coordination via information technology for the purpose of service integration and detection of service gaps: the Jamaica Service Program for Older Adults (JASPOA) in New York City built a data-base system to coordinate a number of agencies serving the aged. In general, information and referral systems tend to require and develop cooperation and some coordination (Levinson & Haynes, 1984). There are, at least, questions of a political and organizational sort, if not a technical and intentional sort.

How do the environment of service, the services, and the roles of each of the actors change when information technology is involved in social work practice? Can we classify the positive and the negative aspects of these changes? Information technology would seem to offer the best available information and service to each and every client, regardless of location, via communications networks, information and referral services, bulletin boards and, especially, expert systems. But we question the ability of many clients to use such services, unaided by others, and the willingness of any professional to play "second fiddle" to a machine. Autonomy of action and discretionary judgment may be threatened, while the ability to serve, and especially to serve well, may be dramatically enhanced. We need to explore and classify the impacts and effects carefully. This is the essence of Palombo's proposed statement in Chapter 8.

What can and what should social work contribute to the development of information technology? The normal assumption is that there is a unidirectional flow from technology and science to social work, but there is mounting evidence that there is a reciprocal opportunity. The dependence of successful technological applications upon human acceptance suggests the need for contributions in value clarifications, ethical analyses, change strategies, group dynamics, team-building, adaptation strategies—areas in which social work can contribute. Similarly, social work can contribute by identifying its own special needs with respect to information technology in order to stimulate appropriate technological developments.

How can we enable the application of the creative potentials of colleagues to the development of information-technology applications in teaching and practice? This question subsumes two other questions: Should this be our mission? And, how can we most effectively distribute the motivating information to those in other areas of the field?

How can we get the appropriate tools into the hands of others? This would require a positive answer to the question, "Should this be our mission?" and it would require definitions of what is to be done, what tools are required, and to whom they should be distributed.

Do we need to develop a catalogue of the technologies that social work organizations now use in order to proceed to the next step? It was suggested that in order to pursue change we must first document the current state of technology utilization in social work organizations, both practice-oriented and educational. Do we need to do that, and can information technology help us in that task?

What could be done with information technology that could not be done otherwise? What new possibilities and opportunities does it offer? What means to avoid previous obstacles and the disadvantages of existing problem solutions does it offer? These are some of the most challenging questions in our encyclopedia of ignorance. The answers are bounded primarily by our creativity and insight. The most significant step in human development occurs when we move from using a tool in the way for which it was intended and begin to use it in ways the inventor never foresaw (e.g., computers used as tools for communicating instead of calculating).

Should the replication of systems be encouraged, and how? The general feeling seemed to be that much duplication of effort occurs because individuals and organizations do not know of the systems being developed by others. This suggests that we need some formal process of building awareness and information exchange.

Beyond the establishment of some exchange mechanism is the question of whether such technology transfers are in fact possible and worthwhile. The general suggestion seemed to be that conceptual transfers were preferable to literal system transfers, that is, the conceptual basis is transferred and then implemented in a particular way suitable to the recipient. This may require much more work than a literal system transfer (turnkey transfer).

How can social work use the new communications technologies such as cellular radio, and prevent their misuse? Cellular technology can provide mobile communications between any two served points on the earth, and accurate tracking of any transmitter, providing remarkable opportunities for voice, data, and video exchanges between individuals in the field and the office. It also makes possible tracking the movements of individuals — for example, chronic schizophrenics or those under "house arrest." There would appear to be both opportunity and responsibility for the field of social work to make use of and advocate, in general, the appropriate uses of these technologies.

What problems, adverse consequences, or misuses should social work try to anticipate and/or try to prevent? Given its concern for the quality of life, social work would seem to have both the opportunity and the responsibility for active involvement in the development of the new information society. Given its expressed interest in preventive rather than restorative models of action, the field should engage in anticipating difficulties and actively moving technological applications away from these difficulties and toward approaches that are preferred in human terms.

How can social work capitalize, for its own development and the welfare of its clients, on the changes brought by information technology? Here the reference of the moment is to the "microcomputer culture," the opportunity for "organic" systems-development processes and a new level of access to information via microcomputers and telecommunications. Social work can capitalize on the new opportunities to network professionals via electronic media and thereby speed information exchange, mobilize action groups in less time, and so on. The profession can also be the means for the "less fortunate" to gain access to these developments for personal or community benefit. What are needed are understanding, plans, resources, and actions.

This question also raises the issue of whether the field needs to take each of the successive steps taken by commerce and government (the leaders in information-technology use), or whether it can avoid some of those steps by taking advantage of the latest technology. A discussion of the stages of information-system development is contained in Schoech's work (Schoech, 1982, pp. 155–168, and Schoech & Schkade, 1980), and more recently, in Martin's (1984) work.

How should the priorities be set with regard to which tasks within an organization are to be supported by information technology? Systems are usually first built to meet the needs of top management (i.e., financial systems, evaluation systems, etc. [LaMendola, 1981]). But Keen (1983) has suggested that there are areas of activity more deserving of support, in terms of organizational benefits, than those at the "top." It was also suggested that by supporting the lower levels, fewer decisions would arrive at top-management's doorstep as crises. The problem is that system builders want top-management visibility for their own personal reasons, and top management often chooses to meet its own needs first. So the issue is whether these decisions will be made on political bases or on the basis of rational analyses of need and effect.

Our discussions indicated that systems designed to support and enhance the service-delivery process would also provide the data required to meet the needs of management. This suggests that systems development should begin with the fundamental transactions of the organization and not with its more abstract needs. The experiences reported by Newkham, Pruger, and Hammond, in Chapter 5, indicate that substantial participation of the service-givers must be a principal, not incidental or auxiliary, element of a design philosophy. Can the organization's needs in strategic planning, control and evaluation be served by such a design process, which, for lack of a better term, has been called *bottom-up*? Are there real fundamental differences in the information required to meet the needs of managers and service-givers? If so, what are they? LaMendola (1976) has provided us with some foundation knowledge in his dissertation work.

Do we know how to build systems expressly for meeting the communications needs of social workers?   Discussions identified the needs social workers have for sharing information, and accessing information, for the purposes of remaining current, resolving difficult problems, finding special resources, and for improving the quality of care and for being accountable. One of the lessons learned from the Heart of Texas system (Newkham, Chapter 5) is that its existence improved the communication among caseworkers via standardized data that could be exchanged easily. Are there special requirements for communicating in a field that is oriented toward long text records, concern for process as well as outcome, and the use of nonverbal information?

Is social work prepared to move ahead to the next level of information-technology applications?   There is much concern over the lack of standardized definitions of terms, standardized data elements, and uniformly structured data bases in social work. The information and referral field provides an example of the difficulty of finding common bases for describing social-service activities. The attempts to develop national data bases in public welfare (Tatara, 1982) illustrate the political, the organizational, and the technical problems of developing uniform data sets. The field of information and referral has also identified the lack of common definitions for services and service characteristics as a problem.

The question then becomes, "Must all the pieces be in place, must all the standards be developed, before starting to apply information technology?" The suggestions made by Vallee, in presentation and discussion, regarding an "information marketplace" (also see Nora & Minc, 1980, pp. 136–141, for a discussion of the "informational agora") are relevant here. The field might develop without an imposed order and, over time, sort and select the appropriate and valuable approaches to data and communications. Can the field afford such an approach?

Should we encourage the use of the "organic growth" model of systems development, and how can we best do that? Given the state of social work organizations, overburdened and without adequate resources in funds and technical knowledge, starting with small prototype systems that grow would seem appropriate (the "organic growth" model). However, there is concern that with limited resources one cannot afford to experiment, one needs to implement "sure things."

Given that it is appropriate, how does one counter the well-developed culture of formal systems analysis and design? How can the field be educated to this new culture? Does the new culture presume a base upon which to build, that is, a base of established data systems and reporting mechanisms, an understanding of how to collect and use information? How can we get professionals to explore what the available and affordable equipment can do, rather than wait for the resources to buy the elaborate equipment that is in vogue at that moment?

Is there a need to continue the discussion process that was initiated by the conference? Many viewed the conference as a ground-breaking event that identified issues but could not resolve them or even fully define directions to be taken. What should be the next steps, if any, in this process?

PRINCIPAL CONFERENCE AGREEMENT

After much discussion and with some difficulty, the conference participants accepted and endorsed the following positions as generally acceptable and worthy of further consideration and action:

The Purpose of Information Technology in Social Work Practice

Miller offered the following proposal, from his view as an economist, in an attempt to bring order to the listing and discussion of issues:

> The objective of information technology is to inform the production and distribution process in the social-service system for the purpose of improving the efficacy of that process/system.

Miller explained that by production and distribution process he meant, for example, service awards, service delivery, and the organization of social services. He went on to say that efficacy meant simply doing a task or activity better, whether that be administering, evaluating, serving, or helping.

Much of the discussion dealt with the understanding of efficacy and its connection to values. Given that efficacy is "the power to produce effects or intended results; effectiveness" (Guralnik, 1980, p. 445), it becomes clear that our values and ethics affect the definition of the desired or intended effects and thereby our specific understanding of efficacy. This was ultimately the conclusion of the discussion of this proposal, and apparently Miller's intent in his choice of words. Thus, while we will debate which specific results are intended because of differing value systems, we can agree that the purpose of information technology is to inform the production and distribution process so that the selected results can be more effectively achieved.

We agreed that we want to be more informed about what we are doing, why we are doing it, how we are doing it, and how well we are doing it. We are concerned not only with the end point but with the process as well. It is vital that we recognize this as a statement of purpose for information technology in social work practice and distinguish it from a definition. This is an assertive, intentional statement, not one that is descriptive in general, or even descriptive of current usage.

To further the utility of this statement, Miller proposed five categories of actions that would help to bring about achievement of this purpose.

Description of the production and distribution process   This might include information systems about accountability, identification of changes in systems that could lead to better decisions, models of professional practice, software scales to measure service effects, text-oriented data bases for capturing process records, and anything else that would help to describe a process.

Implementation of the process descriptions   This includes development of understanding of the barriers to innovation and change, for example, concerns of the field regarding technology, resistance to change, and ethical values that hinder progress.

Transfer of information   In order to make the innovations and creations readily available. This includes educational processes, curriculum development, networking, establishment and operation of bulletin boards, and development of technical standards. In fact, it relates to whatever will enable the products of our collective creative activity to reach all of us and become a part of the field of social work.

Resource development and acquisition   The need to provide the support for these activities.

Defining relationships   The above categories should be considered and related as an entity to the field of social work, while defining how that relationship and the field will change.

In a very simplified form these categories of action could be summarized as:

- Model-building
- Simulation and exploration with the models
- Dissemination of the results
- Funding for activities
- Impact analysis

This overarching statement of purpose was also challenged as being too limiting. That is, much of service is giving information, evaluating information, interpreting information, and so forth, and as such can be provided via information technology. This raised the question of whether the term *inform* was too delimiting. It is not as delimiting if one accepts the rare or obsolete senses of the word, that is, "to give form to," or "to form or shape [the mind]" (Guralnik, 1980, p. 722). Nonetheless, it seems that information technology may not only shape the production and distribution process, but may become a central part of it. Clearly, Miller's proposal is just a beginning statement and will be the subject of further discussion and amendment.

A Design Philosophy

Systems can and should be thought of as organic entities, and as growing from the needs of the service providers and clients. These systems can evolve, beginning with simple concepts and simple equipment involving initially small investments, and they can in that process of growth and development provide for the needs of administration and evaluation as well.

Because they are based upon the needs of clients and their service providers, systems shall be supportive of the service recipient, the service, and the service-giver. This means system design will require the significant participation of all users and affected groups in the design process. Further, given the dynamic quality of humans, their needs, and the service processes, the system must be as flexible as possible and must be designed for change — it must be based upon principles of feedback and adaptation.

With the advent of microcomputers and computer networks, diversity of design and implementation, especially prototyping, shall be encouraged until a clearly superior design or implementation becomes available for standard use. The concepts, implementations, and results of these diverse designs shall be freely communicated to foster technology transfer via a marketplace phenomenon, that is, a place to shop for ideas, not necessarily a place to purchase ideas in the commercial sense.

While this philosophy was not specifically debated in the same way as Miller's proposal, it is a synthesis of tacitly accepted principles that arose in various presentations and discussions.

Next Steps

In response to a strong need for closure among the conferees, Vallee proposed the following:

> Group meetings can do many things — from getting to know someone, to setting strategy, to decision-making and problem-solving. There is nothing wrong with a group simply setting information exchange as a goal. Therefore, let us agree that:
>
> - There is a technology out there that is affecting all of us in many different ways.
> - There is a continuing need to inform the community, for example, via a clearinghouse, and experiments with electronic conferencing.
> - The group has identified a series of issues and has questioned many assumptions about the use of technology; this is a resource for implementers and practitioners.
> - The Silberman Fund could serve the field by setting up a mechanism to disseminate the experiences of specific groups with information technology when it is relevant to others.

This proposal is founded on the observations that the technology is out of control and that its developers do not have any concept of where its development will take us, nor do they show any concern for examining or regulating their own actions (Sackman, 1975, pp. 83–87; Vallee, 1982, pp. 5–11; Christiansen, 1984). Further, it recognizes that the conference did develop at least a beginning list of issues that represent our doubts about where we are going, our ideas and concepts about information technology and social work practice, and a sense of a preferred direction of movement. Vallee recommends continued communications among the interested parties via a low-tech clearinghouse (to assure access to all, at present) and experimentation with high-tech networking among those with a high need to communicate. The objective is to achieve synergy of our actions via communication and information transfers. This proposal recognizes that like the field as a whole, the conferees were not ready to develop policies or an overarching strategy for the development of information-technology utilization in social work practice. It also recognizes the importance of information exchange, and tacitly underscores the need for more interdisciplinary activities. **In summary, it recommends investment in intra- and intercultural technology transfer directed toward the full development of the human edge.**

Appendixes
References
Bibliography
Index

APPENDIX A

CONFERENCE PARTICIPANTS

Dr. William Butterfield
Associate Professor
The George Warren Brown School of Social Work
Washington University in St. Louis
St. Louis, MO 63130

Mr. Richard H. Calica[1]
Executive Director
Juvenile Protective Association
1707 North Halsted St.
Chicago, IL 60614

Dr. Al Cavalier
Director, Bioengineering Program
Department of Research and Program Services
Association for Retarded Citizens
2501 Avenue J
Arlington, TX 76006

Dr. Kathleen Christensen
Deputy Director
Center for Human Environments
Graduate Center, City University of New York
33 West 42nd Street
New York, NY 10036

1. Member, Conference Planning Committee

Ms. Connie J. Cobb[1]
Evaluation Coordinator
Office of Planning and Coordination
Minnesota Department of Public Welfare
St. Paul, MN 55155

Dr. Joan DiLeonardi
Vice President for Planning,
    Research and Quality Assurance
Children's Home and Aid Society of Illinois
1122 North Dearborn Street
Chicago, IL 60610

Dr. John Flynn
Professor
School of Social Work
Western Michigan University
Kalamazoo, MI 49008

Dr. Marilyn Flynn
Professor
School of Social Work
University of Illinois — Urbana
1207 Oregon Street
Urbana, IL 61801

Mr. William J. Garrett
Assistant Vice President
United Way of Tri-State
99 Park Avenue
New York, NY 10016

Mrs. Carole A. Geiss
Publications Consultant
8 Meadowlark Lane
Huntington, NY 11743

Dr. Gunther R. Geiss, Chairman[1]
Professor
School of Social Work
Adelphi University
Garden City, NY 11530

1. Member, Conference Planning Committee

Dr. Margaret Gibelman[2]
Council on Social Work Education
1744 R Street NW
Washington, D.C. 20009

Mrs. Arlene R. Gordon
Associate Executive Director
Program Planning, Evaluation, Research and Training
New York Association for the Blind
111 East 59th Street
New York, NY 10022
Now:
Director, The Lighthouse
National Center for Vision and Aging
111 East 59th Street
New York, NY 10022

Dr. Kenric W. Hammond
Chief, Inpatient Psychiatry
Veterans Hospital
116A
11201 Benton Street
Loma Linda, CA 92357

Dr. Yeheskel Hasenfeld
Associate Dean
School of Social Work
University of Michigan
1065 Frieze Building
Ann Arbor, MI 48109

Dr. John C. Henderson
Associate Professor of Management Science
Sloan School of Management
Massachusetts Institute of Technology
50 Memorial Drive
Cambridge, MA 02139

Dr. Walter W. Hudson
Professor
School of Social Work
Florida State University
Tallahassee, FL 32306

---

2. Contributed scenario, unable to attend

Mr. William Koerber
Director of Computing Activities
School of Social Work
Columbia University
622 West 113th Street
New York, NY 10025

Dr. Walter LaMendola[1]
Social Work Department
Allied Health Division
East Carolina University
Greenville, NC 27834
Now:
Director, Information Technology Center
Graduate School of Social Work
University of Denver
Denver, CO 80208

Dr. Risha Levinson
Director, Service Development Division
School of Social Work
Adelphi University
Garden City, NY 11530

Dr. Harold Lewis[3]
Dean
School of Social Work
Hunter College—CUNY
129 East 79th Street
New York, NY 10021

Ms. Patricia Ann Lynett
Director, Office for Interactive Technology and Training
Social Work Department, Bldg. 77
University of West Florida
Pensacola, FL 32561

Dr. Leonard Miller
Associate Professor
School of Social Welfare
University of California—Berkeley
2223 Fulton Street
Berkeley, CA 94720

1. Member, Conference Planning Committee
3. Member, Fund Grant Committee

Mr. Jim Newkham
Director, Outpatient Services
Heart of Texas Region Mental Health
    and Mental Retardation Center
P.O. Box 890
110 South 12th Street
Waco, TX 76703

Dr. Charles O'Reilly[1]
Dean
School of Social Work
Loyola University
Chicago, IL 60611

Mr. Joseph Palombo
Dean
Institute for Clinical Social Work
466 Central Avenue, Suite 12
Northfield, IL 60093

Dr. Robert Pruger
Associate Professor
School of Social Welfare
University of California — Berkeley
Haviland Hall
Berkeley, CA 94720

Dr. J. Wendell Ramey
Exective Director
Mon Valley Community Health Center
Eastgate 8
Monessen, PA 15062

Dr. Bruce Schimmig
Consultant
Academic Information Systems
IBM
15300 Shady Grove Road
Rockville, MD 20850

1. Member, Conference Planning Committee

Dr. Dick Schoech[1]
Assistant Professor
Graduate School of Social Work
University of Texas at Arlington
P.O. Box 19129
Arlington, TX 79019

Dr. Theodore J. Stein[2]
School of Social Work
New York University
3 Washington Square North
New York, NY 10003

Dr. Jacques Vallee
Vice President, International Operations
SOFINNOVA, Inc.
Three Embarcadero Center
Suite 2560
San Francisco, CA 94111

Mr. Mark Vermilion
Manager, Community Affairs
Apple Computer, Inc.
20525 Mariani Avenue, M/S 23-L
Cupertino, CA 95014

Dr. Narayan Viswanathan[1]
Director, Doctoral Program
School of Social Work
Adelphi University
Garden City, NY 11530

Dr. Lynn Harold Vogel[1]
Assistant Professor
School of Social Service Administration
University of Chicago
969 East 60th Street
Chicago, IL 60637
Now:
Medical Center
University of Chicago
Chicago, IL 60637

1. Member, Conference Planning Committee
2. Contributed scenario, unable to attend

Dr. Douglas Warns
Vice President, Management Information Systems
United Way of America
United Way Plaza
Alexandria, VA 22314

Dr. Wandal Winn
Department of Psychiatry
University Hospital
600 Highland Avenue
Madison, WI 53792
Now:
Alaska Treatment Center
3710 East 20th Avenue
Anchorage, AL 99508

APPENDIX B

THE INFORMATION TECHNOLOGY AND SOCIAL WORK PRACTICE CONFERENCE

Information technology, the synergistic combination of computers, information systems, and communications systems, is making inroads on what some consider the last professional bastion of human values and human concern—social work. Are those who valiantly defend us against the onslaught of mechanistic thinking, automation, and dehumanization the Luddites of today, or are they the visionaries who may protect us against an undesirable future? The opportunities offered to us by high technology are quite attractive, yet we know that there are substantial and, often, hidden costs attached. Therefore, we must concern ourselves with defining the appropriate applications of high technology, especially information technology, in social work.

The primary inroads have been in administrative, evaluative, and record-keeping activities. These applications have, in most instances, made demands upon the service-giver's time and energy for additional data-recording, without returning much of value to the service-giver, the client, or the service process. The focus has often been solely upon efficiency or detection of fraud and abuse, rather than upon the effectiveness or the quality of the service. Finally, little has been done with this technology to enhance the education or training of service-givers.

These statements encapsulate the themes that moved us to write this volume and that informed the writing. This appendix presents a detailed description of the processes of organizing, conducting, and documenting the conference, together with an evaluation of the conference. The processes were unique in the innovative and conscious determination to explore the application of information technology to conference building and execution while building and executing a conference on information technology. For this reason a formal evaluation was conducted and is reported later.

CONFERENCE PURPOSES

The Lois and Samuel Silberman Fund has chosen as its basic goal the "improvement in the quality and competence of persons preparing for work or working in social-welfare programs." With this as its focus, and faced with an increasing number of unsolicited proposals involving computers, the Grant Committee of The Fund recognized the need for guidelines for its investment decisions regarding computer applications in the social-welfare field. It invited one of the editors (Geiss) to organize and chair a group to examine the problem and devise a process for responding to this need for guidance. The Conference Planning Committee (identified in Appendix A, "Conference Participants"), with the aid of some members of the Grant Committee, then defined the broader and emerging domain of information technology as the technological focus, and social work practice as the applications focus. These foci emerged as we came to recognize the need to work well into the future in order to avert immediate obsolescence in this rapidly changing environment.

A working conference of experts, which would contribute to the creation of this book, was selected as the most appropriate vehicle to meet the needs of The Fund and the field it serves. The Planning Committee then defined the conference purposes:

- To broaden the social work profession's utilization of information technology.
  - To define information technology as it applies to the social services.
  - To explore the opportunities to apply information technology in the social-service-delivery process.
  - To examine the appropriate and necessary roles for social workers in the development and evolution of information-technology applications.
- To suggest directions for the development of information-technology applications in the practice of social work.
  - To identify opportunities for change in the education and training of social workers for direct practice.

- To identify particularly attractive innovations and directions for research and development.
- To identify the issues, especially ethical issues, created by adopting, or not adopting, information technology in the service-delivery process.

Along with these purposes, the Planning Committee identified the following major issues for discussion at the conference.

- What is the state of the art in information technology vis-à-vis its utilization in the social services?
- What are the opportunities for development, and which are the preferred directions of development, of the field of social work via the utilization of information technology?
- What steps are required to encourage the immediate use of information technology by the social work profession?
- What actions are required to enhance the long-term development of the utilization of information technology by the social work profession?
- What investment guidelines and project priorities would be most appropriate for The Lois and Samuel Silberman Fund?

CONFERENCE DESIGN AND DEVELOPMENT

Using the stated purposes and major issues for guidance, the Planning Committee, with the encouragement and insightful support of Mr. Samuel J. Silberman, Dr. Thomas Horton, and Dean Harold Lewis (members of the Grant Committee), set about designing a novel conference and a novel conference-development process (electronic conferencing via computer). The Planning Committee decided to invite papers that would inform participants about state-of-the-art innovations in social work practice, and what had been learned by implementing and operating these innovative applications of information technology. This meant that the innovations had to have been in place long enough to allow for the accumulation of operating experience. Laboratory experiments were not acceptable because they would not inform us of the practice issues and difficulties. Further, within a brief span of space and time, participants had to be acquainted with the broadest spectrum of possibilities that might serve as the springboard for a discussion of the future prospects. The Committee selected the first four papers that appear in Chapter 5, "The State of the Art: Concepts, Applications, and Case Studies" with great care and chose to require participants to read the papers in advance of the conference so that the discussions could be focused on developing the implications and extrapolations of these experiences. These papers were prepared according to specific guidelines to provide relatively uniform structure and content for ease of comparison and discussion.

While the papers provide the insights of four operating and design experiences, we felt that more was needed to inform the deliberations. Consequently, we decided to request that participants encapsulate their own views of the opportunities, barriers, and issues related to information technology and social work practice. These views are contained in the problem scenarios that are presented in Chapter 4, "Internal Views of Opportunities and Threats: Scenarios." Each of these scenarios represents an actual case, a combination of cases, or an extrapolation of cases, and, obviously, the concerns of the scenario's author. While the original plan was to present a few scenarios, the chairman took the liberty of including all of the scenarios submitted, in order to provide a broader grounding in our "realities." Random arrangement was chosen as the mode of presentation to avoid imposing a personal perception of order upon others who may perceive quite differently.

We selected the keynote presentations after an extensive search for individuals who had unique insights into the issues inherent in relating information technology and the concerns of helping people and, especially, social workers. Specifically, we searched for experts from outside of the field to provide the expertise and views only outsiders could add. The keynote speakers were informed that their primary task would be to disturb and break down whatever traditional views might be held by participants and, by stimulating and challenging them, open the free thinking and brainstorming that needed to be done. The choice of subjects and speakers seemed to arise naturally, although it was not always easy to gain commitments from people who were quite busy with other demands. The final attraction for the keynote speakers was the opportunity to contribute to a field just entering upon automation and information-technology utilization, and one that is devoted to helping others less fortunate than they. The subjects of networks, ethics, and the impact of decision support systems on organizations and professionals are, in hindsight, still the best choices of the many available, based on their potential impacts on the field, their currency, and the concerns of the field.

The search for speakers was conducted via other experts, automated literature searches to identify productivity and the general gist of positions and, when possible, hearing the candidate speak at a major meeting. The search for participants went along somewhat similar lines, although there the Planning Committee had much personal knowledge of colleagues. Some serendipitous discoveries also helped. These occurred in two forms: accidental meetings at public conferences, and publications or contributions that came to the attention of committee members serving as journal peer reviewers. The significance of these comments, to us, is in identifying and emphasizing the value of access to large human- and technical-information networks.

Perhaps the most unique aspect of the conference-building activity was the use of the Electronic Information Exchange System (EIES) at New Jersey Institute of Technology, Newark, New Jersey. This experimental system, built with National Science Foundation funding, under the direction of Dr. Murray Turoff, provides electronic mail, conferencing, and notebooks, along with a host of document preparation and formatting services. It serves a host of scientific, educational, and not-for-profit activities, and is unique in its built-in optional social-evaluation process. This gave us first-hand knowledge of the new world we would explore at the conference. It also meant that the geographically dispersed Planning Committee could build the conference with frequent contact via EIES and telephone conferencing, despite travel demands and varied work habits.

The Planning Committee members met together, physically, only twice in the 15 months during which the conference was prepared: once to open the process, and once at the mid-point. The telephone conferencing was used for discussions needing on-the-spot discussion and resolution, and to be sure to periodically include those few members who were not able to connect with EIES because of a lack of access to the required equipment. Perhaps the most significant observation was that EIES usage was highest at the outset and whenever there was a pressing issue to engage all members; otherwise participation varied considerably, and even the originator had to be reminded to sign on occasionally to receive mail. Costs were significantly in favor of EIES over site meetings. The monthly charge for six members on EIES, including document-storage charges—for instance, the Conference Plan, which was being reviewed and built on-line—approximated 1 to $1\text{-}\frac{1}{2}$ one-hour telephone conferences, and one-eighth the cost of eight members meeting for one day (including one night in a hotel and airfare). EIES not only provided a means to terminate "telephone tag" but it also gave us a record of our messages, made us give a bit more thought to our messages than we would have done in a conversation, and gave us access to others using the medium. The system is designed for off-line composition—in the sense that it provides for on-line short-message composition—and the connect charges tend to encourage uploading and downloading of larger documents. This also seems preferable for writing, editing, and reading of long texts.

CONFERENCE PLAN

The following is the Conference Plan, as distributed to participants prior to the conference and with the background papers and scenarios.

THE LOIS AND SAMUEL SILBERMAN FUND
INFORMATION TECHNOLOGY AND
SOCIAL WORK PRACTICE CONFERENCE
June 9–12, 1984
Wye Plantation, Queenstown, MD

Conference Process

Participants will receive background papers and problem scenarios one week before the conference and will be expected to arrive having read these materials. The keynote speakers have been selected to provide challenging and stimulating discussions relating to the general conference purpose and will serve as resource persons and consultants during the remaining discussions. The background papers will not be presented but will be discussed in the context of the problem scenarios. The ensuing discussions should provide opportunity for brainstorming and should result in the development of guidelines for the utilization of information technology in the fields of social work practice and education. The development of the conference proceedings will be open to all participants, as observers and commentators. Access will require the availability of a terminal or personal computer, a modem and either UNINET or GTE's TELENET.

Conference Schedule

SATURDAY, JUNE 9, 1984

3:00 PM Participants arrive at Wye Plantation. (About an hour and a half from Washington National Airport.)

6:00 PM Cocktails on the boardwalk patio (weather permitting) or in the Commons Room of the Conference Center.

7:00 PM Dinner in the Dining Hall.

8:00 PM Convene in the Conference Center.

Welcome and introductions, Dr. Geiss.

Conference charge, Mr. Silberman.

SATURDAY, JUNE 9, 1984 *(continued)*

8:30 PM Keynote presentation: "Information Society and Human Values."
Kathleen E. Christensen, Ph.D., Deputy Director, Center for Human Environments, Graduate Center, City University of New York.

Discussion until 11 PM.

SUNDAY, JUNE 10, 1984

Coffee and continental breakfast for early risers.

10:00 AM Keynote presentation: "Societal Consequences of Information Technology: Problems and Cautions."
Jacques Vallee, Ph.D., Vice President, International Operations, SOFINNOVA, Inc., San Francisco.

Discussion until Noon.

Brunch at Noon in the Dining Hall.

1:00 PM Keynote presentation: "The Evolution of Information Technology: Impact on Organizations, and Professional Work; and the Role of Users in Systems Development."
John C. Henderson, Ph.D., Sloan School of Management, Massachusetts Institute of Technology.

Discussion until 3:00 PM.

3:45 PM Cruise on the Wye River to St. Michaels for dinner.

4:30 PM Maritime Museum tour or sightseeing in St. Michaels.

5:30 PM Gather at Terry Cabin for cocktails and dinner.

8:00 PM Board boat for trip back to Wye Woods.

9:00 PM Return to Wye Plantation for casual conversation and after-dinner drinks in the Commons Room.

Planning Committee meets with authors in the Conference Center Meeting Room to discuss procedures for Monday and to assign "housekeeping" chores.

MONDAY, JUNE 11, 1984

7:30 AM Breakfast

DISCUSSION OF PAPERS AND PROBLEM SCENARIOS

8:30 AM to 10:00 AM
"Information Technology Applied to Facilitating Professional Work."
Author: Jim Newkham
Coordinator/Discussion Leader: Walter LaMendola
Rapporter: Connie Cobb

10:30 AM to 12:00 PM
"Information Technology in Support of Service Delivery."
Author: Robert Pruger
Coordinator/Discussion Leader: Richard Calica
Rapporter: Narayan Viswanathan

12:00 PM to 1:00 PM Luncheon

1:00 PM to 2:30 PM
"Information Technology in Direct Service to Clients."
Author: William J. Garrett
Coordinator/Discussion Leader: Dick Schoech
Rapporter: Charles O'Reilly

2:30 PM to 2:45 PM Refreshments

2:45 PM to 4:15 PM
"Information Technology in Professional Preparation and Delivery of Services."
Author: Patricia Lynett
Coordinator/Discussion Leader: Lynn Harold Vogel
Rapporter: Gunther R. Geiss

4:15 PM to 5:30 PM Recreation and rest

5:30 PM to 7:00 PM Cocktails and dinner

GENERAL DISCUSSIONS:

7:00 PM to 9:00 PM
General Discussion Period 1
Discussion Leader: Connie Cobb
Rapporter: Walter LaMendola

TUESDAY, JUNE 12, 1984

7:00 AM
Breakfast (Please bring your luggage to the Conference Center
to facilitate departure on time.)

8:00 AM to 10:00 AM
General Discussion Period 2
Discussion Leader: Charles O'Reilly
Rapporter: Dick Schoech

10:00 AM to 10:30 AM Coffee break

10:30 AM to 12:30 PM
General Discussion Period 3
Discussion Leader: Narayan Viswanathan
Rapporter: Richard Calica

12:30 PM to 1:30 PM Luncheon

1:30 PM to 2:30 PM
Closing Session—Conference Summary
Presenter: Gunther R. Geiss
Rapporter: Lynn Harold Vogel

3:00 PM (Sharp!) Departure from Wye Plantation.

MONDAY, JUNE 18, 1984

Participant expense reports due. Requests for EIES accounts due.
Mail to Dr. Geiss.

MONDAY, JUNE 25, 1984

Participants receive travel expense reimbursement.

MONDAY, JULY 2, 1984

Participants' written comments due for inclusion in proceedings.
Mail or transmit to Dr. Geiss.

MONDAY, JULY 9, 1984

Rapporters' written summaries of discussions are due.
Authors' final paper revisions are due.
Mail or transmit to Dr. Geiss.

MONDAY, JULY 30, 1984

Final draft of proceedings delivered to Fund.
All EIES accounts are to be terminated.

○ ○ ○ ○

CONFERENCE OPERATION
AND DOCUMENTATION

We used information technology wherever possible in the conference-building and -management process. Part of the experiment was to determine whether the technology would permit doing the same task with less resources. The great majority of conference preparation was done by the chairman, with little staff support other than his trusty word processor and a conscientious human technical editor (Carole Geiss). Air-travel arrangements were handled by one travel agency with a direct computer-to-computer link with American Airlines' SABRE reservations system. This made the many changes in flight schedules and coordination of arrivals and departures relatively easy. The ground-travel arrangements were handled with the aid of a simple dBASE II program, again for ease of changes and coordination. The selection of participant invitees (40) from the list of over 100 candidates was also handled with a dBASE II program that recorded and sorted candidates, and assured that our selections represented a good cross-section of the field of participant candidates.

Perhaps the most useful of the applications was a dBASE II program used to index and retrieve comments contained on the 15 ninety-minute tapes recorded at the conference. The chairman (Geiss) used a variable-speech-control tape player (variable-speed playback with pitch adjustment) to listen to the tapes at higher-than-normal speed and thereby identified significant comments, on tape and in his conference notes, according to topic area, subject area, speaker at the time the comment was interjected, person making the comment, and tape identity and tape-counter position. Thus, using the DBMS, we retrieved comments, by a variety of information characteristics, and thus identified their tape positions for relistening. This proved invaluable in writing this volume, for assuring comprehensiveness and accuracy of statements, in words, context, and spoken nuance.

At the conference, a word processor was used to provide immediate printed feedback of the session content to participants. This was done by assigning a Planning Committee member as discussion leader, and another as session recorder. The former focused on conducting the discussion, while the latter kept notes, supported the leader, and kept track of time. Immediately after the session, the assigned team prepared a summary on the word processor, and the technical editor reviewed it and produced a copy for distribution to all participants before the next session. These served as reminders of discussions during the conference, and assisted discussion leaders in preparing the elaborated summaries contained in this volume.

We also used the DBMS program to prepare the keyword index to the scenarios, one (alphabetical) as contained here (at the end of Chapter 4) and distributed with the scenarios, and another, alphabetical within the field of practice of the scenario author. These, especially the latter, were intended to help discussion leaders anticipate issues and conflicts among participants, and to help them identify connections between the background paper they would discuss and the scenarios.

Finally, and throughout, the entire array of paper products needed at the conference was prepared by word processing, and xerographic reproduction. The background papers were received on paper and then placed on the word processor by the technical editor. The scenarios were treated similarly. The keynote papers prepared after the conference were, in two cases, received on disks from the authors' word processors and converted to our format by Dick Schoech. This occurred because of an uploading problem with EIES, which began after the Conference, and which was never satisfactorily solved. This entire document now resides on disks with the conference chairman and The Bookmakers, Incorporated, in Wilkes-Barre, Pennsylvania. This form of preparation has permitted more license in preparation and the freedom to edit and change with less concern for staff distress and expense incurred.

The uniqueness of the entire process led us to commission the evaluation that follows.

INFORMATION TECHNOLOGY AND
SOCIAL WORK PRACTICE CONFERENCE:
AN EVALUATION
**by Connie J. Cobb and
Walter F. LaMendola**

In 1983, The Lois and Samuel Silberman Fund convened a group of persons who were experimenting with new forms of information technology in the field of social work or who had concerns about the manner in which schools of social work could respond to new uses of the technology. The Fund sought to gain guidance and direction for its own policy development. The Fund was also interested in stimulating a process that would contribute to information-technology advances in social work education, practice, and service delivery. The outcome of the meeting was an agreement to enlarge the group into a planning committee. The Planning Committee, under the leadership of Gunther Geiss, was charged with developing a plan for a possible conference on information technology in social work. The plan was to be submitted to The Silberman Fund for approval. A plan was developed, approved, and resulted in this conference.

The members of the Planning Committee began the work process by sharing their concepts of new forms of the use of information technology in social work. The discussion raised concerns for ethical issues, for the modification of practice by the utilization of this new technology, and for the preparation of social workers to understand and utilize new tools. The committee agreed that social work students should be trained to use new forms of information technology.

The committee, after much discussion, set the following purposes and objectives for the conference:

- To broaden the social work profession's utilization of information technology.
  - To define information technology as it applies to the social services.
  - To explore the opportunities to apply information technology in the social-service-delivery process.
  - To examine the appropriate and necessary roles for social workers in the development and evolution of information-technology applications.

- To suggest directions for the development of new information-
  technology applications for social work practice.
  - To identify opportunities for change in the education and
    training of social workers.
  - To identify particularly attractive innovations and directions
    for research and development.
  - To identify the issues, especially ethical issues, created by
    adopting, or not adopting, information technology in the
    social-service-delivery process.

In order to further their stated purposes, the committee members
proposed the gathering of a group of persons who were leading the field
or stimulating the use of innovative technology. They endeavored to
provide some common ground among the participants by inviting
keynote speakers who would stimulate the thinking of participants and
force them to consider areas and issues that do not always surface in the
world of work. They wished to examine not only where this rapidly
developing technology may be moving in the future but also the ethical
issues that must be addressed. The committee sought to solicit "state-of-
the-art" commentary by commissioning four papers reflecting major
facets of information-technology applications in social work.

In setting the conference agenda, the committee attempted to create
an atmosphere that would stimulate participants not only to share the
ideas and concerns brought with them but also to entertain new philosophies. The Planning Committee hoped that this conference could
be the beginning of a growing network of persons who would carry forward the initial work of the conference and contribute to the development of new social work information technology. In order to help
establish rapport among participants and to maintain their focus, the
committee chose an isolated setting in a rural area — The Wye Plantation, a facility of the Aspen Institute for Humanistic Studies, outside
Washington, D.C.

The agenda was designed to move the participants through a variety
of experiences that could lead to accomplishment of the conference
goals and objectives. A key part of the conference was the preparation
expected of all participants. Each person was asked to prepare a
scenario in advance of the conference. A scenario was defined as a problem that could potentially be resolved, or which might arise, through
the use of information technology. The scenarios, along with the commissioned papers, the biographies and vitae of invitees, the description
of the conference purpose, and the agenda were mailed to the partici-

pants with a request that they be read as preparation for the conference. Conferees arrived with some common experience and some knowledge of those who would be their companions for the next four days.

The conference began with the three keynote addresses followed by group discussions. These were followed by discussion periods to be centered around the four commissioned papers. Each discussion period began with the Discussion Leader introducing the topic and relating the paper to appropriate scenarios, issues, and concerns. The author of each paper was to participate as a respondent to issues raised by the group. Following the four paper-discussion periods, the agenda called for moving through three successive general discussion periods, each of which would refine and further distill the concerns and philosophies that emerged in early sessions. These were to be followed by a conference summary by the conference chairman.

Preconference and postconference evaluation forms were completed by the participants. An analysis of the responses formed the basis for this evaluation.

Advance Materials   Participants commended the members of the Planning Committee on their decision to send commissioned papers and scenarios in advance of the conference. Many felt that their thoughts were more focused in anticipation of the conference and that it was valuable to have read the papers in advance. The conference materials in general were regarded as clear and informative. Many respondents commented that other conference planners should adopt the practice of providing papers in advance of the actual conference.

Scenarios   The scenarios were positively regarded by most participants. They were valued for providing insight into the concerns of other persons attending the conference and for providing a real-world focus to the proceedings. Some found them useful and stimulating; others reported that they tired quickly of repetitious problem descriptions. Most found the exercise of preparing the scenario a positive one that focused their thinking. Several wondered if the scenarios had any utility beyond the conference.

Preconference Analysis   The preconference evaluations indicated that participants were impressed with the quality of conference planning and materials and were looking forward to the conference with positive attitudes. Many participants related their pleasure in being invited and in the diversity of backgrounds and interests of their fellow conferees.

Keynote Addresses   The postconference evaluations indicated that the keynote addresses were well received. Most participants rated the speakers' presentations as good or excellent. Only 9 out of a possible 89 ratings indicated a below-average or poor assessment. Many persons commented on the quality of discussion following each keynote. While some persons would have liked more social-service orientation in the presentations, others appreciated the exposure to the areas of interest discussed by the presenters. Dr. Jacques Vallee's discussion of the future of technology and his description of hardware were rated most highly by participants. Dr. Kathleen Christensen's discussion of the ethics of technology utilization was considered most thought-provoking and was mentioned most frequently by participants in their evaluations.

Discussions of Papers   The papers were considered by the participants to have been well done. Indeed, many were disappointed that the group discussion wandered too often and did not focus clearly on the issues presented in the papers. This segment of the conference elicited discomfort. Participants commented that group-process techniques were not effectively used to achieve conference goals. As the day wore on, the discomfort level appeared to increase. The discussion of the first paper received the highest rating. Each discussion dropped in rating from the preceding one. Based on comments, this did not appear to be related to the subject of the paper but rather to a growing desire to focus discussion.

General Discussion   The first general discussion session was cancelled at the group's request. Participants very much wanted time for interaction with fellow conferees. Participants were concerned that there was no plan for generating the set of guidelines that was an anticipated product of the conference. After 2 full days of discussing general social work/information technology subjects, participants were not willing to continue at that level. The agenda was revised to fit the perceived progress of the group. The following day, a general understanding of common themes emerged. This was reflected in the participants' ratings of the session.

Conference Summary   The conference chairman summarized the proceedings at the last session. He reviewed the purpose of the conference, described where it had been and appeared to be going, and he outlined some next steps to further the conference goals. This session was rated as excellent or good in quality by a majority of the participants.

Postconference Analysis   The keynote addresses achieved the purpose
of stimulating conference participants and exposing social work participants to expert views of the ethics of information, promises of and
pitfalls in the use of information technology, and emerging issues in the
use of decision support systems. Each keynote address raised specific
issues of importance to social work, but those issues are imbedded in
each area and require time and consideration before they can be clearly
articulated. The ethics area is closer than each of the others to the surface of social work values and concerns. It also represents an area that
has been studied by social work professionals. For that reason, it pro-
voked a direct discussion of ethical frameworks and their relationships
to information technology and social work. It is in this area that social
work has a unique and important task. As an applied profession that
deals with the relationships between people and their environments,
social work can provide direction in what turns out to be the most
troubling set of questions posed by technologists, computer scientists,
information professionals, politicians, and many others: What is the
ethical use of information? By what set of values should the use and application of information technology be judged? What is there in new
forms of information technology that is of social value, social benefit, or
social good that reduces stress and alienation, increases the coping
capacity of people, and increases environmental responsiveness? It
seems that conference participants perceived these notions more clearly than those posed by the other keynote addresses. The conference
participants wanted a more focused, task-oriented process. Many were
bothered and uneasy about how their discussions could result in
guidelines usable by The Silberman Fund. There was also an emerging
recognition that there were significant value discrepancies between
clinicians and administrators that were not being brought clearly and
directly to the surface. Participants felt that more time should have
been taken to address these issues directly and determine how they
might play out in the infusion of new information technology into social
work practice.

However, the innovative format used by the conference planners had
an unanticipated effect. By reading the background papers beforehand,
it seems likely that the participants felt no need to focus upon discussion of the contents of the papers. In effect, the group of participants
already had formed ideas of the common themes and issues that were
contained not only in the papers but in the scenarios. Those common
themes and issues could not emerge easily if attention to specifics of the
papers had to be addressed. The result of conducting the separate
discussions of the papers frustrated movement beyond the common

themes and issues. During the discussion of the first paper, all of those themes and issues appeared. With each succeeding discussion, the paper became incidental to restatements of those themes, restatements that became more and more strident because they could not be pursued in their own right without seeming to slight the discussion of the paper. At the same time, while the diversity of the backgrounds of the conferees was stimulating and was perceived positively, it would seem likely that the diversity had other effects. One effect was that the group could not sustain discussion in a particular professional area such as direct practice, without either losing involvement of others or risking more open disagreement about the substance of proposed guidelines or priorities. As a result, participants requested more time to talk freely with others outside of the large-group setting. This request can be understood as a felt need for the development of small groups or constituencies that had to be formed to deal with sustained, particularistic practice issues. The conference ended with this need vaguely perceived and understood, and certainly not articulated. Many participants referred to the need to network, and some special-interest groups were formed but not all sustained their work. It seems clear that the second step must be the gathering of persons from the social work community, some of whom attended this conference, who are representative of practice areas. Their agenda must be to develop guidelines and priorities for the professional community, in the context of what occurred at this meeting.

These conclusions seem to be supported by the two factors that participants felt would have made the conference more successful: greater recognition of emerging group processes, and the explicit development of guidelines and recommendations for The Silberman Fund to use in its grant-making process.

Participants reported that while their attitudes and professional goals had not been changed by the conference they clearly had been influenced. Most reported that they were encouraged to proceed with a direction in which they had already been moving but now with the confidence that they are "on the right track." Some expressed the opinion that their horizons had been broadened and that their understanding of the scope of the high-technology applications deepened considerably. Some indicated that they had now formulated ways to move toward incorporating new forms of information technology into their practices, agencies, or school curricula. Others felt they had been made more aware of the pitfalls involved in introducing new forms of information technology to their fields. Most mentioned that they had gained new appreciation for the importance of networking and communication in the information-technology area. Although the conference was often frustrating and sometimes painful, participants generally came away deeply affected by having participated in the process.

Asked what they regarded as most valuable about the conference, a unanimous, uproariously buoyant vote went to bringing the "right" people together and presenting them with a forum for sharing common and diverse interests, ideas, values, concerns, innovations, applications, and understanding. All participants commented on the pleasure they experienced in having 4 days to meet with people who are also pioneering in this technology. Participants also expressed positive feelings about the respect that was evidenced for the expression of opinions or values not commonly held by the group. The conference has initiated a thoughtful movement toward exploring and promoting applications of information technology in social-service delivery, practice, and education. Participants often indicated that the conference helped them to think about how values impinge on or affect all our decisions in technology transfer and adaptation, and on how broad are the applications and implications of information technology. In the words of at least one attendee, "I thought I knew this area quite well, but this has been a very humbling experience!"

REFERENCES

Alavi, M., & Henderson, J. C. (1981, November). An evolutionary strategy for implementing a decision support system. *Management Science, 27,* 1309–1323.

Allen, T. J. (1977). *Managing the flow of technology.* Cambridge, MA: MIT Press.

Alter, S. L. (1980). *Decision support systems: Current practice and continuing challenges.* Reading, MA: Addison-Wesley.

Anderson, R. E. (1983, September 29). Statement of Ronald E. Anderson. In *Computers and education: Hearings before Subcommittee on Investigation and Oversight of Committee on Science and Technology, U.S. House of Representatives,* 64 (pp. 345–373). Washington, D.C.: U.S. Government Printing Office. Also contained in Anderson, R. E. (in press), Monitoring the effect of computers in education. In R. E. Anderson (Ed.), *Topics in computer education: National educational computer policy alternatives.* New York: Association for Computing Machinery.

Anderson, R. E., Welch, W., & Harris, L. J. (1983). *Computer inequities in opportunities for computer literacy.* Minneapolis, MN: University of Minnesota Center for Social Research.

Anér, K. (1979). *New views, computers and new media.* Report by Commission on New Information Technology. Stockholm. Liber Förlag Stockholm.

Arbib, M. (1977). *Computers and the cybernetic society.* New York: Academic Press.

Augarten, S. (1984). *Bit by bit: An illustrated history of computers.* New York: Ticknor & Fields.

Baran, P. (1973). 30 services that two-way television can provide. *The Futurist, 7*(5), 202–210.

Baumohl, J., & Segal, S. (1981, September). Toward harmonious community care placement. In R. D. Budson (Ed.), *Issues in community residential care* (Chap. 4, pp. 49–62). San Francisco: Jossey-Bass.

Beauchamp, T. L., & Walters, L. (Eds.). (1982). *Contemporary issues in bioethics* (2nd ed.). Belmont, CA: Wadsworth.

Beer, S. (1959). *Cybernetics and management.* New York: John Wiley and Sons.

Birnbaum, J. S. (1982, February 12). Computers: A survey of trends and limitations. *Science, 215,* 760–765.

Blumer, H. (1966). Preface. In H. M. Vollmer & D. L. Mills (Eds.), *Professionalization* (p. xi). Englewood Cliffs, NJ: Prentice-Hall.

Boorstin, D. (1974). *The Americans: The democratic experience.* New York: Vintage Books.

Boyd, L. H., Jr., Hylton, J. H., & Price, S. V. (1978, September). Computers in social work practice: A review. *Social Work, 23,* 368–371.

Branfman, F. (1984, Fall). Unexplored America: Economic rebirth in a post-industrial world. *World Policy Journal, 2*(1), 33.

Braun, L. (1983, June 27). *Report on educational technology.* Greenvale, NY: New York Institute of Technology.

Braun, L. (1983–1984). Report on educational technology. *Journal of Educational Technology Systems, 12*(2), 109–136.

Brauns, H., & Kramer, D. (1984, July). *Social work in an information society: New challenges and opportunities.* Berlin: Fachhochschule für Sozialarbeit und Sozialpädagogik.

Brawley, E. (1983). *Mass media and human services: Getting the message across.* Beverly Hills, CA: Sage.

Brian, S., & Miller, H. (1971). *Problems & issues in social casework.* New York: Columbia University Press.

Briar, S. (Ed.). (1983). Current and future trends in clinical social work. In A. Rosenblatt & D. Waldfogel (Eds.), *Handbook of clinical social work* (pp. 1057–1058). San Francisco: Jossey-Bass.

Brill, E. D., Jr. (1979, May). The use of optimization models in public sector planning. *Management Science, 25*(5), 413–422.

Britton, D. W., & Elverhoy, R. (1981). Making peace with the computer. *Public Welfare, 39,* 4–6.

Brod, C. (1984). *Technostress.* Reading, MA: Addison-Wesley.

Bronowski, J. (1973). *The ascent of Man.* Boston: Little, Brown.

Byrnes, E., & Johnson, J. H. (1981). Change technology and the implementation of automation in mental health care settings. *Behavior Research Methods & Instrumentation, 13*(4), 573–580.

Carr-Saunders, A. M., & Wilson, P. A. (1933). *The professions.* Oxford: The Clarendon Press. (See also 1964 edition, London: Frank Cass.)

Champine, G. A. (1980, November). Perspective on business computing. *Computer, 13*(11), pp. 84–99.

Childers, T. (1975). *Information-poor in America.* Metuchen, NJ: Scarecrow Press.

Chin, K. (1983). Software for your psyche. *Infoworld, 5*(36), p. 27.

Christiansen, D. (1984, June). The issues we avoid. *IEEE Spectrum, 21*(6), p. 25.

Clemence, R. V. (Ed.). (1951). *Essays of J. A. Schumpeter.* Cambridge, MA: Addison-Wesley.

Coggeshall, I. S. (1984, February). Variations on a theme by Oppenheimer. *IEEE Spectrum, 21*(2), pp. 70–86.

Comprehensive Community Services, Inc., Chicago, IL (1982). Analysis of management information systems survey. *Computer Use In Social Services Network Newsletter, 2*(1), p. 4.

Computerizing the adoption search. (1984, October). *Personal Computing*, p. 37.

Cortes, M., & Bocock, P. (1984). *North–South technology transfer: A case study of petrochemicals in Latin America.* Published for the World Book. Baltimore, MD: The Johns Hopkins University Press.

Cyert, R. M., & March, J. G. (1963). *A behavioral theory of the firm.* Englewood Cliffs, NJ: Prentice-Hall.

Da Cruz, F., & Catchings, B. (1984). Kermit: a file-transfer protocol for universities, Part I: Design considerations and specifications. *Byte, 9*(6), pp. 255–278.

Dahlman, C. A., & Westphal, L. E. (1981, Fall). The meaning of technological mastery in relation to transfer of technology. *Annals of the American Academy of Political and Social Science, 458*(81), pp. 12–26.

Denning, D. E., & Schlörer, J. (1983, July). Inference controls for statistical databases. *Computer, 16*(7), pp. 69–82.

Diebold, John. (1984.) *Making the future work: Unleashing our powers of innovation for the decade ahead.* New York: Simon and Schuster.

Duncan, R., & Weston-Smith, M. (1977, paper 1978). *The encyclopaedia of ignorance: Everything you ever wanted to know about the unknown.* New York: Pocket Books.

Durden-Smith, J. (1982, January/February). Seeing inside your body—safely: Nuclear magnetic resonance. *Technology, 2*, pp. 32–39.

Elam, J. J., & Henderson, J. C. (1983, April). Knowledge engineering concepts for decision support system design and implementation. *Information & Management, 6*(2), 109–114.

Eliot, T.S. (1962). *Collected Poems, 1909-1962.* New York: Harcourt Brace Jovanovich.

Ellul, J. (1964). *The technological society.* (J. Wilkinson, Trans.). New York: Random House.

Evans, C. (1979). *The micro millennium.* New York: Washington Square Press/Pocket Books.

Feigenbaum, E. A. (1983, November). Artificial intelligence. *IEEE Spectrum, 20*(11), pp. 77–78.

Feigenbaum, E., & McCorduck, P. (1983). *The fifth generation.* Reading, MA: Addison-Wesley.

Fischetti, M. A. (1983, January). Probing the human body. *IEEE Spectrum, 20*(1), pp. 75–78.

France puts Diderot in the limelight. (1984, September 14). *Science, 225,* 1132–1133.

Frankena, W. (1973). *Ethics* (2nd ed.). Englewood Cliffs, N.J.: Prentice-Hall.

Geiss, G. R. (1981, Fall/Winter). Systems design and documentation: An essential relationship facilitated via HIPO diagrams. *Administration in Social Work,*

5(3/4), 145-167.

Geiss, G. R. (1983, Winter). Some thoughts about the future: Information technology and social work practice. *Practice Digest, 6*(3), 33-35.

Geiss, G. R. (1984, May 11). High tech and the future of social work practice and education. Keynote presentation at 15th Annual Symposium, *The Impact of Technology: Changing the Face of Social Work Practice and Education,* Graduate School of Social Work, University of Utah, Salt Lake City, Utah.

Geiss, G. R. (1985, February 19). *The romance of Hy Tech and Socie L. Work.* Invitational paper presented at meeting of CSWE-APM, Washington, D.C.

Geiss, G. R. (in press). Information technology: Human impacts and educational policy. In R. Anderson (Ed.), *Topics in computer education: National educational computer policy alternatives.* New York: Association for Computing Machinery.

Geiss, G. R., Schoech, D., & Viswanathan, N. (1982). Joint ventures in computer based policy analysis and information systems: Opportunities for public agencies and universities. In *Proceedings: Twenty-Second National Workshop on Welfare Research and Statistics* (pp. 25-39). Washington, D.C.: U.S. Department of Health and Human Services, Social Security Administration, SSA No. 13-11979.

Gifford, S., Shaw, C., & Newkham, J. (1979). *Community health automated record and treatment system (CHARTS).* Unpublished manual. (Available from Heart of Texas Region Mental Health Mental Retardation Center, P.O. Box 1277, Waco, Texas 76703.)

Gilliam, H. (1977, November 16). Home computers: The surprizing social costs. *San Francisco Chronicle,* p. 6.

Goldstein, C. M. (1982, February 12). Optical disk technology and information. *Science, 215,* 862-68.

Gorry, G. A., & Scott Morton, M. S. (1971). A framework for management information systems. *Sloan Management Review, 13*(1), 55-70.

Goulet, D. (1977). *The uncertain promise: Value conflicts in technology transfer.* New York: IDOC/North America.

Greenberger, M., Aronofsky, J., McKenny, J. L., & Massy, W.F. (1973, Oct. 5). Computer and information networks. (Adapted from *Networks for Research and Education — Sharing Computer and Information Resources Nationwide.* Cambridge, MA: MIT Press, 1974.) *Science, 182,* 29-35.

Greenes, R. A., Pappalardo, A. N., Marble, C. W., & Barnett, G. O. (1969). Design and implementation of a clinical data management system. *Computers in Biomedical Research, 2,* pp. 469-485.

Greenwood, E. (1957, July). Attributes of a profession. *Social Work, 2*(3), 44-55.

Guralnik, D. B. (Ed.). (1980). *Webster's new world dictionary of the American language* (2nd college ed.). New York: Simon and Schuster.

Guterl, F. (1983, November). Next-generation impacts. *IEEE Spectrum, 20*(11), pp. 111-117.

Hayes-Roth, F. (1984, June). The machine as partner of the new professional. *IEEE Spectrum, 21*(6), pp. 28-31.

Hedlund, J. L. (1974, February). Critical issues in clinicians' acceptance and use of computer systems. *Journal of Hospital & Community Psychiatry, 25*(2), 103–104.

Heller, P. D. (1985). *Technology transfer and human values: Concepts, applications, cases.* Lanham, MD: University Press of America.

Henderson, J. C., & Schilling, D. A. (1985, June). Design and implementation of decision support systems in the public sector. *MIS Quarterly, 9*(2), 157–169.

Herbert, E. (1983, January). Minis and mainframes. *IEEE Spectrum, 20*(1), pp. 28–33.

Huber, G. (1984, September). Issues in the design of group decision support systems. *MIS Quarterly, 8*(3), 195–204.

Jaffe, C. C. (1982, November–December). Medical imaging. *American Scientist, 70*, 576–586.

Johansen, R., Vallee, J., & Spangler, D. (1979). *Electronic meetings: Technical alternatives and social changes.* Reading, MA: Addison-Wesley.

Judson, H. F. (1984, November). Century of the sciences. *Science '84, 5*(9), 41–43.

Kagle, J. D. (1984). *Social work records.* Homewood, IL: Dorsey Press.

Kahn, A. J. (1973). *Social policy and social services.* New York: Random House.

Kanade, T., & Reddy, R. (1983, November). Computer vision: The challenge of imperfect inputs. *IEEE Spectrum, 20*(11), pp. 88–91.

Kay, A. (1984, September). Computer software. *Scientific American, 251*(3), pp. 53–59.

Keen, P. G. W. (1980, Spring). Decision support systems: Translating useful models into usable technologies. *Sloan Management Review, 21*(3), 33–44.

Keen, P. G. W. (1983, June 29). Wrap-up presentation. *DSS-83: Third International Conference on Decision Support Systems.* Boston, MA.

Keen, P. G. W., & Gambino, T. J. (1982). Building a decision support system: The mythical man-month revisited. In J. F. Bennett (Ed.), *Building decision support systems.* Reading, MA: Addison-Wesley.

Keen, P. G. W., & Scott Morton, M. S. (1978). *Decision support systems: An organizational perspective.* Reading, MA: Addison-Wesley.

Krieg, A. F., & Shearer, L. K. (1981). *Computer programming in ANS MUMPS: A self-instruction manual for non-programmers.* College Park, MD: MUMPS Users' Group.

Kuhn, T. (1970). *The structure of scientific revolutions* (2nd. ed.). Chicago: University of Chicago Press.

LaMendola, W. (1976). *Management information system development for general social services.* Unpublished doctoral dissertation, University of Minnesota, Minneapolis.

LaMendola, W. (1979). A personal computer based human service organization information system. *Proceedings of the National Computer Conference* (pp. 433–436). New York: IEEE.

LaMendola, W. (1981, Fall/Winter). Feasibility as a consideration in small computer selection. *Journal of Administration in Social Work, 5*(3/4), 43–56.

LaMendola, W. (1981). Some effects of microcomputer based information systems in human service organizations. In G. E. Lasker (Ed.), *Applied Systems and Cybernetics* (Vol. 3, pp. 1429–1432). New York: Pergamon Press.

LaMendola, W. (Ed.). (1984, Summer). MUMPS [Special Issue]. *Computer Users in Social Services Network Newsletter, 4*(2), 5–11.

LaMendola, W. (1985, Spring). The future of human service information technology: An essay on the number 42. *Journal of Computers in Human Services, 1*(1), 35–49.

LaMendola, W. (1985, February). *Information technology: Importance and prospects.* Paper presented at the National Conference of Deans of Graduate Schools of Social Work, Washington, D.C.

Lessin, A. (1982, May 20). Smart card technology and how it can be used. *American Banker*, pp. 4–7.

Levinson, R. W., & Haynes, K. S. (Eds.). (1984). *Accessing human services: International perspectives.* Beverly Hills, CA: Sage.

Lewin, K. (1947). Group decision and social change. In T. M. Newcomb & E. L. Hartley (Eds.), *Readings in social psychology* (pp. 330–344). New York: Holt.

Lockheed, M., Nielsen, A., & Stone, M. (1983). Sex differences in microcomputer literacy. In *Proceedings of the National Educational Computing Conference* (pp. 372–375). Baltimore, MD.

Loftus, G. R., & Loftus, E. F. (1983). *Mind at play: The psychology of video games.* New York: Basic Books.

Long, F. A. (1978). Technological innovation for the U.S. civilian economy. In W. Goldstein (Ed.), *Planning, politics, and the public interest* (pp. 106–142). New York: Columbia University Press.

Lynn, K. S. (Ed.). (1965). *The professions in America.* Boston: Houghton Mifflin.

Majahan, V., & Muller, E. (1979). Innovation diffusion and new product growth models in marketing. *Journal of Marketing, 43*, 55–68.

Martin, J. (1981). *An end-user's guide to data base.* Englewood Cliffs, NJ: Prentice-Hall.

Martin, J. (1984). *An information systems manifesto.* Englewood Cliffs, NJ: Prentice-Hall.

Mason, R. O., & Mitroff, I. F. (1973). A program for research on management information systems. *Management Science, 19*, 475–485.

Mason, R. O., & Mitroff, I. F. (1979, Winter). Assumptions of majestic metals: Strategy through dialects. *California Management Review, 22*(2), 80–88.

Massy, W. F. (1974). Computer networks: Making the decision to join one. *Science, 186*, 414–420.

Match made by computer in adoption. (1983, May 23). *NY Times*, 1, 10:1.

Mayer, M. (1983, August 8). Here comes the smart card. *Fortune, 108*, pp. 74–77.

Mayo, J. S. (1982, February 12). Evolution of the intelligent telecommunications network. *Science, 215*, 831–837.

McCorduck, P. (1979). *Machines who think.* San Francisco: W. H. Freeman.

McGuire, J. F., & Cooper, R. M. (1983). The Veterans Administration's approach to hospital automation. In R. Dayhoff (Ed.), *Proceedings of Seventh*

Annual Symposium on Computers in Medical Care. New York: Institute of Electrical and Electronics Engineers.

McHale, J. (1972). The changing information environment: A selective topography. In *Information technology: Some critical implications for decision makers* (p. 187). New York: The Conference Board.

Meadows, A. J., Gordon, M., & Singleton, A. (1982). *The Random House dictionary of new information technology.* New York: Vintage Books.

Media therapy controls asked. (1984, September). *The NASW News,* p. 19. Washington, D. C.: National Association of Social Workers.

Meldman, M. J., McFarland, G., & Johnson, E. (1976). *The problem-oriented psychiatric index and treatment plans.* St. Louis: The C. V. Mosby Co.

Mogavero, L. N., & Shane, R. F. (1982). *What every engineer should know about technology transfer and innovation.* New York: Marcel Bekker, Inc.

Morrisroe, P. (1984, January 9). Living with the computer. *New York,* pp. 22–31.

Naisbitt, J. (1983, November). Computertrends. *IEEE Spectrum, 20*(11), pp. 110–111.

Naisbitt, J. (1984). *Megatrends.* New York: Warner Books.

National Academy of Engineering. (1984). *Cutting edge technologies.* Washington, D. C.: National Academy Press.

National Association of Social Workers (NASW). (1983). A computerized tracking system for deinstitutionalized clients. *Practice Digest, 6*(3), 24–25.

National Science Foundation. (1983, May). *The process of technological innovation: Reviewing the literature.* Washington, D.C.: National Science Foundation.

Newell, A., & Sproull, R. F. (1982, February 12). Computer networks: Prospects for scientists. *Science, 251,* 843–852.

Newman, F. L., Burwell, B. A., & Underhill, W. R. (1978). Program analysis using the client oriented cost outcome system. *Journal of Evaluation and Program Planning, 1,* 19–30.

Nimmo, R. P. (1982, February). *Executive order regarding ADP policy in DM&S medical operations.* Washington, D.C.: Veterans Administration.

Nolan, R. L. (1979). Managing the crisis in data processing. *Harvard Business Review, 57*(2), 115–126.

Nora, S., & Minc, A. (1980). *The computerization of society.* Cambridge, MA: MIT Press.

Oettinger, A. G. (1971). Communications in the national decision-making process. In M. Greenberger (Ed.), *Computers, communications and the public interest.* Baltimore: Johns Hopkins Press.

Office of Technology Assessment. (1984, February). *Technology, innovation, and regional economic development.* Background paper #2. Washington, D.C.: Congress of the United States.

Orwell, G. (1948). *Nineteen eighty-four.* New York: Harcourt, Brace.

Ouchi, W. (1981). *Theory Z.* Reading, MA: Addison-Wesley.

Parker, E. B., & Dunn, D. A. (1972, June 30). Information technology: Its social potential. *Science, 176,* 1392–1399.

Perrolle, J. (1983, August). *Computer-generated social problems.* Paper presented to the SSSP in Detroit. 59 pages.

Peters, T. J., & Waterman, R. H., Jr. (1982). *In search of excellence: Lessons from America's best-run companies.* New York: Harper and Row.

Profession of social work: Code of Ethics. (1977). In J. B. Turner, R. Morris, M. Ozawa, B. Phillips, P. Schreiber, & B. Simon (Eds.), *Encyclopedia of social work* (pp. 1066–1067). Washington, D.C.: National Association of Social Workers.

Rabi, I. I. (1970). *Science: The center of culture.* New York: World Publishing.

Rawls, J. (1971). *A theory of justice.* Cambridge, MA: The Belknap Press of Harvard University Press.

Reddy, R., & Zue, V. (1983, November). Recognizing continuous speech remains an elusive goal. *IEEE Spectrum, 20*(11), pp. 84–87.

Reinhold, R. (1984, March 29). Reasoning ability of experts is codified for computer use. *New York Times,* 1, 1:4.

Robinson, A. L. (1984, May 11). Experimental memory chips reach 1 megabit. *Science, 224,* 590–592.

Rockart, J. F. (1979, March/April). Chief executives define their own data needs. *Harvard Business Review, 57*(2), 81–93.

Rockart, J. F., & Flannery, L. S. (1981, December). The management of end user computing. *Proceedings of the Second International Conference on Information Systems,* pp. 351–363.

Rockart, J. F., & Scott Morton, M. S. (1984, January/February). Implications of changes in information technology on corporate strategy. *Interfaces, 14*(1), 84–95.

Rockeach, M. (1973). *The nature of human values.* New York: Free Press.

Russell, L. B. (1979). *Technology in hospitals: Medical advances and their diffusion.* Washington, D.C.: The Brookings Institution.

Sackman, H. (1975). Computers and social options. In E. Mumford & H. Sackman (Eds.), *Human choice and computers* (pp. 73–87). Amsterdam: North-Holland; New York: American Elsevier.

Sackman, H. (1967). *Computers, system science, and evolving society.* New York: Wiley and Sons.

Schein, E. H. (1961). Management development as a process of influence. *Industrial Management Review, 2*(2), 59–77.

Schinke, S. P. (1983). Data-based practice. In A. Rosenblatt & D. Waldfogel (Eds.), *Handbook of clinical social work* (pp. 1077–1094). San Francisco: Jossey-Bass.

Schoech, D. (1982). *Computer use in human services.* New York: Human Sciences Press.

Schoech, D., & Arangio, T. (1979, March). Computers in the human services. *Social Work, 24*(2), 96–102.

Schoech, D. J., & Schkade, L. L. (1981, August). *Human service workers as the primary information system user.* Paper presented at 1981 Urban and Regional Information Systems (URISA) Conference, New Orleans, Louisiana. 10 pages.

Schoech, D. J., & Schkade, L. L. (1980, Summer). What human services can learn from business about computerization. *Public Welfare, 38*(3), 18–27.

Schumpeter, J. (1935, May). The analysis of economic change. *Review of Economic Statistics*, pp. 2–10.

Scott Morton, M. S. (1983, January/February). Implication of changes in information technology for corporate strategy. *Interfaces, 18*(1), 82–88.

Servan-Schreiber, J-J. (1985, Summer). On the computer revolution: An interview with Fred Branfman. *World Policy, 2*(3), pp. 569–586.

Shannon, J. (Ed.). (1973). *Science and the evolution of public policy*. New York: Rockefeller Press.

Sidowski, J. B., Johnson, J. H., & Williams, T. A. (Eds.). (1980). *Technology in mental health care delivery systems*. Norwood, NJ: Ablex.

Simon, H. A. (1960). *The new science of management decision*. New York: Harper and Row.

Sines, J. O. (1980). The use of computers in the delivery of mental health care: The necessary background conditions. In J. B. Sidowski, J. H. Johnson, & T. A. Williams (Eds.), *Technology in mental health care delivery systems* (pp. 3–16). Norwood, NJ: Ablex.

Smith, D. (1984, May). The verdict on videogames. *Link:Up, 1*(8), pp. 18–21.

Snow, C. P. (1959). *The two cultures*. Cambridge: Cambridge University Press.

Snow, C. P. (1963). *A second look*. Cambridge: Cambridge University Press.

Sprague, R. H., Jr. (1980, December). A framework for decision support systems. *MIS Quarterly, 4*(4), 1–26.

Sprague, R. H., Jr. & Carlson, E. D. (1982). *Building effective decision support systems*. Englewood Cliffs, NJ: Prentice-Hall.

Stein, T. J., & Rzepnicki, T. L. (1983). *Decision making at child welfare intake*. New York: Child Welfare League of America.

Stewart, F. (1979, July). *International technology transfer: Issues and policy options*. World Book Staff Working Paper No. 344. Washington, D.C.

Tatara, T. (1982, November 5). *A report on the VCIS design meetings with participating state agencies*. Washington, D.C.: American Public Welfare Association.

Timson, G. F. (1980). The file manager system. In J. T. O'Neill (Ed.), *Proceedings of Fourth Annual Symposium on Computers in Medical Care*. New York: Institute of Electrical and Electronics Engineers.

Trowbridge, A. (1972). Preface. In *Information technology: Some critical implications for decision makers*. New York: The Conference Board.

Turkle, S. (1984). *The second self: Computers and the human spirit*. New York: Simon and Schuster.

Turner, J. B., Morris, R., Ozawa, M., Phillips, B., Schreiber, P., & Simon, B. (Eds.). (1977). *Encyclopedia of social work*. Washington, D.C.: National Association of Social Workers.

Tushman, M. L., & Katz, R. (1980, November). External communication and project performance: An investigation into the role of gatekeepers. *Management Science, 26*(11), 1071–1085.

Tydeman, J., & Mitchell, R. B. (1977). Subjective information modelling. *Operational Research Quarterly, 28*, 12.

Urban, G. L., & Karash, R. (1971, February). Evolutionary model building. *Jour-*

nal of Marketing Research, 8, 62–66.

Vallee, J. (1982). *The network revolution: Confessions of a computer scientist.* Berkeley, CA: And/Or Press.

Veatch, R. (1977). *Case studies in medical ethics.* Cambridge, MA: Harvard University Press.

Waltz, D. L. (1983, November). Helping computers understand natural language. *IEEE Spectrum, 20*(11), pp. 81–84.

Ward, B., Runnallo, J. D., & D'Anjou, L. (Eds.). (1971). *The widening gap: Development in the 1970's.* New York: Columbia University Press.

Ware, J. (1984, May). From Algol to Andromeda — The mega wars story. *Link:Up, 1*(8), pp. 18–21.

Watson, H. J., & Carroll, A. B. (1976). *Computers for business: A managerial emphasis.* Dallas: Business Publications.

Ways, M. (1972). The question: Can information technology be managed? In *Information technology: Some critical implications for decision makers* (p. 3). New York: The Conference Board.

Weinstein, S. B. (1984, February). Smart credit cards: The answer to cashless shopping. *IEEE Spectrum, 21*(2), pp. 43–49.

Weizenbaum, J. (1976). *Computer power and human reason: From judgment to calculation.* San Francisco: W. H. Freeman.

Whisler, T. L. (1970). *Information technology and organizational change.* Belmont, CA: Wadsworth.

Whitehead, A. N. (1948). *Adventures of ideas.* Gretna, LA: Pelican Books.

Whitehead, A. N. (1929). *The aims of education and other essays.* New York: Macmillan.

Wiener, N. (1949). *Cybernetics: Or control and communications in the animal and the machine.* Cambridge, MA: The Technology Press of MIT.

Wilson-Ress, J. (1983, January 17–23). Indianapolis RCI computer matchup aids orphans. *Indianapolis Business Journal,* 10.

Zimmerman, J. (1979). *Introduction to standard MUMPS.* College Park, MD: MUMPS Users' Group.

Zimmerman, J. (Ed.). (1983). *Technological woman: Interfacing with tomorrow.* New York: Praeger.

Zuboff, S. (1981). Psychological and organizational implications of computer-mediated work. CISR *Working Paper* #71, Cambridge, MA: MIT Center for Information Systems Research.

BIBLIOGRAPHY

Abshire, G. M. (Ed.). (1980). *The impact of computers on society and ethics: A bibliography*. Morristown, NJ: Creative Computing.

Anderson, C. M. (1975, Fall). Information systems for social welfare: Educational imperatives. *Journal of Education for Social Work, 11,* 16–21.

Anderson, R. E., Hansen, T., Johnson, D. C., & Klassen, D. (1979). Instructional computing: Acceptance and rejection. *Sociology of Work and Occupations, 6*(2).

Anderson, R. E., Klassen, D. L., Krohn, K. R., & Smith-Cunnien, P. (1982). *Assessing computer literacy,* (Publication #503). St. Paul, MN: Minnesota Educational Computing Consortium.

Blasgen, M. W. (1982, February 12). Database systems. *Science, 251,* 869–872.

Boston Systems Group. (1983, January). *Decision support systems bibliography* (2nd ed.). Boston, MA: The Boston Systems Group.

Braun, L. (1983–1984). Report on educational technology. *Journal of Educational Technology Systems, 12*(2), 109–136.

Cohen, V. B. (1984, January). Interactive features in the design of videodisc materials. *Educational Technology,* pp. 16–20.

Coyle, H. F. (1983, March). *Computer literacy for social workers: Recommendations for developing course content.* Paper presented at Annual Program Meeting of the Council on Social Work Education, Fort Worth, Texas.

Currier, R. L. (1983, November). Interactive videodisc learning systems. *High Technology,* pp. 51–60.

Date, C. J. (1983). *Data base: A primer.* Reading, MA: Addison-Wesley.

Dery, D. (1981). *Computers in welfare: The MIS-match* (Vol. 2, Managing information). Beverly Hills, CA: Sage.

Dworaczek, M. (1982, June). *Social aspects of automation: A selective bibliography* (Public Administration Series: Bibliography #P–1236). Monticello, IL: Vance Bibliographies.

Erdman, H. R., Greist, J. H., Klein, M. H., Jefferson, J. W., Salinger, R., & Olson, W. (1981). Clinical usefulness of a computer program for psychiatric diagnosis. In *Proceedings of The Fourteenth Hawaii International Conference on System Sciences* (pp. 802–817). New York: IEEE Press.

Evans, C. (1979). *The micro millennium.* New York: Washington Square Press/Pocket Books.

Feigenbaum, E., & McCorduck, P. (1983). *The fifth generation.* Reading, MA: Addison-Wesley.

Forester, T. (Ed.). (1985). *The information technology revolution.* Cambridge, MA: MIT Press.

Fransecky, R. B. (1974, January). *Telecommunications and community services* (Contract No. HEW–OS–73–201). Department of Health, Education, and Welfare, Office of Telecommunications Policy (HEW Report No. 73–142). Cambridge, MA: Abt Publications.

Fuller, T. K. (1970, December). Computer utility in social work. *Social Casework, 51,* 606–611.

Gripton, J. M. (1981). Microcomputers and word processors: Their contribution to clinical social work practice. In C. E. Lasker (Ed.), *Applied systems and cybernetics, Vol. III.* New York: Pergamon Press.

Harrell, K. F. (1983, July). *Computer systems and software: National standardization* (Public Administration Series: Bibliography #P-1254). Monticello, IL: Vance Bibliographies.

Hedlund, J. L., Vieweg, B. W., Wood, J. B., Cho, D. W., Evenson, R. C., Hickman, C. V., & Holland, R. A. (1981). *Computers in mental health: A review and annotated bibliography,* (DHHS Publication No. ADM 81–1090). Washington, D.C.: U.S. Government Printing Office.

Herrick, W., Schubothe, H., Miller, L. C., Jr., Winn, R., Monteforte, V. R., Hall, J., Minton, E. B., Downing, G., & McGill, M. (1981). *Computer assisted rehabilitation service delivery.* 8th Institute on Rehabilitation Issues. Dunbar, West Virginia: West Virginia Research and Training Center.

Hiltz, S. R. (1984). *Online communities: A case study of the office of the future.* Norwood, NJ: Ablex. (Evaluates the Electronic Exchange System [EIES].)

Johnson, J. W. (1979). The state of the art of instructional computing. *Proceedings of the National Educational Computer Conference.* New York: IEEE/ACM.

Jonassen, D. H. (1984, January). The generic disc: Realizing the potential of adaptive, interactive videodiscs. *Educational Technology,* pp. 21–24.

Kasschau, R. A., Lachman, R., & Laughery, R. (Eds.). (1982). *Information technology and psychology: Prospects for the future.* New York: Praeger.

Keen, P. G. W., & Scott Morton, M. S. (1978). *Decision support systems: An organizational perspective.* Reading, MA: Addison-Wesley.

Krieg, A. F., & Shearer, L. K. (1981). *Computer programming in ANS MUMPS: A self-instruction manual for non-programmers.* College Park, MD: MUMPS Users' Group Publications.

Linvill, J. G. (1982, February 12). University role in the computer age. *Science, 215, 802–806*. (Manpower resources for computer age, university–industry opportunities)

Manning, D., Thompson, B. P., Ebner, D. G., & Brooks, F. R. (1983, November). Student acceptance of videodisk-based programs for paramedical training. *Technology in Higher Education*, pp. 105–108.

Martin, J. (1978). *The wired society: A challenge for tomorrow*. Englewood Cliffs, NJ: Prentice-Hall.

Martin, J. (1981). *An end-user's guide to data base*. Englewood Cliffs, NJ: Prentice-Hall.

Martin, J. (1984). *An information systems manifesto*. Englewood Cliffs, NJ: Prentice-Hall.

McCorduck, P. (1979). *Machines who think*. San Francisco: W. H. Freeman.

McNichols, C. W. (1984). *Data base management with dBASE II*. Reston, VA: Reston.

Meadows, A. J., Gordon, M., & Singleton, A. (1983). *The Random House dictionary of new information technology*. New York: Vintage Books.

Meany, K. (1984). *Computers in social work: An annotated bibliography*. Iowa City, IA: Iowa School of Social Work Research Center, University of Iowa.

Meindle, J. D. (1982, February 12). Microelectronics and computers in medicine. *Science, 215, 792–797*. (Decision-making, tomography, ultrasonic imaging, patient monitors, aids for the handicapped)

Mumford, E., & Sackman, H. (Eds.). (1975). *Human choice and computers* (Proceedings of the IFIP Conference on Human Choice and Computers, Vienna, April 1–5, 1974). Amsterdam: North-Holland.

Naisbitt, J. (1984). *Megatrends*. New York: Warner Books.

National Institute of Mental Health, Series FN No. 4. (1980). *A client-oriented system of mental health service delivery and program management: A workbook and guide* (DHHS Publication No. (ADM) 80–307). Washington, D.C.: U.S. Government Printing Office.

Nora, S., & Minc, A. (1980). *The computerization of society* (First English language ed.). Cambridge, MA: The MIT Press. (Original work published 1978)

Norman, C. (1981). *The God that limps: Science and technology in the eighties*. New York: W. W. Norton.

O'Shea, R., & Eisenstadt, M. (1984). *Artificial intelligence*. New York: Harper and Row.

Pagels, H. R. (Ed.). (1984). *Computer culture: The scientific, intellectual, and social impact of the computer* (Annals of the New York Academy of Sciences, Vol. 426). New York: New York Academy of Science.

Parker, D. B. (1976). *Crime by computer*. New York: Charles Scribner's Sons. (Privacy legislation and computer abuses)

Peters, T. J., & Waterman, R. H., Jr. (1982). *In search of excellence: Lessons from America's best-run companies*. New York: Harper & Row.

Pogrow, S. (1983). *Education in the computer age*. Beverly Hills, CA: Sage.

Quality Education Data, Inc. (1983). *Microcomputer data.* Denver, CO: Quality Education Data. (Survey data on inequities in computer access in public schools)

Rosenberg, J. M. (1984). *Dictionary of computers, data processing and telecommunications.* New York: John Wiley and Sons.

Sackman, H. (1967). *Computers, system science, and evolving society: The challenge of man–machine digital systems.* New York: John Wiley & Sons.

Sackman, H. (1971). *Mass information utilities and social excellence.* Princeton: Auerbach.

Schank, R. C. (1982). *Dynamic memory.* New York: Cambridge University Press.

Schoech, D. (1981, Fall/Winter). Selected bibliography related to the use of computers and information systems in the administration of human services. *Administration in Social Work* [Special issue], 5(3/4), 171–181.

Schoech, D. (1982). *Computer use in human services.* New York: Human Sciences Press.

Schwartz, M. D. (Ed.). (1984). *Using computers in clinical practice: Psychotherapy and mental health applications.* New York: Haworth Press.

Seidel, R. J., Anderson, R. E., & Hunter, B. (1982). *Computer literacy.* New York: Academic Press.

Slavin, S. (Ed.). (1981, Fall/Winter). Applying computers in social service and mental health agencies: A guide to selecting equipment, procedures and strategies [Special Issue]. *Administration in Social Work,* 5(3/4).

Smith, R. C. (1984). Technical management of a microcomputer-assisted learning project. *Computers & Education,* 8(1), pp. 197–201.

Smith, R. L. (1972). *The wired nation.* New York: Harper Colophon Books.

Sprague, R. H., & Carlson, E. D. (1982). *Building effective decision support systems.* Englewood Cliffs, NJ: Prentice-Hall.

Stein, T. J., & Rzepnicki, T. L. (1983). *Decision making at child welfare intake.* New York: Child Welfare League of America.

Turkle, S. (1984). *The second self: Computers and the human spirit.* New York: Simon and Schuster.

Tydeman, J., Lipinski, H., Adler, R. P., Nyhan, M., & Zwimpfer, L. (1982). *Teletext and Videotex in the United States.* New York: McGraw-Hill.

Vallee, J. (1982). *The network revolution: Confessions of a computer scientist.* Berkeley, CA: And/Or Press.

Vance, M. (1983, July). *Computer crime: A bibliography* (Public Administration Series: Bibliography #P-1255). Monticello, IL: Vance Bibliographies.

Vance, M. (1983, July). *Management information systems: Monographs* (Public Administration Series: Bibliography #P-1250). Monticello, IL: Vance Bibliographies.

Wakefield, R. A. (Ed.). (1984, January). The home computer, families, and the mental health professions. *Monograph 1 of series on impacts of home computer use on professionals serving families.* Bethesda, MD: American Family and Washington, D.C.: National Center for Family Studies.

Weinberg, G. M. (1971). *The psychology of computer programming.* New York: Van Nostrand Reinhold.

Weizenbaum, J. (1976). *Computer power and human reason.* San Francisco: W. H. Freeman.

Wilson, J. (1982). *New information technologies for the nonprofit sector* (Report of a Joint Conference of The Foundation Center and The Aspen Institute held at Wye Plantation, Queenstown, Maryland). New York: The Foundation Center/The Aspen Institute for Humanistic Studies.

Winston, P. H. (1984). *Artificial intelligences.* Reading, MA: Addison-Wesley.

Worcester, C. (1983). Interactive video—a new video. *Performance and Instruction Journal, 22*(9), 14–16.

Zimmerman, J. (1979). *Introduction to standard MUMPS.* College Park, MD: MUMPS Users' Group Publications.

NAME INDEX

A

Adams, Charles F., Jr., 75
Alavi, M., 94
Allen, T. J., 95, 105
Anderson, Ronald A., 284, 290
Anér, Kerstin, 57
Arangio, Tony, 246
Arbib, Michael, 55
Aronofsky, J., 56
Atanasoff, John Vincent, 46
Augarten, S., 33

B

Barnett, G. O., 255
Bateson, Gregory, 27
Bawcom, L., 168
Beauchamp, Tom L., 81, 83, 90
Beer, Stafford, 54
Berry, Clifford, 46
Birnbaum, J. S., 31
Bismarck. *See* von Bismarck, Prince Otto
Blumer, H., 20
Bocock, P., 4
Boorstein, D., 76
Boyd, L. H., 235
Branfman, Fred, 312
Braun, Ludwig, 207
Brauns, H., 287
Brawley, Edward, 331
Brian, S., 309
Briar, Scott, 21
Britton, D. W., 245
Brod, C., 333
Bronowski, Jacob, 7, 19, 45, 51, 59
Buchanan, Bruce, 34, 46

Buckley, Lisa, 240
Burwell, B. A., 172
Butterfield, William, 111
Byrnes, Elizabeth, 322

C

Calica, Richard H., 133, 165, 228, 360, 361
Carlson, Eric D., 22, 28, 29, 93, 95
Carroll, A. B., 28
Catchings, B. (Da Cruz, F. &), 262
Cavalier, Al, 113, 145, 185
Champine, G. A., 31, 32, 34
Christensen, Kathleen E., 47, 49, 50, 72, 281, 283, 303, 306, 318, 332, 359, 367
Clemence, R. V., 8
Cobb, Connie J., 143, 184, 360, 364
Coggeshall, I. S., 34
Cooper, R. M., 255
Cortes, M., 4

D

D'Anjou, L., 313
Da Cruz, F., 262
Dahlman, C. A., 4
Denning, D. E., 286
DiLeonardi, Joan, 141, 248, 294, 295
Duncan, R., 281
Dunn, D. A., 56
Durden-Smith, J., 40

E

Eckert, J. Presper, 46
Elam, Joyce, 97, 99
Eliot, T. S., 267

TOPIC INDEX

[EDITORS' NOTE: This index has been designed as an example of the richness of information that would be available in an informational agora or marketplace. While it may have less structure and be less compact than some would prefer, it offers the opportunity to browse or shop, as though in a marketplace, and, hopefully, imposes less of our particular view than would otherwise be the case. We would be very interested in feedback from users regarding the utility of this approach.]

Scenarios *(continued)*
  definition of, 109
  keyword index, 155–157
  purpose of, 110
  range of, 110
Scenario-writing, 109
Schizophrenics, chronic, location of, 336
Schools of social work, computer-use survey, 165
Science:
  and culture, 6, 7
  exponential growth of, 5
Scientific society, 19
Screening Hospital Admission/Readmission
    Emergency (SHARE) Form, 174
Script, sample page, 196
Seattle, Washington, 237
Second Industrial Revolution, 276
Second self, 47
Security kernel, 256
Self-diagnosis computer software, 244
Self-help groups, 69–70
Self-help software, 166
Self-therapy computer software, 244
Senior citizen services, 221–223. *See also*
    In-Home Supportive Services *and*
    Multipurpose Senior Services Project
Senior meal programs, 237
Service:
  conception of, 162
  evaluation of, 332
Service delivery:
  concrete services, computerized, 235–239
  goals of, 230–231
Service-delivery issues, 308. *See also* Informa-
    tion-technology applications, direct-
    service-delivery issues *and* Decision
    support systems
Service-delivery system, 307
  dehumanize, 307
Service facilitation:
  definition of, 163–164
  exemplar, 168–182
  understanding of, 164
Service Facilitation Information System (SFIS), 164
  serving the client, 164
  and social work values, 163–164
Service integration, 184, 323
  fails to survive, 248
Service organizations, 98
  public-sector, 98
Service profession(s), 301
  centrality of values and ethics, 301
Service quality, 244, 247. *See also* Quality of care
Service standards, 244
Service-opening registries, 237
Services:

to frail elderly, 221–222
long-term care, 221–222
Shared data-base strategy, 262
Shearson American Express, 91
Silberman Fund. *See* Lois and Samuel
    Silberman Fund, The
Simulation:
  of decision behavior, 222
  of social agencies, perfectly functioning, 222
Skill hierarchy, 197
Smart card, 87, 283, 303
  enhances autonomy, 88
Smart terminals, 261
Social alternatives, 314
Social analysis, 102
Social caseworker, new roles, 67
Social change, 267, 268, 329. *See also* Change
Social changes, 9
Social choice, expression via technology, 314
Social development and technological develop-
    ment, 8
Social group, formation of, 66
Social inequity relief via information
    technology:
  access to experts, 333
  access to information, 333
  access to other resources, 333
  access to services, 333
  power of information, 333
Social innovation, 184
  and political and economic forces, 184
Social opportunity via information utilities and
    "wired nation," 57
Social problems related to information
    technology:
  "chilling effect" of "being observed," 42
  conformity, 42
  employment dislocation, 42
  inequitable access to information, 42
  invasion of privacy, 42
  loss of diversity, 42
Social revolutions, technological roots of, 268
Social Security Act:
  Title IV-A, 191
  Title XIX, 113, 114, 185
  Title XIX, paperwork burden, 185
  Title XX, 190, 202
Social services, 277. *See also* Public social
    services
  adoption, 241
  delivery site, 247
    impact of information technology, 247
  ethical principles, 80–82, 89
    conflict in, 87–88
    duty to protect client, 80–81
      human dignity, 82

✳

ABOUT THE EDITORS

Gunther R. Geiss is Professor, School of Social Work, Adelphi University, Garden City, NY. He has served as Acting Chairman of the Research Sequence, was founder and Chairman of the Management Sequence, founder and Director of the Post-Master's Certificate Program in the Management of Human Services, and is a member of the doctoral faculty. He has also served as Consultant to the Provost with regard to academic information technology.

He is a graduate of the Polytechnic Institute of Brooklyn, holding the BEE (summa cum laude), MEE, and Ph.D. (Electrical Engineering) degrees, with specializations in computing, systems analysis, and automatic control systems. Support was provided by scholarships from the Polytechnic, and Electronic Engineering Representatives; and a National Science Foundation Cooperative Graduate Fellowship. He has been Adjunct Professor of Electrical Engineering at Polytechnic's Graduate Center at Farmingdale, and has taught quantitative analysis in Adelphi University's School of Business, and environmental systems in the Marine Science Institute at Adelphi. Prior to becoming a full-time faculty member, he worked for 8 years in the Research Department of Grumman Aerospace Corporation, where he was responsible for the control theory research group; and for two years he was an officer and director of Poseidon Scientific Corporation. He has also done research on professional unemployment with the National Society of Professional Engineers.

Dr. Geiss is a Senior Member of the Institute of Electrical and Electronic Engineers, and a member of the Association for Computing

Machinery (ACM), Sigma Xi, Tau Beta Pi, Eta Kappa Nu, and the Council on Social Work Education. He has served on the ACM Task Group on National Educational Computer Policy Alternatives and contributed to the ACM monograph, *Topics in Computer Education: National Educational Computer Policy Alternatives.*

Narayan Viswanathan is Professor and Director of Doctoral Education in the School of Social Work, Adelphi University. He teaches social policy and social-welfare administration in the undergraduate and graduate programs.

He earned his Master of Arts degree at the University of Delhi, and the Master of Science and Doctor of Social Welfare degrees at Columbia University. Dr. Viswanathan has held faculty positions at the Madras School of Social Work and Tata Institute of Social Sciences in Bombay, India; he has been Associate Professor at the Jane Addams Graduate School of Social Work at the University of Illinois in Chicago; and he was Director of the Institute of Social Work in Colombo, Sri Lanka.

Dr. Viswanathan is a recipient of the Award of Excellence for undergraduate study in philosophy and economics in India; the Willard Straight Fellowship and Asia Foundation Fellowship for graduate study at Columbia University; and a National Science Foundation Award for East European studies in Poland.

DATE DUE			
DEC 1 0 2001			